The Rising Down

ALEXANDRA HARRIS

THE RISING DOWN

*Lives in a
Sussex Landscape*

faber

First published in 2024
by Faber & Faber Limited
The Bindery, 51 Hatton Garden
London EC1N 8HN

Typeset by Faber & Faber Limited
Printed and bound by CPI Group (UK) Ltd, Croydon, CR0 4YY

A CIP record for this book
is available from the British Library

ISBN 978–0–571–35052–0

Printed and bound in the UK on FSC® certified paper in line with our continuing
commitment to ethical business practices, sustainability and the environment.
For further information see faber.co.uk/environmental-policy

2 4 6 8 10 9 7 5 3 1

for Caroline Garrett
and her family

～

'I suddenly found myself thinking
of the places and people of my own
infinitesimal past.'
WILLA CATHER, *My Ántonia*

'Local records are peculiarly silent —
except indirectly — about large sectors
of past thought.'
ALAN MACFARLANE, *The Family Life
of Ralph Josselin*

'Los flam'd in my path, and the sun
was hot
With the bows of my mind and the
arrows of thought.'
WILLIAM BLAKE to THOMAS BUTTS,
'composed while walking from
Felpham to Lavant'

Detail from Richard Budgen's map of Sussex, 1724
showing Chichester, the western Sussex downs,
and the Arun valley

CONTENTS

CONTENTS

SQUINT

Sometimes, when I'm in the midst of other things, marking essays, or listening to friends with a glass of wine getting warmer in my hands, there appears to my mind's eye a slightly lumpy white surface. It's the sunlit south wall of Hardham church. I can see it now.

The lumpiness comes from the rubble below the limewash. The church was built from heavy blocks of this and that, sandrock, greensand, flint, each smoothed and shaped as best the men could manage during those months of building a thousand years ago when their arms ached from the mallet and from hoisting up the stones with ropes to lay one course after the next. It's thought they carried bricks over from the ruins of the Roman posting station, which was a good source of materials in the late eleventh century, even after six hundred years open to the weather. They brought clay tiles too, still mortared together with the lime that had been slathered round them when Britannia was newly conquered. I imagine that the local labourers recruited for the job had known the old and broken walls since they were young; they'd played on Sunday afternoons in a strange tiled pit. They dug out the shiny glazed chips with fingernails and arranged them in new shapes on the ground, or tossed them like knucklebones to be caught on the backs of their hands. Grass grew up between the shards and later cattle were put to graze there, with streams running on three sides of the meadow.

Heringham it was called then, and Heriedehem in the Domesday survey, meaning a settlement of the people of Heregyð, whose name could be shortened to Here. Whoever Here was: a Saxon woman who owned this place and gave her name to it, when women had the right to own land and sell it if they wanted.[1] After the stones, perhaps long afterwards, came render and limewash, the native paint of the downs, made with chalk burnt in kilns to form quicklime and slaked with water. Then more layers over the centuries, each one gleaming at first. I like the sheen and the smoothness of this paint over the unseen surface of the stones. But there's a break in the smoothness: a sharp shadow, lowish down at the chancel end. It's a gash, reaching almost but not quite through the full thickness of the wall. A violent cut, but carefully made. It was clearly intended to go right through, but has been blocked up on the inside. The recess is painted over in thick white, so that the edges are soft and homely-looking, as if it's always been here and ought to be here. But it's not homely. It runs obliquely into the wall, at an angle so odd you have to get up and peer in. It's sculptural, like a modernist carving; you can enjoy the shape for a moment as you might enjoy one of Ben Nicholson's abstract constructions made from white and light.

No, this isn't modernist; it's eight hundred years old. It forms a slanting shelf on which you can lay your hand, but I'm reluctant to put my hand there. It makes me think of putting a hand through flesh, of Thomas poking his finger into the wound. Many times I've stood apprehensively beside this shadowed shelf. It's common to cut windows in walls, of course, and this is only another sort of window, like the shapely lancets high in the nave. How plain and straight they look by comparison, open-eyed, letting the light in.

This cut in the wall once gave a sightline through to the altar. A simple lean-to construction would have stood on the side of the church, forming the cell in which a holy recluse came to live. From the cell, the slanted window allowed a view of the altar and nothing else. The oddly shaped gash in the white south wall tells us, in the language of windows and stones, about things that happened at Hardham and left no other physical trace.

By 1253 an anchorite was living here, someone who had chosen to be stoppered up, walled in, to worship God on this very spot and see no more of the world than a narrow shadowed room. There's a record of money being left to this enclosed person, the 'incluso', by the Bishop of Chichester, Richard de Wych, who died that year and was later a saint. 'Item incluso de Heringham dimidiam marcam.'[2] Half a mark: enough to register his continuing support of the man sitting upright in his tomb day by day. 'Incluso' indicates a male hermit rather than the more common 'incluse'. Richard remembered too, with the same sum, the 'incluse de Stopeham' and the 'incluse de Hoghton', the women shut in at Stopham, just a mile or so upstream, and Houghton to the south, where the downs meet the water meadows. When the anchorite died at Hardham, in the cell that was already prepared as his grave, others succeeded him. Fragmentary records suggest that a Prior Robert lived here and died in 1285, bequeathing the cell to a female follower.[3] They were all held in place, anchored by the church as a ship might be anchored in a harbour; they also took on the role of anchor and were deeply respected for it, providing the still weight that would fix and shelter the church.

I must have seen this closed window as a girl of ten or eleven. I remember a frisson of shock, but mostly I was pleased to have learnt a new word, 'squint', which I stored up among the other architectural words that showed me what to look for in buildings. The wall paintings inside the church were the reason for going to Hardham, and when I lobbied for a family detour in the car from the main road into the little track by the church, the pictures were the attraction. Because we went so infrequently, because years could pass without our entering the little church that stood a mile away from our local chemist and railway station in

Pulborough, the paintings were an amazing discovery each time, leaping from the gloom. As for the squint, I didn't appreciate the physicality of it until much later, when I had read about the lives of anchorites.

The man who came to this spot to surrender the world would have been preparing himself for several years, taking spiritual guidance, living with what he intended to do. As he went about the routine of his days, he carried with him the idea of the cell walls. When he walked down a corridor, he thought of not walking again. He probably lived locally, and may have been one of the Augustinian canons at Hardham Priory just across the fields. In that case he knew the dampness of the place; he knew his skin would be clammy with wet through the winter and the air heavy in his lungs. He knew that each part of his body would protest with aches and fevers.

The priory was spacious and built with graceful craftsmanship. Through the trees, before the land drops down to the river, you can still see the arches, long since made part of a private farmhouse. They rise on slender moulded columns and curve gently to finely carved points. Three portions of blue Sussex sky are framed in quatrefoils. The man, if he was there, thought his way from these upward arches into a tiny room with the door nailed up. He thought of his body chafing at constriction, and then thought of the wall as an extension of his body. He decided that this was what he wanted. A sponsor was sought, someone who would pay for the building of the anchorhold and for an attendant who would prepare basic meals.

Apart from the deep recess of the squint, there is no trace of the cell at Hardham. It is likely that the walls were made from wattle and daub, and reeds cut from the marshes to make a thatched roof sloping up to join the church. Workers pounded at the chancel wall to make the required hole through to the altar. An awkward job: blocks to be pulled out, re-cut, re-inserted. The opening needed to form a funnel, narrowing towards the chancel interior, directed so as to reveal the cross and the Eucharist raised above it. It was a window and a not-window, an anti-window, its eye trained on the circle of the Host. This was the 'chirche-thurl'. Anchorholds usually had this and one other window, known as the 'huses thurl' (the house-hole or parlour-window), positioned on the other side of the cell.[4] All transactions with the world had to go through this window. Food and water were passed in, and waste was passed out. Brief conversations were permitted, for example with those who sought religious guidance. But the opening was to be kept curtained at all times.

A Mass was said, the cell blessed. The episcopal seal was laid upon it. Richard of Chichester made the sign of the cross and said the last rites over the body of the man who went in through the one-way door, dust to dust. Tuesday came, Wednesday, and the recluse did not see them. In winter the great yew tree in the churchyard stood out with velvet magnificence.[5] It was becoming famous; people said it was so old it had been a sapling in the first flush of new life after the Flood. Three travellers took shelter in its hollow innards one night while the storm dragged at the branches above them. Workers stretched out their legs on the grass in its shade. On a late afternoon in August, a heat haze sat over the fields and the cows moved heavily towards the river. The aching man held himself upright though his muscles had no strength. By the dim light coming through the black curtain, he followed the words of the prayer book.

It was that kind of hot August afternoon when I last went to Hardham, walking along the side of the road from Pulborough, on the verge overgrown with nettles, blinking dust out of my eyes. There was the sweet smell of wood on a saw-yard truck, straw flying off an overloaded tractor, a clanking skip with swinging chains, commuter cars, school runs, all following the Roman road, fast and straight. The hamlet is little more than a lay-by. There's a hedge to screen the traffic, but a few conifers are all that stand between sixty miles an hour and the stillness of the cottages. Willow and ash branches are pulled into the wake of each lorry as it passes. Only once in a while does someone put out an indicator, slow to a halt and let a queue build up behind them while they turn into the lane by the Saxon church.

No one turned into the lane that afternoon. On the road, people were driving home from work, looking forward to finding the children in the paddling pool or laying the table on the patio. I lifted the latch of the heavy church door, grateful to the warden who must come over each day with the keys and hang out the sign saying 'OPEN'. Each return here feels privately ceremonial. I step into the cold as into a pool, and it is all there in the half-dark: font, pews, chancel arch and the pictures of wheels and beasts, bodies that seem all abdomen, tensed, shaped like pears or teardrops.

For a thousand years people have been stepping into the shadows of this church and letting their eyes adjust. At first the paintings were bright. St George tilted his spear; Joseph lay suspended in a dream. From the altar, the priest could see the Last Supper; he could bless the table in the picture as well as the altar at which he stood. In the picture the disciples were packed closely together, their legs all stretched the same way, haloes fitted one behind the next. Around the chancel arch, the months of the year rose and fell, each a figure with a task. Labourers, yeomen, cooks, serving girls, bargemen: all saw the dove flying to the Virgin Mary, who folded her arms as she received the blessing. They saw the green haloes of the saints and angels, shining out in the precious paint made from malachite, which was only used for haloes and which was the colour of a copper pot left for years in the rain.[6]

The walls were whitewashed, the paintings hidden. The commandments were on display for all to read in English. 'Thou shalt not make to thyself any graven image.' People were still stepping into the cool nave. A section of whitewash was removed during building work in the 1860s and traces of colour appeared behind it; then all the interior walls were scraped to reveal row on row of pictures. Architects and restorers came, hoping to stabilise the paint. Art historians worked out the sequence of images and consulted each other: it was the earliest and most complete series anyone had seen.[7] Clive Bell arrived in the 1940s, his mind full of comparisons to painted churches in France and Italy. He had long known the murals at Clayton, a quick drive out from Charleston; these decorations on the other side of Sussex looked to be by the same artists. He made notes about Cluny and Byzantium, the rhythm of repeated forms and the emotional significance of gesturing hands.[8]

Outside and round the back, the white wall was still brilliant in the sun at five o'clock and I was shielding my eyes. There were tall elms here before disease took hold of them. The yew is gone too: damaged by storms, it died at last in the middle of the nineteenth century. But I like the bright and open patch of hummocky grass. Over the low fence, arable fields, and beyond them, where the land becomes watery, the wild brooks take over: thick rushes, sedges, purple grasses loud with crickets, ditches and drains, dark, silent water running in channels. A raised causeway made by the Romans cuts across the marsh. The 'incluso de Hardham' saw none of this. He came here especially not to see it.

As a child I used to make a telescope with my two hands and peer through the tunnel at a world I could edit in order to try out other places. I could point the telescope at an umbrella pine and be in the Mediterranean, or at a wooden beam over our garage and I'd be on a Jacobean farm. I'm still doing it. A figure walks out along the familiar path to the church where a small crowd has gathered. He leaves behind him the space of the cloister, vegetable gardens, a fishpond. He leaves the grass and the light. In he goes and the door is closed. This happened here, and it seems impossible as the sky glows a deeper and deeper blue.

For about two centuries, solitary enclosure was a venerated form of existence. In Sussex, where the practice seems to have been especially common, most people in the 1200s would have passed by an anchorhold on a regular basis. The village anchorite was a familiar presence, though one they would never see. The extremity of the surrender was encouraged by religious leaders, who helped with instructions on how to carve the abyss of dark time into routines of devotion. Rule books decreed an intricate choreography to keep the mind trained on the task of continual prayer: fall to the ground at this word and this word; make a cross over the bed with two fingers, four times, here and here. This is how the day starts, continues and ends.

A male anchorite might follow a book adapted from the Rule of St Benedict. Women, whose bodies were thought to require different kinds of control, followed the guidance set out in *Ancrene Wisse*, or other books like it. The language was sometimes beautiful, opening images to the starved eye. 'Saplings are hedged round with thorns so animals do not eat them while they are tender. You are saplings planted in God's orchard.' 'Ye beoth yunge impen i-set i Godes orchard; thornes beoth the heardschipes thet ich habbe i-speken of.'⁹ An anchoress might re-fresh herself with the thought of her soul as a vital sapling, bright green, unfurling upwards, but those in the churchyard were hidden from her. 'What is more depraved than the eye?' asks the book. 'All the openings of your windows should be closed . . . and if they can be more firmly closed, they should be more firmly closed.'¹⁰ So men and women de-prived themselves of sight at Houghton, at Stopham, at Hardham.

At this deep-silled squint, I'm looking into a past so alien to me that I can only concentrate on it for a few minutes at a time. This is what can happen if you investigate the uneven stones of a wall. In a churchyard three miles from where I grew up and made my plans for life, at least three people rejoiced to bury themselves alive. Here, in a place more vertiginously strange the more I learn of it, they sought to erase their in-dividuality where I tried to grow confident in mine. Already I'm turning away towards the open expanse of the water meadows. I want to walk along the riverbank with the setting sun in my eyes.

PART I

1. THE VISITOR

Never go back, they say, but for me the return was a revelation. Midway upon the journey of my life I found myself in Sussex. I paused and sat down on the verge. I followed paths so familiar that I knew where the puddles would be. And there they were: the skiddy place at the foot of a stile even in high summer, and the milky ruts in the chalk margins of a brassica field, dried smooth in the heat and starting to crack. I waited for the sun in certain spots, knowing which ridges of turf would show up in the low light before dusk, anticipating the slight rise in the wind after dark. Home, I thought. But of course it wasn't home – or at least, I wasn't. I hardly knew the place at all.

Wide-eyed as a first-year student, I was amazed by how much there was to think about. Starting to explore a fairly obscure patch of rural England, I felt a whole new syllabus opening up, my assumptions up-ended by new forms of thought and understanding. What had been background became foreground. The downs acquired names and their sides were sorted into scarp slopes and dip slopes. 'The path on the bank' became the Greensand Way. Pulborough Sandrock distinguished itself from Amberley Blue, which sounds like a butterfly but is a heavy malmstone, quarried along sunken lanes and giving its sheen to local buildings. I had thought with all the blandness of ignorance that flint was dark grey and chalk was white. But the 'upper chalk' has a different character to the 'lower chalk'. Flint can appear anywhere on the spectrum from near-white to near-black, the darkest dug from the deepest mines and lightening as it weathers. Nodules of flint have chalk-like casings, the dark centres revealed only when the flint is cracked open.[1]

It is a well-known pattern: the grown-up goes back to the first place and draws, as if on tracing paper, an adult world over the contours of childhood. The bold shapes beneath give structure to the more cautious and self-conscious pencil lines above. The new kinds of knowledge both emphasise and obscure the old routines. There is another kind of layering because the rediscovered place is no longer alone: it is part of a shifting constellation of places lived in or imagined over the years. I was often elsewhere when I was thinking about Sussex, so that what I saw as I crossed platforms at Birmingham New Street was sometimes the arch of North Stoke church, its bevelling carved in a soft clunch that powders very slightly to the touch (PLATE). It would rise as a creamy rainbow across the track with a train pulling in underneath.

I am fascinated by these composite places we all make, and by the way we use memory, each of us differently, to work out where we are. It's one of the reasons that I wanted to watch what happened when people I associated with other landscapes set foot on earth I knew. When he visited Sussex, John Constable drew the working life of watermills on the River Arun almost but not quite as he drew the mills he had grown up with on the Stour. W. H. Hudson, one of the most celebrated writers of the South Downs, grew up on the plains of Patagonia and found on the barer reaches of the Sussex hills a strange kinship with the place he had left. Looking across the downland turf he was also looking – with a squint or a slant view – at South America. Looking, and touching and hearing. 'It is the likenesses that hold me', he reflected, describing the 'home feeling' that came to him on chalk uplands.[2] The yoking of Patagonian plains and Sussex downs is a striking example of the very common, complicated, unpredictable habit humans have of making places from other places, so that nowhere is simply itself.

Trains on the Arun Valley Line run from London Victoria (platforms 15–19) to Crawley and Horsham, after which the carriages are quieter.

There's a change in the rhythm of the engine as we slow through a cutting and round a bend on the approach to Pulborough; the people who recognise that low sound gather up their coats and stand by the doors. I used to get out there, and my father would be in the car at the front of the station, or on the platform for special occasions, then came the last four miles to the house. Now he lives in Chichester and I stay on the train as it goes south. Marshes open out on either side and the downs are there, a solid green wave that never comes to shore. Grass, water, riverbanks, then the grey right angle of Amberley Castle rising out of the brooks, as if it had reared up in a great geological event, solidifying above the fluid ground.

A moment later Amberley is answered by Arundel, all turrets and filigree piled on the hillside, but it's not the castle that makes me want to interrupt the passengers opposite me in the carriage who are head-down in their phones as I would be on many other journeys. It's the water meadows and the reed-writing of the ditches that make me lean forward to say, though I don't say it, *Look!* It's the tiny, assertive spire of a church right by the river, the glimpse of a bridge with no sign of how you might get to it. It's the secret life of those few houses. It gives me a glittering eye, this stretch; but I'm not the ancient mariner waylaying others with my story. I'm the guest, hoping that someone here will hold me with their eye and tell me about the place.

⌒

'Local' has so often been associated in modern culture with 'minor', but for at least seventy years local work has been attracting some of the most groundbreaking historians. Thinkers from many other disciplines are increasingly attentive to subjects that have been undervalued because they are provincial, regional or rural.[3] In the new contexts of the twenty-first century, local is major. As we adapt to living more sustainably and resourcefully, attending to the frustrations, dilemmas and

13

richness of what's nearby, a great diversity of experience comes down to us from those who have been here before.

I tried to think my way into lives distant from my own yet so close that we have sat under the same trees. At every turn I encountered powerful varieties of local vision. Reading about one place and widely various notions of place, I discovered the wealth of stories to be met with if we focus in tightly, if we start from the ground and ask who has known it.

I tended to assume, when I was growing up, that art and literature came from somewhere else. That was fine because art travels. It collected me from the driveway of a bungalow outside Storrington and took me to panelled rooms of court intrigue or remote clifftops. When I started to read the great books of place in my teens, I projected myself into Wessex plains and Yorkshire moors. Occasionally, a local spot would stir into new life as a version of one of these legendary settings. From a particular ridge on sandy, root-riddled Sullington Warren I thought I could see the balding, thin-soiled expanse of Egdon Heath. The gorse was encouraging in literary terms: this could be a place for the furze-cutting that was so often mentioned (and in that, at least, I was right). In my mind's eye I parked the reddleman's caravan on the common. I discovered the magic by which writers could show me my own surroundings without ever having visited. Had I set down my Hardy and Brontë novels, though, and asked who knew this gorse, these streams, the enquiry would have set me on many new paths.

Decades later, my growing reading list sent tendrilled feelers into canal-building and barges, sheep-breeding, botany, warren management – only the logic of place could make sense of the assortment. Concentrating on the close at hand, I think I learnt more world history than at any other time in my life. I traced the journeys of migrant pioneers to Western Australia and Canada, and read the memoirs of displaced Poles making new homes after the war. I made notes on Quakers who left Sussex for America, merchants and their trade routes, diplomatic missions, French ironworkers, religious exiles. William Blake's idea, conceived on the Sussex coast, of 'a World in a Grain of Sand' kept urging me to look for the world as it might appear in this patch of southern England.[4]

⌒

The quantity and variety of local records, and the care with which they have been catalogued and interpreted by archivists, have me in awe. Yet coming as I do from the study of intricately recorded literary figures I am confounded by the vast gaps and silences. Without diaries or letters or descriptions of table talk, I keep chafing at the difficulty of discovering anything beyond the barest external facts of people's lives. When I look at the hearth-tax records for 1670, I am amazed by the evidence of so many addresses and by what social historians are able to do with it. But the numbers give little clue as to what men and women dreamt about over their fires. Were the images that rose in their hearths associated with plough-shares or lovers or fish or saints? Did they find any pleasure in the high paths over the downs, or in the lower sheltered lanes?

The local materials that have long been a mainstay of historical research are much less commonly used by those writing about the arts. Yet stories of human imagination are double-stacked and neatly folded in regional archives, if only we can find ways to unfold them. Here are generations of men, women and children, walking, sometimes reading, mourning changes to loved places, catching their breath at a view, and sometimes deprived of any view at all. Here are stories of places known and valued in ways that won't be found on the National Gallery walls or in volumes of pastoral poetry – though the perceptions of celebrated artists and all sorts of other people deserve to be explored not separately but side by side.

Slowly I began to grasp the distinctive rhythms of local research: the leaps between stepping stones as one source led to another, the pointilliste effect produced by the sporadic survival of documents so that you might know the name of every householder in Amberley for 1779 because a single year's window-tax returns have survived. You have to learn where these pools of light are. Each area has its different lights.

The search boxes on Ancestry.com assumed I was looking for my own family history. 'Enter the name of your ancestor'. I entered names that had nothing to do with bloodlines, feeling that those in a place before me were forebears of an equally significant kind. I started to keep an eye out for particular people in the crowd of history, as if I knew them. Many of their names were familiar: they were still common in the area. These were the names of people I knew when I was growing up – Hills and Jupps and Bellchambers – but now they were reappearing in Tudor, Georgian and Victorian circumstances. The Aylings were irrationally linked in my mind to Mrs Ayling, the Storrington playgroup leader who had us all in a circle while she played the accordion. Aylings in the records kept coming through the centuries, stretching and folding behind Mrs Ayling as she squeezed the bellows and tapped her feet.

In the early phase of my Sussex visits, when I had no idea of writing more than an essay or two on writers in the area, a great and unexpected gift appeared. My old schoolfriend Caroline was helping her mother to leave her home and move into the other sort of home. I knew Elizabeth well, or had known her, because she was my history teacher at school as well as my best friend's mother. Now dementia was taking its brutal course, and it was too hard for Elizabeth to carry on without round-the-clock care. It had been too hard all year. The terrified calls to Caroline, four times a day, eight times a day, had changed to alarming silences. There had been disasters and hospital stays. The care-home fees necessitated that the old house be rented and Caroline was trying to clear out her mother's things.

We were talking on the phone as we have done every week since we left school and left the Arun, passing our lives along the wires between Oxford and London, Liverpool and Exmoor, Oxford and Dartmoor. She was keeping as much furniture as she could, sending the Sussex chairs to have their rush seats re-woven, and measuring her standard-issue 1970s sitting room to see what would fit. She was sorting through the thousands of books collected by her parents in their life together studying the world around them: natural history, especially entomology for John, local geography and history for Elizabeth, all kinds of archaeology, map-making, hydrology, ironworking, woodworking, agricultural and industrial history between them. The books formed a double portrait.

Elizabeth had wanted to write about the Arun and for years she had been collecting anything relevant to the river and the valley. Caroline was lifting examples from crates on the other end of the line and her toddler was pulling at her ankles. *The Roadmender. The Arun Navigation.* We tried to think whether any library would take them. Caroline asked if I'd like some myself. The titles sounded almost comically obscure. I was not yet involved with roads and rivers and didn't expect to be. I asked if I might have a few.

Three boxes arrived a fortnight later. Out came giant scarlet volumes of the *Victoria County History*, offering extraordinarily concise and well-documented entries on parish after parish. Here were not only the affairs of church and gentry but details of warrens, fisheries, the building of barns and opening of quarries. Out came antiquarian studies of an earlier kind: gilt-tooled nineteenth-century volumes with gothic-script headers and fold-out pedigrees meant to assert the noble continuity of families in an age when this was a prime constituent of 'history'. Armorial shields were printed in the margins as if you might run a finger down the column to reach three sinister gloves pendent argent tasselled and say 'aha!' Out came *Wealden Glass* and *Dew Ponds*; I saw glass-blowers appearing in the woods and sheep coming to drink at the round pools up on the high downs, which are mostly now abandoned and dry. Out came *The Roadmender*, which on inspection turned out to be a contemplative text by Margaret Barber, who published as Michael Fairless. A picture showed her in the bed to which spinal disease confined her; she was happiest when she imagined herself as a Sussex road-mender, breaking flints. Everything was stranger and more full of life than I'd had the wit to imagine.

Lifting volumes five at a time, I remembered the tight-squeezed sitting room where they used to belong, on the hill above Pulborough, in the 70s estate built on the old glebe field. Caroline would sit on the low sofa, John in a brown velour armchair reading through thick glasses, Elizabeth at the table copying a map onto tracing paper for her history of the Arun. The point of the house was the window at the front. You could see down the paved path, over the car, over the ornamental cherry standing alone in the lawn opposite, up and over the roofs to the wild brooks in the distance. John died rapidly of a cancer that was incurable by the time he saw the doctor. Elizabeth carried on for several years afterwards, transcribing tithe surveys and working out how the water meadows were used. She understood where the peat was dug and where common fields had been enclosed for private use. I hadn't appreciated what she was doing or the specialist knowledge that went into it.

In the Bodleian I found that the publications of the Sussex Archaeological Society were on open shelves in Duke Humphry's Reading Room. This is an inner sanctum where biros are not allowed and the inhabitants always look to be reading in Latin. But up in the gallery was Topography: Sussex. A volume fell open at 'Excavations on a Romano-British Site, Wiggonholt, 1964'. Wiggonholt is, like Hardham, one of the hamlets on the edge of the wild brooks. To me, it was a sloping meadow, sometimes with a bull in it, a few stone houses, and an ancient one-roomed church with a high-backed bench that catches the sun by the porch. It was a favourite walk from the nearby RSPB café. Wiggonholt was a turning off the open stretch of road running fast and straight from Storrington to Pulborough. An old section of the road had been left as a lay-by, and I was taken there for my first driving lesson. Forwards and back I went, uncertain of the clutch.

Now objects rose up from beneath the grass and tarmac: a bronze trumpet brooch with acanthus leaves, a stylus for writing, fragments of rare Samian jars made by potters in the Auvergne whose names were stamped into the clay feet. In Oxford, where I had read my way through Milton and Joyce, the clay pots of Wiggonholt were incongruous and radiant. My own place was there on the shelf; it was a subject of scholarly attention. I stood in imagination on the ragged grass and pineapple weed as the cars went by, held by the idea that under me, behind me, there was another language, a different way of life and a frigidarium leading to a hot bath. There were fragments of red porphyry from Egypt: 'porfido rosso antico', the Romans called it, attracted to what was ancient even to them.' Our house was a mile away, and now I looked at the map I could see that the course of a lost road from the Wiggonholt bathhouse cut straight through our garden. The dotted line crossed the map like a perforation: 'tear here' and tear through time. My parents painted our dining room Porphyry Pink, which seemed exotic given that the other rooms were Magnolia. But porphyry had been here long before us.

For a while I stayed clear of the topography section, which offered such distractions. I had an essay to write about seasonal drama in the Renaissance. But when I checked through Philip Henslowe's notebook, treasured by scholars because Henslowe, theatre impresario, was at the centre of the London world in which Shakespeare worked, a footnote led me back to Sussex. Only part of the original notebook had been published, the rest of it apparently containing nothing of literary interest; for more information, I was directed to the *Sussex Archaeological Collections*. Henslowe had a brother, John, and he used the notebook first. John's brother-in-law, Ralph Hogge, owned one of the major ironworks in the Sussex weald, and John wrote up the records of the firm. Day by day through the 1570s, he itemised the sums 'pad to Nycolas Sleppon for his Cuttunge of Tymber in the fforest', for carrying a ton of shot to

London and so on, tons delivered and sent out, the furnaces burning with ferocity in forest clearings, a heavy industry in full swing.[6] For a time Hogge had a Crown-granted monopoly on iron ordnance, so that every English gun and cannonball began from Ashdown Forest.

Ashdown was some miles north-east of the places I knew. Nevertheless, I was struck by the diptych of the London theatres going on side by side with the logging, the digging of ore and the stoking of flames, leaving their records in the same volume. I had looked at the famous part of the diary; now it was time to turn it upside down and start from the back, which was really the front, since John at the ironworks used it first. Finding out about Sussex would prove to be like that: it was like turning history upside down and starting from the back, which to the people who lived in the weald and the downs was very much the front. I filled up my own back-to-front notepad and started another.

⌒

The Old English 'dún' meant simply a hill. It's the dún that gave us sand dunes. In the Blickling Homilies, Christ preaches 'on Oliuetes dúne'.[7] The Down of Olives is a marvellous thought – Christ delivering his sermon on a grassy slope with the chalk at his feet and rampion straining in the breeze – but clearly dúne was a generic word, used for all kinds of high places. The general meaning gradually acquired more specificity. A fourteenth-century encyclopaedist explained carefully that, 'A downe is a lytyl swellynge or arerynge of erthe passynge the playne grounde . . . and not retchyng to hyghnesse of an hylle.'[8] This sounds like what we now call downs. Swelling is still a word much used to describe them; 'arerynge' is good too, a version of 'a-rearing', as in rearing up. By the sixteenth century, 'down' was distinctly associated with chalk sheep pastures. The Tudor poet Barnabe Googe offered a vision of peace in his third eclogue: 'I . . . thought it best to take my sheep / And dwell upon the down.'[9]

The western Sussex downs are more wooded than the hills to the east, and the tree cover has made the history round here more secretive. Earthworks disappear under depths of leaf mould; brushwood fills in former trenches.[10] Most of the villages are sheltered by land rising around them, which makes them different from villages in Norfolk, say, where you can see from one church to the next, or in Oxfordshire where if you find a hill, you can see tracts of the midlands. In the downs, you often come upon places by surprise. A friend lit a roadside beacon once on a November afternoon when he was expecting me, knowing that a visitor would be liable to miss the spot.

For most of its human history the Arun valley was isolated. Proximity to London, as the crow flies, meant little when an impassable band of Wealden clay was in the way. Well into the eighteenth century, overland travel was either onerous or impossible except for a few months in the summer. Goods coming into and out of the downs were transported by river, or by the seaborne 'coasting trade' round to London or west to Portsmouth. There are strong traditions of people living here without wanting to be easily observed. The area's powerful Catholic families sustained recusant networks with necessary discretion through the post-Reformation centuries of intolerance.[11] Others have come – even in the twentieth century – to shake themselves free of networks, to be private. You could drive through Fittleworth regularly without noticing the lane up to the smallholding where in the 1920s Ford Madox Ford lived almost self-sufficiently with his partner Stella Bowen, recovering himself from the double horrors of the war and his marriage; he raised pedigree black pigs and thought his way towards his novel *Parade's End*. Laurie Lee left the Ministry of Information to live, under the radar, in a caravan outside Storrington. Ivon Hitchens had another caravan towed into the woods at Lavington Common and stayed for the next forty years, painting shadowed, secretive hollows and millponds.

The long, high path on the top of the downs stretches from above Winchester through Hampshire and Sussex and out to the white cliffs of Beachy Head. You can look across the Channel to where the same band of chalk continues, reappearing from under the sea. Sussex men who went to the Front in 1915 and 1916 were surprised to find themselves among the familiar contours and flora of chalk country.[12] The path is almost as old as human life on the hills, long predating any notion of England or France. There is evidence for Mesolithic activity on the ridge, and by the time of the Iron Age the track was already very ancient. It has been a busy highway. It still is – on sunny Saturdays when off-road bikes weave around the groups of walkers.

I love to be up there pounding into the wind on the white road. But soon I drop down to a lower path. I would have been no good in the Iron Age. Unless you are a very hardy shepherd, it's mostly in the foothills and valleys that life is lived. When I think of the downs, they are not falling beneath me but rising in the distance; I've always thought of them as rising. They rose beyond the playing field of my junior school in Storrington, so that when I came eleventh out of twelve in a running race there was still that rounded green wall, glimpsed beyond the football posts and the boundary trees, standing for something that was not to do with coming first or last. They rose in the seven o'clock dusk on Wednesday evenings when the window was open in the upper room at the village hall where children went for 'ensemble' class, or semi-controlled playing of all available musical instruments. I liked to tap the xylophone and hear its chimes answered by church bells from across the field. I was nine or ten, I suppose, and already conscious of turning from the brightly lit room, where someone was shaking maracas, to look out at the hills in the night. I think I was aware of something grand and inviolable out there, but I didn't understand much about the land around me and wouldn't have known what to ask.

⌒

The value accorded in British culture to local knowledge has altered significantly over time; it has many histories of its own. In a book that has stayed with me through my years of local thinking, the literary critic Fiona Stafford describes a transformation in the relationship between poetry and places. Eighteenth-century shifts in moral and aesthetic attitudes established the ground for a new kind of specifically rooted writing that the Romantic poets brought to full realisation. 'Local detail ceased to be regarded as transient, irrelevant, or restrictive, and began to seem essential to art with any aspiration to permanence.'[13] I was surprised to realise how pervasively the classical taste of earlier periods had directed attention away from particular instances to a search for abstract ideals, and how marked was the change when it came. It was philosophical and political as well as aesthetic. It amounted to 'the discovery of local truth'. Romantic poetry expressed, and encouraged, a new kind of faith in ordinary external surroundings, and in personal observation. This came with profound implications, following the principle that 'even the poorest agricultural worker could attain deep knowledge of his own world, so that, when he saw a wren, his perception differed entirely from that of the passing traveller'.[14]

Drawn to this history, I wanted to ask how it worked in my own local place; that seemed a logical step though I could see it would be hard. I wanted to reach back behind Romanticism, asking what regional areas might look like, feel like, if art and literature paid them little notice. I hoped to get some glimpses, too, of how people in Sussex encountered the emerging cultural emphasis on 'local truth'. Would it affect the way they valued and investigated their surroundings, or shape what they saw from the window?

My own new interests were awoken by finding Wiggonholt archaeology in the Bodleian, an affirmation of the place having significance beyond its bounds. But that experience was not available to Sussex readers in the seventeenth or eighteenth century. Even while England was having its antiquities inspected, its soils surveyed, its temperature taken, its mountains sketched and scenic routes recommended, the reputation of Sussex remained doubtful. There was no consensus about its being an area of historical interest or landscape beauty. The antiquary John Aubrey knew it would be full of things worth looking at; a rare figure in his passionate attachment to local detail a century before Wordsworth, he had a rich feeling for lowland landscapes and the history of ordinary human goings-on. In the early 1670s he 'perambulated' Surrey, commissioned by the cartographer John Ogilby to make a historical survey of the county. Knowing from experience that even the most solid-looking monuments can be shattered by time and war, Aubrey committed himself to recording the remains of major and humble things alike, foraging for parish registers and measuring earthworks. By 1673 he was looking forward to the next county. But it was not to be. 'I should have been glad to have surveyed Sussex', he reflected sadly when Ogilby called off the project and left him in the lurch.[15]

The *Compleat History of Sussex* published by Thomas Cox in 1730 had to serve as a reference point for the next hundred years, though it was a small part of a national project and short on original research.[16] The major work of a county history was taken on by the lawyer, politician and tireless antiquary William Burrell, who amassed an enormous collection of sources in the 1780s. For two weeks each Whitsun holiday for more than a decade, he employed one of the finest topographical artists in England, the Swiss-born Samuel Hieronymus Grimm, to travel with him on his Sussex tours.[17] Burrell and Grimm visited even the smallest village churches, working out the age of arches, matching families to monuments. For the first time, the history of rural Sussex was being studied, and the thought of it grips me. Grimm sat in the fields above Pulborough and made a drawing of 'Upper Mount', all that remained of what was probably a motte and bailey (PLATE). Expertly, in pen and ink, he caught the rough hump of the earth, the windblown trees and the view across the valley from this greensand foothill to the main line of the downs. If he went into the church at Hardham he would have found the walls plainly whitewashed; he made no drawing there. Perhaps on a hint from locals, he found his way over the fields to the farmhouse that incorporated the ruins of Hardham Priory. He drew a close-up detail of the carving around the chapter house arches, showing the stylised leaves on the capitals: exceptional medieval sculpture in a farmyard. And he stood back to sketch the whole building in its setting, so that even now, a little faded, this modest wash drawing gives a powerful sense of space and distance: the open site under a wide sky, the low meadows beyond (PLATE).

The following Whitsun, Grimm was at work in Arundel, Chichester, and at the dissolved priory of Boxgrove in the countryside between them. The Benedictine guesthouse had been patched up for use as a barn. Grimm put two figures at the entrance, gesturing up at where a great hall once bustled above them. With delicate ink outlines and cool eggshell colouring, Grimm gave definite character to every arch and gable. In all, he made thirteen hundred watercolours, most of which now live in the British Library along with Burrell's notes and gatherings of manuscripts. But the book was never finished.

Samuel Hieronymus Grimm, *Inside of the Refectory of the Priory at Boxgrove*, 1781

Other visitors came with their different interests. The account of western Sussex in Daniel Defoe's 1724 *Tour through the Whole Island of Great*

Britain brimmed with enjoyment. He duly noted the seats of nobility (Arundel Castle; Petworth House 'with its elbows to the town'); but, in a way that would still be unusual a century later, he was equally interested in Petworth's 'good well built' houses, Chichester's thriving corn market and the export of Arun mullets to London. Keen for conversation, he surveyed places by finding out how people lived in them. The success of a bull-breeder stayed in his mind more vividly than any bishop's palace or unearthed inscription. The roads through the clay were dreadful, but riding the twelve miles between Arundel and Chichester he rejoiced in the 'most pleasant beautiful country in England'.[18]

In the 1760s and 70s the naturalist Gilbert White regularly travelled almost the full extent of the South Downs, or 'Sussex Chalk-hills' as they were called then, from his Hampshire home in Selborne to his aunt near Lewes. He tried to convey the distinct character of the chalk landscape. 'Perhaps I may be singular in my opinion,' he ventured, 'but I never contemplate these mountains without thinking I perceive something analogous to growth in their gentle swellings and smooth fungus-like protuberances, their fluted sides, and regular hollows and slopes, that carry at once the air of vegetative dilation and expansion.'[19] He had the sensation of a land alive and growing; it sounds almost as if it is breathing. Fungi: among the most mysterious kinds of organism. Peel the velvet skin from a mushroom and suddenly you are peeling turf, skinning the mound of a hill to find chalky flesh beneath. White was less concerned with measuring the downs against received ideas of beauty than with their living presence and what it felt like to be near them.

But few people were drawing or writing about these swellings and protuberances. They were not widely talked about as either beautiful or sublime. William Gilpin, who had a tenacious influence on perceptions of all kinds of British landscape, toured Sussex in 1774 (though his account wasn't published for another thirty years) and evaluated its views and textures according to his grammar of 'Picturesque' composition. The Arun region scored highly. From Bury Hill he looked down on the 'windings' of the river between 'beautiful tufted groves and buildings; among which Amberley Castle is conspicuous'. The rugged drama of the scarp was best, he decided: the hills 'break down *abruptly*, and often form promontories, projecting in beautiful perspective, into their several vales'.[20] Was the Arun to be the next destination for those in search of the Picturesque? No. Gilpin's general pronouncements on downland were too scathing. The bareness of the hills he found distasteful, and where stone showed through the turf it gave a 'blank glaring surface'. 'Chalk disfigures any landscape.'[21]

When W. H. Hudson began his 1900 book *Nature in Downland* and reached for the literature of Sussex, expecting to immerse himself in the imaginative life of his forebears, he found little on the bookshelf. There had been no Wordsworth in the area, finding permanent forms for what he felt as he looked and walked and listened to the stories of local people; there was no John Clare or George Crabbe of the downs. Percy Shelley, born to the north, near Horsham, wrote not a word about his native county and got out as soon as he could. Hudson's conclusion to his search was that 'Sussex, or any part of it, can hardly be said to exist in literature; or if it has any place there and in our hearts it is a mean one, far, far below that of most counties'.[22]

The 'discovery' of Sussex came late, but in the first years of the twentieth century it gathered pace. Soon after Hudson lamented a whole county's absence from literature, Rudyard Kipling moved to Bateman's and started to write of talkative spirits rising up from the ancient ground, spirits rhyming and gossiping as they remembered lives long ago, 'Yes before the Flint Men made the Dewpond under Chanctonbury Ring.'[23] Modernist artists and writers found particular affinities with the bare chalk and high beacons of the eastern downs – to such an extent that 'Sussex Modernism' is now a celebrated phenomenon.[24] Sussex Modernism was what made me want driving lessons on my seventeenth birthday in 1998: I was anxious to set off east towards Eric Gill's Ditchling, Lee Miller's Farley Farm and, most of all, towards the paths walked by

Virginia Woolf. Later, in my thirties, it was the untold – the mystery rather than the known thing – that took hold of me. Rather than go off towards my cultural heroes I would wait, read and watch to see who had lived just where I stood. In the event there was no need for patience: the merest scratch of the topsoil was all it took.

⌒

In biology class once, we traipsed out to the area of grass next to the Astroturf. The teacher had brought equipment in the form of white wire squares or 'quadrats', which were to be thrown on the ground. We then examined what was framed by the square. It's one of the basic methods used by ecologists. I don't remember what we found. We probably raced to list moss and clover, claimed praise for our rapidity and reverted to gossip about other things. I've remembered the square, though, and its way of focusing the mind. I remember how it made the earth at my feet newly visible. And I've seen now what people with deep knowledge and long-honed skill can do with such squares. For the two-by-two kilometre 'tetrad' that includes Pulborough, the plant list published by the Sussex Botanical Recording Society runs to 479 species.[25]

Local historians don't go around with wire squares but they choose units of study that work a little like quadrats, adapted to patterns of human set-tlement and community. The question of how to select sample areas and how to extrapolate from findings in one place is central to their discipline. Scholars might work by parish, or by groups of neighbouring parishes. Or it may be more helpful to consider agricultural regions, areas made coherent by similar topographies, farming practices and economies.[26]

As the books on my Sussex shelf accumulated, I made use of an imag-inary quadrat that landed where, forty years ago, I landed. I explored the area around Pulborough and downriver to Arundel, with excursions across to Chichester, the county town, which became my western limit. In my life as a critic of art and literature I was used to studying time periods – anything from a century to a single year. But this patch-work, this testing of the ground, was new to me.[27] With each day's reading I was learning its possibilities. Magnetised by certain places, choosing particular figures to follow, my methods were very unlike those of a social or economic historian making a steady survey. The stories demanded other kinds of response. As they established their own rhythms and patterns of imagery, time pooled and eddied. Currents of memory flowed in and out like the tidal river.

The artist Richard Long once took an Ordnance Survey map and drew a ring around the Cerne Abbas giant in Dorset. He walked every lane within its circumference over a six-day period. It was an artificial ritual, a propitiatory offering to the giant, perhaps. The perfect circle within which all the walking took place demonstrated just what we don't ordinarily do. Life creates odd-looking maps. What shape is a place, after all?

The locality that became my subject was defined by the Arun, and a stretch of the downs, and the orientation towards Chichester as commercial and cultural centre. Chichester was the place for being born and dying: I was born in 1981 at the hospital there, St Richard's, named after the bishop who gave money to the anchorite. I knew the road from home to city and back again; I knew the places where friends and relatives lived. When I shaded the familiar miles on a map, there was no name for the shape they made – it was certainly not a circle or a square.

The measure I really worked by might best be described as one of magnification. There are place names that stop me if I hear them away from Sussex, out of context. If the characters in a novel suddenly go to Pulborough or a book on Roman Britain mentions Bignor, the words stand out from the page. The detail bristles. It's as if the donor in a Van Eyck painting had held his glasses over just that passage. This phenomenon is part of my subject, and I have tried to see how it works for others too. I've watched for the moments when people in the past have felt suddenly alert to the significance of their place or caught sight of it from a new angle. It may be an Arundel gentleman reading Camden's *Britannia* in the 1630s and wanting to give the River Arun a fuller write-up in the story of the nation. It may be a poet in the 1790s realising that her childhood landscape had inspired other writers before her.

I let each chapter grow from a moment of startled noticing or finding: a document or a painting, a date stone or a lump of concrete, a voice overheard. Each suggested a different kind of exchange between local lives and wider worlds. The closer I looked, the more complex and far-reaching each subject became. I began to think of how a quadrat might also be a kind of window, simultaneously constraining and enlarging the view. It was nothing like the lonely window of the recluse but one that revealed thousands of people, all going about their lives. Their voices were sometimes hard to catch, but if I listened I could pick up fragments of what they were saying. In the bright space of the window, I could watch the people passing. And occasionally, with luck, effort and a library card, it felt possible not only to look at them, but for just a moment to look with them: to see what they were seeing as they crossed the fields under the downs.

The last item I unpacked from Caroline's boxes of her mother's books was a thin stray that had slipped down the side of the main piles. A pocket at the back held a map of the Arun intricately marked with weirs and ferries, keyed to a text that seemed to be a river atlas, chronicle, price list and address book combined. It was a printed edition of a seventeenth-century manuscript. I was supposed to be reading a thesis on Wordsworth that day, but a few paragraphs of this anonymous book introduced an author with a sense of place stronger than any I had encountered in writing before the 1780s and the 'discovery of local truth' that shaped Romanticism. The writing combined practical knowledge with a joyous use of language. Wouldn't Wordsworth have been interested in such a thing? I launched on *The High Stream of Arundel.*

2. HIGH STREAM OF ARUNDEL
A water bailiff and the river

In that small and obscure volume I found the voice of a Sussex man in the 1630s who loved the River Arun and wanted to write about it. He was a water bailiff, responsible for the business of the river from the Port of Arundel right up to the furthest navigable waters at Pallingham Quay north of Pulborough, on the far side of the downs, at the edge of the Wealden iron country. It was his duty to receive and record fees due on imports, to regulate fishing, and to keep a record of swan-marks showing who owned which birds. But there was so much else to say about this great stream that had run through his life. He had known it as a boy in the 1590s, his family had lived beside it for centuries, and the Earl of Arundel had made him its overseer. He knew the voices and habits of fishermen and bargemen as much as he knew the voices of the gentry whose lands and swans he could tell you blindfold. He liked the idea of a history – not a book to be printed, perhaps, but notes to pass on. He would record what he had done 'during the time of his Water Bailyship being 26 yeares & upwards'. More than that, he would be the biographer and the geographer of the Arun, naming its 'heads and risings', the smaller streams that found their ways through Sussex, the byways that came to make their acquaintance with the highway, the 'High Stream' that was his responsibility, his subject, the scene of his life.¹

There's barely a soul on the river now. A few pleasure boats are moored at Arundel, but upstream it's lonely and silent except for moorhens, ducks, and swans. You can stand on the bridge at Offham and it's so quiet you can hear the reeds shaking. The bailiff's river was busy with ships, barges, lighters, intricately engineered with quays, its tides carrying populations of watermen, some of them known on the river

for as long as anyone remembered, others bringing goods on their foreign ships and leaving on the next ebb. In the wetlands around the
High Stream the osier beds were thick with willow, and floods ran out
over the great acres of the wild brooks (that was their name in the 1630s
as now) where drowners and meadmen worked their sluices.[2]

The water bailiff took me on a tour of my native places as I had never
seen them, including the ferry crossings, 'the ancient weares on the sayd
streame' and the 'sundry kinds of fishes therein'. He wrote as if he were
rowing downstream, talking as he went. On we go past the 'old demolished Fort' at Pulborough, under Stopham Bridge to the 'Turning-stream'
where the major tributary the Rother (he called it the West-water) joins
the Arun. Antiquities, natural history and present usage are all essential
to the portrait of the river. Moving out across the plain between Hardham
and Wiggonholt to another crossing point, the stream runs on:

> It hasteth under the Bridge by Greatham part whereof was sometimes
> the land of Sir Henry Tresgose. But by the way it taketh in a little
> Riveret that springeth from the foot of the Downs at Chantrey Farm
> in Storrington whence, driveing certain water mills, it passeth from
> Sillington . . .

That's a 'riveret' of my early childhood, rising at the end of the lane
where I went to primary school, and still gushing with surprising force
after wet seasons. Whenever a new tributary joins the main channel,
the bailiff gives an account of its life – the mills it has turned, the lands
it has watered:

> From Houghton-Bridge by many crooks and turnings, leaving South
> Stoake & Offham on the West . . . it hasteth down neere to the antient
> Abbie de Calceto . . . and so under Arundell-bridge which Bridge when
> in decay ought to be repaired by the Borrough of Arundell . . .[3]

His interests and values shape every line. Always he names the
landowners past and present: the pattern of ownership is integral to the

landscape he loves. But he knows the business of both the nobles and the workers. The practical matters of bridge-repair and fishing times are not filed separately under admin, but central to the story. The proper way of doing things is that which is time-honoured, so he asserts the customs of the river.

'If the ancient lawes . . . bee not observed', says the bailiff, 'some one may happily take the whole benefitt of the river to himselfe or destroy the fish.' So fishing is closely regulated in the well-ordered river society of the 1630s that this text aims to preserve. Fishermen are 'tenants in common' of the stream, asked to act as 'under guardians' to the bailiff: they too are custodians, upholding the rules. The bailiff is at his most vigilant during the 'fence month' in spring, when the fish and the swans are breeding. Nothing then must disturb their peace and freedom in the waters. Fishers must keep open all their 'weare-gates, weeles, shutting netts, and other engins whatsoever'. For the rest of the year, standard rules apply. No eel spears on the High Stream. No green timber to be used in the water, lest the sap kill the fish. The mesh of nets needs to meet the regulation inch and a half from knot to knot, 'siz'd according to the ancient brase pin' kept at Arundel Castle.⁴ 'Weeles, and fish potts', must be of such a size that the bailiff 'may easily thrust his hand flatt-wise to the middle': any smaller and they will be cut up.

These 'wheel' traps were not allowed on the main river, but they were much used on the streams across the levels where there were thirty weirs at least, all with names and addresses. The bailiff knew every ditch and inlet in what had always been to me simply 'the wild brooks'. He could arrive unbidden at any time for an inspection, though he had to blow his horn, in warning, at your gate. The water bailiff is a Prospero waving a different world into life. I can almost hear it across the levels, the sound at sunset of all the nets being pulled in and the weir doors opened for the night.

For each stretch of water he describes the customary register of inhabitants at each time of year: for instance how the fish would move 'to the deeper Reaches that lie among the winding Hill, the better to keep off the Winter Storms' and 'here rest they, close garrison, till the returning Summer'.[5] His delight in the yearly rhythm of the river is palpable in the energy with which he tells the story:

> And now, having sent forth their Scowts to clear the Coast [the fish] presently disband & leave their Winter quartering and joyfully break up their Garison running, shooting Leaping & Foraging every where seeking for shallow Fords to Road in where I shall leave them.[6]

The text was edited and published in 1929 by Joseph Fowler. I looked at the name. Could it be a hoax, an elaborate 1920s game of fish and fowl? Investigation quickly revealed that Fowler was a clergyman, a keen geologist, and ran a boys' school outside Arundel. He was also, so far as I could tell, a skilled researcher. He had tracked down two eighteenth-century copies of the bailiff's guide, which seem to have been issued to successive water bailiffs when they took office. The text was in two parts: the first set out the history and character of the river and the second was more of a directory, with information that should be kept up to date. Much to his frustration, Fowler could not find the original of the first part, but the second was in the Duke of Norfolk's archives and could be dated by internal evidence (like the up-to-date payment of swan fees) to 1636, with additions made until 1640.[7]

The author never names himself, but he refers to 'the bailiff's house at Stopham'. This is a good clue, since there were only ever a few houses in Stopham. In February 1642, when the adult men of each parish were required to swear their loyalty to King Charles and the Church of England, there were thirty-seven men resident in the parish whose names were listed and submitted to the Crown.[8] Fowler saw that only one of these was of the right age and standing to be the water bailiff. By deduction he found the probable author: William Barttelot, whose house was either the handsome manor farm next to the church, or Ford Place right by the river.⁹

In the archive room at Arundel Castle, among wax-sealed pedigree rolls and bundled letters from forgotten controversies, I read the bailiff's manuscript: one part (the customs and swan-marks) written in a rapid seventeenth-century hand on loose sheets, the other (the history and topography) copied in steady copperplate into a later parchment-bound notebook dated 1713.¹⁰ The 1630s document had not been decoratively presented in any way: no hand-drawn title page or binding of the sheets together. There was not much to suggest it marked the culmination of many years' work on the river and was meant to last. But the blotless fluency suggested this was a fair copy of a text worked out elsewhere; in that sense, care had been taken. Whether or not this was the bailiff's own handwriting, these were his words. Here he was, talking, gesturing. The water bailiff, or William Barttelot. Let me risk it and call him Barttelot. Wearing lightly his four hundred years, this gentleman of Stopham comes striding out from the pages and asks that I consider seventeenth-century culture from his point of view.

Barttelot was a keen reader of history, marvelling at the 'learned labours' by which William Camden in his *Britannia* had sought out the lost names of places throughout the country and revived them with, 'as it were, a second birth'.¹¹ *Britannia* was a county-by-county survey of Great Britain and Ireland, researched by Camden on an enormous scale with the aims of restoring 'Britain to his antiquity' (Celtic, Saxon and especially Roman antiquity), recording the current state of its monuments and (as if this weren't enough) providing a topographical portrait of these 'flourishing kingdoms' in the present. It had been repeatedly enlarged since the first edition in 1586 and available since 1610 in an English translation that proved popular with a growing public of readers who did not lead lives of Latin-speaking scholarship but were keen to learn about their country. Barttelot knew Latin and might have used any of the editions; he had read other books by Camden too. The work of those who recovered the past seemed to him fertile, creative, a way of giving new life. 'A second birth' he says: the phrase suggests how closely Barttelot associated Camden's project with a wider 'renaissance'.

But Camden had his limits. Barttelot was exercised about his calling the river the Arun instead of the 'High Stream' or *Alta Ripa* as Barttelot was sure it had been called in ancient times. 'Lett it not seeme strange that the right name of a River should pass by a Learned Gentleman un-seene, that was a Strainger to those parts.' Barttelot pressed his case for the river name, but he was also making a wider point. No scholar could know everywhere intimately, even with help from correspondents. The history of the country couldn't all be written by one Londoner. Infor-mation was often 'hidd in the custody of private men' or preserved in the language and customs of a place. Camden had every county of Great Britain and Ireland to think about, and needed to attend to strategically important sites along the south coast, so the gaps in his survey of Sus-sex were understandable. The wealth of history to be found in villages was not Camden's emphasis (or that of any widely known writer at this time): 'The inner parts of the county being thick set with villages have nothing very remarkable.' Nothing to detain us here. The manor houses and churches went unmentioned. Camden made haste, 'sometimes *per saltum*' says Barttelot, 'for he over pass'd the Priory of Boxgrove, lying almost in the Rode between Chichester & Arundell'.[12]

There's baffled amazement in Barttelot's tone. How could Camden have missed Boxgrove? *Per saltum*: 'by hopping', leaping ahead with a hop, skip and jump. Barttelot imagined the great scholar rushing along the Arundel road, leapfrogging one of the most significant buildings in the county: a major Benedictine monastery, its cloisters empty and ruined since the dissolution, but its church — almost on the scale of a cathedral — open to anyone who turned off the road. The water bailiff knew the fine tombs of Boxgrove and the flowers that soar above. In the 1530s, the painter Lambert Barnard had hoisted himself on scaffolding to decorate the vaulted ceiling through the whole length of the monastic choir with a pattern of scrolling vines and hanging grapes, roses, daffodils and dianthus, each section of ceiling growing with a different plant to make a garden in the air.[13] Camden mentioned none of it and when he got to Arundel he was quickly ready to move on. 'Besides the Castle and the Earls, Arundell hath nothing memorable' he wrote, dealing at a stroke with the port, water meadows, wooded hangers, the ruins of the Maison Dieu with its white clunch innards now exposed to the wind.[14]

In private rooms across the country others were making, like the bailiff, revisions and additions to the larger story. As part of an investigation into early modern 'local consciousness', one recent scholar has studied seventeenth-century copies of *Britannia*, looking at notes made by readers in the margins. Often the annotations relate to a particular area, drawing attention to features absent from the text – like a 'cleere riveret' in Surrey 'so full of the best trouts'.[15] *Britannia* encouraged men and women to think of the nation as a coherent whole, but people were also reading, thinking, writing and feeling in local terms, taking up their pens to add regional knowledge to the national account. The Arun bailiff could see that the discoveries of those who travelled might be joined with the insights of those who stayed. There was no established model of a local history for him to look to (though that would change in the century to come); he wrote what he cared about and what might be of use.[16]

He looked for traces of former ferry-points, like the one in the north-east of Stopham parish ('Passagium de Fishium'), near the seat of the Combes 'of which there is nought remaining now but the Plot of ground, moated round'. There was another ancient crossing place in Wiggonholt, giving access to the parish of Hardham ('alias Herringham' he added, wanting to include the old names which held histories bound up in them), vanished except for the causeway across the levels that once led to it.[17] Barttelot was a field archaeologist, reading the lines in his landscape. He liked to hypothesise around place names and his guesses were good ones, like his explanation of 'Steeple Rye' for a stream near Amberley 'on which there stood antiently a steeple'. He didn't mean there was a church there, but a fishing weir set with large wicker cones. The steeple-shaped traps would be laid with their open ends facing into the current so that eels could swim in but not get out. Fisheries are fugitive things that leave fewer traces than churches, but for Barttelot the history of a place was in the wicker steeples lowered into the water as much as towers pointing into the sky.

The bailiff was experimenting as a local historian and also as a literary stylist. River-writing was a phenomenon in the seventeenth century, and it took established forms. Rivers were currents of national identity, and lived in poets' and readers' minds as allegorical figures. Great rivers might be attended by flowing trains of pageboys and maids lining the path of a ceremonial progress to the sea. A stream might be a virgin bride, courted by a lover and then joined in confluence. The result was sometimes a bland kind of artifice: once expressed in terms of nymphs, rivers with different environments and ecologies soon start to sound the same. But these mythologies insist on natural phenomena having characters, narratives, self-determining energies; they suggest the animate life of waters.

The Thames commanded most attention, eulogised as the living current of national prosperity, but a few determined writers felt that their own places were also fit for poetry. William Vallens of Ware in Hertfordshire left the mainstream for a Thames tributary, the River Lea. His 1590 *Tale of Two Swannes* was a blank-verse tour, mixing literary motifs of noble swans and watery marriages with a gazetteer of real things to look out for, the wonders of his area: abbey ruins, smart houses and 'a rare device . . . but newly made': a special lock for maltsters' boats.[18] It was not the usual stuff of poetry, but in this direction lay new ways of looking. Samuel Daniel, who was regarded by many contemporaries as a successor to Spenser, wrote warmly of West Country rivers whenever he saw the chance and was conscious of pulling against the currents that drew poetry to London and to the court. 'No, no, my Verse respects not *Thames* nor *Theaters* / Nor seekes it to be knowne unto the Great', he wrote with evident regional pride in his 1592 *Sonnets to Delia*. His subject instead was a river of Hampshire and Wiltshire: '*Avon* rich in fame, though poore in waters, / Shall have my Song, where *Delia* hath her seat: *Avon* shall be my *Thames* . . .'[19] The modesty was confected, since the poet's 'Delia' was at least in part the Countess of Pembroke and her seat at Wilton House was hardly lowly, but the argument for local attention is clearly made.

Daniel would return to regional subjects.[20] He wrote a masque in which the country's rivers appeared on stage, bringing their riches to the court. *Tethys' Festival*, with production design by Inigo Jones, was staged in 1610 as part of the investiture celebrations for the new Prince of Wales. The gist of the drama was that he should not seek imperial conquest but concentrate his patronage and stewardship on the bountiful waters of home. A call, then, to value what one has before pursuing colonial expansion. All the dancers carried gifts from their respective rivers. Lady Arundel, Aletheia, played the River Arun, dancing out of an ocean cavern as a nymph. What she presented as her symbolic offering is not recorded. Perhaps it was a basketful of the famous Arundel mullets, generally acknowledged, says the bailiff, as 'the best and fatest in England, and of a most pleasing taste'.[21]

The riverine masque genre reached its height at just the time the bailiff was writing. Milton's *Comus* gave voice to Sabrina, the nymph of the Severn, on whose shores at Ludlow Castle the drama was first performed in 1634. More influential for many regional readers, though, was Michael Drayton's poem *Poly-Olbion*, an epic survey of the country in which the land itself – and the woods and rivers – spoke of what they saw. Drayton made a literary progress, in two volumes of 1612 and 1622, through the 'rivers, mountains, forests, and other parts of this renowned isle of Great Britain', presenting a description of it all, 'with intermixture of the most Remarkable Stories, Antiquities, Wonders, Rarities, Pleasures, and Commodities of the same'. The Isis prepared for marriage to the Tame, and all the Cotswolds arranged flowers for the bride. The whole country was dancing a masque. This was geography in high Jacobean style. I'm almost sure the bailiff knew it; there are echoes of it in his prose.

Drayton was distinctive in combining the fantastical language of a national pageant with a degree of topographical and ecological exactitude. Sometimes his nymphs speak with sharp and urgent regional knowledge, complaining of wrongs done to the fabric of the land. His Sussex resounds with the distress of 'hollow woods' cut bare to stoke the Wealden furnaces.

RIGHT Inigo Jones, design
for a water nymph, 1610

BELOW William Hole, map
for the 1622 edition of *Poly-
Olbion*, showing the nymphs
of Lavant and Arun

They cry out in sorrow, wondering at men who allow 'the holiest things to perish': 'These iron times breed none that mind posterity.' The 'clear Lavant' tells Chichester the dreadful news.[22] The firmly artificial literary conventions of personified woods and rivers seem here to rediscover their origins in ancient perceptions of nature's animus and agency. Drayton has the trees speaking for themselves, and the Arun ('which doth name the beauteous Arundel') echoing with their groans.

As if taught by Drayton, the water bailiff tries the style: a stream runs 'half dead with feare' from the noisy ironworks; 'the water nimph, thus scared and comfortless goes coldly on to Rudgwicke Furnace'. But he can't decide whether the stream is male or female (must it be either?), and he associates Rudgwick with comfort, probably because the parish had long been a Barttelot family home. In his text, the nymph 'finds a Fire there rests and warms', soothed rather than violated by industry. The bailiff suggests his care for the woods and streams by knowing their names. He nods with momentary enthusiasm to a literary culture of water spirits, but is soon attending to his environment in more practical ways. The water nymph and her sister Hamadryades (a Greek dryad bound to a tree) set off towards the next bridge, forgetting their Greek to advise in plain English 'how it ought to be repaired by the Tenants of Amberly and Bury'.[23]

The water bailiff on the High Stream sounds like none of the courtier-writers of his time. He read and respected literature and tried a personification or two as we might expect. But he called a swan a swan. The Arun is not a nymph in a ceremony of Britain but a particular river, the background and foreground of a busy life. He was a provincial gentleman writing a bit of local history and a manual; there was not much art about it. Yet there's a mix of poetry and practicality in his book, and a bold sense of place, that we won't often find in the high literature of the seventeenth century – and that it's hard to find in art at all before the Romantics made local feeling a virtue. We can't know what the Sarahs and Janes and Johns and Samuels of the parish registers felt for the river that ran fast and deep at Offham bend and wide through Stopham levels.

But it's from unsung documents of practical life that we're most likely to glean a clue.

⌣

Since childhood I have known the sight of Stopham Bridge in the fields beyond Pulborough, unused now, its edges lost in withies and willow-herb. Seven stone arches, finely engineered in the fourteenth century, still rise over the wide river. It's a structure that can appear soaring or hunkered, its character changing with the water levels. When the floods are up, or the winter tide is in (it's tidal here now, though it wasn't before eighteenth- and nineteenth-century planners straightened several down-stream bends), the currents lap at the roofs of the arches. The bridge is in up to its shoulders and looks beaten, but the path above remains dry. The Barttelots kept this impressive piece of civil engineering in good repair for six centuries. The traffic was rerouted over a concrete and metal-railed bridge in 1986. Now walkers linger on the old stone para-pets and watch the ducks.

We often went past the turning to Stopham village. 'Carry on past Stop-ham': it was a staple of local directions. It was a Sunday and special-days direction because it led towards my great-uncle and -aunt in Sutton, or to the garden centre, which was a standard destination for 'getting out' when anyone was fractious or in need of a new indoor fern. All that familiar ground, and yet when I turned down the lane to the village last year, I'm sure it was for the first time. In the church, half a mile from the main road, there were Barttelots everywhere: glowing in bright glass in the windows, sculpted in marble monuments around the walls. The long red carpet down the central aisle had the look of protecting what lay beneath. Should a visitor disturb it? I peered under one end and started to roll it back.

Two brass figures appeared, and two more. There, very tall and thin, were the oldest of the brass people: John Barttelot, who died in 1429, and his wife Joan, each pressing their long hands together in prayer, each standing firm on a little mound of earth, incised with clumps of grass. Among the drapes of Joan's dress was a miniature dog. Then came their son John, who went with the Earl of Arundel to fight in France. I rolled the carpet and unrolled time, rolled and rolled as a whole family appeared. There it was: stretching up the aisle. Row after row, they were gathered in assembly. They lay with their feet towards the altar so that if they sat up just a little on a Sunday they could watch the communion. People see cities suddenly appearing in the clouds or mountains above the sea; the brasses, revealed for a moment, glistening, from under the carpet, were a strange and complete vision like a Fata Morgana.[24]

William and his older brother Walter had grown up with the sight of their brass ancestors in the nave, a map of time, a way of counting back.[25] Some of the brass people were relatives they remembered. They had known their great-grandfather William, who had lived to the age of ninety-seven and presided at Stopham as an ancient man when the boys were still learning the names of the fish. Before him, behind him: John and Joan, Richard and Petronilla. The engravings were old and worn, but by 1630 Walter had plans for Stopham church. He wanted Barttelots to shine in the very fabric of the building. He commissioned an artist to make painted glass windows with ancestors kneeling in them; the signature 'Roelandt' suggests Roelandt Savery from Utrecht, one of the best-known Flemish artists of the time. As for the brasses, the old figures were to be repaired, and new brasses made in commemoration of his parents.

The man he chose for the job was the mason and monument-maker Edward Marshall, only just liveried but with a London yard and major commissions to his name. Marshall could do a classically wreathed head in marble when required, and stone sculptures were certainly what most clients wanted in the 1630s.[26] But Marshall was also expert in the tradition of memorial brass engraving that had flourished through the Middle Ages and he understood that, for those who cared about it, brass carried strong associations of longevity and continuity. In 1631, leaving instructions for a monument in his will, Archbishop Samuel Harsnett (former Bishop of

Chichester, former keeper of swans on the Arun) had asked that his figure be cut in brass. And he stipulated: 'the Brasse to be soe riveted & fastened cleane through the Stone as sacrilegious handes may not rend off the one without breakinge the other'.[27] This was a man who had lived among the severed stone limbs and wrenched plaques of Reformation England. Edward Marshall engraved an image that looked both ancient and strikingly immediate. Then he set to work on the Barttelots of Stopham.

Walter and William saw their brass parents laid into a tablet of Petworth Marble, quarried just to the north of Petworth, at Kirdford; a limestone close-set with winkles, it is not a true marble but it polishes to a sheen. It would hold the Barttelots forever, or near enough, among all the fossil shells held fast in the stone. Their father, Richard, looked imposingly large in armour, though he was standing on a tiled floor that made it seem as if he had just come indoors. Their mother was on one side, and their stepmother opposite, both women in fine ruffs and long veils, praying together now as if they had known each other all their lives. Walter had written to the Heralds' College to check the coats of arms for his parents, and Marshall engraved them: three left-hand gloves pointing downward, four crescents, the tower crest that remembered John's leading the capture of Fontenay Castle after Agincourt. There was also a crest newly granted: a swan.[28] The monument to John was restored, so that he stood on a re-tufted hillock, hands steepled in prayer, heraldry above. John and the other medieval people were re-laid in new tablets of local marble and set in the aisle.[29]

Walter wanted even more of the family gathered in the church, and so Marshall made a series of plaques engraved with the children of each generation. They were screwed into the stone under the appropriate parents, these groups of children in twos and fours and fives, all wearing Carolingian best no matter which century they had lived in. Many of them had skulls floating over their heads, which meant they had died young. Under the large figures of his mother and father, Walter had a little plaque installed that showed himself and his siblings:

His lost sister Ann.

His lost brothers, Edward and John, shown the size of schoolboys
though dressed as men with capes and garters, death hovering over
their heads like a thought, or a cloud, a bone-cloud cut in brass.

Walter himself in armour at the head of the line-up.

And William: moustache and pointed beard of the Charles 1 kind,
doublet and breeches, suavely slouched boots with spurs.

It was too generic to be much of a portrait, but still it was him: a man who
wrote about the river and talked with fishermen, a man of brass and swans.

The church memorials give no indication of William Barttelot's domestic life, but the parish registers do. His wife, Anne, came from the
large Strudwick family in Wealden Kirdford, a centre of glass-making,
iron-smelting – and marble-quarrying. The River Kird flowed past the
furnaces to Wisborough Green where William and Anne lived for parts of
the year. This was their home parish during the 1630s, though William was
also 'of Stopham'; they moved regularly between the two and had property
in both. Their daughter Mary was christened six months after they married
(probably conceived during the engagement, which would not, I'm told,

have been uncommon at the time) and another baby, Ann, came in 1630. Barbary was baptised and buried at Stopham in January 1635. After this came a son, Richard, who lived. Anne had another decade of pregnancy and childbearing ahead. Elizabeth, Charity, Barbara – her name recalling the lost Barbary. At Christmas 1643, when the Royalist garrison at Arundel Castle was surrounded and held under siege by Parliamentary forces, Anne had seven-month-old Barbara crawling around while Richard was a schoolboy of seven and a half. Then came Robert and Rosa.[30]

⁓

It was said that you could ride from Stopham to Horsham on Barttelot land. For the seven years I was at school in Horsham I went by the King's Highway instead, or rather I was taken, day after day, by parents who sacrificed swathes of their lives to the school run. Half an hour each way, morning and afternoon, up into the weald and back into the downs. Three families shared the duty on rotation, different rules and atmospheres reigning in each of the three cars. One was from Burpham, a muddy, adventurous, country car that bounced through potholed lanes while playing music from CDs that had lost their cases, and stopped on summer afternoons for ice creams at Wisborough Green. The other two were cars of rural suburbia: velour-seated, spotless, put away in garages. We sat in our kilts, wedged in between satchels and art portfolios and smelly sports bags. We dozed in the mornings and giggled in the afternoons, and I can barely remember what we saw from the window through all those hours. The rhythm of the crossroads and roundabouts comes back to me, though, in the morning sequence, each slowing and acceleration freighted with the knowledge that we were approaching, that only ten minutes, five minutes, were left of dreaming before the day began. Billingshurst changed from a village to a large town in those years, flags fluttered at the entrances to new estates, and a bypass swept across the fields; I remember the sense of weightlessness on that smooth arc of road.

For centuries this was one of the most difficult routes in Britain, when wheels and hooves and boots were sucked down into clay. But the weald could not do without the downland, or the downs without the weald – or the 'wilde' as it was called then. It was the Sussex wilderness, thickly forested, hospitable only to those who knew it well. Estates in the downs often stretched northward (as the Barttelot estate did); marriages that united downland and Wealden properties were much encouraged. The forests were hiding places in times of trouble, 'secret and reserved places for the Inhabitants of the County' as the water bailiff put it. But the villages were populous with workers and this was an area of heavy industry, forging the iron that made tools, ships and – crucially, in the coming years – cannon.[31]

The river was the best road between inland Sussex and the coast. Ships of ten tonnes or more could be anchored in the deep central water of the Arun, though most cargoes were loaded onto flat-bottomed river-barges and transferred to ships in port at Arundel for onward transport by sea. Incoming goods, likewise, were rolled, levered, lifted from ships to barges for the journey upriver past South Stoke, Amberley, Pulborough.[32] At the Port of Arundel, the cargoes and charges were logged. Every vessel was the bailiff's business. Reduced fees for Ryers and Cinqueportmen, half a hundred oysters due to him from each oyster boat in harbour.[33]

A fisherman rowed over from Greatham and walked up to the bailiff's house with the sum of six shillings eightpence in his pocket. The money paid, he was taken to where the swans stood in a pen, startled and watching. He got hold of them one at a time, and held them while the bailiff punched a tiny hole in the beaks on the right side, and cut the left wing tip. Then he carried them through the garden and out of the gate: the big tense bodies breathing under his arm, necks supported in his hand. Orange bills travelling past cut yews, white arcs of neck carried over the fields, and then a release into water, energy let fly in splashing and spread of wings, then bodies recomposed, necks erect, feathers twitched and settled, silence.

Anthony Jutton of Greatham had failed to pay for his swans. They were left to him by his father, but an inheritance charge was due and this had not been paid. Jutton was still a child, overseen by an elderly guardian, and the family was in considerable flux. The bailiff had seized the swans. Jutton's boatman was sent over with the money. Recording the incident, the bailiff names him: 'Pratt, that had been fisherman on the high streame forty yeares.' He knows the man. The young swans were given the customary Jutton mark, and 'putt to ye river againe'.[34] The bailiff told the story with pleasure at the spectacle of it: the old fisherman and the great white birds.

Swans in the 1630s had a language clipped into them, a runic alphabet of ownership that now seems disturbing. Two holes on the right of the beak and a slit in the inner blade of the left foot; one notch on the left of the beak and the right heel cut. District swan-herds like the bailiff, appointed as deputies to the Master of the Royal Game of Swans and Cygnets, kept books or rolls in which every mark was recorded, with the details of its owner. This went on in almost every region of England.[35] Splendidly painted swan-rolls survive from the Broads, the Isle of Ely, the rivers Yare and Witham, beaks arrayed as a kind of heraldry. If there was ever a painted 'swan-roll' for the Arun, it has not been found. But the water bailiff recorded the markings in words next to the names of their owners. Successive bishops, he noted, had paid to inherit the mark that belonged inalienably to Amberley Castle, the bishops' palace, and so it had passed (three notches on the beak and a butted wing) from Lancelot Andrewes, bishop 1605–9, his sermons never to be forgotten, to Samuel Harsnett (later engraved in brass) to George Carleton to Richard Montague, each paying a fee to the bailiff – for whom it was all modestly lucrative.

Swan protection was strictly enforced according to statute – until, of course, it was time for the birds to be eaten.[36] The rules were devised with the protection of human property in mind, not the liberty of swans. Nobody must disturb the nests in breeding season, and the bailiff had a duty to crack the ice if the river froze. Disputes were brought before Courts of Swan-mote. The biggest event in the river calendar was the annual swan-hopping, or 'upping'. This was swan census day, when each bird was counted and registered and the year's new cygnets given the mark of their parents.

Swan-upping still takes place on the Thames over several days each July, the ceremonially dressed 'uppers' progressing upstream in skiffs, checking but no longer 'marking' each swan as they go. It's a famous occasion for its bird-grappling waterborne pageantry, but other water-ways across the country also have their histories of swan counting. In the 1630s, the second day of August was the date for upping on the Arun. Every swan-owner or his representative was required to attend, and all fishermen were needed to help. Each bird had to be tethered with a long-handled swan hook, lifted up from the water into a boat or straight onto the bank where marks could be read and new ones issued. 'Rowers and waders' worked together, quickly surrounding and manoeuvring the brood. Cygnets had one wing 'butted' or pinioned to prevent flight: they were robbed of the freedom of the air. The bailiff noted each upping in his book, and a tuft of feathers was taken from the bird's head to show it had been registered. When the census was complete all along the river, there was dinner, hosted by the bailiff, for everyone involved.[37]

⌒

I took the train to Arundel each day in the summer after my first year at university. I had a job in the café at the castle, so I walked in my poly-ester uniform across the causeway from the station, in through the lower castle gate, up the hill past the keep and into the noise of steel forks being tipped by the hundred into cutlery-holders, and instructions shout-ed over the clatter of the washing-up and the radio. I was an object of suspicion, fresh from college. They didn't want me to clean the plates; they wanted me out of the café altogether and selling ice creams. I presumed it was a way to get rid of me, but perhaps it was simply that no one else liked days alone outside.

There was an octagonal wooden hut on the grass by the keep: I unbattened the shutters, put out the sandwich boards, and sat at the counter under the window. There could be twenty minutes between customers, so I started taking a book. Surreptitious at first, I propped *The Faerie Queene* under the ledge where it couldn't be seen. Then I offered a customer a stanza with his Magnum, and the next customers wanted a stanza too. The Magnums were overpriced, but people buying ice creams are happy, or at least hopeful. We read the words together sometimes, the American sightseers, the retired local women, the parents with push-chairs, the uncles and husbands and I.

Pictures appeared in succession, each framed and distinct in the square form of Spenser's nine-line stanzas: a dragon with waving wings snatching up the Red-Crosse Knight; Avarice on his camel laden all with gold. Pictures passed in the open window before me, framed by the shutters of my wooden hut as the days went by and heat yellowed the lawn. Swans would come on excursions from Swanbourne Lake, the millpond in the valley between steep downs north of the castle. They preened quietly on the grass until some enchanted child would creep too close, offering a bite of Twister, and a mother would pull him back in panic. On a grey day with no visitors, making my way through Book 3 of *The Faerie Queene*, I met the horrible rape of Leda by the god Jove embodied as a swan, much aestheticised by Spenser. I looked up at the birds on the grass in disgust, their rough beaks nibblingly insistent, the hosepipes of their necks searching and stretching. I turned the page. That story was a violence to all swans.

All the rivers of England and Ireland flowed into the riverine pageant of *The Faerie Queene* Book 4. The effect is of looking from a great height, yet we can see fish in the currents. Dart, Stour, Winbourne,

Mole (running underground): I loved the familiar names jostling in this fantastical literary world. Except – not all rivers. Now, reading it again, flicking past phrases I underlined in the ice-cream hut, I see there is no Arun. It was the river that served the nation's furnaces and brought grain to Elizabethan London, but has no place in the Faerie Queene's realm. Perhaps Spenser knew nothing of it or, like his contemporary William Camden, hopped over much of Sussex *per saltum* when he looked at the map.

History did not hop over Arundel. The bailiff's employer, Thomas Howard, Earl of Arundel, made his will in 1641 because he knew that trouble was coming. As Lord Marshal of England, he was one of the most prominent officers of the King, though he dreaded some of the military roles that fell to him. Whenever he could he had turned his attention from matters of state to the study of art, visiting painters across Europe and assembling, at Arundel House in London, one of the greatest collections ever made. 'My lord of Arundell' the bailiff called him, loyally reciting the family pedigree. But they would rarely have met; the Earl had never spent much time at his Arundel home – a warlike castle when what he wanted were picture-hung rooms and a garden. By 1641 his position was perilous. The power and the anger of Parliament were rising against the King. The pictures and sculptures were crated up by the hundred and sent to Europe, then Thomas Howard secured his own exit.

The Earl was not in England in February 1642 when every man over the age of eighteen was ordered to swear allegiance to 'the true Reformed Protestant religion' and to both King and Parliament. Over and over, in every parish, the oath was taken in front of the minister and churchwardens. Up and down the Arun the census was taken. In Stopham the rector wrote down the names. Thirty-seven adult men:

John Harwood
- Richard Gardener
William Barttelot, gent.[38]

The gentry and clergy, the Arun fishermen, the shopkeepers and needle-makers in Chichester, the brewers and blacksmiths in Arundel, all were sworn and counted in a desperate attempt to unite the nation behind Crown and Parliament.

The Earl spent time in Antwerp and then moved to Italy and settled near Padua. He funded from a distance the army he raised for the King. In small bids against the ruination of his estates, he sent messages to stewards about what should be done. He longed to know how the new gardens were doing at Albury in Surrey, the house where he had been happiest; the steward was to take care that 'Roses Chesimine wodbines & ye like sweetes be planted'.[39] The great stone fortress at Arundel had not been his favoured place for gardening, but in any case the time for planting there was over.

War came to the castle. Most of Sussex was under the control of Parliamentary forces by autumn 1642, early in the protracted conflict that would run on for most of the decade in other areas. The ground-swell of popular feeling across much of the county was for Parliament, while most clergy were loyal to the King as were some of the influential gentry. Towns and villages were divided against themselves.[40] In Arundel and the surrounding area, dominated by ancient Catholic families, even close-knit communities were split. Parliamentary loyalties were not to be relied upon in this stretch of countryside. A Royalist counter-attack succeeded in taking the garrison at Arundel Castle, and troops set about securing the town as a stronghold. But a major offensive was coming.

The Parliamentary army under William Waller moved in from Hampshire in mid-December 1643, having taken Alton and with Arundel next in line. The ground was frozen hard, and the approaching troops covered the distance quickly. They stopped at Petworth, attacking the precariously held garrison there and returning Petworth Park to Parliamentary hands. Then it was south through the downs on 19 December and by evening Arundel was surrounded. With reinforcements due to arrive, Waller pressed the Royalists back within the castle walls and trapped them there: an estimated fifteen hundred people. Forces moved in from across the south to hold the siege. As the days passed, reports came out from the castle that food was critically low. The attacking army targeted the water supply. The account despatched by Waller to London explained that 'the course of a Pond was turned . . . so that now the Enemy began to be distressed with thirst'. It's thought that the upper millpond at Swanbourne was drained. Within the walls, the only remaining water became contaminated. That was fatal. Dysentery and typhus spread through the overcrowded, captive community, and continued to spread after the surrender, killing Parliamentarians and their Royalist prisoners alike in the shattered streets.[41]

Wenceslaus Hollar, *A Prospect of Arundel Castle and Town*, 'Fecit 1644', but it was an act of memory and memorial: by 1644 the castle had been blown open to the sky and this scene no longer existed

I don't know whether the bailiff went to fight or whether he found other ways to protect the old order of the river as it had been under the Earl. On the death of his brother Walter, he had inherited the manor of Stopham. He and Anne still lived there, by the Arun. A son, Richard, was baptised in August 1645 – his name entered into the Stopham register by the rector, who liked to keep his records in Latin. Then a daughter at the end of 1646, while the King was held prisoner. There is no sign of William Barttelot having to forfeit his property. He was able to hold minor public office as one of the county treasurers in 1649, so he must have co-operated with the parliamentary administration, or actively supported it.[42]

What did the revolution mean for swans and the system of swan-marks on the Arun? The legal process by which the Royal Swan-herd had as-signed marks was defunct, there being no royalty. In the flux, when it was unclear who if anyone owned the swans, they were widely considered fair game for all. Rumour had it that republican garrisons cooked every swan on the Thames. There were a few left on the River Len near Leeds Castle in Kent by 1651 when soldiers there were instructed to hold back since 'great spoil' had already been made of fish and swans.[43] It was an odd light in which to be thinking about the English Commonwealth. Local history had brought me here, to a question about the status of swans at a time when the constitution of a new society was being worked out day by day.

Firm evidence is very scarce, but a scrap or two suggests an attempt to translate the old system into the reconfigured framework of government; the official who validated a Lincolnshire swan-mark in 1651 signed him-self 'Swannerd to ye Commonwealth'.[44] When Amberley Castle was sold off (the bishops were deposed; church property was Parliament's to sell), it came with 'swanns and Game of swanns'. But how the purchaser assert-ed his right to them in the 1650s remains unclear because almost certainly there was no bailiff to oversee swan-marks.[45] The household and staff of Arundel Castle had been broken up, the title of Earl abolished.

From this perspective of a profoundly changed nation, we might look back on the bailiff's work as an effort of saving up. He had recorded the old customs of the Arun in their last moment of certainty, before all was reconfigured in the crucible of the revolution. Perhaps even in 1636 he felt it coming.

William Barttelot lived to see the Restoration. He made a good old age – seventy-four – and died in the winter of 1666–7. He made his will at the end of January. I pored over the writing of a long-ago clerk, learning about William Barttelot from the arrangements he made while dying. To his 'loving wife Anne', for the course of her life, he left a bedstead and the furniture in the kitchen. I went on with gritted teeth. But there was care in the list of objects he named for Anne: the coloured curtains, pewter dishes, a brass skillet. She may have been ill already – she would not live beyond that year – and William ensured these things wouldn't be carried off under her nose. The rest of his goods and chattels, after expenses, went to their daughters. This didn't include the house itself, though, or his land holdings. These he left to three 'loving friends', all local men; they were probably involved in business together (there were certainly debts to be paid) and the bequests were part of a working relationship between neighbours who were almost family. William named the parcels of land in Rudgwick and Stopham, the plots of his life: coppice ground called Hides Copps, Assetts, Jupps, Harwoods, meadowland called Bathpoole.[46]

At the house, an inventory of goods was taken. The record of it, kept at the West Sussex Record Office, is like a parody of a tantalisingly illegible document, straight out of *Tristram Shandy* or Virginia Woolf's mock-biography *Orlando*. It's an enormous hole with fragments of page around the edge. A few discernible phrases emerge from the ruin and I write them in pencil on a blank sheet.[47] Hovering as if in mid-air, the solid objects of a life:

> Boulster
> > Flocke
> Bushell
> Item one long table one little table
> > a milke traye

William's name and dates were recorded on a floor-plaque at Stopham, but there were no more brass pictures. Edward Marshall, the engraver, was doing fewer monuments by then: after serving as King's Master Mason in the 1660s he passed the business to his son, whose workshops would be at the heart of the great re-building after the Fire of London. Anne Barttelot did not stay long after her husband: she was buried at Stopham that summer. A new water bailiff may have taken office on the Arun but no evidence has emerged. The next recorded bailiff was Laurence Eliot of Yapton Place, who took the role in 1713 and was given a copy of the history and customs, written out in the notebook that survives in the archive at Arundel Castle.[48] I have no idea how he thought about the river and its history. There had been a revolution and a counter-revolution. Some of the book's instructions were no longer relevant. But it was still his job to regulate fishing. The copying of the book suggests some investment in the pre-war customs. It seems likely that when he went to inspect a fisherman's weirs and nets, he followed the old courtesy of blowing his horn at the gate.

3. A TEACHER'S BOOKS

Caroline rang after her weekly visit to the home. Her mother was still on tenterhooks, she said, keeping an eye on the hallway with exhausting vigilance. I could visualise where she was, having gone along with Caroline a few weeks before. It was as good a place as it could be, run by skilful, attentive staff, with a giant fish tank by reception and each room entered through a painted and brass-numbered front door. When I was there Elizabeth wanted to read and repeatedly opened books to begin, but worry arrested her at the first lines. The long habit of reading told her there would be pleasure as she settled with the book, but there was only bafflement where pleasure had been. Reading is the greatest safety I know when trouble comes. But for Elizabeth that haven was unreachable. Reading had closed its gates and there was no getting in.

At school we knew Elizabeth as 'Mrs G'. She was mainly a Geography teacher, but she also covered part of the A level History syllabus and it was History classes that I had with her for a year in Lower Sixth. The Russian Revolution. She gave us maps, of course, insisting that it mattered where things happened. We labelled Archangel and Murmansk. My essay on economic development came back with a B+. It was let down by geographical mix-ups, said the pencilled note. I was to think again about the distance between places and how this might affect the argument.

The Russian Revolution exam required us to interpret a range of sources. For this, Mrs G coached us patiently week by week. We peered at photocopied images of Stalin greeting labourers and read Soviet newspaper reports. 'Whose point of view are we getting?' she would ask. 'Whose voices are we not hearing?' She drummed it into us: 'NOP: nature, origin, purpose'. We all wrote it in the front of our files, and underlined the words in several colours. Whatever the source, ask its nature, origin and purpose.

Caroline sent eight more boxes of books, including a full run of the *Sussex Archaeological Collections* since 1847. I set them all out in order, a century and a half running along the extra bookshelves I'd wedged under the stairs. Brown spines shading into maroon. The Sussex Archaeological Society is one of the oldest county history groups, though analogous societies were established in most counties of England in the mid-nineteenth century. I started to read my way through the early volumes, looking around the Victorian museum of it all. 'Archaeology' in these journals, or 'collections', might mean reports on excavations – and there were certainly many spades being taken to the tumuli of the downs and urns being carried out. But the term was capacious enough to include investigations of ancient buildings, and analysis of many kinds of objects from tradesmen's tokens to church paintings. These were also 'collections' of historical documents, often transcribed from manuscripts. In the first volume, the editor offered a translation of St Richard's will from the medieval Latin (half a mark to the 'incluso de Heringham', the man sitting at Hardham in the dark). Another founder member of the Society discussed a remarkable document in Volume 2, a record of the 'ancient customs' of fishermen in Brighton as agreed by the fishermen themselves in 1580. Immediately, of course, I was comparing their customs and ways of describing them with those of the bailiff on the Arun.

But it was another series of books that took up long-term residence by my bedside table. In 1901 a distinct organisation, the Sussex Record Society, was formed with the particular aim of publishing original documents with historical significance for Sussex. Again, this was a common pattern across the country: 'record societies' worked to make a great range of sources easily available. New texts appeared every year through the twentieth century, from every region, and in the twenty-first century they keep coming. Merchants' books from Exeter, travellers' tours from Northumberland. My inherited library included a selection of the Sussex 'records', and I bought more of my own. Their usefulness to the specialist historian was clear, but what was I doing taking someone else's ancient account books to read on the bus?

It wasn't so much for specific information as for the angle on the world that each volume suggested. Having tried to think about the Commonwealth from the point of view of swans, I was ready for anything. Virginia Woolf suggested that 'biography will enlarge its scope by hanging up looking glasses at odd corners'. These Sussex books were looking glasses hung at odd angles to the history of my childhood places; their angles on national and international history were even stranger, and more revealing. They were full of close-up details, but I could feel them enlarging my scope.

Clergymen's inventories, school logs, tax returns: many would have been incomprehensible to me in the archive, even had I known to consult them. What a gift to the common reader these well-edited volumes were. As well as the voices, and the points of view, it was the forms that were so involving, each pushing to the fore certain kinds of knowledge or expression. The records of an estate steward suggested lives told in terms of land use, and disputes about it. The inventories listed furnishings room by room so that you tried to imagine people's lives according to the number of joint-stools in their parlour, the presence or absence of a Turkey carpet.

The water bailiff had gone silent after 1640. But the records of the Sussex law courts held up a kind of mirror, or a thousand mirrors, to life as it went on in the towns and villages around the Arun. In the *Quarter Sessions Order Book* published by the Sussex Record Society, Elizabeth had marked passages revealing the damage and repair of roads and bridges. I started with the roads and then caught sight of the people coming and going over them. Not only the roads, made and unmade, but a whole panorama of Sussex seemed to unfurl itself across the pages, bright with the specificity of objects and known places, and dark with the record of poverty and desperation in communities paying the price of war.

4. QUARTER SESSIONS
What the court heard

At the four corners of the year, Easter, midsummer, Michaelmas and Epiphany, local courts met to settle disputes and matters of county business, as they had done since 1388 and would continue to do until reforms in 1972. With only two interruptions they went on through the years of the civil war. While the future of the country was in the balance and then as the republic established itself, the Quarter Sessions courts attended to the irritations and tragedies of individual lives, the licensing of traders, the care of immediate surroundings for the common good. These civil matters were followed by criminal cases, most often assaults and minor thefts; difficult cases were referred to the Court of Assize, which sat twice yearly for the whole county. Without fail, the Clerk of the Peace, William Alcock, turned out to present indictments and advise the assembled magistrates, ensuring that all the proceedings were recorded in the large Sessions Rolls, and the final judgements set out in the Order Book.[1] As I started to follow its threads of human stories, it felt like moving among the multiplying, half-glimpsed plots of a modernist novel.

Eastern and western Sussex had separate sessions, except at midsummer when the court met at Lewes for the whole county, and officials from the Arun region made their dutiful round trip of seventy or eighty miles to get there. Western sessions in the 1640s were held mostly at Arundel or Petworth, occasionally at Chichester, Horsham or Midhurst, always on the Monday and Tuesday following the appropriate feast. William Alcock then had a day to cross the county and it all started again with the eastern sessions on Thursday and Friday.

The Justices of the Peace were appointed by government, and the names of those commissioned as JPs changed during the 1640s as prominent Parliamentarians took the place of men with known allegiances to the Crown.[2] So Thomas May of Lavant, for instance, who presided as a Justice in 1642–3, had by the following year been designated (in the language of the time, which standardised spitting contempt in even its basic administrative processes) a 'Delinquent'. He was banned from public office, and his property in Parliament-held Chichester had been confiscated. Herbert Morley was one of those who became a regular on the bench, sitting at both eastern and western sessions. His estates were at Glynde in the east, but he served as governor of Arundel Castle once it was secured by Parliament. Morley, Cowper, Stapley: powerful names in the new structures of Sussex. They were all working on national committees, helping to establish a republican administration; but they were also needed in the work of local decision-making, shaping the pattern of Sussex lives however mundane the rulings seemed.

The courts licensed 'badgers', or travelling salesmen, but only for a year at a time – so that Hugh Feild of Pulborough had to apply each Epiphany to continue his days on the country lanes selling butter, eggs and poultry. They set the standard wages for servants, and the standard price of beer. The frequent closure of alehouses on charges of disorderliness may reflect a Puritan crackdown, though the sheer number suggests that houses on every street were opening to drinkers. In Arundel alone, twenty were closed down at Easter 1645; again and again people were warned to 'surcease from keeping Alehouse', and constables ordered to take down the signs.[3] But more promising drinking places were supported: a yeoman in Cocking could sell drink at his home, with men from Pulborough and Petworth providing sureties. A Houghton gardener got his licence. Was his alehouse in the village or down by the river, I wonder, where walkers and bikers now pack the outdoor tables at the Bridge inn on sunny afternoons?[4]

A continuous stream of disputes concerned the cutting of hedges, the scouring of ditches, the repair of lanes: each one trivial, but all together the vital stuff of human beings living as neighbours. The records give a powerful sense of places intimately known and used. A common spring had not been dredged at West Stoke (at the foot of the downs near Chichester). It was the parishioners' responsibility to keep such water sources clean, and they were ordered, under the law, to do it. Two local men certified to a subsequent court, albeit two and a half years later, that it was done.[5] Stall Lane in Pulborough was in bad condition; who was going to sort it out? At Easter 1645 a group of parish representatives stood charged with neglecting it. The group included the prominent local figure Christopher Coles, who would soon marry the bailiff's niece, Jane Barttelot, and who was the bailiff's 'loving friend'. Coles often took a lead on parish problems, but he drew the line at Stall Lane and claimed costs for wrongful indictment. By the next session it had been agreed: young Henry Streater, who had land around the lane, must make it good – and so he did.

The mending of bridges was a particularly fraught subject because the work was expensive and if a bridge failed a whole area could be cut off. In this, as in many aspects of local administration, a filigree of civil laws, common laws, manorial customs, ancient rights and unwritten understandings were brought to bear. There were county bridges, borough bridges and parish bridges, classed according to their use and strategic importance. Questions of responsibility were constantly negotiated. Who would mend the Houghton clappers? Could a tax be levied for Greatham repairs? The military manoeuvres of the war had been hard on these bridges. Behind the repair orders slowly negotiated through the 1640s lay the events of terrifying days when armies had watched for each other's advance and tried to close off their routes. The events, for instance, of 7 December 1643 when a small advance guard of Parliamentary men rode through the narrow lanes to see if Houghton Bridge were 'laid' or not, and so whether the approach to Arundel could be made from Parham. 'The day was misty, especially on those high hills; so was the night', remembered Edward Apsley of Worminghurst; only by the moon could they find their way.[6] The Order Book does not, of course, deal in memories of tense nights in mist and disappearing moons; it records that where a bridge was damaged 'for the benefitt of the Country' repair costs should be shared across large areas or 'rapes', and local Justices should collect in the payments.[7]

Like magistrates' courts today, the Quarter Sessions dealt with miscellaneous transgressions from drunkenness to trespass. Some of the group offences prosecuted may have been acts of protest. A whole group of Sutton men (all respectable people: husbandmen and the village blacksmith) appeared on charges of having felled trees belonging to the Earl of Northumberland, who owned almost all the land around them.[8] Then there were the petty thefts. Items stolen:

apple pies	chisel	thatching-rods
apron	chicken	wheels
axe	cloth	well-bucket.

A version of local life could be sketched from this list of modest items, things that people wanted and could not easily afford to buy.

The most difficult and disputed cases were often those concerning arrangements for people who could not support themselves. It was the responsibility of individual parishes to provide for those unable to earn a living, and who might otherwise, for a great range of reasons, become destitute. They might be orphan children, or single mothers or elderly people with no savings to fall back upon or family to take them in. Or they might be mentally unstable. Seventeenth-century clerks and churchwardens had standard words for summing up infinitely various kinds of distress, generally designating people as 'melancholy' or 'distracted'. Parishes must pay for their own parishioners: that was one of the contracts around which this society was organised. It was the only kind of welfare provision to be relied on, an affirmation that each parish was a community responsible for its members. But the question of who exactly its members were, who really belonged and who could be sent on elsewhere, was often open for debate.

And so, among hundreds of 'resettlement' hearings that determined the fate of vulnerable people in western Sussex in the 1640s, there came the case of Mary Owden. The Justices in Arundel heard the story in October 1643, and the clerk summed it up in the Order Book:

> Whereas Mary Owden wife of Henry Owden late an Inhabitant of Westaldrington in the parish of Portslade and since gone to Sea being now a distracted woman was receaved by a kinsman of hers into the parish of Southstoke by whom she hath beene kept without charge to the said parish till now of late her kinsman dying she is or wilbe a parish charge.[9]

The bare facts of her life are run together in this condensed prose, pooled in a dependent clause. She and Henry had lived near Portslade (down on the coast west of Brighton), and Henry went away to sea. You only have to pause a moment for the possibilities to multiply. She was insane, he could not stand it, and he went to sea. Or he went to sea, and her grief escalated into something more frightening. Or she lived alone quite capably after his departure, and then her health deteriorated.

Henry was from a large local family. There had been Owdens at Aldrington since at least 1284, when an earlier Henry Owden paid a peppercorn rent to the lord of the manor in the form of a single red rose. The presence of extended family did not help Mary when she needed it, but there was someone to the west, on the Arun, who could provide a home. She moved, or was taken, the twenty miles or so to South Stoke, a tiny hamlet in a bend of the river, two miles across the water meadows or over the down from Arundel. She lived there with her kinsman for 'divers yeares'. On his death, the parish overseers immediately worried about her becoming their responsibility and asked the court what should be done.[10]

The Justices at Arundel ordered that Mary Owden be sent back to her former parish, Portslade, and provided for there. But, as frequently happened in these cases, the 'receiving' parish objected. At Lewes a few days later, representatives from Portslade argued that Mary Owden was nothing to do with them. It was now 'made appeare' that the Owdens had not lived in Portslade for at least seven years, having moved before Henry's departure. In any case, ran the argument, Mary had been in South Stoke long enough to be considered resident there.[11] The Justices asked South Stoke to look after her for the moment, until the matter could be discussed further at the Assizes.

Their reluctance to leave her as an ongoing cost to South Stoke, where there were so few residents to share it out, was influenced by their sense of her kinsman in the hamlet having done the right thing by her for those 'divers yeares'.[12] The courts in general spent much time in pursuing family members who, according to the law, should be made to care for dependent relatives; here was an example of a man who had taken responsibility in just that way. Yet, in bringing Mary to his home and dying before her, he had landed his parish with hefty bills to pay. The court did not want to set any precedent that put relatives off hosting vulnerable kin; people should not attract the censure of their neighbours if they made room in their homes for those who would otherwise have no home at all.

Mary stayed on in South Stoke before her case came to court again. If she was well enough she would have sat in church on Sunday, taking her pew with the others: Cobbies, Hollands, Palmers, Randalls, Sowtons, Stockes and Styants.[13] For all the astonishing detail to be found in local archives, there seems to be no way of discovering anything about her life there. Did she understand where she was? Gunfire and alarms would have been audible from the village that winter as the castle downriver stood besieged. Perhaps she heard it all. Her resettlement case was due to come before the county court, but we cannot know what happened there because the Assize papers for 1643 and spring 1644 are missing – their loss another sign of a county in hiatus. That's it: that's all I can tell. There are no texts or brasses to go by. So she slips back into the crowd, only a name, and the pages of the Quarter Sessions turn to new disputes and pleas.

Each year local gentlemen deemed trustworthy were appointed to the two 'Treasurer' offices, one responsible for taxation revenue to be spent on 'Charitable Uses', the other for funds designated for the support of 'Maimed Soldiers'. In 1649, for example, it was the turn of William Bart-telot of Stopham, the man who was probably the water bailiff before the war, to be Treasurer for Charitable Uses. Now he was responsible for receiving money, keeping accounts and making disbursements according to the Charitable Uses Act of 1601, a pioneering piece of social legislation which specified 'releife of aged impotent and poore people', 'Supportacion Ayde and Helpe of younge tradesmen Handicraftesmen and persons decayed' and other causes.[14]

'Charity' levies were of great importance in the years of the civil war and after, when poverty was an urgent problem. The fighting had left citizens homeless or needing to build up their businesses again from the ground, and it was the role of the courts to make some provision for these disasters. In Chichester the whole suburb of St Pancras had been burnt to the ground during the siege of the city in December 1642, leaving many of its former residents on the streets. It was the area around the East Walls where many of Chichester's needle-makers lived and worked. The trouble was on such a scale that it was agreed the cost of relief should be shared across eighteen surrounding parishes. The residents of Eartham, East Lavant and Boxgrove therefore found themselves taxed for the support of destitute people who had formerly been the needle-makers of the East Gate.[15] It was William Barttelot's duty to oversee collection of the money, but every parish found a reason not to pay.

There was much for the courts to do in assessing the claims of the maimed soldiers (Parliamentary, not Royalist) who returned injured to their parishes, and those of widows whose soldier-husbands were killed. The problem was lack of money to pay them. Taxes were not raising sufficient funds to support the large numbers who needed help. Payments were badly in arrears by 1645 and new levies ordered.[16] The veterans John Blount and Gregory Earle of Chichester received a paltry forty shillings before their pensions were increased to £4 and £3 respectively. The forty shillings awarded to Martha Carpenter in January 1647 at Arundel could not have gone far in supporting her life as a war widow.[17] Anne Bettes-worth of Lavant did much better. A large pension of £10 was agreed, reflecting her family's contribution to the Parliamentary campaign. Her husband William had 'lent £50 being the one halfe of his estate' to the war chest; he had served as Corporal of the Horse at the Chichester garrison and died (one of many) at the siege of Taunton.[18] In her written petition to the court, Anne presented her plight in emotive terms:

> Your poore peticioner his wife is utterly undone shee being great with childe when her husband was slayne & shortly after delivered of 2 children, ever since w[hi]ch time shee hath beene weake & sickly & full of greeffe & sorrow & soe like to contynue noe way able to gett her liveing & therefore like to perish for want.[19]

She was in a bad way but had the confidence and connections to assert herself through every possible avenue. She gathered endorsements from leading local Parliamentarians, including several Justices, all petitioning on her behalf.

Royalist veterans and widows had no chance of such support, it being illegal under the Commonwealth regime for public money to be spent on those who had served the Crown. Some who survived the ordeal long enough (many reduced to years of begging) would renew their petitions after the Restoration, and at last receive a pension.

The Quarter Sessions Order Book is a record of the extraordinary and quotidian going on side by side. Through violence and political tur-moil, efforts were made to maintain the common amenities of local life. A chalk pit had been left open near the road at Boxgrove, causing a haz-ard. Those who had dug there must be fined, and the pit enclosed.[20] The bridges at Houghton and Greatham were again in disrepair. Perhaps it was William Barttelot, who knew of their long history and had written about it, who brought the matter to the court's attention. The bench or-dered that 'speedy and effectuall' action be taken to set them right.[21]

5. SIC VITA

The seats in South Stoke church

Six winters running, in January when cottage rents are at their lowest, I went with friends to stay at South Stoke, the hamlet outside Arundel where Mary Owden lived for a time. We always arrived in the dark, headlights showing the steep-sided cutting where the road goes through chalk, and then we were out the other side, with the open river valley to our right, the space and the huge view tangible but not yet visible. The road leads nowhere except to the fields, large farmhouse, grey flint-and-brick rectory, six other houses and the church close in among them with its strange, slim spire, a Victorian addition with a fanciful hint of Normandy chateau. It is a powerful place for me, as near as I know to what T. S. Eliot calls 'significant soil', though I have no long-standing connections to attach me there.[1] Significance builds in many unofficial ways that escape the records and clear reasoning.

I read the entry for the parish published in 1992 as part of the revised *Victoria County History*, with its bright shards of detail hard-won from the archives. I read the names in the parish registers and the roll-call of twenty-nine men who took the Protestation oath on 13 February 1642, compulsorily swearing their allegiance to the Church of England and the King; I tried to imagine the women of the parish who were not required to give their names since their allegiance was of less consequence.[2] I thought of the water bailiff passing on the river, which at that time took a wide meander across the brooks. That 'old' river channel still makes its arc between Offham and Burpham and skirts wide around South Stoke, but the water stands placid; the fast current flows on the 'new' cut made by Victorian engineers in a tight horseshoe around the village on its spur of rising ground. Squinting, I tried to reroute the river.

I demolished the great flint wall running for miles over the hill, built when the park around Arundel Castle was expanded and enclosed in the eighteenth century. The down was open grassland, though intricately portioned into sheep 'leazes', which tenants leased for grazing. In the churchyard I changed the fairy-tale chateau spire for the plainer 'Sussex cap' that was there before.

Standing in the lane one day after the walk back from Arundel, wanting the last of the low sun before going indoors, I tried putting my pin in the map of time, somewhere near where the bailiff and the Order Book had ended and left me. A winter afternoon in 1663 – who stood here then? 1663. I floundered round for some bearings. Pepys and Evelyn were keeping their diaries, the theatres were open, John Dryden was writing a comedy. The Restoration! I said it aloud, as if the word might take on some meaning relevant to this hamlet where there were definitely no theatres and, alas, no diary that survived. It was silly to be looking at the rectory windows when they were clearly later than the Restoration; there had been a timber-framed house on the same site in the seventeenth century and it was those unknown windows – wooden sills? Small panes set into a leaded grid? – through which someone looked out on 1663. Different windows, then, but in the same place: right next to the churchyard.

Who was at the window? I had written down the names of the rectors and checked my list.

> John Sefton, rector of South Stoke from 1662. Brasenose College 1627, BA 1631; will proved 1679. Also rector of Winchfield in Hampshire from 1660.

Now that I put it to the test, the information I had blithely copied from the Clergy of the Church of England database seemed full of puzzles. Winchfield was forty miles away. But here was something to start from: a new rector in the hamlet.

The Reverend John Sefton cleared a space on his table and spread out a large sheet. He drew a rectangle, which was the nave, and sketched the pulpit in its corner. Then the pews, six on each side, and two extra ones at the back on the north side. He had done it too quickly, the lines wavered, the first rows were too large and the last ones were squashed to fit. The first names were easy: he filled in two rows without a pause. The seven Sowton children from Offham he arranged in order of age, though he thought on Sunday the eldest girl had been in the middle and was probably in the habit of keeping her siblings under control. He tried to picture them all together, in order, but they wouldn't sit still.

It was a tiny parish, a few houses around the church, three in the fields, the others in a cluster downriver at Offham, where the barges came up to a landing stage and there was a new quarry opened in the side of the hill. He would serve them this year; he would try to settle them in the true faith. Who knew what preaching they had had all this time; the churchwardens wouldn't tell. He could guess. The thing now was to be steady, keep to the prayer book, and bring the words of the service back into their lives. He and they were starting again.

One of the books I read at South Stoke, while I was thinking about the forms in which local histories have been written, was a text from Shropshire. Richard Gough had spent most of his life in or near the village of Myddle. In the last years of the seventeenth century he wrote an account of the topography and local antiquities of his place according to the framework established by county historians like Robert Plot. But he found that there was no room in orthodox 'chorography', or place-writing, for much of what he wanted to set down about Myddle and its people. He tried something different. He drew a plan of the church, St Peter's, labelled the pews, and wrote a portrait of each member of the congregation, seat by seat. He made a decorative title page: *Observations Concerning the Seats in Myddle and the Familys to which they Belong.*[3] The manuscript was found among his papers when he died. He had invented a method of group biography; no one seems to have used it before, or since.

Fourth pew on the south side: Stocke family, John, husbandman. South Stoke six years. Wife Anna, two boys c. six and ten, lately joined by Anna's sister and mother.

Sefton wondered what he could put down that would help more, but all he could remember was the size of the man's great hand clutching his hat, the sloping shoulders, the reticence, and the quickness with which his wife made up for his not saying anything at all. He would come to know them. There would be people under these names. From the window by his table he had a wide grey-green view over the orchard and the garden wall to the water meadows. He would walk near the river often, he thought. It would be a way to meet people incidentally, at their work. Studying the pattern of greens now he could make out the banks and the ditches. Just behind the Stockes there sat two elderly shepherds, brothers, and the Hollands. The Holland man ran the ferry – he was probably there now, on the water.

Fifth pew south side: Isaake Holland, fisher, boatman.

Having delivered two Arundel gentlemen to the far bank, Isaake Holland made his way back across the tide, moored, and fed the stove that kept his fingers from freezing. There was a wait now until the quarrymen finished for the day and wanted the ferry. In the mornings they had brown hair and black boots and later they were visions of white and grey, the chalk sitting in their beards like the powder on grand men's wigs.

An hour after ebb tide, the water was coming steadily. The fish kept low through the winter in this deepest stretch of the river, twenty feet, twenty-five feet down in the dark where the currents hardly found them. The hooks didn't find them either. The fishing lines were slack. Tench, dace, bream, sitting out the winter in the depths like Old Ayling by the fire at Hollands.

Isaake adjusted himself on the stool to watch the hanger change as the sun caught it. 'The mountains also shall bring peace,' he said aloud, 'and the little hills righteousness unto the people.' He was learning psalms: it was a new idea since Christmas. They had Psalm 72 on Sunday for Epiphany and it didn't hurt to say it over. It was good for the cold and the waiting. 'He shall come down like the rain into a fleece of wool.' It meant the Lamb of God would come from above. He could see that now he turned the words around, but he liked the plain daylight meaning too: rain on fleece. At first the oil in the wool resisted the wet, and you could see the drops coming off the sheep as they came off his coat. But the wool clotted together and was saturated. He watched the lines and floats in the water, moving lightly under the arching rods, nudged by the wake of a passing branch. Just above, on the low hillside, he could see the ewes gathered towards Peppering barn. They would be soaked and resilient, sides swollen out in pregnancy.

I looked at the entries in the registers, where the same names (Sowtons, Stockes, Rixhalls) paired and parted in the pattern of marriages and burials. I didn't know how I could tell who was a shepherd or ran the ferry or who worked for who. Names in a landscape were all I had. Very occasionally, South Stoke residents were mentioned in other kinds of records – in the court orders or in the 'presentations' made by churchwardens to the Bishop of Chichester, for example, in which they were obliged to report on their neighbours' transgressions. Thomas and Marya Duke had contravened the code of conduct for parishioners along with six other neighbours in 1664. They were drunk, or sleeping with each other, or playing cricket on Sunday – or possibly 'sowing discord' of a political kind – but the churchwardens did not say.[4] News of their proscribed behaviour revealed little of what I wanted to know about. No record of this sort was likely to indicate whether the ferryman liked to look at the hill.

I gave some of the parish names to the people I was imagining. Except for John Sefton the rector, and the minister he replaced, these are fictions, based on hardly a scrap, fictions made from the materials of the place, the political and religious contexts I was trying to grasp as I went, and a long-held interest in how different people know and respond to landscape. I would certainly be wrong about what the ferryman saw, but it seemed right to keep wondering about him.

I read that 'a chalk pit at Offham was worked from 1724 or earlier'; it was shown on Richard Budgen's pioneeringly accurate map published that year.⁵ Consulting the map, I thought the pit looked a large and established feature. If chalk was quarried at Offham in 1663, some of the labourers would have been in John Sefton's congregation.

Seventh pew north side: Sam Cobbie, labourer.

Every block of chalk revealed more chalk behind it, never seen before, and astonishingly clean. It was a year now since they opened the Offham pit, slicing into the hanger to make a white cliff. They skinned the earth like a rabbit and the flesh under her was bright white. The flesh was bone; she was all bone. The picks swung into her sides and brought lumps of white tumbling to the white ground. Sam Cobbie was sick of it and still amazed.

The Burpham boys were up above him, laughing at the joke they'd been telling all week, and the rockfalls kept coming. No one had died yet. He'd get a few loads barrowed to the landing now and Doick would bring the barge up on the tide in the morning. But the shovel was heavier every time he plunged it into the rubble.

As soon as the white was exposed, it was vulnerable. It started to look grey. The parts of the pit not worked since spring were stained yellow and green, and grass was established already in cracks where morsels of soil had crept in. Sin, sin, sin: they had to keep standing in church to confess it. Here you took away the tarnished chalk and behind it was another start, but the soil and dust fell into the cracks. He didn't know if the Burphams felt it too.

The dry rock had dried him out. His fingers were prunes, his voice croaky with the dust that was in his mouth and under his nails and in the raw places on his knuckles. By noon each day he was rationing his thoughts of soft grass, food, flesh, all that wouldn't powder in his hands. Even his blood felt sluggish, thickened with chalk dust. He told his mother it was the same as when she put flour in the sauce to thicken it. By the afternoon, anyway, he had seen enough white and entered upon four hours of pure labour. Then, just before dusk, he could see the end coming – the dew, the walk home – so that for a few moments the white glowed again. He walked to the road with the Burphams and left them by Stocke's cherry trees. They cut towards the river and the ferry.

'A rabbit warren called Pughdean existed between the 1490s and 1787' said the *Victoria County History*. I printed sections of the maps with the warren marked, and walked in search of the place where it used to be. 'A warrener was recorded in 1660 and later.'

Randall was the name. John Sefton noted the warrener particularly, having spent time on a warren himself. So tall he was that his pale head floated on top of all the others, or that's how it seemed from the front of the church. The woman's name was Alice. They were over there in the steep valley behind Swanbourne. He stared at their names, which were silent.

Fifth pew south side: Robert Randall, warrener. Alice Randall, his wife.

This was the strange hour, this one now in the afternoon, when the light was grey, and the warren looked a desert waste, and the stench from the storeroom was meaningless, not connected with the fur she would skin off or the pot that would boil with the meat cooking into its dark stew. Sometimes she sat that hour by the window, powerless to do the chickens or start the dinner, unmoored in this estuary of time. They had said she mustn't marry the rabbit-man though he was dependable enough, because how would she stand the days in that strange house? It was a good house, she had said, and that was a fact: brick on the ground floor (which was for traps and nets and hanging the meat) and timber above, a high house to give the keeper a view of things: high and dry, she had said when the cottages by the river had their backs foot-high in water, best house around. It was only in the afternoons she was at a loss, and only then that her good house was lonelier than a boat at sea. The acres of thin turf stretched away on all sides, and here was her good house empty of any life except Robert, who would be out til late, and downstairs a pair of ferrets and eighteen rabbits three days dead. The quiet was heavy, as if the hummocky earth absorbed all the sounds ever made and buried them. Nothing moved. A few scatterings of newly disturbed chalk showed grey.

But there it was, the change in the sky: not grey now but a bird's-egg blue, with the gibbous moon rising between two hillocks, and then a glow of pink and gold, which pulled up the mazy paths and gave them purpose for a moment before they whitened. The humps of earth were great big pillows now. Though the sky was still blue, the land was dark and two lights appeared just over and beyond the sod wall that kept her in. They were the millhouse lights, her beacons. And now she could answer them: she prodded at the fire and lit a taper. She was ashore. She could not have explained what had been wrong.

Underneath, in the half-darkness of the storeroom, eighteen rabbits made faint shadows on the brick wall. Each had one leg threaded through the hamstring of the other, between the sinew and the bone, and from these crossed limbs they hung.

Two boys, standing in the lane by the warren wall, dared each
other to call out to the coney-catcher. *Coneyman will catch you,
coneyman will catch you.* They could see, very dimly, his tall form
coming over the mounds, bending and advancing. He was checking
the nets, was he? Securing the pegs which held them. The boys
wanted to be asked to help, to scramble over the wall and grasp a
rabbit by its hind legs when he passed it to them with his big gloved
hands. They wanted to get away and be home. The burrows were
strange shadowed shapes now; nostrils for the earth when it was
breathing. If the tunnels went deep enough, and people said they
went miles and miles, they would go down to hell. They were the
chimneys of the underworld. 'Mr Randall!' shot out Samuel. He was
thwacked in the stomach and they ran. Mr Randall heard them come
and heard them go. He might have liked the company.

But there was the first coney, and the second. He took the big
struggling warmth in his arms, feeling the kick in the thickness
of his oil coat. There were more skirmishes, one rabbit in the net,
another throwing it off and bolting, white scutt zig-zagging in the
distance, on and on out of sight, past the lodge and towards the
river.

*Third and fourth pews north side: Simon Stiant, yeoman. Jane Stiant,
his wife. May Stiant, his sister. Six children.*

Simon Stiant slowed his horse as he came over the last rise and saw
the village ahead of him: lights in the windows at the farmhouse,
lights at Hollands, and behind them the dark shapes of the barns. He
loved this last stretch downhill to the door. There was a group of
bustards on the down, and the woods below were fading. The road
would take him down into the little globe, which would hold him
steady. They were dice in a pouch, May said, the river drawn round
them as a drawstring pulled fast and she wanted to be out of it. But

he wanted to be home, where the sky was larger than anywhere else. They felt their opposite things more strongly every year.

'We'll never have a minister like it again,' Jane Stiant repeated, sliding a knife under the rabbit skin. The kitchen was gloomy and disarrayed by the afternoon's efforts; flour had stuck to splashes of grease around the table legs. She was alone with her God now that Henry Staples was gone, 'ejected' for not accepting the prayer book, as if he should have conformed to any kind of worship that suited. He said she must endure it and make herself open to receive the heat of the Spirit in her blood. She slipped the grey cord of intestine into a bowl while picturing heaven as he described it.

May was not to be drawn on the subject of the Spirit and found a reason to look in the larder. Jane pressed on, with a new angle. 'I've seen you friendly as a bramble bush with this new one, calling at the rectory on any purpose that comes into your head, but he won't want to know about people like us.' Mr Staples would always cross the field to ask their health if he saw them in the garden. 'I told you what he said before he went?' Yes, she had told everyone several times.

But no one had been watching the children. One of them (it was Anna, who was now sucking on a sugar stick while George reddened with guilt) had put the cream jug under Aunt May's feet so that May kicked it over and screamed as the broken handle spun down the cellar steps and a pond of cream spread over the tiles. She let them clear up around her while she whisked egg whites in furious silence. 'The new man has travelled,' May said after a while. 'The new man has been in Africa. And he is not new. He was curate in Slindon when you were playing dolls, Jane.' She sent the children out to watch for their father.

George appeared at the door again. 'What is Africa?'

Henry Staples had been minister at South Stoke through the years of the Commonwealth. Anglican clergy loyal to the King had been expelled from their livings as soon as Parliament took control, and Staples was one of the Puritan clerics who took their places at the heart of parishes throughout the country. His small, even handwriting records baptisms in the register from 1648, though it wasn't until 1654 that he was officially appointed as registrar by one of the county officials responsible for carrying out Parliament's 'Ordinance for Ejecting Scandalous, Ignorant and Insufficient Ministers'.[6] Peering at the photographed pages of the ancient book that had outlasted so many writers and so much change, I could see that the neat hand went on recording the baptisms of South Stoke children, several of whom were his own. And I could see that after 1659 there were no more entries in this hand. With the Restoration, Staples was himself ejected. The record of appointment was crossed through. The parish register told in its changing handwriting part of the story of the revolution. John Sefton had arrived in the midst of profound hiatus, hope and pain.

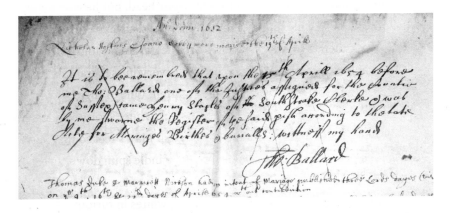

The rector made a note next to the pulpit.

Myself. John Sefton.

Once, when he left school, he had made a plan like this, drawing out the classroom he had known for seven years. He kept that sheet. It went with the vandals of course. Tipped into a fire somewhere, or into the river. The sentiment had all been knocked out of him so that he didn't miss things like that.

He had his rooms in the cathedral, and he had this damp rectory with its orchard and its view. The windows were warped, the doors didn't close, every hole in the plaster had its own community of spiders and woodlice. Walking in the garden last night, with the sky an arc about him and the thick, breathing quiet of the water meadows beyond the wall, he had felt closer to God than anywhere.

He would buy books again, and he would lend them out. English books for the country people: there were several around here who could read well, the women especially. He would have shelves made downstairs so that they could come and choose. The pages would spot and wrinkle, but this cool damp was a heavenly dew compared with the wet heat of the tropics. Lord God keep me and settle me.

Sixth pew south side: Hannah Holland. Ruth, her daughter, now widowed, and her two children.

Hannah took her red-faced granddaughter in her arms and went out into the lane for a cool-off. The grizzling stopped, and there was a cheek resting on her neck. The sky was almost white now, the valley a dim purple and then grey. All the detail was absorbed into the mass of land. Sparrows in the malthouse eaves, starved fieldfares working fitfully in the hawthorn. The peace was broken by barking. Stiant dogs were racing round in a fight now with Fuller dogs.

She had seen her boy ride away up the lane to a night meeting at Pulborough. He said he was only going that far. She heard the guns at Arundel, and he had never come back round the shoulder of the hill to find her standing there. She waited. So many days she had waited.

Hefting the baby, she waited there. The view ought to have changed, she thought. Enough blood had been lost, enough raising of dust from one county to another and frantic signings and protestings to make some indentation on the face of the land. It was the ejection of the minister that had brought back the worry just lately. But the valley still opened beyond the meadows. 'The kingdoms of the earth,' the minister used to say.

Isaake Holland glanced back to where he had left the Burphams at the landing. The two whitened ghosts were moving vigorously past Peppering and nearly home. They were always laughing. He checked the boat, locked the hut, felt the lightness of his fish baskets with shame, and was glad of going home to Hannah again, after all these years.

Third pew north side cont.: John Ayling, labourer. Grace Ayling, his wife. John Ayling, his father.

Old Ayling sat all winter on the settle at Holland's, coming in as soon as the door was open in the morning and leaving when Hannah tipped him out at night. He shrank as the days went on, drying out, receding into the corner until she didn't notice him for hours at a time. It was a kind of curing, in the warm room. Hannah didn't mind his being there all day while she worked, if it was only for a month or two. Last year he resumed life on Valentine's Day; she remembered that. He had drawn himself up straight, shaken her hand solemnly when he said goodnight and next morning was over on Milne Field sowing barley.

The early-seventeenth-century brick chimney is still there, as is the clunch base, visible from the outside where a few initials have been scratched into the soft stone as if it were a local monument. The huge hearth inside, with its ledges and oven, had clearly been intended for cooking on a serious scale.

The pews were filling up; the plan was good. For pleasure Sefton marked in the tower. Inside, the tower arch rose very slender and high at the back of the nave, stretching up into the darkness where the bell hung, unseen, glimpsing the world only through the little louvred window that let the sound out. He made a tiny sketch.

Bell.

'Bryanus Eldridge me fecit' it said. It was a new bell, made at the Eldridge foundry in Chertsey and brought down on the river in '57. For the final stretch up from the landing stage it was strapped onto a wagon that needed oxen to pull it into the churchyard. It came with a twin, a new bell for Slindon. Two men arrived from the foundry with scaffolds to hang it, and the first ringing was for a christening, little John Sowton, though he was gone now, sick with the fever just when he could walk.

Fifth pew south side: John Dudeney, manor farm shepherd. Tom Dudeney, his son.

There were three lengths of binder left: that would be enough. John Dudeney had brought up onto the hill the last two hurdles for mending and his basket stuffed with binders. The job was nearly done. He smoothed the last three strands, softening the little knuckles and knees, pulling away a few seed heads. Withbind, travellers' joy, old man's beard. All summer it thrust out its sappy limbs, so soft and full you wouldn't think it might age this way; but it was good for this mending. He studied the edge where the rods had cracked and come loose. Then he was sewing the wood together, one hand gripping the rough split willow, the other looping the binders through and around. It was ready to be stacked with the others in Lower Field where the pens were waiting.

He pushed himself up, basket over shoulder. Jack had raced off, skirting the left of the flock. Warm bodies pushed slowly around his legs; the crowd of backs surging around him. Over the hill, the valley opened. There was the Sowton flock already folded, and an upright shape that must be Tom, holding open the gate into Surrey Field.

Seventy-eight ewes, and Tom counted them in, from the bright green of turnip tops to the brown-grey of the field where the turnips were foraged to the roots, which stuck up in trodden, broken chunks among the flints. There was a few days' feeding left in here. The ewes set to the roots without pause. His eye followed the thin animal he had kept in sight all afternoon. She was on her feet and had settled to feeding. He watched. His father was coming down the hill. Above him in the south-west sky, the folding star was suddenly bright. Tom started along the lane, between the dark hedges, past the field where the lambing pens were waiting, hurdles making their tight wall against the weather to come.

Fourth pew north side: John Cobbie, woodsman. Anne Cobbie, his wife. Joan Martin, my housekeeper.

Joan went to bring in the last bits of washing from where they lay on the hedge. A white hedge, wrapped up like a New Year gift. Still damp, but they'd had an airing. Two sheets, six cloths, four napkins. Edges together, halves, quarters. Folding, folding. Standing a minute at the back gate into the brooks, she saw the ferry come across. There was only the dinner to do now, and the feed to take over to the horses at Calves Croft, and she should check whether the boys had done the chickens. And if the shed door was still wedged shut, she should ask Sam to look at it before tomorrow though he'd be tired out. And then she would have another poem.

It was the book Mr Sefton had lent her. Mr King's poems. Mr King, or his lordship: the bishop. The rector had known him years and years, since before the wars he said. It was a change from the Bible anyway. These poems were very sudden and full and then over.

The star is shot and man forgot: that had happened last night. There were beautiful pictures: a falling star, a flying eagle, bubbles on the water, and men were like those stars and eagles, the poem said: a flash of light and they were gone. Sic Vita.

> The wind blows out, the bubble dies;
> The spring entombed in autumn lies;
> The dew dries up, the star is shot;
> The flight is past, and man forgot.

There was a bird up there now over Perry Hill, lumbering into the air on immense, rapid wings. She stayed watching as she realised the size of it. A bustard was it? Shepherd's turkey, the old people called them, though she'd never known a shepherd eat one. Like to the falling of a star or as the flights of eagles are. The damp sheets were cold and heavy.

The rector, peering across the churchyard from his window, saw figures moving in the light at Holland's. Someone small, it was the young widow, came out with a bowl, and wandered between the gravestones while she stirred whatever it was. Behind her the fine brick chimney showed in outline against the sky. He wanted to go over to the inn; he would like to sit and talk with the men and then with the young woman when she had finished serving, but he shouldn't, or couldn't. They would seize up; he would spoil their dinner.

Another chapter of Davenant on St Paul would do instead. Bishop of Salisbury before the wars, a Cambridge man, and he wrote well – he woke up the old questions. Non posse quenquam simul sapere coelestia et terrena. No, you couldn't attend to earthly things and salvation at the same time. *Agros, boves, uxores*: distractions. That was Luke 14. But he couldn't go into the barns this moment and tell the cowmen to stop thinking of their cows because they were distractions. He found the passage he had marked last night. *Sapere*: to know. He felt he might come to know the earth here. And as for the sky, *coelestia*?

'Two days off full moon' Ruth called from the back. John Sowton studied the almanac tacked up by the fire and found the day. 'Full on Thursday.' A spatter of fat or gravy had obliterated the rest of the week.

At the turning of the tide, the river stood high and silent. Rising fish left groups of bubbles that spun and burst. The moon lit the flooded path that ran around the edge of the brooks at the foot of the down. It lit the top bars of the gates and the dole stones in the wet grass, the white streak of a coot pushing out from the bank and then another.

Joan Martin adjusted the rushlight to make it burn more slowly. 'And as you see the dying taper waste / By such degrees does he to darkness haste.' She read until the flame spluttered out and the last grease dripped into the saucer.

Light reached down into the burrow entrances and the rabbits were cautious.

Orion passed sideways over the rectory, and the twins of Gemini swam silently after him. Not minding the cold, Grace Ayling pushed open the bedchamber window to see them.

6. A CHURCHMAN'S BOOKS
Following John Sefton

'Africa?' the child asked. All the evidence I can find suggests that John Sefton, the new rector of South Stoke after the Restoration, had indeed gone away overseas while Parliamentary forces consolidated their power in his own country. The details are lost in the upheavals of the dangerous years when his possessions were repeatedly confiscated, but the odd traces of his life that I have collected suggest a more mobile and complicated existence than I had associated with Church of England clergymen in Sussex. Conjuring an evening in 1663, I had wanted to imagine the unknown people of the hamlet, the warrener's wife and quarryman, the shepherds up on the hill; my roughly sketched-in rector might encounter them all, but I didn't intend to write his history. Except that every trace of him kept me looking. His life was a thread I could almost, not quite, follow through the extraordinary terrain of the mid-seventeenth century, and through the familiar places of my childhood.

An early appearance of his name and signature comes in a deposition book of 1638 when he acted as witness in a legal case. The entry records that he had been living in Eastergate and Oving (just outside Chichester) for the last two years, that he was about twenty-eight, and had been born in Bignor.[1] So he was a native of these few miles around the Arun and the downs.

I've sometimes visited Bignor and followed the village street round in its loop. Wondering which was Sefton's childhood home, I realised it may have been the rectory; few other households round here would have had the means to send a boy off to a theological education. Perhaps his father was the rector. I checked the clergy inventories transcribed in a volume published by the Sussex Record Society – a book brimming with the itemised possessions of busy and vanished lives. And there it was: Bignor 1632, the inventory of John's father, Reverend Thomas Sephton, or Sefton. His household goods were valued so that probate could be granted and his will executed – a will that left the beds and pewter to his wife Ellinor, and divided the rest among three sons.[2] The middle son, John, was to have 'no more bedding than that he already hath with him in Oxon'; the undergraduate had depleted the family linen cupboard. John's inheritance included all the books, though he was to give his step-mother and brother 'such English books as he can best share'.[3]

A whole family background opens out from these few documents. Unless there had been major redecorating, the furniture listed in the inventory would have been the furniture of John Sefton's childhood in the 1610s:

> 6 turkey-work cushions in the hall
> 2 settles and an old chest in the parlour
> Yellow curtains in the bedroom over the front door.

There was a buttery, bakehouse and milkhouse, and a barn stocked with barley, wheat and hay. There were pigs and chickens, and two horses. As for the books, they are all rolled into one heading with 'other things in the studye'.[4] It was not a large collection, being valued at a modest £5, but it was something worth passing from father to son, and it seems that these books mattered to the whole family. Ellinor was clearly a reader who would appreciate a share of them. She had probably been given no chance to learn Latin, so that much of what her husband and his sons read was closed to her. She was only to have what John could spare, but there were English books coming her way.

In his younger days Thomas Sefton had been licensed as a teacher, coaching boys from Sutton and the surrounding area in the 3Rs and Latin.[5] Presumably he taught his own sons alongside other children who came to the rectory for lessons. The standard texts of a seventeenth-century schoolmaster, pored over by a generation of local boys, may have been in the study at the end of his life and among those he bequeathed.

John was about twenty-two when his father died, and had doubtless accumulated some books of his own as an Oxford undergraduate. Drawn back to Sussex, he was serving his curacy at Slindon, a flint village six or seven miles south of the old family home in Bignor. After this he seems to have been installed as the rector at Burton, one of Bignor's neighbouring parishes, a place associated with the Catholic family at Burton Park. His reputation was high enough by 1640 for him to be elected master of Collyer's School in Horsham, a grammar overseen by the Company of Mercers. In the Mercers' archives a modern historian of Collyer's found remarkable evidence of his changing fortunes. Sefton was commended in 1642 for 'extraordinary worth and diligence' and given a pay-rise; by autumn 1644 he had lost his job. A petition for his removal had been raised in Horsham, signed by the Puritan minister and local men who supported Parliament. Sefton was 'addicted to superstitious courses as bowing to the communion table', they said. They also complained that he was too often absent from Horsham, attending to a lucrative living elsewhere – as 'parson of South Stoke'.[6] Really? I'd been getting him wrong. He was there in 1642–4, much earlier than I had understood.

It was in remote South Stoke that he carried on his High Church rites when it was dangerous to do so, 'continuing to preach up loyalty and obedience to the king after the Rebellion brake out', as the historian John Walker put it fifty years later (relying on reports from Sussex correspondents) in his *Attempt to Recover the Numbers and Sufferings of the Loyal Clergy*. Known loyalists were sacked from public positions as soon as Parliament had control; Sefton was duly expelled from Collyer's, Burton and from South Stoke. It was more than expulsion: the republicans wanted him locked up. 'Sir John Fagg, a colonel in the Rebel Army came with a Troop of Horse to apprehend him.' Sefton got away, and would spend the coming years on the run as a wanted man.[7]

For a time he lay low near Slindon, living 'for a considerable time in a Lodge (or Watch-House) belonging to the Warren called Gumber'.[8]

This is what Joshua Thornton, the vicar of Sutton in 1712, told Walker. Thornton, too, had become a kind of historian, making enquiries about what happened in Sussex during the interregnum. For some in his congregation it was all in living memory; others took their pick from the lively oral culture of partisan war stories, refined with each telling. Thornton's local research suggested that Sefton's time on Gumber Warren may not have been too desolate an exile. He 'resorted thither as he did to his other friends' houses', so it wasn't a case of camping in a lonely building as Thornton initially assumed. The whole Slindon estate was in ally hands, the home of the recusant Kempe family, though that was little protection when Sir Garrett Kempe faced the sequestration of his property on a major scale. Kempe paid large fines to rent back the lands that had been his, filing the requisite confessions and pleas to the Committee for Compounding with Delinquents.

The watch house is long gone. Even the site of the large warren is no longer known, centuries' worth of pillow mounds having disappeared under park and farmland, though the later 'Warren Barn' may indicate the place. Hilaire Belloc's joy in the 1920s has made the name of Gumber famous. 'Lift up your hearts in Gumber, laugh the Weald / And you my mother the Valley of Arun sing.' For Belloc this was a place of homecoming: 'Here am I homeward and my heart is healed.'[9] Sefton was at home in this country too, but he was also living in exile.

Across England expelled clergymen were taking refuge with friends and supporters, deciding on the kinds of work and worship they could continue in their new circumstances. There were many stories (passed on and improved) like that of the Petworth curate Oliver Whitby who escaped being shot, was found months later hiding in a poorhouse, fled, and spent days concealed in a hollow tree. Henry King had only just been made Bishop of Chichester in 1642 when Parliament ordered the abolition of all bishops. Chichester was besieged that December, and clergy property subsequently confiscated. Most upsetting for King was the destruction of his personal papers ('the moniments of my course in Study through all my Life') and the seizure of his books, a library of several thousand volumes formed over decades and including many gifts from friends.[10] Piles of them were lugged across to the deanery and left in the ruins until the Committee for Compounding with Delinquents sent instructions about what to do with them.[11] Henry King himself moved repeatedly over the ensuing years, staying in the various households of his siblings, establishing private communities of prayer but always regretting his 'sad retirement'.[12] It seems that he was able to buy back some of his books in 1652, though most had suffered from their years exposed to the damp. Sefton, meanwhile, left the green hills of Slindon and is said to have 'fled to the East-Indies'.[13] Walker records no further details of this journey at all.

He made his way back to Britain, and to Burton, while the Puritans were still in control. It's possible he wanted to be part of the activist networks working to overthrow the regime. He may have longed to be back and accepted the risks. The later accounts of his return have the texture of truth in their detail. Walker records the 'care and pains he had taken to come over the hedges to his house by a back way'.[14] The native returned by stealth, like a burglar, though it was he who would be burgled. The authorities were quickly on him: 'a great man of those parts went into his study and rifled it'. Among the papers taken or destroyed, it was said, were the manuscripts he had written while abroad, including 'disputes he had with several heathens'.[15] He had to disappear again, but a decisive moment of Royalist uprising was drawing near.

Sefton was safe as soon as Charles reached London. His life was remade quickly: he was installed as a canon of Chichester cathedral and given the living of Winchfield in Hampshire. It took some time, though, for 'loyal clergy' to be re-instated in all parishes. In 1662, nearly twenty years after the great wave of expulsions that unseated priests across the country, there came the Great Ejection. This time it was hundreds of Puritan ministers or 'lecturers' who were expelled, many of whom were long settled and loved in their parishes.[16] The ejected minister at Slinfold, for example, was Matthew Woodman, descendent of a protestant martyr, a scholarly thinker whose collection of books was among the largest in Sussex; he and his nine children were left without home or income.[17] John Goldwire had to leave his church in Arundel; his son was forced from the pulpit at Felpham. There were departures from Bignor, Singleton and East Dean.

This was the tumultuous moment in which Henry Staples, who had ministered in South Stoke for a decade, faced expulsion. He made his way to Ireland where he could continue to preach. Many stories were told of how he talked with common people. Later, when the eulogies of these persecuted men were written, Staples' virtues were vividly emphasised. 'Wherever he went, and with whomever he conversed, his Lipps dropp'd as the Honey Combe.' 'As he happen'd to meet with Strangers on the road he endeavour'd to drop something that might be for their good.'[18] At South Stoke, John Sefton was made rector in his place.

It was common practice at the time for Church of England clergy to hold several livings in 'plurality'; many of those who had suffered for their loyalty were now given two or three parishes, which meant multiple incomes from rectory estates. Church regulations stipulated that the parishes must be within thirty miles of each other, and that the incumbent must reside in each parish for a 'reasonable' part of the year. That could be freely interpreted. Many pluralist priests barely saw one or more of their parishes, renting out the rectories, and delegating ministry to curates. So did Sefton spend much time in the little hamlet on the Arun?

From 1672, when Sefton was made a canon residentiary, his home was probably in the cathedral close at Chichester. But I may have been right that he spent time at the timber-framed rectory house, churchyard on one side, water meadows on the other. He had clearly been attached to the parish before the war, when he was meant to be elsewhere. Sefton had lived most of his life in downland villages, and his friendships with nearby rural priests were strong. It seems likely that, at least for a time in the 1660s, Sefton got to know the community of South Stoke and made a place for himself there that was different and complementary to his place in the cathedral, where a seat was reserved for him, labelled with his name.[19]

Most of the evidence for Sefton's later life is contained in the will he made the year before his death in 1679.[20] His heir was his 'loving brother' Joseph, who had spent his life as a farmer in Sutton (a yew tree he planted in 1666 still grows in the churchyard) and who, when he came to make his own will, asked to be buried across the fields in his native Bignor.[21] The will shows that John Sefton had two servants, Elizabeth Cotterall and Joan Martin, to whom he gave money, clothes and linens. He left money to the poor of Winchfield, Sutton and South Stoke, and to widows in Chichester: bequests that map the geography of his life.

The will is, strikingly, a record of friendship: gifts are carefully selected for men, women and whole families. There was a three-volume Bible for his 'good friend' Thomas Musgrove, who had been priest in a series of downland parishes through the 1660s and 70s. Hannah Woodward (wife of another rural Sussex priest) was to have the use for her lifetime of a large and fine volume: a 1638 Book of Common Prayer. Did anything survive from the small library that once lived in the study at Bignor, passed on to Sefton by his father? Most had probably disappeared with his papers and other possessions during his years in hiding and exile, but later he built up a large library of his own, and would pass it on.

Sefton's will ends with a list of a hundred volumes bequeathed to Chichester cathedral on the proviso that the vicars' hall be repaired and opened as a 'publicke library'. So we have both a reading list and a sign of Sefton's investment in shared learning. Not that he was imagining families borrowing poetry and histories and field guides. His aspiration was to foster theological study and the promised books constitute a bracing syllabus of Greek and Hebrew Bible commentaries and contemporary treatises. There were editions of Ambrose and Augustine and Cyprian; Bartolemeo Platina's *Lives of the Popes*; all five volumes of Matthew Poole's enormous and recently completed 'synopsis' of biblical critics.[22] I suppose I had hoped to find him reading Izaak Walton's biographies and John Evelyn's *Sylva*. Perhaps he was doing that too. But Platina's *Lives*; Poole's *Synopsis*; Davenant's exposition on St Paul: this was his world as a theologian.

The bequest was part of a larger local effort to re-establish a library in Chichester after the seizure of the cathedral's books and of Henry King's personal collection. King himself tried to reassemble his library during the 1660s and after his death his son gave a large portion of those recovered volumes to the cathedral. Now Sefton arranged for his books to stand binding-to-binding on new shelves with King's, and with volumes that King had inherited from his friend John Donne when he, too, passed his library on.

～

At South Stoke in the mid-eighteenth century, one of Sefton's successors decided to annotate the register. He took up the book that both Staples and Sefton had used, and against the chronology of parish baptisms he added another kind of chronicle. 1648 (he circled the date): 'Ye horrid murder of Charles ye 1st.'

> 1650 This is the second year of the usurpation & interregnum; & by right the second year of the reign of Charles ye Second.

1658 Cromwell Tyrannus moritur
1660 Caroli Secundi Restauratio

History inscribed in a rural hamlet, still charged with feeling a century after the events of the revolution, the records of that time still being written and revised.[23]

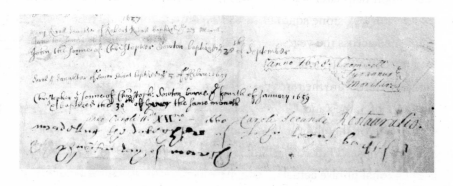

On a bright December day, long after I'd gleaned all I could from John Sefton's will, I steered a giant hire car precariously through the lanes to Sutton and sat looking in through the kitchen door at my great-uncle and -aunt. I was on a chair by the herb bed; they were just inside, wedged between the cooker and the table: a classic Covid gathering. They leaned towards each other, framed in the opening. There were biscuits and coffee, and a tot of whiskey in my uncle's cup. He was frail, defeating disaster with every small manoeuvre, but under my aunt's supervision they were coping masterfully with the task of being elderly in a remote village in a pandemic that meant no one except a daily nurse could go inside. Bright-eyed, with his beautiful voice, my uncle asked about a radio programme I'd made and that he'd half been able to hear. They could only keep a small part of the garden up, my aunt said, which seemed to mean there were fewer varieties of winter lettuces and beetroots coming up in the sheltered beds under the flint wall. The nurse had wrung a chicken's neck that morning and they would have a stew for lunch.

I walked over to Bignor afterwards and tried the door of the church. In the cared-for emptiness – plain plaster walls, vases of holly by the chancel arch – a familiar name appeared suddenly from a huge tablet that I must have passed many times before. THOMAE SEFTONI. There followed a long inscription. I deciphered as much as I could that morning, and sought help later with the Latin. Gradually the church wall-plaque told its story. A stone square of condensed biography and feeling communicated across the years.[24]

VIDE VIATOR: look, traveller. Yes, I was the traveller, stopped and looking. Here were the remains of Thomas Sefton, who lived in the happy years of James and Charles, before peace was broken. He saw the golden age of the church. His homeland, 'PATRIA', was Lancashire, and Brasenose, Oxford, nursed him – or rather, in the amazing but conventional phrase actually used, he sucked at the breast of Brasenose. He reached his climacteric (the age of sixty-three) and died. He left three living sons. The eldest was a surgeon who sailed three times to India ('INDOS') and died at Surat. This was John Sefton's brother, who must have spent his boyhood among the cushions and yellow curtains of Bignor rectory, became a surgeon, and lived his life between England and India. The Surat he knew was the largest of the Mughal ports, a city of ship-building and cloth markets, and the centre of English East India Company trading. I imagined the crowds, and the young man from Bignor among them.

Then came lines on John Sefton, the second brother, the churchman who had unexpectedly fascinated and eluded me. MINOR BIS AFROS FUGIENS FUROREM / BELLI (HEV) CAROLI SENSIT RUINAS. He went twice to Africa, fleeing the fury of war (alas); he saw the ruin of Charles. Africa: not the East Indies as Walker had it in *Sufferings of the Clergy*. The horror of the revolution and regicide is given here as the defining context of John's life, not his settled career after the Restoration, his parish in South Stoke on the edge of the marsh, his canon's stall in Chichester cathedral. The story of the third brother is presented as a happy contrast (O FELIX FATUM!) to John's forced exile. TERTIUS LARI LITANS: he kept the lares, the household gods. He died peacefully, an old farmer.

VADE VIATOR. The traveller is urged to pass on, not disturbing Thomas Sefton's bones. And I do pass on, back to the spaceship hire car, back to Chichester then Oxford (breast-feeder of undergraduates). In the Oxford libraries I read about ejected and restored clergy across England, turning from local to national stories and back again. Who has been speaking to me in these Latin lines? They must have been engraved after all the Sefton brothers were gone: after 1681, that is, when the old farmer with his happy homely fate left his Bignor and Sutton property to the next generation of Sussex Seftons. Yet it sounds like one of the brothers talking, like John or someone very close to him, remembering and envying his father, passionately missing England as it was in the 1630s, fraught with anger and sadness at the ruination he had seen, understanding a tranquil home to be a blessing indeed. It's an act of witness and recording, this long epitaph, part of a much broader effort to inscribe the century's events in stone, in books, in memory. 'Let us keep memorials of those sufferings' wrote a loyalist minister in Suffolk when his persecution ended; John Walker was still collecting the evidence in the 1720s.[25] Nonconformist thinkers were, at the same time, writing the memorials of those who suffered on the opposing side of the argument – hence the record of the honeycomb dropped across England and Ireland by Henry Staples who, to bring that other story to an end, died after being thrown from his horse in 1686, while visiting friends near Chichester.[26]

It is characteristic of this elusive history that when I searched for some of Sefton's books in the catalogue of Chichester cathedral library, they were not there. The terms of the bequest seem not to have been fulfilled. Sefton had wanted the vicars' hall to be a public library, but it was not opened, and Sefton's books were not listed among cathedral acquisitions. There must have been some disagreement or delay. But the cause of a city library was not lost. The cathedral's historian in modern times,

Mary Hobbs, records the growth of the cathedral book collection in the early eighteenth century, its new home in the beautiful painted Lady chapel from 1750 and, at last, certainly by 1769, its status as a library, where men and women alike could not only sit and read but borrow books and take them home.[27] At least one of Sefton's volumes was there in the Lady chapel. When his friend Mrs Woodward died in 1722, the Book of Common Prayer she had been left by Sefton was passed on to the cathedral, with a label remembering Sefton's wishes.[28]

If you stand in the dusk and choose a date, if you find a name in the parish registers and follow where it leads you, the story is not likely to be an immediately vivid or full one. It won't be like tracing the life of Henry King, celebrated writer and deposed bishop, whose letters and elegiac poems survive. But you may find an inventory of furniture, a hedge leapt, a confusion of Africa, India and the East Indies, an unattributable epitaph, a list of a hundred books.

7. CIDER IN STORRINGTON
Discoveries of a Baptist farmer

West Wantley: I knew the name immediately. I was staying in a pub room above Storrington High Street, and had spread out the map to plan a walk. West Wantley. It came back to me with an impression of an overhung lane and water: an old house beside a millpond, gabled stone walls. I don't think I've invented the memory of going there because the narrow lane and the stone house at the end of it were familiar when I went to look. My tentative knock at the door received no answer that morning, but looking up I could make out the eroded letters on a date stone. R-H-M 1656.

A few hundred yards away was the comfortable, deep-carpeted house where my best friends, twin sisters, used to live. It was where we spent large parts of our childhoods trying to be in the sixteenth or seventeenth century. With or without props from the dressing-up bags we performed a series of Tudor and Stuart existences more absorbing to us than anything in the present, except perhaps the trampoline. We wrote vehement letters, pressed our plastic rings into the red wax, and sent them by messenger to London. We sat in window seats holding tiny Latin prayer books we had made for ourselves with A4 paper and Sellotape, not knowing Latin. Cultivating highly partial and fantastical notions of how anyone lived in the 1600s, we had little idea about rural history except for a passionate interest in Elizabethan manor houses and the temporary country retirement of those not welcome at court. The big farmhouse that lay just through the garden laurel hedges and across a field must have exerted some appeal. But I don't think we left aside our court fantasies for long enough to consider the life of anyone on a farm in Stuart Storrington.

R-H-M 1656. Richard and Mary Haines were newly married and had overseen the renovation of the old West Wantley house inherited by Richard from his father when he came of age. They had kept the medieval core, but the builders had refaced the main range in brick and stone, made a handsome two-storey porch, laid polished flag floors, and re-roofed it with durable Horsham stone. With six bedrooms, and a parlour large enough for a table and thirteen chairs, there was space for a substantial household, perhaps with several indoor and outdoor servants living in, though the records give no hint of anyone beyond the family. There were five fireplaces, a fact that speaks of a middling-sized house and a lot of domestic work to do. It's a fact known to us because hearth tax was payable each year from 1662, though in West Sussex only the receipts from 1670 survive. Five hearths for Richard Haines. The main fireplace downstairs was rebuilt when they moved in as a huge brick recess, with ovens, salt cupboard and curing ledge.[1]

The timbered rooms went largely unaltered. They would have been recognisable to Roger Wantley who owned them in the 1400s, before the estate ('lands, tenements, rents and services in Sullington and Storrington called West Wantele') passed to members of the Barttelot family who farmed here until the 1550s, ancestors of William and Walter on the river at Stopham.[2] But that was all history. There was enough to think of in the present. 1656: Richard was twenty-three and starting out with his wife.[3] The upstairs windows looked towards the corn, wheat and barley fields. The date stone marked the beginning of their life there.

It was a death-date too. Their daughter was just past a year old when she died. A second child, a boy, lived for a month. There may well have been other pregnancies that did not reach full term. But there were also healthy children: Gregory was born in 1658, Richard in 1661, John in 1663 and a daughter Mary in 1666. A seventh child, Stephen, born in 1668, was buried the following month. Like many other women of her time, Mary was almost continually pregnant for fifteen years. She bore the loss of three children in infancy, and brought up four others.[4]

As far as records go, Mary is silent. Her husband on the other hand won't stop talking. Richard was an inventor, an entrepreneur, a social reformer, a hatcher of schemes. He was absurd, ingenious, irrepressible. Once he had published a first pamphlet there was no looking back: he went into print with his personal quarrels, his agricultural and economic research, his modest proposals for the achievement of national prosperity. These tracts, which we can download today with a mere few clicks, allow us to hear the voice and follow the ambitions of a Storrington man who, because he had a taste for pamphleteering, left much more of himself to posterity than anyone around him.

Not that he was writing for posterity, setting down knowledge for the future as the water bailiff had done a generation before; his mind was on the present and how to do things more effectively. The Wealden iron industry, he thought, could be prosperously expanded if only attention were paid to woodland management. No nymphs fled groaning from frightful furnaces in his imagination. He was more worried by Britain not being self-sufficient in iron. Also: 'The neglect of Iron-work has been a main Cause, that our woods are so much decayed, and so many Coppices grubb'd up and converted into Tillage.' Those woods must be looked after: coppices tended, underwoods preserved. This rural man of business was clear-sighted about ecology when the economy of his region depended on it.[5]

At home, his farm was increasingly a laboratory in which new processes were trialled. It was his own Storrington branch of the Royal Society. John Evelyn was developing his treatise on horticulture; Robert Hooke was working out the movement of the earth on its orbit. Aware of these contemporaries, keenly pushing himself into the midst of the 'culture of improvement', Richard Haines was finding a way to extract hop-clover seeds from their husks. This mattered because hop-clover (or nonsuch trefoil) grows on even the flintiest or sandiest ground. It could transform the fortunes of farmers on difficult soils by providing a reliable food crop for livestock.[6] He knew enough about it from the flinty ground on the downland side of the parish and the sandy heathland of the commons.

What did he see when he looked up towards the green slope of the downs above Storrington and Sullington? He saw *potential*, among other things: the thin, chalky soil was ground for agricultural improvement.

Asked to picture the life of a gentleman farmer here in the 1660s and 70s, I might well have made assumptions about an energetic but uneventful existence, squarely focused in the parish. I would imagine him on Sunday walking with Mary up to the Saxon stone church on Sullington Hill. The children would run round the yew tree, which was eight centuries old already and is still there. Haines would say his prayers in the nave, alongside the thirteenth-century knight in chainmail who stares at the ceiling from his marble bed next to the pews. He would smoke a pipe with the neighbouring farmers (Barns Farm, Cobden Farm) and frown over the estate accounts after dinner.

He didn't. Instead, he rode, or drove with the family, the twelve miles or so up into the weald to join the Baptist congregation in Southwater near Horsham. He ran serious and long-term risks in doing so: nonconformist meetings were illegal under the Conventicle Acts of the 1660s and 70s. But this punitive regime strengthened the determination of those fighting for the freedom of worship. Haines was in open and dangerous defiance of the ancient parish church that was meant to be the centre of his life.

The names of the Haines children were all entered in the Baptism section of the Sullington register like the other parish babies, a fact that puzzled me until an experienced and sharp-eyed archivist suggested I look again. The entries were different from all the others. They did not say 'baptised' but 'born': it was the birth dates that were given. 'John Haines the sone of Richard & Mary Haines was borne ye nintenth day of August in ye year of our Lord 1663.'[7]

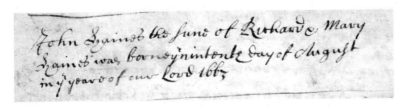

These children would make their own preparations for baptism when they were old enough. The variation of a single word in the register was the sign of their parents' resistance to the state religion. So, while John Sefton followed the Book of Common Prayer in South Stoke, and Henry Staples preached his honeycomb words in Ireland, while a new Baptist assembly met just outside the city walls of Chichester and discussed the possibility of lives in America, Richard Haines rode to Southwater.

What drew him there? The minister, Matthew Caffyn, was known across the South for vehement preaching and for the fierce disputes he stoked within and between dissenting communities. *Deceived and Deceiving Quakers Discovered*, he titled his attack on fellow nonconformists in Horsham: *Their Damnable Heresies, Horrid Blasphemies, Mockings, Railings*. He preached in villages throughout Sussex and Kent, fighting duels of words with those who challenged him. Caffyn was the son of a Horsham farmer, but he had been adopted and sent to Oxford by Lord Onslow of Wisborough Green, an MP before the King dismissed Parliament, a man who fought for the Commonwealth in the years of Caffyn's youth. Caffyn's religious radicalism was strong from the first: he was expelled from his college, All Souls, for his views on baptism. No dissent at the university was allowed. By the age of seventeen Caffyn was back in Horsham and preaching at Southwater – which would be the centre of his religious life for the next sixty years.[8]

Haines became a close friend of this charismatic, querulous, raging minister. Then in 1673–4, suddenly and completely, they fell out. The trigger seems to have been Haines' intention of seeking a royal patent for his clover-cleansing method. Disgusted at this ungodly profit-seeking, Caffyn launched a campaign to discredit him in every way, refusing to stop until the Storrington farmer had been excommunicated by the congregation.[9] There must have been something else going on, I assume, though perhaps the rage is comprehensible. Yearly in and out of jail, Caffyn devoted himself to resistance. Haines had become treacherously complicit with the Crown, seeking recognition and patronage as his way of doing business. When he rode off to London to bend the ear of Lord Shaftesbury, or dedicated his proposals to the King, he was looking for state sanction and acceptance.

Thrown out by the religious community he had chosen, Haines did not walk away. He went into print with *New Lords, New Laws* (1674), the 'new Lord' being the false apostle Matthew Caffyn who thought it his right to invent laws about what Baptists might and might not do. Haines apologised for his style: neither nature nor education, he said, had furnished him with accomplishments as a writer. This was true, and here Caffyn had the better of him. Haines knew it, and proceeded at length, undaunted, to denounce him as the 'Idol of Southwater', a dissimulator worthy of Machiavelli, a pretend saint whose toxic behaviour must be stopped before spreading 'like a Gangrene' through the body of the Baptist assembly.[10]

Haines reported several dreams — with disclaimers that though they might be the result of indigestion, they might also be visions from God, especially since they came to him after days of prayer and fasting. In one there was a great fire at the meeting house, and when it abated the congregation was safe but the pulpit was empty. Caffyn the preacher was nowhere to be found, and a bright key was left gleaming on a nail. Then Haines dreamt of trying to get his patent. A church appeared in his way, blocking the street, and he knew that to proceed he must climb over its 'stately steeple'. 'Which I did.'[11]

Crudely and vividly expressive, full of striving and arm-waving, symbols dangling as plump low fruits for interpretation, these dream narratives have something of the quality of the woodcut prints blazoned on so many of the period's religious tracts and broadsides. Dreams themselves are often like that. Haines was publishing a fragment of autobiography, but in common with many other writers of dreams in the seventeenth century he was meaning to talk about God and truth and the church rather than personal ambition, thwartedness and an obsession with patents that could not now be dislodged. He turned the steeple-scaling episode into a tale of perseverance and triumph: he got his desired audience with the Earl of Shaftesbury and secured the patent. He went home to West Wantley and poured out the whole story in his book. 'I have never been exercised in such publick endeavours', he began; from now on his public endeavours would never stop.[12]

He must have employed a farm manager to keep the estate running while he embarked on research into the economics of poverty relief schemes – unless it was Mary who took charge of everything in his absence. Richard set off for a tour of the Netherlands, observing Dutch projects for employment of the poor in manufacturing. He was immediately translating what he saw into the British context and expanding it. Every county in the land, he said, should have one or more large almshouses where inhabitants would be employed as flax-spinners. Those currently reliant on parish poor relief would be accommodated by these purpose-built 'working hospitals', which were really live-in linen factories.[13] Rather than being dependent, people would contribute to the economic growth of a nation that could, in return, support its workers.

Variants of this idea, widely diverging in detail and political motivation, would still be legible in the union workhouses of the 1830s and in many kinds of public work projects across Europe and America.[14] In one giant plan Haines looked to increase national prosperity by building an efficient, co-ordinated British linen industry, reduce the amount that householders must spend in poor relief contributions and provide secure employment for the poor themselves. One of his publications on the subject advertised nothing less than *The Prevention of Poverty*.

As he grew in conviction he imagined transformed English landscapes planted with hemp and flax for linen-making. England 'might so easily become the Garden of Europe'; it would take only a little improvement of the soil. He had experimented, of course, at home. 'Any indifferent good Land, Chalky, &c. from the foot of the Downes to the Sea-side, with double Folding or Dunging, and twice Plowing, will produce Hemp in abundance.' And in the weald: 'many Thousand Acres of the Wild of Sussex will produce Crops of Flax'.[15]

Each new project sprang from Haines' immediate surroundings in Sussex. He saw how a local problem might be solved, and how the solution might be adapted across the country. He always relished multiplication sums. He imagined two thousand spinners on average working in each county almshouse; hence, across fifty-two counties, upward of a hundred thousand spinners.[16] Part of the point of bringing workers together in large factories, rather than encouraging cottage enterprise, was that such economies of scale would justify investment in a new kind of mechanised spinning machine – a contraption too complex and expensive for any cottage parlour.[17] To most independent cottage workers, with settled homes and families, almshouses were dismal spectres. But the seeds of another idea lay in Haines' plan: one not necessarily linked with poverty but with new models of work. His visions of progress were first glimpses of the Industrial Revolution.

To the obvious objection that spinning had always eluded mechanisation, that there was no such thing as a spinning machine, Haines flourished a new set of letters patent. He had been working with a partner in London, and they secured a patent in 1678 for a machine that had multiple spindles turned by one crank.[18] It would allow 'from six to one hundred spinners' to produce linen and worsted thread 'with such ease and advantage that a child three or four years of age may do as much as a child of seven or eight years old'.[19] That proud claim comes to us across the gap of time and sends out its shock. Here was the prevention of poverty for the glory of the nation as the Storrington farmer imagined it: a vast workshop fitted with machines and row upon row of tiny children subdued to the rhythm of treadle and loom. It looked to him a better scene than many he saw around him in London and in the Sussex countryside: vagrant children not yet strong enough for farm work, subsisting on anything they could steal.

The scheme outlined by Haines very nearly passed into law. The proposals secured wide support and a bill was due to be brought before the Commons. But it was never heard.[20] This was not a good time for making agricultural or industrial history because other kinds of history were taking centre stage. The question defining current politics was whether the King's Catholic brother James should stand as heir to the throne or be excluded from the succession. As the 'Exclusion Crisis' intensified and the rifts between factions deepened, the problem looked intractable. Parliament was prorogued and then dissolved by Charles II in early 1681, before meeting for a single week in Oxford, when its business was not with almshouses but with the future of the monarchy, the constitution and the nation's fragile peace.

At West Wantley, attention turned to apples. Richard Haines had a new plan for the advancement of national prosperity. It was more modest this time, though when he had done his multiplication sums he was sure it would have a palpable economic impact. He walked through the estate, much of which was now given over to fruit bushes and orchards. He saw in the rows of gooseberries, in the Golden Pippins and bitter crab apples, a glistening future of British wealth. He proceeded by trial and error and a lot of drinking, and by 1683 he was confident: he had hit upon a way of making cider every bit as 'pallatable and pleasing . . . strong and Chearing' as French and Spanish wine.[21]

The trick was to distil cider twice over, add the resulting spirit to a hogshead of normal or 'simple' cider and leave it for three months, unstoppering it for five hours every ten or twenty days. Variations on this basic method promised a whole range of new drinks. A sweet version would be a rival for malmsey (or 'canary'), and he had worked out the best way to make the required syrup (with forty egg whites for each gallon of sugar water, to be mixed in and then skimmed off). Wormwood might be added to help digestion. The juice of other fruits might be added to the apples, or used instead: 'Pears, Wildings, Crabbs, Cherries, Goose-Berries, Currants, and Mul-Berries' in many permutations.[22]

Haines persuaded Henry Goring, a pillar of the Sussex gentry community, to invest in a share of the business; they signed articles of agreement 'concerning Mr Haynes secrett touching Cyder'. Such support was helpful as he made his application for a patent. Then Haines was ready to go public with his secret, vigorously explaining its significance in a tract that over-spilled the bounds of a pamphlet and grew to the size of a book: *Aphorisms upon the New Way of Improving Cyder, or Making Cyder-Royal Etc.* Here was a home-produced drink that would stop the British buying foreign wine at great expense. Haines envisaged that a Cyder-Royal Office would soon be established in London;

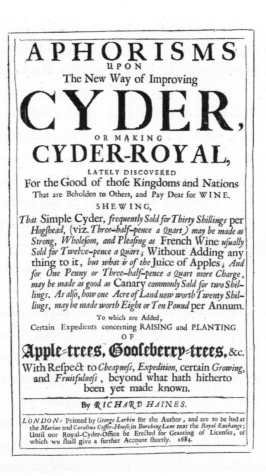

for the moment, he left copies of the book at the Marine and Carolina Coffee-Houses near the Royal Exchange, where merchants and investors would find it and spread the word. He was already envisaging production on a giant scale, and arguing that tax on the new liquor would be windfall for the Exchequer: 'In any Country where there shall be One-Hundred-Thousand Acres Planted, the King or State may Raise to themselves Six or Eight Hundred-Thousand Pounds per Annum.'[23] A hundred thousand acres. The figure sounds more appropriate to the traders in the Carolina Coffee-House than to English orchards, though as an ambitious estimate it was about right.[24]

Haines wanted to think and act internationally. He had toured Holland in his quest for good systems of poor relief, and now he dedicated his cider 'to all Kings, Princes, & States, Who have No Wines of their own'. At the same time, and despite his nonconformism, he was very much a patriot, arguing for national economies of production and consumption. He thought local drinks a good idea on health grounds, 'the juice of vegetables growing in our own soil, and under the same influences with ourselves', being more likely to agree with British stomachs than juices brought from different climates.[25] This had logic at a time when the body was understood in terms of four delicately balanced humours, and doctors emphasised a finely tempered relationship between the microcosm of the body and the hot-cold-wet-dry conditions around it. An early advocate of low food miles, Haines urged the efficiency of local production.

Here was a small-scale farmer who understood himself in relation to communities of inventors and reformers in Europe and America. He had a powerful sense of himself as a citizen of his beloved Great Britain, a businessman in England's prosperous capital and a farmer in Sussex. He belonged to a parish, and had duties in it: he signed as churchwarden in 1683 and rode uphill to the church among the yew trees. Moving across these spheres he was defiantly proud of his class. Despite the pompous letter to princes and the bandying about of royal appellations (further rebuke to Caffyn), he cared about lower-to-middling families, those with no Latin or fine rhetoric and more energy than education.

He wrote as a yeoman. Metaphors stuck with him when they were grounded in the physical world. There is no sign that he read Shakespeare, or Milton, or even Bunyan. When he described the proper planting of orchards, there was no memory of Thomas Browne's ample sentences, no Garden of Cyrus invoked as he described the layout of trees. He explained how to use pond mud instead of dung, how to stop the cider from 'Huzzing and sputtering', how to prepare the cask by burning coriander seeds.[26]

'Tho' Princes and Nobles are the Highest and most Refined part of the World, yet they are but few.' He didn't really mind what they drank at their tables. His cider was for the 'thousands of good Country-Gentlemen, multitudes of Citizens, substantial Yeomen'.[27] It was also for women, and children from twelve months old. But what Mary Haines thought about any of it, we do not know. Home brewing and cider-pressing were generally women's tasks in the seventeenth century – until tracts like Haines' began to promote them as advanced arts, requiring ingenuity and yielding a patriotic juice of which a man could be proud.[28] Perhaps Mary had one less job to do. More likely she was fruit-pressing, barrel-cleaning, decanting, unstoppering and re-stoppering.

Haines' way of imagining national prosperity in cider terms was not wholly eccentric. Cider was broadly understood as a national drink, flowing amber-gold through English veins as blood flowed red, as plentiful in apple districts as ale in hop-growing areas. Its symbolic freighting only deepened in the decades after Haines secured his royal patent. John Phillips' poem *Cyder* (in two volumes of Miltonic blank verse) appeared in 1708 and influenced a new genre of what became known as English Georgic. Phillips showed his wit by stretching his humble subject to its limits, but he was genuine in his desire to celebrate the apple-presses ('theme as yet unsung'). He thought of how Virgil in his *Georgics* had sung of harvest times, grafting and pruning.[29] Phillips came from a Herefordshire family with large orchards, though as a young man he spent most of his time in Oxford, where he stretched out his undergraduate career to last a decade. Proud feelings for the 'native soil' he had thus far mostly escaped were fused in the poem with the alternative fruits of a life spent with friends and books in college rooms.

Like Haines he argued that no one need look for 'Foreign Vintage, insincere and mixt' when there was English cider to be had from the 'bounteous Womb' of our 'native Glebe'.[30] But Phillips was a very different thinker to Haines, and the contrasts are audible in their apple-talk. For Phillips, assertively Tory, 'Cyder-Land' is the real England. His version of Cyder-Land had taken arms for the King in the civil war, when 'all her Pruning-hooks extended into Swords'. The men of orchards fought to subdue the 'Atheist Rebels' who were 'bent to Ill / With seeming Sanctity'.[31] Phillips, born long after the Restoration, thought of his orchard inheritance in terms shaped by the war of the 1640s: his cider carried in its frothing juice a tradition of King and church and land. Haines' cider was the toast of a brave future that would be shaped by men willing to think and drink differently.

Mary died in November 1684 and was buried in Sullington churchyard. Richard seems to have based himself in London after this, overseeing the sale of cider from a vault on Newgate Street and Three Crown Court in Southwark.[32] He needed to scale up the business if he was going to earn back some of what he had invested in experiments, advertising and premises, but he was interrupted. He was fifty-two when he died the following May and was buried at Christ Church Newgate Street.

In Sussex, two local administrators went over to West Wantley to make the inventory of the deceased person's assets that was necessary before probate could be granted. They walked through the rooms of the big farmhouse. In the bedroom over the porch, the one with the gable window: one feather bed, one bolster and blanket. In the hall below: five chairs and a settle, a table, twelve pewter dishes and twelve wooden plates. The document they wrote out has not survived but a copy made soon afterwards is tied into a roll of legal documents in the National Archives. A Victorian genealogist found it there while researching a different subject; the information reached Charles Haines in the 1890s, while he was writing about his seventeenth-century ancestor. I had only to tap the names into the catalogue, place my order in the reading rooms at Kew, and unfurl the list of things counted and valued on a summer day in Sussex in 1685.[33]

It was June, and the year's cereal crops were still in the fields: the assessors added up the acres. They toured the barns, estimated the worth of the ploughs and harrows, and checked over the livestock: ten oxen, nine hogs, seven pigs, yearlings, heifers, some good horses.

> Five hogsheads of cider
> Three gross of glass bottles

The hogsheads of cider they valued at £2 each. They noted the hundreds of glass bottles stacked up, waiting to be filled with cider. Three gross: 432.

Outside, the apples were beginning to form; the gooseberries were plump and bitter, ready for picking; but the bottles would not be filled. The bottles gleamed in their emptiness. The bottles, it transpired, were on credit. A glass-seller in Southwark sued in Chancery for his unpaid bill.[34]

In 2013 a planning application was made for a new estate on the greenfield land neighbouring West Wantley. I knew I'd heard the name more recently than those childhood visits to my friends and this was why. The case was famous locally because the proposed development, for 102 houses, would encroach on the green gap between Storrington and neighbouring West Chiltington, a gap that was already only a few fields' width. Many felt it would expand Storrington decisively from a large village to a town, and if that was almost inevitable it mattered how the urbanisation was managed. The character of the whole area was in question, and so too was the specific history and character of West Wantley Farm. The old farmhouse was Grade II* on the register of 'listed buildings' and therefore protected by law as a 'heritage asset'. The 'setting' was protected along with the physical buildings. But what exactly constitutes a setting? The National Planning Policy Framework defines it as the 'surroundings in which a heritage asset is experienced'. 'Its extent is not fixed and may change as the asset and its surroundings evolve.'[35] It may extend well beyond the grounds of the property itself, but you can't touch it or cite its dimensions by the metre.

When their initial applications were knocked back, the developers brought an appeal and an inquiry was opened in January 2014.[36] Over several days in late winter, the planning inspector walked the paths around the site. There were hundreds of measurements to check and sightlines to assess. He agreed that the new development would answer to the pressing need for housing in the Horsham District Council area, particularly affordable housing. He could raise no objection in principle to use of a greenfield site outside the current built-up area of Storrington: with many new homes needed, development would have to occur beyond existing settlement boundaries. This was in line with both local and national policy.[37] But he needed to interpret planning law in relation to this particular place.

'The wider landscape to the north, east and west of the site, although not subject to any policy designation that reflects particular visual worth, is nonetheless attractive and resolutely rural.' Having visited a range of 'viewpoints near and far', he decided that the development would not be too obtrusive from a distance. His concern was for close-up views glimpsed from the road and from footpaths, snatches of open field, signals of town giving way to country. There's not much along that road you'd stop to admire; you wouldn't reach for the camera, but after careful examination the inspector found local 'character and appearance' to be defined by those fields. Dense building in this 'transitional' area would be 'incongruous and jarring'.[38]

As for West Wantley House, the Listed Buildings Act required decision-makers to have 'special regard to the desirability of preserving the setting' of a registered building. The National Planning Policy Framework went further: 'where a proposed development will lead to substantial harm to a designated heritage asset, consent should be refused unless it can be demonstrated that the substantial harm is necessary to achieve substantial public benefits that outweigh the harm'.[39] The inspector had therefore to balance degrees of harm against the public benefit of new homes. Assessing evidence from English Heritage and conservation officers, he sought to understand the historic significance of the house in order to judge what most defined its setting.

Some historic sites take much of their meaning from association with particular people. Representatives of Horsham District Council described West Wantley's links with famous figures, especially with Percy Bysshe Shelley, whose father owned it: the place was linked with one of our great Romantic poets, they argued. But the inspector did not set much store by this connection. Nor did he emphasise the presence of Richard Haines.[40] The setting to be protected was that of a functional farmstead, in use since the fourteenth century, something made and experienced over generations. He looked outwards from West Wantley and back towards it from many directions, asking how the house would have related to the land around it. The inspector found it 'reasonable to assume that a farmer would wish to keep an eye on his land from within the house'. This meant an open aspect to maximise sightlines. Boundary planting around the new estate might create a screen, but it could not return open views and a 'sense of rural isolation' to the farmhouse setting.[41]

The language may sound dry, the case may sound minor, but this was a direct investigation of what value should be accorded to a long-established farm landscape in contemporary Britain, what kind of heritage was to be protected, and from whose viewpoint, and for whose benefit, and to what effect. English law takes historical seeing seriously: in this case it asserts the importance of what farmers and their families saw year after year. 'Views over the land to the south of West Wantley House would have been available from its upstairs windows.' The fact that very few people were currently able to see these views did not lessen their significance as part of the listed asset; access might in any case change over time.[42] The inspector considered carefully the footpath running along the southern side of the garden: this was the perspective from which the public could get some sense of the house and setting. 'Anyone walking from west to east along the right of way will register the isolated location of the listed building and will retain that impression when proceeding to the elevated part of the footpath from which the proposed development would be readily visible.'[43] It is striking to find in a formal appeal decision this weight given to the experience of people on a little-known footpath, and to find that those anonymous pedestrians are generously credited with sensitivity to their surroundings.

The inspector concluded that the development would bring 'substantial harm' to the character of the area. The impact on the setting of West Wantley would not be 'substantial' but it would be 'significant and irreversible'.[44] The appeal was dismissed; the houses were not built. Haines' view is preserved, but not because it was seen by Haines or by any other individual associated with the house over the years. The case was not about personalities. It was about the relationship between town and country: not spectacular landscape but 'attractive countryside', what Ford Madox Ford might call 'just country'. And it was about the character of an ordinary, ancient Sussex farm. The rural surroundings of West Wantley survive now for the passer-by on the footpath, today and tomorrow, who is trusted to 'retain the impression' of the place as he or she goes by.

PART II

8. THE LONDON MODEL
Building work in Chichester

In the city of Chichester in 1711 a master mason worked on designs for a grand new house. He had to think about ceiling heights in proportion to the windows, the construction of the roof and the price of the tiles. The client was Henry Peckham, a young merchant who would come to be known as Lisbon Peckham, probably because his head and his account books were full of wine shipments from Portugal, and so as to distinguish him from other Henry Peckhams in a family that had been in the neighbourhood for generations.[1] His grandfather was still well remembered by those who could think back to the 1650s and 60s. Sir Henry Peckham: the older people of Chichester knew him by repute. He was repeatedly returned to Parliament as MP for the city. As a Justice of the Peace he was a trusted figure on the bench at Quarter Sessions (hearing settlement cases, ordering that Anne Bettesworth's pension be paid in arrears). He steered a moderate course in Commonwealth politics and was knighted when the King returned to court.[2] But there had been trouble in the Peckham family since then.

The young Henry, still in his twenties, wanted to commission the best house in town for himself and his new wife Elizabeth. The money was entirely hers, or it had been until the marriage put most of it at Henry's disposal. She might have lived independently as a widow. But something drew Elizabeth Albery, in her early forties, to the Chichester merchant fifteen years her junior. Whether that was friendship or sex or some hidden entanglement, the records do not say. She had lost her husband and only child. Henry made 'pretensions of great love and kindness', Elizabeth said later.[3]

Henry's motivation for marriage was plainer. His father had left the family deep in debt. With fierce effort, his mother managed to hold on to their farm in the country south of the city, including the Dutch-gabled brick house where Henry spent most of his boyhood.[4] She ran the estate herself, with nothing to spare for errors or comforts. Henry was not, by the sounds of things, very helpful. Set up with a legal training, with prospects of a reliable income if he applied himself, he rebelled, was 'impudent', and left.[5] By early 1711 he was making headway as a merchant but was far from riches. Elizabeth made him a wealthy man, and they agreed to build a new home for themselves in the city.

Most of Chichester's housing was still timber-framed, but there were several recent buildings of a different kind that showed what prosperous domesticity might look like in modern times. Edes House, completed in 1694, set the standard. The deep eaves were bright with white-painted modillions; Portland stone dressings gave solidity and lightness at once.

East Street looking towards the market cross, painted by an unknown artist, c.1715. Robed aldermen process into the Swan, with the big inn sign hanging above them.

Tall gate piers at the front were topped with urns holding stone pineap-
ples. At just a few other prime sites, wattle-and-daub walls had been pulled
down to make way for brick elevations with large sash windows, emphatically symmetrical, lined up in equal numbers each side of boldly pilastered
front doors. At the corner of South Street, a house had just been rebuilt in
brick with a stucco cornice. And the pride of East Street was the coaching
inn, the Swan, with its new brick facade, a first-floor balcony and an enormous, eye-catching painted swan sign suspended high over the street.[6]

A county town in the 1710s. People in East Street passing the sign
of the Swan and the hat shop further along. Dissenters walking out of
the East Gate to the Baptist and Quaker chapels beyond the walls. Orchards and market gardens around the edge of the city. A three-mile ride
through the flat country to Dell Quay where corn and timber are loaded
for the coasting trade to London. Ships coming in, fifty tons, seventy
tons, from Holland and Portugal.

Henry and Elizabeth showed optimism and imagination in choosing
their new address: a corner plot currently occupied by an old malthouse
in the area called the Pallant. The lanes here, in the south-east quadrant
of the circular walled city, were dominated by the malting and leather
industries.[7] As soon as you turned off East Street you were in among
the leather sheds and liming houses. There was at least one tannery and
tanning brought the stench, coming and going with the breeze. At the
tight crossroads was the leather market, where the curriers brought their
goods to be stamped and valued, and dealers showed their wares to buyers at stalls they kept around the wooden cross. If the Peckhams liked
this location, then the stonemason Henry Smart would design something
distinguished. It needed to be private and separate from its surroundings, yet also a landmark for everyone to see.

The house that Smart planned was never made. He presented a 'fframe
or modell' to the Peckhams, which was probably a series of plans and elevation drawings. Professional architects were rare at this time: even for
a large project it was usual for a master tradesman to propose a 'model'

based on another building or designs in a pattern-book, adapt it to the client's needs, and oversee the work.[8] Henry Smart presented his ideas. The Peckhams went off to London soon after, where they saw architecture that impressed them more than anything their Sussex builder proposed. They came home with drawings prepared by an architect in the capital, and asked Smart to price them up.

Here was a moment of direct competition, or conversation, between ideas from London and what a local craftsman was offering, and in the early 1700s there were many such conversations. Traditional vernacular buildings were beginning to look old-fashioned now that classicism was the guiding spirit in modern architecture across the wealthier cities and the stately homes of Europe. In London, the major buildings that had emerged after the Great Fire seemed to define a new kind of national style. The City churches, the Royal Hospital Chelsea, the magnificent frontages at Hampton Court by Christopher Wren: these boldly expressive versions of classicism showed the possibilities of an English baroque that was now being adapted in the design of private homes. Some features of the style were responses to building regulations introduced after the Fire – brick parapets, for example, rather than wooden eaves, safety measures that became marks of a modern idiom.[9]

It's not known who in London did the drawings for the Peckhams or whether they were based on an existing house, but they reflected the proportions and decorative details increasingly appearing in the terraces and squares of the capital. Henry Smart and his fellow tradesmen could see the new structures in pattern books, but there weren't yet many opportunities locally to make their own contributions. If the nascent 'national style' in architecture was to spread through England's regional cities, there were big questions ahead about how it would be adapted to local materials and needs, and how regional clients and craftsmen would make it their own.

Mrs Peckham 'liked best the London model'. Work began accordingly.[10] Smart's 'fframe' was not needed, and he applied his skills instead to realising the chosen design. A fine and costly house was constructed at the crossroads in the Pallant. Five years later Elizabeth Peckham left her husband, filed a complaint against him for spending her money, and took him to court.

The financial settlement was not straightforward. Since the money had been hers in the first place, Elizabeth wanted serious recompense. Henry argued that most of her money had been spent on the house at her behest. It was she who had wanted the London design. It was she who had kept ordering changes after the house was finished. The lawyers needed to clarify the cost of the house, and the extent to which Elizabeth had approved the expenditure.

⁓

I unrolled the Chancery documents at the National Archives and had to ask for help in managing the heavy parchment sheets, pinned at the corner in a bundle and all trying to roll themselves back up again. Having read about the case, I was hopeful of finding some further hint as to why the Peckhams chose the London design, and what their Chichester builder, Henry Smart, was offering instead. This was optimistic: there were no design statements, or aesthetic creeds, or arguments over local and cosmopolitan values. But the file was rich with life. A lawyer had been sent down to Chichester to interview the builders as witnesses – and here, in the brown ink of a long-ago clerk, were their statements. Henry Smart, builder. Richard Clayton, carpenter. John Pryor, joiner. Richard Morey, bricklayer. If you needed evidence of what was spent on the house at whose order, these were the people to ask.

On 14 October 1717 they were summoned to the Black Horse, across East Street from the Pallant, and questioned one by one. John Pryor, the joiner, stated that while he was wainscoting a chamber, Mrs Peckham 'came into the room and ordered a partition and a door to be made in the middle of the partition to make the chamber more private'.[11] John Channell, the carpenter, was clear that 'where she disliked anything she had it altered'.[12] The Chancery rolls take us into the half-wainscoted parlours of a house being built in Chichester three centuries ago, and into the room at the Black Horse where the witnesses gave their versions of events.

It's rare to hear the voices of early-eighteenth-century Sussex workmen talking about what they do. These people leave many physical traces – in the walls they build, in the intricate rune-like language of carpenters' marks pencilled or incised on beams, in the close-guarded code of mason's marks – but names and words are thin on the ground. Even here, their statements are mediated by legal clerks as they write up the evidence in long-winded formulations. Still, we can catch their tones. And we get a strong sense of the woman at the centre of it all, Elizabeth Peckham, who cared a great deal about this house, and about the skill of the craftspeople who were making it.

The tradesmen had not been left to get on with the London model: revisions were made at every stage. Mrs Peckham was frequently on site, guiding the work. The builders had the skill to move doors and reposition walls as required, negotiating with a client who 'did often come and inspect'.[13] Elizabeth was clear from the first about the kitchen. The London model located it in the basement, but Elizabeth was not having that. She thought it 'too cold & damp for herself and servants & directed the same to be built on the back side of the house'.[14] The carpenters tried to persuade her otherwise, but she was not willing to consign her maids to airless gloom. The kitchen would go in the back courtyard, leaving the whole underground realm of barrel-vaulted cellarage to be used for Henry's wine and other shipments.

Above the cellars rose a seven-bay brick frontage in Flemish bond (header, stretcher, header, stretcher), the work of the bricklayers Edward Lawrence and Richard Morey. It was boldly decorated with a bevelled string-course, rusticated quoins giving an emphatic outline, and lintels decorated with emblems. The windows shone in the light, thirteen tall sashes at the front, and more in the attic behind the pediment. A staircase gave access to a rooftop platform from which you could see the whole city, looking down into the cathedral precincts, over the orchards and – at a pinch, with a pocket telescope perhaps – across the plain to the harbour.

Down at street level there was uncertainty over the front steps. Henry Peckham would not approve them until Elizabeth expressly agreed the design.[15] Then Smart got to work, cutting and rounding off the treads on a flight of ten steps (John and Hannah Edes' house was similarly elevated) leading up from the churned lane to the panelled door in its extravagantly moulded frame.

Visitors would arrive in the airy entrance hall with its wide oak staircase drawing the eye upwards. Smart was asked to make mantelpieces using large marble tables that had belonged to Elizabeth's brother. The joiners John Pryor and James Burley worked on the panelling: shaving and sanding until the parlours were elegantly lined. It was probably these men who decorated the staircase, carving the side of each tread with motifs suggestive of domestic comfort. Oak flowers droop from oak vases; carved smoke curls from oak pipes, as if two companionable smokers had set them down in the course of an after-dinner conversation.

Outside, the market square was unrecognisable. The cross was gone, the stalls where hides had been checked and stamped since anyone could remember had been dismantled. The tanners were trying to put their businesses together again on the other side of East Street. Henry Peckham had pushed through the change, urging the city council to relocate the market. Sitting over their agenda at the Swan, the mayor and aldermen struggled to make the decision, but once assured that Henry was offering a new site for the market, they let it through.[16] There was a clearer view now for the Peckhams from their windows.

Other timber buildings were demolished to make way for houses of the new kind. Soon the city's builders would be receiving enquiries and instructions: a three-bay house to be designed on East Pallant, a family home with a music room on North. Clients looked up at the Peckham facade, gauging the proportions of the rooms. Those with enough money had a choice to make – should they entrust local builders with the design or ask a London man?

On every side, Chichester was a city of contrasts and people could feel it changing. Well into the 1720s, when a boy called James Spershott was growing up, it had 'a very mean appearance'. There were no pavements, only a 'broad stone or two at most of the Doors'. The Roman city walls were 'in a broken ragged condition' 'overrun with ivey'. As an old man in the 1780s, a retired joiner who knew the town's language of wood and stone, Spershott wrote his recollections, wanting to record for his children how the place had changed and prospered. He remembered 'Night Freaks' and drunken revellings, bull-baiting, 'cock-scailing' even in churchyards (where players took aim at a tethered bird and tried to stone it). Loud and threatening groups of people had made a strong impression on him as a boy. Footballers played in the streets 'to the advantage of the Glazier'. That was the raucous outdoor world that might at any moment go smashing through the expensive windows of North Pallant. [17]

Elizabeth had not been born to wealth. She grew up in a village on the coast near Worthing, daughter of the vicar of Ferring. At thirty she married another local clergyman, and they lived first at Houghton on the Arun, then Hunston outside Chichester. It was her brother who made a fortune, leaving Sussex parish life to pursue East India trade. He made his sister his beneficiary, and died in 1710. She was almost immediately drawn into matrimony, though she spent time negotiating the marriage settlement: £50 a year of her own inheritance she managed to keep for herself.[18] In the matter of the house she was assertive, stepping decisively into the role of discerning client.

Within four years of it being finished, work began again. The kitchen and other 'offices' – brewhouse, wash house – were not right and Richard Clayton was called in. He was a carpenter, but probably employed other trades to work for him. The Peckhams were both there when he arrived and a barely controlled scene unfolded. Henry announced that he had built the kitchen to please his wife, and said that 'it should be pulled down and rebuilt to please her'. Clayton was told to follow her directions. As for Henry Peckham, he would leave them to it. He was going to London, 'and would not meddle with it having had trouble enough about it already'.[19] We can almost hear the slam of a door.

Henry Smart the mason was not at first involved in the re-building. He had started work on the Duke of Richmond's vast estate, Goodwood, in the downs north of Chichester, and he would be employed there for the next fifteen years.[20] But he had time to do Mrs Peckham's paving when his skill as a stonecutter was needed. He laid new floors in the wash house as instructed. Mrs Peckham, he told the lawyers, 'did mightily approve'.[21] She knew good stonework when she saw it. But she would not be going back and forth for long to the well-floored laundry. By the end of 1716 she had had enough and moved out.

Elizabeth embarked on a new phase of life after the Chancery settlement. She used some of the money wrestled back from Henry to lease a farm east of the city, though I'm not sure whether she moved there. She was living in Chichester when she died thirty years later, in 1749, leaving gifts to many local friends and relations in her will. She wanted her best furniture saved for her great-nephew (dressing table and glass, armchairs in the 'best parlour', 'my green bed in the fore chamber with the bolsters, pillows, bedstead, curtains and vallens'). She specifically bequeathed him, too, a large Bible, *The Whole Duty of Man* and anything else that should be 'thought fit' from the bookshelves. Her emphasis on the religious volumes gives us a hint that though she had some very secular concerns about her wainscoted rooms, she was a pious woman. She was, after all, the daughter and widow of vicars. Her first husband, John, was the man she still wished to be buried next to (as quietly as possible) – and so she was.[22]

Henry Peckham stayed at the North Pallant house and tried to get on with business. In 1717 he was appointed as 'Customer' (or customs receiver) of the Port of Chichester for a year, also known as 'city water bailiff'.[23] Presumably he knew the bailiff who was his counterpart on the River Arun, Laurence Eliot from Yapton, who had in a parchment notebook the river's history and customs as they were compiled in the 1630s. It was the last time Peckham held a major role in the city. A long but undistinguished career followed, as a merchant and local politician. At the time of the 1741 general election he was to be found trying to win votes for the Tory candidate by importing a hogshead of rum liquor or 'shrub' for the pleasure of citizens who might give their support to anyone by the time they had drunk it. His Tory allegiances divided him from the city's Whig communities, but there seem to have been other problems. Civic status eluded him, despite being four times nominated for mayor.[24]

For the master mason, Henry Smart, things were different. He became a prominent figure among the Free Masons, first as a member of the Swan Lodge in Chichester, named for its meeting place at the Swan.

He went on to the Cross Keys Lodge in Covent Garden, where he was nominated as a Grand Steward in 1728.[25] He must have been regularly in the capital, where all around him, street by street and square after square in Covent Garden and Soho, London models were being built. A classicised modern city was rising in brick and stone.

Was Smart interested in the architectural grand schemes of his time? His employment on the Duke of Richmond's Goodwood estate put him close to noblemen and their architectural projects. New kitchens were being built at Goodwood in 1724, to designs by the celebrated Scottish architect Colen Campbell, architect to the Prince of Wales. This was the man who had remodelled Burlington House. Henry Smart, as estate mason, was surely involved. He knew all about kitchen extensions, but this one (no records of which survive) would have been on a level of grandeur beyond anything in North Pallant.[26]

There were complex and varied patterns of connection between regional craftsmen and the more celebrated figures at the centre of their cultural worlds, and I had little hope of finding out about the particular case of a Chichester builder. Then a clue appeared. I was looking at the three lavish volumes of Colen Campbell's *Vitruvius Britannicus, or The British Architect* (1715–25), the essential guide to contemporary classical building in early-eighteenth-century Britain. There were large plan and elevation engravings of buildings from Somerset House on the Strand to Dalton Hall in Yorkshire, and an emphasis throughout on neo-Palladianism, recalling and anglicising the sober, spacious formality of Andrea Palladio in Renaissance Italy. The third series included ambitious designs (never realised) for a new Goodwood House. The Duke of Richmond had several copies of this book, but there too in the list of subscribers (from Joseph Addison Esq. to Sir John Vanbrugh, knight) was the name of Mr Henry Smart, mason.[27]

Smart's investment in this pricey volume suggests how closely he was engaged with the Goodwood plans and their aesthetic context. Smart, and just a few other master craftsmen who were also subscribers, pored over the engravings and considered the growth of classical style in England.

Work by Smart may well survive, unlabelled, in the garden pavilions, stables and dairies of Goodwood Park, and in the streets of Chichester. A well-laid stone floor and sculpted gate piers can mediate in their own way between pattern-book styles and the particular ground of a long-known place.[28]

There were private sorrows. A family monument in the cathedral cloister, carved in stone of course, tells me that Smart lost his wife, Martha, in 1729 and their son, Robert, in 1740. The register of apprentices (printed by the Sussex Record Society) shows that soon afterwards he took on a boy called William Lever, committing to train him at the mason's yard for the standard seven years.[29] In his middle age Smart was one of the most respected people in the city. He was elected mayor for the year 1751, and continued as an alderman. All through the 1750s until his death in 1760 he had a significant voice in decisions about the city. His name is still there in the cloister, alongside the names of the wife and child he lived so long without.

The Black Horse inn on St Martin's Lane closed in 1730 and the site today is occupied by Marks & Spencer's food hall. In its different way, this too is a meeting place. The brightly lit refrigerated aisles have their evening regulars who go in looking for dinner. They greet each other and exchange brief comment on current events in the place where the eighteenth-century locals came for a beer, and the tradesmen sat to be interviewed by the lawyers from Chancery.

The Peckhams' house is now Pallant House Gallery, which holds perhaps the finest collection in the world of modern British art. Work by David Jones and Ben Nicholson hangs against the wainscoting made by John Pryor and John Channell in the 1710s. Henry Smart's flag-stoned floor in the hallway is polished to a shine.

Outside, the gate piers still support the two stone ostriches that have been drawing surprised smiles from passers-by for centuries. Lisbon

Peckham had an ostrich in his adopted coat of arms, symbol apparently not of heads in the sand but of endurance since the birds will eat hard objects like stones. I can't find any mention of who designed and carved the Pallant ostriches. Were the bird-topped pillars all part of the London model? It seems more likely that they were designed and made by Henry Smart, working from book illustrations or prints. In the 1720s there would be ostriches for inspection in the Duke of Richmond's menagerie at Goodwood Park, and as an employee on the estate Smart would have the opportunity of seeing them. But the stone ostriches predate those arrivals and are works of imagination.[30] It seems not unreasonable to imagine that in 1713 a small audience gathered round to watch while two large and intriguing crates were hoisted from a cart. People stood around in the lane, leaning on sticks, laying down baskets that contained shopping and borrowed books. A slightly built man came over from the last of the leather sheds to see what was happening.

The mason's boy pulled armfuls of straw packing from the first crate and Smart began to ease out the contents, nudging and manoeuvring until he had it clear and stood back with a flourish. There in the lane: a stone beast with a tall neck, white and proud and odd and cheerful-looking. 'A goose!' said someone's daughter. 'A phoenix,' said her mother, 'the bird that comes from fire.' William Collins the hatter, who had a side view, had discounted sheep and camel and realised the hind part was not legs but a tree branch to prop up the body. Moving forward, seeing the sculpted plumage, he thought of the sign of the Swan inn with its great flapping bird raising its wings over East Street. Laurence Eliot, overseer of swan-marks, wondered that anyone could get a swan so wrong. But no, this must be a bustard and what a fine choice that was. It was a wonder bustards could fly at all, what with the size of them, and yet they were powerful when they got up over the downs, and the sight seemed to him so unlikely that he always stopped to watch. Excellent meat and lots of it. This sculpture was a splendid thing, but not, on reflection, like a bustard.

There was a big rump of feathers at the back that made Ann Cox think of plumed hats waving on the way to a dance. 'Endurance!' muttered a round man in a clerical gown who had put on his glasses to see. He thought it was an excellent creature: stout and solid, flamboyant without being voluptuous. The second was unpacked now. He considered the stoniness of the fast-running birds. He lifted them into flight – flying stones – and then remembered that ostriches don't fly and brought them back to the ground.

A gust of wind loosened the bundled straw; a few stalks of it lodged in the velvet of Miss Cox's coat. For a moment, Mr Collins thought it might be his part, as an alderman, to welcome the stone bird to the city. The scene was momentous, he thought. But he only mentioned to the stranger next to him – who seemed to be more apron than man, a leather apron stiff with years of the city's juices – that the beak was good. A good beak for the first ostrich of Sussex.

9. EASTER CHALK

I planned to find Andy Goldsworthy's *Chalk Stones* at Easter. I had read about the fourteen large chalk balls he had placed between Cocking Down and West Dean in 2002, but I wasn't sure any of them still existed. At the time of installation, geologists predicted that they would be deeply eroded after two years and would break down completely soon after that. Goldsworthy had the chalk cut from Duncton Quarry, the only chalk pit still in use in the western downs. He worked in the quarry to shape each enormous chunk into a sphere about six foot high, not perfectly geometrical but expressively globular. Heavy-lifting equipment was required to haul them to the various positions Goldsworthy chose along a route down the hillside. Some were to be prominent, others to loiter in the gap of a hedge or sit cushioned on grass and silverweed in the verge.[1]

It rained continuously through Maundy Thursday and Good Friday. The drains overflowed in Chichester; families with tired faces struggled along the pavements in search of holiday entertainment. Water pooled in the rain coverings of buggies and poured off the awnings of shops. I postponed my chalk walk for a better time and then started out anyway. I needed a marker, some central axis around which the indoor days could arrange themselves. The *Chalk Stones* I had seen in photographs worked on my mind with a strange mix of weightlessness and gravity. Chalk was rolled away from the tomb. The round white boulder stood aside from the entrance, budged just a few inches, marking the difference between death and life.

Dark would come early on this day that had barely got light, and I had left it too late to go far. Just a rapid there-and-back, up the scarp and a little way along the ridge. The wet was running in streams over the flinty path ahead and the report of gunshots hung in the air. Somewhere in the coverts there were pheasant shooters. The guns stopped, which was unnerving; had I walked into their range? Flints and bright chalk had been thrown up by ploughing and the ribbed papery husks of harvested maize lay about with stone in them. The sweetcorn had long ago gone off to freezer compartments, and here in the rain were the pale relics, weathered sheaths holding flint cobs. The guns began again. And then, round the corner, where the hedges end and the path runs bare over the hill, there was a *Chalk Stone*. I have never had so overwhelming a sense of being greeted by something inanimate in the landscape. It was to do with the fullness of the answer, I suppose, to the stone I had imagined. 'Are you still here?' I had asked, coming through the rain. And there it was, patient, plump, quiescent, imperfect.

Chalk and flint are made together. Geologically they depend upon each other in a partnership of opposites. Chalk is among the softest lime-stones, powdering to the touch. There is nothing jagged or sudden in a chalk landscape: the hills have been eroded to curves. The harder kind of chalk, from the lower layers of sediment, can be used in building, though it weathers too readily to be much use outdoors and is better for interior masonry. A chalk wall can crumble, but there's a kind of clemency in its ready answer to the touch of human hands.

Flint is used for cutting and for killing. It can be sharpened to a knife blade or shaped to an arrow. In these lethal forms it made life possible for those who sent it plunging into the flesh of birds, rabbits, deer, boar, mammoths. So many flint arrows were made in the downs that you can still find them pointing out from a ploughed field or from cleared undergrowth. They may break but they won't erode so most of the flints ever carved are still present somewhere near the surface of the ground.

A landscape of chalk and flint is the giant ossuary of ancient seas. South-east England was a seabed for sixty million years before emerging into the light. A further drowning followed, adding a final layer to the sediment. The sea was alive with single-celled plankton called coccolithophores, perpetually reproducing and dying, their tiny shells falling to the floor where the calcium accrued.[2] Each layer weighed down previous layers, which solidified under the pressure. The skeletons of other marine organisms were formed of silica. Dissolved in water, this flowed into gaps between layers of chalk. Like fillings in teeth it closed up the holes. The liquid silica hardened in the calcium moulds, becoming much harder than what surrounded it.

The North and South Downs once formed the sides of one large chalk range, which rose in a dome over what is now the weald (over Crawley and Horsham, over schools and stations and shopping malls). It stood open to the weather and the chalk eroded, exposing the more ancient clay beneath. That giant white hill, which no human ever saw, bulked massively into northern France with no break along the way. Water rose in the glacial lake of the North Sea and the lake spilled over its bounds. Floods washed across the chalky land bridge and flints carried in the currents scoured the soft rock. Water flooded into a fissure and (what was it like? The calving of an iceberg or the judder of an earthquake? Or was it the quiet rising of water in an estuary?) in that ancient season an island was made.

⌇

Goldsworthy grew up in West Yorkshire, and moved north to Dumfriesshire, exchanging slate and gritstone for granite and red sandstone. He was a visitor in Sussex. 'Coming from the North, from the Scottish borders, as I do,' he said, 'the idea of digging a hole and finding it white seems totally contradictory.' As visitors often can, he brought to the place a new kind of perception. The chalk was strange to him in a way it could not be for those who walked white paths all their lives. He was a traveller crossing into another geological realm. 'Dig a hole up North and it's black and stony and dark and earthy. So to dig a hole in Sussex and find chalk, so absolutely pristine and pure and white . . . was like finding the sky in the ground.'³

The sky in the ground. It's any tunneller's dream of digging and digging through to the light. Or it's the radiance of buried wonders. When characters in cartoons dig in the right place for treasure, a glow radiates up from the hole: here be shining gold, or white. The chalk ball had greyed and greened with time, but still it gave an uncanny impression of having landed from elsewhere: a meteorite, if not a cloud or a solidified portion of the sky. It looked out of its element, a parked wanderer, yet the whole hill is made of this. What it resembled most was a giant snowball. Goldsworthy made a group of outsize snowballs once, and set them down in the streets of London on Midsummer's Night. They were pieces of escaped winter, trespassing on the opposite side of the calendar for a few hours before melting.

The chalk ball will melt eventually, but for now it was defying expectations. A long-woolled sheep looked over the fence at the stone. The stone started to look like a sheep. The stone and the sheep stood wet under the grey sky, one warm to the touch and one cold.

10. NATIVE STRAINS
William Collins' places

The Vicars' Close in Chichester has always seemed to me a place of peace and beauty. There's a single row of terraced cottages, low and protective-looking, medieval with Georgian upgrades, sash windows fronting onto small gardens where roses flop over box hedges. Walking past, on the path leading through to the cloisters, there's often something that makes me pause. There'll be a column of honeysuckle scent or a lamp switched on in a low-ceilinged room among books and chairs.

Here, on a Sunday evening in the late 1750s, a woman read the Bible aloud and a man sometimes corrected her. Perhaps it was warm and they had the window open. Certainly their voices were audible to the Reverend Richard Shenton who was walking in his garden close by. He was used to hearing unhappy sounds from that direction. Ann Collins had undertaken to shelter her brother, once a promising writer, long since declared insane. People passing through the cathedral precincts said they heard him crying out. That Sunday, it was the quiet that struck Richard Shenton. He remembered it much later, when asked for any recollections of William Collins the poet:

> I heard a female (the servant I suppose) reading the Bible in Mr Collins'
> Chamber. Mr Collins had been accustomed to rave much & make great
> Moanings: but while she was reading or rather attempting to read,
> he was not only silent but attentive likewise, correcting her Mistakes,
> which indeed were very frequent, thro' the whole 27th Chapter of
> Genesis.[1]

I don't know whether it happened quite like that; Shenton may have sharpened the details in the telling. Nor do I know which was the

Collinses' house — only that it 'abutted the cloister'. But the scene is infinitely sad.

Shenton is recalling a very ill man who gained, perhaps, a short spell of relief while the Bible was read aloud. He must impress upon us the incompetence of the reading woman. Though the subjects at hand are mental distress and a fleeting peace made possible for one person by another, Shenton needs to get it clear that the servant is making a mess of the Bible. Was she in fact a servant? He lived close enough to hear her voice, but didn't know who she was.

A voice with no particular owner, then: just a female voice in the evening air, trying to make sense of the extremely convoluted passage in which Jacob pretends to be his brother Esau, and claims the blessings of his father. So she read: 'He smelled the smell of his raiment and blessed him, and said, See, the smell of my son is as the smell of a field which the Lord hath blessed: Therefore God give thee of the dew of heaven, and the fatness of the earth, and plenty of corn and wine.'[2]

The dew of heaven and the fatness of the earth: those things stand clear from the narrative of Genesis. Collins spoke a few words but was mostly quiet as he listened, and he is invisible in this fragment of a story, as he was mostly invisible in the last years of this life.

It's easy to call William Collins a 'Chichester poet': he spent his first thirteen and much of his last nine years in the city. It's harder to be sure what the phrase might mean. He is not in any emphatic way a poet of place. He did not choose to begin life in Chichester, nor to go back there when he was too ill to live alone. As a young man he wanted to be in London. Thinking about Collins we're not going to learn much about any of the obvious local subjects. We won't see through his eyes the downland plants or ancient sites, or who was who in 1750s Chichester. With Collins we can enter into the midst of British literary culture and ask how places were imagined and valued by a highly ambitious young poet in touch with the major thinkers of his time. We can see, as Collins saw, rural, provincial and metropolitan cultures questioning each other, shifting in their relative status. His contemporaries were asking, quite consciously, where mattered. Where might poetry live?

The terrain Collins inhabited most intensely was that of literature. He lived in Chichester and Soho, but his addresses could more accurately be given as Milton's Eden or the Bower of Bliss in *The Faerie Queene*. Schooled in Latin and Greek from the age of five onwards, his mind ranged over 'Hybla's Thymy shore' or 'Paphian hills and fair Cythera's isle'.[3]

What did Sussex mean to him? Nothing about Collins is very easy to get a grasp on. He slips away from definitions and co-ordinates, which may be what keeps drawing me back. He strives in his odes for a kind of landscape evocation that is abstract and general, levitating above the quirks of topography. The 'Ode to Evening' (1746) swells outward to evenings of each season, surveying the late gleam of 'some sheety lake' on a lone heath, and 'dim-discovered Spires' beneath a nameless representative mountain, settling nowhere, folding distant views into one breathtakingly condensed sequence of thought and image.[4] It's nowhere, yet for generations of readers it has created an atmosphere so pungent as to seem a place of its own.

⌒

There's a plaque now to mark the place where Collins grew up on East Street, close to the site of the Swan (where Henry Smart met other masons in the 1720s), beside a passageway through to the Oxmarket. It's one of the small local council plaques that bring a scene of civil war cannon-fire or needle-making flickering briefly into the mind as you make your way to somewhere else. William Collins' boyhood home was demolished in the 1920s and rebuilt in an exaggerated Queen Anne style, all quoins and dressings, a giant scrolled pediment above the door. The ATMs of the Halifax building society bleep behind the windows as people go by. Except on Wednesdays, beast-market days when the street was packed with bulls and heifers, pens and dung, it might not have been so different in the 1720s. People walked past, unless they wanted a hat, or they had business with the mayor, in which case they rang at the Collins door.

William's father sold hats. He must have sold a lot of them while pursuing other business interests too because this was a prominent building right in the centre of town (recorded as having a plentiful nine hearths, when West Wantley, for example, had only five).[5] His own father had been a Chichester clergyman, so the family moved between church and trade. He was a hatter from a well-educated, bookish background; the books his father specifically willed to him were probably on the East Street shelves.[6] He ran into debts but he kept up the outward show, living 'in general style' according to one man who knew the family.[7] He may have been 'pompous in his manner' but he was twice elected as mayor, and was concluding a term of office when his wife, Elizabeth, gave birth to a son at Christmas 1721. Their two daughters, Elizabeth and Ann, were already young women; this was a late, last baby. They named him William after his father.[8]

It's not known where he went to school. His parents may have paid a private tutor.[9] Or if the family was already in financial straits, young William may have been chosen for a scholarship at the Bluecoat charity school in West Street or at the Prebendal School next to the cathedral, in which case he would have walked back and forth each day between the house of hats, business and sisters – and a boys' world of Latin grammars.

His father died in 1733 and the following February, at the age of twelve, William went away to Winchester School.[10] His mother kept the hat shop open. The old customers kept coming. The Caryll family from South Harting, where their close friend Alexander Pope would often stay, bought new hats for their household staff. Thirty shillings for three hats in 1735 – Elizabeth wrote out the receipt and hundreds like it – but the finances were precarious.[11] She dealt with quantities of legal paperwork to rent out pieces of property and mortgage others, and made a will instructing her daughters what they should sell to pay off the debts.[12]

Her teenage son was dreaming of more exotic trades than the family hat shop. His *Persian Eclogues* were not published until he was at Oxford, but his friend Joseph Warton confirmed that he wrote them while at school. The whole sequence of poems is a confection of fantasies expressed in the forms of Virgilian pastoral: the familiar form of the classical eclogue has been taken out of school and sent to the alluringly unfamiliar East. Selim the shepherd sings to virtuous maids among the balmy shrubs of Baghdad. Hassan the camel-driver laments 'hapless youth' as he crosses a scorching midday desert.[13] Playing a game of artifice, Collins presented the poems as the work of an unknown Persian author – translated here for the first time into English. It was immaterial to ask whether the 'originals' had really been eclogues, since the ruse was not meant to fool anyone, and much of the attraction lay in the collaging of Western allusions with extravagantly imagined versions of the East. How had Collins come to have the Persian texts? He had received them, he said, 'at the Hands of a Merchant, who had made it his Business to enrich himself with the Learning, as well as the Silks and Carpets of the Persians'.[14]

Here were the gap-year dreams of an eighteenth-century sixth-former. With what now seems outrageous presumption, projecting himself into a world beyond the dorms of Winchester and beyond Chichester harbour, he was posing as Mahamed on the basis of having read bits of Persian history. According to his own invention and the varyingly reliable sources he was exploring, Persian poetry swelled with emotion and richly figurative language; it veritably dropped fatness. In a dim stone room at Winchester, Collins sat among European books and began to see great plump figs, and bright silks unfurled in a bazaar, and a beautiful woman called Zara weeping for a lost lover. He was probably picking up a hint from Alexander Pope, who had intended to write a 'wild' Persian fable and had not done it; Collins, a generation younger, was now asking how poetry might open itself to 'wilder' realms of feeling. In the coming years, British literature and art would burgeon with fantasies of oriental culture.

Collins disliked these poems of his youth when he reread them a decade later, though he made revisions for a second edition. When the Warton brothers came to visit him in Chichester he was too unwell to talk for long, but he gave them a copy of the book. It was a memento of their younger lives together, and their dream of bringing new worlds of imagery and feeling into English poetry.

In the 1760s, by which time ideas about place and the arts were rapidly changing, Oliver Goldsmith spotted something curious about these poems. He thought them attractive but 'not very local', and he was right.[15] If you're going to write about an Arabian desert, why not decide which bit of desert, research it, and put in details of the setting? That was not the way Collins worked, and nor was it expected of a poet in the 1740s. Deep in the architecture of the project was a kind of comparative mythology in which Eastern shepherds, perhaps even descended from those who sang the Song of Solomon, were joined in a common literary language by the shepherds of Western pastoral.[16]

～

The young man who left Oxford in 1743 may have been shaky on Persian but he ranged with ease through the literatures of Europe. He had read his way through the courts of imperial Spain, the universities of Renaissance Italy and Germany. He was going to write a book, an enormous book, about the revival of learning across Europe in the later Middle Ages, ending in 1521, he thought, with the death of Leo X who was for him a figure of heroic stature.[17]

All this was in his mind, but he wasn't sure where to go or how to earn a living. The death of his mother in summer 1744 took him back to Chichester. There would be no more hats trimmed at the East Street shop.

There's no clue in Collins' surviving work as to how the loss of both parents at a young age affected him. There was now no steady family home for him in Sussex should he need it, and he would come to need it. For now he took rooms in London (with a Miss Bundy in Soho) and built his literary plans night by night with his old schoolfriends the Wartons, James Thomson (celebrated author of *The Seasons*), Samuel Johnson and the young actor David Garrick when he was between performances at Drury Lane.[18] At Bedford's and Slaughter's coffee houses Collins was known for his conversation and warmth – and for always needing a loan.[19]

He had an idea of going into the church, or joining the army, or an army chaplaincy to combine the two. He set about gathering support for ordination. 'Don't laugh,' wrote his old schoolfriend John Mulso to their Oxford contemporary Gilbert White, 'this will be the second acquaintance of mine who becomes the thing he most derides.'[20] It didn't happen. Clerical friends advised him against joining the clergy; they heard the hint of derision in his voice or at least the ambivalence. Colonel Martin thought him unsuited to the army ('too indolent' was the judgement that got around).[21] What then should he do?

The trouble was not wilful laziness. It seems more that Collins couldn't control the energies that flared up suddenly into grand projects and then sank. The two letters that survive from what must have been hundreds of dashing, convivial, conversational pages are little capsules of barely contained enthusiasm for music heard, books read and imagined.[22]

Top-ups and bailouts came from his uncle, but Collins was living beyond his means. When he was 'immured by a bailiff' on one occasion, Johnson helped him secure an emergency advance from booksellers for a major edition of Aristotle's *Poetics*. Johnson never forgot his vulnerability and narrow escape that day. 'He showed me the guineas safe in his hand.'[23]

Collins took rooms close to James Thomson in Richmond, far enough from Covent Garden to live more cheaply and good for cultivating a life of stylishly pastoral semi-retreat. He did not get far with his promised *Poetics*, but some of the emotions discussed by Aristotle grew in his mind as complex allegorical figures. He approached them and addressed them, wanting to see where they manifested themselves and how they could be understood. A group of highly worked odes crystallised, including poems addressed to Pity, Fear, Simplicity, Mercy, Liberty, to Peace, to Evening, to all the 'Passions' and to another phenomenon he found sacred and mysterious, 'the Poetical Character'. Confident of their originality, he had them published at his own expense and they attracted almost no attention at all, though later they would be among the most influential literary works of the century.

They are shifty poems, rhythmically elegant yet irregular and disorientating. Part of their strangeness has to do with the way things keep coming close and then falling away into great distances. The bat of the 'Ode to Evening' flits into our path, and then our eyes adjust myopically to see a beetle wind his 'small but sullen horn'.[24] But the poem won't let us settle and situate ourselves – on a country path or in the emptied-out streets of an English town. Collins' evening is not made of place memories like that, but of literature's evenings.

The 'Ode to Pity' begins with an idea of Pity herself, the embodiment of all pity, as a friend with balmy hands, binding the wounds of injured Man. Collins turns naturally to his Greek inheritance, invoking Euripedes, but he makes an unexpected pivot: 'But wherefore need I wander wide / To old Illisus' distant side / Deserted stream and mute?' He need not look to Greece for the songs of pity when they are heard in more familiar places:

> Wild Arun, too, has heard thy strains,
> And Echo, midst my native plains,
> Been soothed by Pity's lute.

This turn from Greece to Sussex is set up in a way that is made to be remarked upon. Everyone knew of the Athenian river Illisus, but the Arun? Partly, Collins is sounding a patriotic note, setting British poetry and feeling alongside the Greek canon. Partly, the Arun stands for any number of ordinary places: Pity is to be found in unsung parts, and readers might substitute their own. But the story told here is one of specific attachment to the scene of past loves and griefs. Here was the 'wild Arun' appearing for the first time in a work of literature, and it was no passing reference but a vote for a more geographically personal and locally invested kind of culture.[25]

It's striking that Collins cannot write about his 'native plains' for their own sake: he has to make them matter by making them literary. 'Pity's lute' is explained in the next stanza. Collins is thinking of the dramatist Thomas Otway, much read for pathos in the eighteenth century. Otway is his poetic predecessor on the banks of the Arun, shown into Pity's rustic home or 'cell':

> There first the wren thy myrtles shed
> On gentlest Otway's infant head
> To him thy cell was shown;
> And while he sung the female heart
> With youth's soft notes unspoiled by art
> Thy turtles mix'd their own.[26]

Collins evokes the sounds of the Arun. The turtles are turtle doves, their soft coo almost audible in these lines, a song often heard in Collins' time (later lost, and recently reintroduced to Sussex by rewilding). He makes Otway part of the natural scene, like the birds, as if raised and taught by the spirits of the riverbanks. It was all a literary fiction: Otway makes no mention in his works of Arun riverbanks or birds, or anything to do with his boyhood in the area, but Collins needs him to be a poetic spirit of the place. Retrospectively, he pours Sussex nature on the little boy's head with a sacramental touch, an alternative or additional baptism.

Otway matters a great deal in Collins' story, and in the growing tradition of Sussex poetry that flows on from it. Collins seems to have felt a special association with him even while at school. He and his friend Joseph Warton installed an Otway 'marble' in the common room when they were prefects, commemorating a literary predecessor who had also been at Winchester. More significantly, he came from the Arun valley. There were not many published poets you could say that about; it was hard to think of anyone else at all.

Otway was born in 1652 at Trotton, a village east of Midhurst where his father was curate. The river here is the Rother, which meets the Arun after miles of meandering beneath the northern slopes of the downs. For Collins it was all one stream – of water, and poetic connection. After a period of exile the family returned to Sussex with the Restoration, when Otway's father was ordained and installed (by the Bishop of Chichester, Henry King) as rector of Woolbeding, a few miles downriver from Trotton.[27] This was the home to which young Otway went in school holidays, and the place in which, while still a young man, he saw his father buried.

Collins would have known Otway's autobiographical poem 'The Poet's Complaint to His Muse', in which boyhood happiness with nurturing parents is ended by the father's death. News of it pierces teenage Otway's ears while he is busy enjoying a banquet of student delights. 'It shook my Brain, and from their Feast my frighted Senses fled.' By his own account, Otway remained profoundly shaken for a long time afterwards. 'The World was wide, but whither should I go?' he asked. That was a question Collins knew well. He too had known footloose student days altered by the death of a parent. His odes of 1746 were dazzlingly confident performances but he was still asking 'whither should I go?' He was still thinking about Otway, who had come from the same place. He described him as an infant on the riverbank, but Otway was a kind of regional poetic father too.

There's no sign that Collins intended to live in Sussex again. He and his sisters sold the family house in 1747. The deeds laid out the domestic topography of what had once been their lives: a large property worth £230, with the Oxmarket passageway on one side that would have echoed with voices and the clatter of deliveries.[28]

It was an ending. Collins returned to Richmond, went to the theatre and talked enthusiastically about a new journal.[29] Yet his new life was soon to break up too. His friend James Thomson contracted a fever which killed him in the summer of 1748. Collins shaped his grief into quatrains.[30] In the spring another guiding figure died. Colonel Martin had been living in Chichester since being wounded in Flanders during the campaign to halt France's conquest of the Netherlands.[31] He had not given up on his erratic scholar-poet nephew. He left a bequest so substantial (£2,000 split between the siblings) that William could live on it for years to come. It was the common fate of the inheriting bereaved: he was financially secure at last and – with childhood home and guardian-uncle gone – less rooted than ever before.

That winter he wrote a long poem addressed to a new friend, John Home, and much concerned with homeliness (though he elegantly avoided the pun). Home had come from Edinburgh to offer David Garrick a play-script, but his play had been refused. Collins came to know him quickly. What remains of their few months' sociability in London is a poetic celebration of all that Home might write if he turned his attention to the voices and stories of Scotland. 'Ode to a Friend on His Return' must be one of the most elaborate letters of encouragement in literature. Here is a glimpse of Collins not as indebted and unreliable, but as he was better known to those who loved his company: warm, and sparkling with conviction about the possibilities of art.

Goodbye and good luck, says Collins, and here's what to write. 'Fresh to that soil thou turn'st whose every vale / Shall prompt the poet and his song demand.' 'Thou need'st but take the pencil to thy hand / And paint what all believe who own thy genial land.'[32] Home would hardly need to exert himself with invention: the stories were all there, rising from the land or passed on through generations. Collins is bringing different ideas of culture into powerful contact. He is thinking of stories that survive in oral folk culture, told in crofts and shiels. He is suggesting a turn away from classical literary subjects (Home's play about Agis, King of Sparta, had not been a success), towards local soil.[33]

How about the story of the 'luckless swain', Collins excitedly suggests, 'late bewildered in the dank, dark fen', and then he is telling it: a Gothically sensational tale of a man caught by rising floods, far beyond help as night sets in. Only his blue spectre returns to the house where wife and children wait for him.[34] Collins toured in imagination the 'quaggy moss' and shivered at the will-o'-the-wisp that might lure you astray. He caught up an echo from *Paradise Lost*, where Satan works like the 'delusive light' that 'Misleads the amazed night-wanderer from his way' and where, in the gathering dusk of the Fall, as the final expulsion comes, angels glide over the ground like evening mist from the marshes.[35] Milton had used his simile of a man 'homeward returning' at the very moment of man's exile from Eden. For Collins, too, 'home' is always a complex idea. The subjects he advises for his Scottish friend may be local but are intensely unhomely, possessed by spirits of lost wanderers.

Did he think of how his own places in Sussex might demand his song? He sounded defensive when he mentioned his 'Southern vale'. 'Confin'd within my Native dells / The world I little know.'[36] He didn't wholly want to be in native dells with his sisters, but by 1750 his periods of psychological distress were worsening and it had become too hard to live independently in London. Collins was involuntarily local: 'While here I sit, my wandering Soul / Is in a distant land'. Yet at a time when the 'learned' and the 'homely' were held in opposition (as they still often are), he advised his friend not to neglect 'his homelier thoughts'. Collins' confidence in rural subjects far from urbane London was more radical than it now sounds. Decades later Robert Burns would write of a vision in which a 'native muse' appeared to him, a muse who seemed to carry in her cloak all the rivers and mountains of Scotland. By the end of the century homely thoughts and native places would be the celebrated territory of the new Romantic writers.[37] But neither Burns nor Wordsworth was yet thought of in the winter of 1749–50 when Collins and John Home told each other stories of the Scottish vales.

From Chichester in November 1750 Collins wrote in delight to the Oxford music professor who had composed a setting for his 'Ode to the Passions'. He loved this tribute to the music inherent in his poetry, and wondered if the composer might set another of his poems.[38] But he was now in the grip of mental illness. Needing to be on the move, he made a series of journeys in the attempt to distract and steady himself. He travelled in France, then tried a stay in Bath. He appeared sporadically in London. He made a return to Oxford in 1754 and took rooms opposite Christ Church, but the old city of books and friends could not help him. The situation was now extremely serious. The Wartons reported that he was 'weak and low', so weak that he could not walk without help. It must have been soon after this that Gilbert White happened to see him 'under Merton Wall' – on the footpath that runs beside the meadow and under the tall limestone wall of Merton gardens, where flowering toadflax and fleabane take hold in the cracks.[39] What he saw was dire: Collins was being restrained and taken away to an asylum.

He was briefly at a lunatic house in Chelsea until his sister Ann brought him back to Chichester to live with her. For all Ann knew this might be for the rest of her life. She was the only family left to help: the parents and solicitous uncles were gone, and her sister Elizabeth had died that summer. Like so many people thrust into responsibility for a 'melancholy or distracted' relative, like the kinsman who housed Mary Owden at South Stoke, she had little option. As she prepared to marry, and to start a new phase of life in her fifties, it was clear that William would be part of the household. And the house that was to hold them was not large. Ann, her husband and her brilliant, unstable younger brother had to negotiate each other in the low rooms of the Vicars' Close.

There is no surviving Collins manuscript dateable to this time, but when the Wartons visited he talked keenly and showed them poems. One was about a prophetic bell at Zaragoza cathedral ringing of its own accord before the death of a king. It was the kind of tale Collins most loved, a chill-inducing superstition from pre-Enlightenment Europe, the kind of tale through which he looked around him at Chichester. 'The Bell of Arragon, they say / Spontaneous speaks the fatal day' – Warton remembered that it began like that, and ended with the poet's own death, marked by 'some simpler Bell'.[40]

It was not the only time he imagined his death; another draft poem was haunted by 'luckless Collins' shade'.[41] Yet he continued to be alive. In the room 'abutting the cloister' he had his collection of rare books, and was apparently reading volumes of Tudor poetry and medieval Italian romance.[42] He may have returned to his 'History of Learning': a friend was shown a 'preliminary Dissertation' 'written with great judgment, precision, and knowledge'.[43] Samuel Johnson tried writing, but there was no reply. He understood that Collins probably could not write back, and felt a sad, frightened kinship. 'I have often been near his state, and therefore have it in great commiseration', he wrote at Christmas 1754.[44] There were no more of the showy, allusive letters, chatting away half in Latin. In 1756 Johnson was still wondering 'What becomes of poor dear Collins?'[45]

John Home's play *Douglas* was staged in Edinburgh that year and transferred to Covent Garden, thrilling audiences with its Highland subjects, as Collins had foreseen. Collins himself was still in his native land, at home and unhomed. Vicars' Close was at this time much more 'closed' than today, with rooms on four sides facing onto a paved central quadrangle with a water pump and small areas of planting. The gate from the street was locked each evening at curfew. Illicit attempts by residents to climb in through their street-side windows prompted a clampdown from the dean.[46]

The Vicars' Close as it looked to Samuel Hieronymus Grimm in 1782

The evidence, though there is not much of it, suggests that Ann Collins was angrily unhappy. Her stepson left a bracing portrait among his notes: 'the sister of Collins loved money to excess, and evinced so outrageous an aversion to her brother, because he squandered or gave away to the boys in the cloisters whatever money he had, that she destroyed, in a paroxysm of resentment, all his papers, and whatever remained of his enthusiasm for poetry, as far as she could'.[47] This was not a neutral view, and we don't hear Ann's own voice at all. Who knows what motivated that irreparably destructive 'paroxysm' – if there was one. Collins was in the habit of burning his own work. Exactly what happened to his papers is not known, but almost everything disappeared.

He died, 'in his sister's arms', in June 1759, aged thirty-seven, and was buried at St Andrew's in the Oxmarket behind his boyhood home. The 'simpler Bell' of that church hangs in a little weather-boarded turret. It tolled the death of a mental traveller and story-lover who had heard in his mind the ghostly bell of Zaragoza. What did he die of? Depression itself does not kill men in their thirties. No one took much notice, except his faithful schoolfriends the Wartons and a few others who remembered the brilliance of his 1746 *Odes*. He had disappeared from London social life, gone 'into the country', and years later people in the literary coffee houses were not sure if he was still alive or dead.

His reputation increased with the 1765 publication of a new edition of the poems accompanied by rapturous commentary on Collins' 'luxuriance of imagination' and 'wild sublimity of fancy'.[48] There was no question for Samuel Johnson that Collins merited space in his *Lives of the Poets*. Johnson was critical of the willed obscurity and 'clogged' lines, but wrote with appreciation of 'Collins, with whom I once delighted to converse, and whom I yet remember with tenderness'.[49]

By the early 1780s Collins was being read more than ever in his lifetime. The enthusiastic John Scott (of Amwell in Hertfordshire) wrote his own version of the *Persian Eclogues* and set out on a pilgrimage to pay tribute at the poet's grave. But he left Chichester in sadness, having found no trace of Collins there. 'The sacred spot I seek, but seek in vain; / In vain I ask – for none can point the place.'[50] Representations were made at Chichester meetings and a campaign launched to raise money for a monument to the native poet the city hadn't realised it had. The Chichester composer John Marsh rapidly wrote a setting of the 'Ode to the Passions' for a subscription concert.[51] The marble monument by the sculptor John Flaxman took rather longer and was eventually installed in 1795, by which time a new generation was discovering Collins. Reading the 'Ode to Poetical Character' in the 1790s, Coleridge felt himself inspired and 'whirled along' with 'agitations of enthusiasm'.[52] Collins became known as a poet of the passions, whose closely wrought classical stanzas gave form to the exhilaration of strong feeling and the trouble of not feeling enough. 'He leaves stings in the minds of his readers,' wrote Hazlitt, 'certain traces of thought and feelings which never wear out.'[53]

11. LIGHT FOOTSTEPS

Ann Gittins remembers

In 1786, when she was nearing fifty, a woman in Norfolk read Collins
for the first time and realised his connection with the Arun valley. How
was it that she had not read him when she lived by that same river, she
wondered aloud, in her 'Lines, occasioned by reading Collins's Poems'.
As a girl she had known his name: he was the madman whose howls sent
a chill through the veins if you entered the cathedral cloisters at dusk:

> My trembling ear has startled at the sound,
> And my quick-glance – brought flitting spectres round!
> 'No spectre shriek'd, 'twas Collins gave the cry' –
> The tale I heard, and heard it with a sigh,
> While chilling horrors o'er my senses ran
> And pity melting for the hapless man.[1]

So much for freakish stories. What young Ann Gittins was not shown
was Collins' poetry, and so she missed out on something that might
have meant much to her. 'O! had I heard the fascinating song!' If only
she had known the work as well as the madness. 'On *Arun's* banks *my*
virgin lyre was strung', she wrote with all the pleasure of recognition;
only now did she understand that a poet had walked the same paths just
before her. They were so close –

> But envious time had shadow'd o'er the scene
> Ere my light footsteps press'd the humid green
> Or sought the oozy margin of the flood –
> Where Collins, plaintive bard! had erst, enraptured, stood.

She conjures him there, in her place, feet on the same grass. She goes

back in imagination, beneath the willows, where 'the rude-rush flourished, and the bramble sprung'.[2]

⁓

Ann Gittins grew up in South Stoke, the hamlet on the Arun where I
had imagined the figures once gathered in the pews. She and her younger
sister Margaret were born after their father Daniel – Reverend Daniel
Gittins – had established himself as rector in the hamlet on the river outside Arundel.[3] The river still curved wide across the floodplain; the bell
was still the one cast in 1656; the parish register still showed how radically
England could change. The old house that had been John Sefton's was
falling apart, and a fine new rectory was built in 1740 for the use of Daniel, his wife Jane and their young family: flint-faced with big windows
looking over the water meadows. This was Ann's world until she married.
    Her father made a highly unusual commitment to the education of his
daughters. His own education had been at Cambridge, and he often told
the family about those precious years of student life.[4] His girls would not
have the chance of similarly collegial debate and companionship at university, or even at school, but they received in a remote Sussex rectory
a serious, if circumscribed, training. Year after year through the 1740s
and 50s, they were set translation exercises or texts to interpret. In the
high-ceilinged rooms, with the river and the downs beyond the window,
the lessons went on in Latin, Greek and Hebrew. There were pictures
and histories in the house as well as religious commentaries. Reverend
Gittins had subscribed (at significant cost) to the Buck brothers' 1737
series of Sussex engravings; the intricate views of Chichester, Amberley
Castle and Boxgrove Priory were probably displayed at the rectory.[5] But
the syllabus for the girls centred on classics and theology.
    Their father was High Church, Royalist and given to immensely
long, ambitious, fiercely hectoring sermons. His parishioners could expect hours of dread on Sundays and extra horror on special occasions.

This too was Ann and Margaret's education. At South Stoke church on 11 April 1744, for instance, the date assigned by royal proclamation for a General Fast, asking God's pardon and assistance in war against Spain, penitence was the order of the day. Gittins denounced the '*Perfidy* and *restless Ambition*' of a 'neighbour nation' where popish pretenders spread poison.[6] It was a penance to sit up straight and listen in the dim nave while the words rolled down the aisles and pushed up over the sills of high windows where spring light came in. Then the words drew closer and were about not nations but fields: '. . . our *Pastures* deprived of their *wonted* verdures', the rector was saying, 'and our *Mountains*, heretofore covered with Flocks, afford us prospects of *desolation*'. He was pointing to all troubles in nature and agriculture as the sign and symbol of contemporary sins. 'Our *Valleys* which, through their abundance, used to *laugh and sing*, have failed in their *Exuberance*.' Emerging into the lane after this, you would have to look anxiously across the valley. The following year, just before Christmas, came another fast and a sermon marking the penitential Advent season. Gittins issued further warnings against Catholic heresy, dealing out from the pulpit obscure threats that hung about in a thick atmosphere of hazard: 'Look but on your *Neighbours* around you and you see *Popery* and *spiritual Tyranny in the Church.*'[7] Ann was eight, and the words streamed on in triumph and rage through her childhood.

⌒

I can't tell from the surviving records what the younger daughter, Margaret, did with her learning. She spent her adult life in the market town of Midhurst, twenty miles or so away in the valley under Cocking Down. Because she remained single she had legal status of her own, and she was active in managing several estates.[8] Ann married, and moved to North Norfolk where her husband, Robert Bransby Francis, was rector in the village of Edgefield near Holt. She was mother to four children, of whom two sons survived into adulthood. She kept up her reading in Greek and Hebrew, and in midlife she started to publish original poetry, biblical translations and boldly dramatised responses to classical texts. *A poetical translation of the Song of Solomon, from the original Hebrew, with a preliminary discourse, and notes* appeared in 1781, followed by *Obsequies of Demetrius Poliorcetes* (1785), and a very expansive *Miscellaneous Poems* (1790).

Really I wanted to know about her feeling for places. Did she retain any attachment to the landscape in which she grew up? Did she love Norfolk's flint churches (as I did, when I first saw them, recognising the flint but not the scale on which it was used)? These were odd questions to ask of a woman who wanted to be discussing Hebrew, so I put them aside and followed her into debates over Arabic nuptial custom, noting the way she argued out her word-choices with university-educated con-temporaries, mostly clerics, who clearly admired her, several of whom had published their own versions of the Bible's most sensually beautiful text, the *Song of Songs*.

Ann Francis' writing is bold and definite, full of material and sen-sory detail. Solomon's style attracted her: she wanted, she explained, to translate 'the *spirit* and *energy* of *Asiatic* poetry into English metre'.[9] Like Collins imagining Persia, she was drawn to the sensuality she found in 'Asiatic' verse and its difference from the voices of northern Europe. She understood Hebrew to be the language given directly by God, and more supple in character than English. She used a compari-son from the water meadows: 'To reduce the Hebrew poetry to English verse, is nearly as difficult as to render pliant like the slender osier the solid branches of the sturdy oak.' That tactile analogy was characteris-tic. Calling on all the sources available to her, including Mary Wortley Montagu's descriptive letters from Turkey, Ann Francis in her Norfolk parsonage tried imaginatively to inhabit Solomon's world, considering (as her footnotes attest) the decoration of Bedouin tents, the clothes of Egyptian ladies, the skin of Zenobia, Queen of Palmyra, the scented trees of Lebanon, the 'green walls' of Eastern topiary gardens.

Her passages of landscape evocation are little short of ecstatic. She wasn't free from the artifice and indoor manners of mid-eighteenth-century pastoral (orbs, flowrets, argent dews), but she takes us with a leaping movement into valleys and hills. The King James translators render the end of Solomon's second song with spare simplicity: 'Until the day break, and the shadows flee away, turn, my beloved, and be thou like a roe or a young hart upon the mountains of Bether.' Ann Francis expands and inhabits this scene. First comes a wondering pause; we are still for a moment on the hillside, and then we see the deer bounding away from us over the heights:

> Before the incense-breathing dawn
> Shall chase the mighty shades away,
> And all impurpled glows the lawn,
> Emblazon'd by the orb of day –
> Turn, my belov'd; – and be thou like
> The youthful hart or roe,
> Which bounding up the path oblique,
> Leaves dusky vales below:
> Which leaps exulting on the topmost height
> Of Bether's mountains, ting'd with orient light.[10]

'Incense-breathing' sounds overdone, but Francis saw that in the Hebrew text dawn was breathing rather than breaking, and that the divine poet must be invoking the morning breeze. She added a footnote: 'Solomon, who had so frequently experienced the comfortable freshness of these breezes . . . knew how to express himself with propriety on the subject.' It was not only Solomon who cared for the veracity of such things: 'That the easterly gale blows brisk at the rising of the sun, I myself have often experienced, when climbing the lofty summit of the Sussex downs.'[11]

Here in a footnote comes a gleam from the past. It tells us that the young Ann Gittins was a walker. She walked not only at politely sociable times of the afternoon, but in the dawn; she did it often, and she noticed the rising breeze. The places she walked were part of the background of her reading, and her reading layered these places with associations. When she visualised the air, light and landscape of the Holy Land she was forming a pattern of contrast and connection. When she walked in Norfolk, or in Sussex, her language for the experience came in large part from the language of the Bible.

~

She had many friends and correspondents. There were lively exchanges with classical scholars and theologians, and the word 'friendship' recurs in her poems, many of which are affectionately dedicated, though even local friends did not mitigate her loneliness at the parsonage.[12] The pattern of her intellectual networks is clear from the large subscribers' list for the *Song of Solomon*, which is dominated by readers in Norfolk and Sussex. The gentry and clerics of Norwich and the North Norfolk parishes all wanted copies (two for the rector at North Creake); so did the celebrated landscape designer Humphry Repton at nearby Sustead; so too did readers in Midhurst, Arundel, Boxgrove and Chichester – and the Duke of Richmond at Goodwood, whose father had sponsored her father, Daniel Gittins, as rector of South Stoke. Not all these were personal friends, but Ann kept up strong connections despite the distance.[13]

Reading Collins in 1786 made the past feel close again. And the old tales of his madness affected her differently now. She thought with adult sympathy of his illness. She wrote of how she grieved at her father's death (in her early twenties), stopped writing, tried to keep going, 'to weave the tissue of succeeding days'. Hope revived, and brought the desire for poetry; she described it in terms of her returning ability to appreciate the dawn. So now she would keep writing, far from fame, far from the centres of literature, remembering Collins and tuning her 'inglorious lyre / In secret concert with the woodland choir'.[14] Paying homage through imitation, Francis wrote her own 'Ode to Melancholy', which is also an ode to evening. She affirms companionship with Collins and with Thomas Gray by listening, with them, for the 'beetle's droning song' and the call of the 'moping owl from time-shook tower'.[15]

And now here am I, reading Gittins, who read Collins, who read Otway. It's not that I'd press her work into the hands of strangers as lasting poetry; and nor is it always easy to sympathise with her thinking. Her anti-Jacobin stance was uncompromising and set her against all radical influence from France and America. For all the broad reading she brought to her theology, her devotion to the institutions of church and Crown made for what seems to have been a narrow kind of patriotism. In the political poems she published in local newspapers, we might catch the tone of her father's sermons.[16] She is not an overlooked hero, she did not shape the history of place-writing, and that doesn't at all lessen my desire to work out how she thought about where she lived.

This encounter with Ann Gittins is a prompt to look beyond those who are obviously and expressly writing about landscape. The history of local feeling is also to be found in such strange corners as the footnote to a Hebrew description of dawn. It suggests, too, how much it can matter for a reader to find that people have written in, or about, a certain area. Seamus Heaney wrote, in a wonderful phrase, that he became a poet 'when his roots crossed with his reading'.[17] Heaney is an outstanding example, but for many thousands of people there has been some analogous 'crossing'. Ann Gittins lived just before the Romantic poets brought loved places emphatically into the realm of literature. There was little Sussex writing for her to find, but she fixed upon Collins and felt her perspectives on her childhood country sharpen as her roots crossed with her reading.

The last work in her *Miscellaneous Poems* is about landscape and memory. It is about what the poet holds saved up, and how it shapes her present. 'Tho' far from Arun's-vale', she begins:

> I rove
> The verdant mead, the beechen-grove
> The stream that winds along —[18]

She could enter into those meadows or study them at a distance like a painting:

> ... pictured on my faithful mind,
> In vivid traits exact, refined,
> Those varied beauties glow;
> The wood ascends in rural pride,
> The Castle frowning o'er the tide
> That peaceful glides below.

She holds up another scene, hanging the two pictures together as a pair:

> Now fix'd on Norfolk's bleaky shore,
> I hear the German ocean roar
> And view the raging main
> As oft at solemn close of day
> I steal along the lonesome way,
> That skirts the sandy plain.[19]

Ann Gittins had been fix'd there nearly thirty years. She had come to appreciate it and in many poems she had observed details of light or the texture of a field path. She can 'scarce restrain the twinkling tear' when thinking of her first home, but the poem is less mournful complaint than acknowledgement: of the solace of memory, and of the multiple dimensions of time and place that make up the apparently fixed scene of the present.

12. MIDSUMMER FLINT

Below the ridge of Cocking Down on Midsummer Day I took a flint in each hand and made a spark. It was visible for an instant in the shade of the steep-sided track: the merest fleck, vanished before it reached the powdered-milk ruts of a path not yet dried out from winter. It would not have been enough to light a scrap of tinder, had I had one, and had I known how to catch one grain of fire, just so, in a char-cloth. But something caught from this mote of light, the first I'd made from stone. The sharp crack and the sulphur on the air were familiar to men and women of every generation before me: serving-girls in the darkness of damp kitchens, readers in the watching hour, my grandmother lighting the kitchen stove in her bungalow under Cissbury Ring.

I walked all morning as the heat grew, out onto high open pasture and down the wooded southern slope. Two farmers mending fences were the only people I saw in four or five hours. I kept company with the clematis, which was shooting out its arms two at a time, covering hedges with its swags of sappy bunting. Watching for a while, I think I saw a tendril growing. And more than ever before I enjoyed the company of flints. I picked them from their sockets in the path and tapped – gently at first, the chink of marbles, pétanque balls sidling into each other, and then with conviction: chink, tap, crack.

Paul Nash thought of flints as eggs one might crack open. 'If I broke all the shells of all my wild stones,' he wrote in 1937, 'I should find that precious yolk which is like precious stones, the black core of the flint.' He found his first 'nest' of them on the chalk downs at Swanage, and another in Sussex, moments from where I was standing. Drawn to the mysterious liveliness of certain flints, he watched them as if they were about to take flight. 'If stones are eggs they are birds too.' Stone birds born from flint eggs.[1]

Every so often I cracked another egg to find its gleaming yolk. The silica of a weathered stone is slightly translucent, so you look past the still surface to faults and fractures below. Pooled rock, rock pools: Nash was right, the yolks look curiously liquid. The dark yolk sits within an outer casing, which occurs in varying thicknesses. If this is the 'white' of the egg, there's no whisking it. It's called the 'rind' and is tough as the silica within, not like cheese rinds or fruit rinds that can be grated or peeled. The breaking-open is known as 'snapping'. A builder will snap open flint nodules to produce sheeny planes, which will form the surface of a wall. They will glitter, especially after rain, and earn their name of 'Sussex diamonds'.

Many of the downland villages are made from flints gathered from fields, picked and sorted, bedded in lime mortars derived from the chalk. Garden walls, barns, cottages, smart houses: all built with flint, some roughly arranged to do the job, some knapped and tessellated with marquetry precision. Slivers of flint are often pressed into the mortar between the main building stones, strengthening the joins and keeping water out of the cracks. 'Galleting', or 'garreting', this is called. Lacy ruffs of gallets, swimming whitebait shoals of gallets: all invitingly intricate but sharp to the touch. Strike a flint and gallets will come off at right angles to the blow. The stone doesn't break where you hit it: don't look for the injury where you think it should be. The shock shoots out sideways through the rocky body; knappers come to know these indirections.

It is a mark of the most skilled flint-workers that they can cut a piece of stone so thin as to be slightly translucent. David Smith, a contemporary Sussex craftsman, has made a chandelier. Only a virtuoso would think of such a thing. The stones have acquired aureoles. The light comes yellow and white through the suspended gallets, brightest at their outer edges where each shard is just thin enough to let it through. Each dark flint island is ringed by beaches.[2]

Marine creatures burrowed through the calcium ooze in the depths of the ancient ocean. Not unlike a great aquatic rabbit warren, I thought, skirting the edge of the old West Dean warren, a hillside continuously burrowed from the sixteenth century to the early nineteenth. On that other scale of time, when there was no one here to make rabbit pie or count the years, when this area was underwater, crustaceans nosed their way through the seabed. Dissolved silica crept deep into the burrows.

Coming out from woods into open sunlight felt like coming up from underwater, though my path was all downhill. The lane zig-zagged on the slope. A scattering of bony flints shone in the crook of a bend. Flints specialise in boniness. You won't find long ones to make a shin or femur but you'll be over-supplied with ball-and-socket joints, knees and knuckles, ankles and heels. The colour depends partly on the biography of each stone – how often in the ice ages it was frozen and thawed, whether it's been ploughed and broken. Near the surface, flints lead disrupted lives and are so fractured inside that they break unevenly. You can snap them open, but you can't work precisely with them: you can't knap them into a straight-edged square or into the blade of an axe.

For workable flint you have to reach deep below ground, and the deeper you go the purer the stone, right down to 'the floor'. Neolithic men and women, whose lives depended on the sharpness of flint arrows and knives, knew this very well, opened the flanks of the hillsides and burrowed in. The downs are pitted with grassed-over entrances to Neolithic flint workings, which show themselves now mostly as sunken thickets, as on the turf slopes up to the fort at Cissbury Ring. Far underground there is a world of nearly black flint and nearly white chalk, though no light of course to show it.

The seventeenth-century poet Henry Vaughan understood his heart as a cold flint that must be violently struck if it were to kindle into divine light. This realisation formed in the extremity of an illness that took him close to death; the illness was to him a divinely wielded weapon battering at his spirit until it yielded some response, 'battering' in a sense close to Donne's use of the word in 'Batter my heart': 'break, blow, burn, and make me new'. *Silex Scintillans* is the name Vaughan gave to the series of religious poems that resulted: the flashing or fiery flint. A woodcut on the title page shows an extraordinary emblem: a flint cut crudely into the shape of a heart, which is both melting and burning. Drops fall downward in molten tears. Fire leaps up from the point at which the stone has been struck by a weapon clenched in a hand held out from a heavenly cloud.[3]

The image strikes like the striking of a flint; it flashes out from the page. The stone has a lumpishness about it, so that we understand the previous state of the heart as mere rocky matter. The tears show us sorrow, but also a process of melting by which the solid heart is made liquid, ready to flow into new and divinely made shapes. Vaughan's *Silex Scintillans* is a work of spiritual autobiography and religious devotion, in which the flint is a figure for psychological states. Metaphors work in two directions: Vaughan's spiritual resistance and battering become part of our understanding of flint.

Emerging onto the side of the A286, there was the usual blinking moment of arrival, the steadying of sea legs that have been used to dipping, curving paths. Here were a scrap of pavement and two-way traffic, gabled estate houses and a bus-stop sign tied to a street lamp. Tap-tap with the flints in my pockets. There it is again: the crack in the night made by an unseen figure with a tinderbox, fumbling with flint, steel and hemp in cold hands. The scratch of my grandmother's lighter, kept on the stovetop, followed by the tamed roar of the gas. She lived at the foot of Cissbury, below some of the very oldest mines, but she didn't have the strength to walk up the hill and see them. Not that she ever expressed any interest in doing so. Perhaps the back garden was enough.

Skilled flint-workers assess the quality of nodules by looking, weighing and listening. They tap with hammers, and the sound rings through the stone in ways which form a map of its construction. The purest silica rings like a bell, sound travelling through the dense-packed molecules. A fine flint is a 'ringer'. Where the structure is irregular, the sound is dull and flat, its quality lost in the cracks. Knappers listen for the right place to strike the stone: a hollow ring at the saddle, high and sharp at the dense compression points. Tap-tap and the rapid strike: again and again through a lifetime for the men who built in the downs, and those paid pennies for breaking stones, and those who made flintlocks by the thousand until silicosis reduced their breath to a straining wheeze and strong bodies to exhaustion.

The Number 60 took me back to Chichester, winding out from field-flint villages to the cobble-flint walls that appear as you near the sea. The character of beach cobbles and field flints is different: cobbles have been rubbed and rounded by two tides a day. Chatter-marks, the crazing or cracks on the surface are called. The chalk which once held them has powdered and washed away, leaving the flints to roll over each other, the infinite bag of marbles that chatter on.

Cobbles, or 'pitchers', wear down eventually if they spend their lives this way. But flints and time give each a run for its money. A flint wall may weather, but it's the mortar and not the stone that wears. Chichester's city walls have been rebuilt many times, the mortars changing and stones re-coursed, but as for this or that flint, few people can tell whether it was worked last year or by a Romano-British builder two millennia ago. Flint-knappers who practise their skills by making arrows are asked to store their productions carefully. A well-made modern arrow is indistinguishable from one made when the tumps on Cocking Down were newly raised.

13. A TEACHER'S PLACES

On the phone, Caroline said her mother doesn't look out of the window any more. We agreed it was best to keep paying extra for the view so it's there just in case. It was only a glimpse of green hillside beyond the road and houses, not a major view of any sort, but an idea of distance can change the feel of everything.

All her life she had known where she was. Most of her childhood was spent in Canada, while her father was working there. Her first understanding of places developed in Ontario – maps, roads, rocks, the scale of houses and the pattern of towns all forming strong contours over which later experience would be laid. Back in England, while a graduate student in Nottingham, she painted on a large blank wall at home what her family remember as 'an amazing map of the south-east midlands': it featured 'towns, villages, lost Roman as well as modern roads'. 'We all loved it enormously and used it like an Ordnance Survey map.' It was accurate to the last eighth of an inch. It was an objective record, and yet a wealth of feeling went into it and remained attached to it.

Elizabeth's first career was as a town planner, working in Camden and Westminster. Her brothers recalled her joy and authority in what she did, whether she was inspecting embassies or night clubs. 'She knew all the dark corners like the back of her hand.' In the planning appeal courts she put the big developers on their mettle. She didn't want promotions that would take her away from work on the ground. 'Looking at plans, checking them against reality, history, context – that's what she loved.'[1]

When she and John married, they moved to Sussex and brought up their daughter in a plain 1970s house painted in Pugin reds and blues, the downstairs crammed like a two-room museum with fossils, pot shards,

Sussex tools and ironwork hinges. An inventory to continue those taken in houses all through the seventeenth and eighteenth centuries recording the coloured curtains in Bignor, the cider bottles in Sullington. Here: oak table, low sofa, velour armchair, butter moulds, butterfly boxes, books. Items in the corner cupboard: architectural models, Roman coins, flint arrowheads, the clay pipes puffed and broken by Pulborough men. It wasn't oppressive because from the windows there was the view of the wild brooks, 'one of the finest views in England' as all the family agreed.

Maps and buildings remained clear to Elizabeth long after other things started to become incomprehensible. The name of the prime minister? No. But there was news on the dating of the Roman marble head that had emerged from a garden in Pulborough and was rescued from a digger bucket. (A third-century Gallienus, the experts thought. An emperor found behind a dog kennel.) It was years later that Sussex slipped away and the clearest geography was that of her Nottingham-shire teens and twenties, the Midlands terrain painted on the wall of the old family house. Inevitably, she lost her hold on that map too. Restless-ly awaiting departure, she packed away the domestic museum that now worried her. She was ready by the door for an unknown journey. She knew there were things she must remember to do, and walked round in raids of trial and error. She could not reach the thing she needed.

Elizabeth no longer had the luxury of being settled anywhere. Yet even now, in sudden moments of complete lucidity, her bearings appeared to be unchanged. When Caroline mentioned a detour taken to avoid a flood on the way, her mother frowned. 'But you should have gone left at the Whitebridge crossroads! The road's much higher there.'

14. ITALIAN LIGHT ON NORTH STREET
George Smith and landscape painting

In the opulent rooms at Goodwood House, where gilt-framed pictures crowd the crimson damask walls, it's not the landscape paintings that catch most visitors' attention – not when duchesses shrug seduction and Princess Henrietta by Lely commands the scene in yellow silks. I glanced at the large varnished views. They looked conventionally Italianate and generalised, though quietly luminous. I went past, and then went back.

In a clearing beneath riverside willows there was an outdoor concert going on: a musician playing the horn, another holding open a book or musical score, a gentleman reclining to listen (PLATE). Where were they? My eye was taken soaring and strolling. A wide distance opened in soft tints borrowed from Claude Lorrain. A town of domes and towers stood dreaming in an apricot sunset on the edge of a bay. Craggy peaks to either side framed a Mediterranean fantasy. But the willows, mallows and mulleins, with the great oak rising above them, combined to look like southern England. The cathedral spire that gave the whole composition its focal point was very familiar. Beyond it the furthest land was reminiscent of the Isle of Wight when seen across the Channel. The picture showed off its fine coherence, but it seemed also to be a kind of collage. It was a mixture of pictorial arcadias and known things closely observed. 'George Smith of Chichester' read the label on the frame, and then I realised that Sussex was there in the making of this scene.

The story of George Smith is that of an artist and his family in mid-eighteenth-century Chichester: a high-spirited man who enjoyed a prospering city where he could meet friends and play his cello, a lover of fresh air and country life, an industrious painter from working-class roots who showed dukes and tradesmen that the places they inhabited might be fit subject for art. It's a story that takes us into the midst of the century's debates about local observation and landscape beauty.[1]

George Smith, *Landscape*, 1763, Goodwood (detail)

The family trade was coopering, much in demand in a port city. The container-shipping of the day was barrel-shipping. Barrels – and kegs, buckets, chests. It was a highly skilled trade, each generation of coopers training the next. George stayed at school long enough to learn writing, and then began in his uncle's shop.[2] Wood was cut into 'staves', expertly carpentered so as to fit perfectly when arranged in a ring to form the sides of the barrel. These were held at one end with iron hoops, usually forged on the premises. The staves were heated under pressure and bent. The apprentice in the cooper's shop, a boy of twelve or thirteen, would have learnt to handle the plane, adze and drawknife, the block-hooks and hoop drivers. He learnt the huge strength and precisely honed effort required to shape planks into firkins, hogsheads, butts, troughs, tubs, casks.

George's father William had been a cooper too, but became a baker, probably when illness left him too frail for continuous physical labour. He was also the Baptist minister at the Eastgate chapel, just beyond the city walls (not permitted within) and next to a bend of the Lavant used as a plunge-pool for the baptisms. In his committed nonconformism he followed his own father, who had been Elder of the first Eastgate meeting house in the 1670s.[3] In that volatile decade Smith senior had been persecuted for his faith and spent time in Horsham jail. He was held there with Richard Haines' old enemy, Matthew Caffyn. In Chichester in the 1710s, in what promised to be a more peaceful and tolerant age, his son, George's father, was up before dawn for the bread-making, preaching on Sundays, negotiating a Baptist missionary voyage to Virginia, and ministering to the local Baptist community in between. He was so 'zealous and assiduous' in his work, according to a later friend of the family, that he exhausted his 'feeble constitution' and died young, leaving his wife Elizabeth with two small girls and three boys.[4]

George was six when he lost this parent he could barely have known. He grew up with respect for hard work, remained a Baptist and found his closest friends in chapel circles. He honoured his family's history of strenuous nonconformity by his resistance to forms of extremism and coercion. Friends observed that he practised his religion in a way that was 'remote from fanaticism'.[5]

Coopers used chalks to mark up the wood for staves; perhaps George chalked his earliest pictures. His elder brother had made drawings whenever he could, and somehow won sponsorship from the Duke of Richmond. Now William was in London, studying art with a portrait-painter in St Martin's Lane.[6] When George was fourteen or fifteen he was allowed to follow – except that with no family money to spare his tutor was to be his brother. Half the education came from being in London anyhow. Picture collections were sometimes opened to visitors, students were rolling in and out of James Thornhill's classes in Covent Garden, and Hogarth (in his thirties, becoming famous) was to be seen in the street or overheard in Old Slaughter's Coffee-House.

George helped William in his new studio on Prince's Street, and their productions must have attracted some notice because a Gloucestershire client commissioned an altarpiece for his private chapel.[7] George went as an assistant and they both stayed in Gloucester for several years. Scenes reminiscent of the steep combes and soft sandstone caves of the countryside south of Gloucester would still be appearing in their pictures decades later. The altarpiece is lost, and so is most of their work from this time except for William's engagingly thoughtful portrait of his patron the Duke of Richmond as mayor of Chichester, and firmly characterised paintings of responsible-looking aldermen, churchmen and lawyers.

The obvious move for George after Gloucestershire was to build his reputation in London, and he did so, but for long periods he left William to run the studio and went home to Chichester, where his sisters and many friends were still living, and where he could paint with his younger brother John.[8] He allowed himself to do some landscapes, and received encouragement from the Duke. The market for landscapes, which was small in any case, was focused on French, Italian and, to a lesser degree, Dutch art. If England was depicted at all it was by Flemish artists commissioned to paint great estates, or it might appear behind a groomed horse or prize-winning bull, or in the dazzlingly detailed antiquarian prints of the Buck brothers. All these forms of art were shaping understandings of the country, but few people could have named an English landscape painter in 1745, when Gainsborough was turning eighteen. Constable and Turner would not be born for another thirty years; the expressive landscape pictures we might recognise as 'Romantic' were still half a century off. George Smith, just past thirty, was committing himself to rivers and trees when it was not an established or profitable path to take.

Richard Wilson, Smith's exact contemporary, the man who would emerge as the pre-eminent landscape artist of his time, left his Welsh home for a tour of Italy in 1750. In Venice he tried the rococo styles of

Zucharelli, and then in Rome he settled in to copy the Claudes. Smith, meanwhile, went sketching on Trundle Down at Goodwood and sat by Swanbourne Lake on the Arun. The Duke, it seems, wouldn't run to the expense of sending protégés on the Grand Tour. The idea may not have arisen: the Tour was for those with money to spend, not for the sons of barrel-makers. So the brothers never went to Europe, and they spent their lives hearing their art measured against paintings and places they had not seen.

Undeterred, they pored over prints, trying to work out how Claude achieved his famous aerial effects. They experimented with layers of subtly tinted glazes, casting a hue over the paint beneath. They read all the pastoral poetry they could lay hands on (Sidney, Spenser and Pope, Ambrose Philips, John Gay and James Thomson), educating themselves in landscape taste.[9] They had no Latin education, but English translations of Virgil and Theocritus were making the classical canon available to new kinds of readers. The history of art offered encouraging precedents. Claude himself had attended a French village school and been apprenticed to a baker, so that he went to Italy as not a painter but a patissier. Gaspar Dughet, the most celebrated pupil of Poussin, was the son of a pastry chef. There was something else a provincial painter may have noticed: Claude was known by the name of his French village, Lorrain, and the Italians had long associated themselves proudly with their places. George gave his name as 'Smith of Chichester' and let his address define him.[10]

Riding out from the market cross, the brothers could be in downland within twenty minutes, following the road up through Lavant to Goodwood, and on further to the Arun, ten miles west. They stood with their backs to the view, held up a camera obscura and saw scenes composed in its frame.[11] They also put the mirror away and looked directly, sketching with boards spread on their knees. In the picture now known as *The Watermill (Sullington, near Storrington)*, the tower of St Mary's stands square in the golden distance.[12] The effect is of a question posed: 'Here is a view of Sullington, and doesn't it seem (from this angle, in this light) a version of Arcadia?'

I was looking at montages, or double-takes, for which there was no equivalent term when George Smith painted a capriccio landscape with a cathedral spire rising from a walled city in a green coastal plain.[13] If this is a version of Chichester, then the modest Lavant has become a great European river. It's not so arbitrary as a cut-out silhouette of a Sussex town pasted onto another background. From up on the downs what you see is the spire, the sea and – just where Smith has conjured a blue mountain – the low grey lozenge of the Isle of Wight. Never has an Italian connection occurred to me when I've stood up there in the wind. But Horace Walpole, looking seaward from a downland garden, saw 'such exact pictures of Claude Lorrain, that it is difficult to conceive that he did not paint them from this very spot'.[14] Smith understood that composite landscape was the very point of Claude, who was seeking the best possible form for each element (tree, cliff, dawn over water) and fusing these perfect parts into fictive ideal wholes. Smith responded with his own Sussex fantasias.

Where Claude and Poussin set the model for landscapes lifted out of time and with universal rather than local addresses, the northern masters like Hobbema and Van Ruisdael tended to prize just the opposite, reaching for the singleness of a gesture, or the precise make-up of a clump of grass. The northern and southern schools of landscape carried on a dance of opposition and attraction.[15] The Smith brothers were powerfully drawn to the northern tradition of winter painting, a genre rich in the sensory possibilities of ice and fire. There was a streak of the mysterious and the fantastical in William that made him turn away, sometimes, from his steady work on portraits and fruit baskets to imagine bare oak branches rimed and moonlit, and how one might pass under them into the hidden world of a firelit cavern where dancers circle through the night.[16]

George liked to work in the diptych form of winter and summer landscapes, made to hang side by side. His 'snow-pieces' remained a speciality.[17] Fusing ideas from Netherlandish frozen rivers with images from James Thomson's British poem 'Winter', he painted the footprints of a child and mother walking home through snow, the complex boles of pollard oaks picked out by frost, the exposed irregularity of post-and-rail fences dipping from path to river.

⁓

In London there were fierce discussions about how British artists as a body might be represented and how exhibitions should be staged. Many chose to put their weight behind the Society for the Encouragement of Arts, Manufactures and Commerce, which promoted developments in fine art alongside new industrial processes and agricultural machines. The Smiths involved themselves immediately, entering the Society's first open competition, in April 1760, for an 'original landscape, own composition'.[18] George won first Premium, and John second. The next year the same, and in 1762 first prize to John. The winning pictures hung in the Society's 'Great Room' on the Strand, where crowds of visitors arrived to see London's first big public display of contemporary pictures.[19] Landscape was only one category among many and a lowly one, but it was beginning to attract attention.

In the lists of exhibitors at the Society of Arts through the 1760s we glimpse other artists, the first generation of great British landscape painters, coming to prominence. There was Paul Sandby, moving from military topography into art, the crystalline translucence of his watercolours animated with lively human warmth; Anthony Devis, whose joyously fluent loops and leaps of ink moved across country subjects; Thomas Jones, the Welshman who was working in Rome after his training with Wilson, sending back pictures alive with the texture of buildings and bright southern light.[20] Thomas Smith presented images of spectacular Peak District and Lakeland scenery, with vertiginous crags and waterfalls. Thomas Smith 'of Derby' and the Smiths 'of Chichester' avoided confusion by styling themselves with local affiliations. They would have known each other's work. Their places told them apart – and also showed their affinity.[21]

⁓

After the Premium successes of the 1760s, all the brothers worked from studios in Sussex rather than London. William had already left the capital and was living in Shopwyck, just outside Chichester, with his wife Hannah. It was a partial retirement though he continued to paint flowers and still life. George took lodgings in London so that he and John had somewhere to stay when they went up to exhibitions, but their lives centred on a 1680s house in North Street. The more expensive houses in the Pallant, where the Peckhams had lived, were a few minutes' walk away. North Street was commercial, in the centre of things, close to Chichester market cross.[22] For George and John the move from London had nothing to do with retirement.

Their audience was growing. The third Duke of Richmond proved as enthusiastic a patron in the 1760s as his father the second Duke had been before, so that George could still ride across Goodwood Park with a new picture to offer. For a large exhibition piece he could ask as much as forty guineas, but he often made smaller versions for the aldermen, merchants and doctors who had money to spend on a picture or two they admired.[23] Walk through the East or West Pallant in Chichester today and you can see their houses: bevelled stone steps to a panelled door shining with brass fittings and sheltered by a deeply carved portico, sash windows to either side.

Like many painters, George offered tuition to children. One of his pupils in 1756 was seven-year-old Charlotte Turner from Bignor Park, who was already reading poetry and intent on art. In twice-weekly lessons with her tutor she applied her small hands to drawing and painting. George also taught Abraham Pether, who developed a particular feeling for night pictures. When Abraham moved to Southampton and built a reputation that was both local and national, he was known as 'Moon-light Pether'. He revealed to his buyers a compellingly unfamiliar way of seeing places; they had all hurried home through dark, muddy streets but Pether showed their towns quietly breathing mystery, made new by the white glow of the moon.

William Pether, a fine mezzotint engraver (and uncle of young Abraham), made a group portrait of the three Smith brothers all together, gathered around a landscape on the easel. William is in a chair pulled up to the painting, looking frail but distinguished as he turns to John who is elegantly relaxed, with a long, pale face that explains why his friends thought he resembled John Locke.[24] George is standing palette in hand, ready for action, looking thoroughly content. The debate and mutual interest between them is clear. The four paintings visible, three landscapes and a still life, represent a collective achievement.

By the time this portrait was published in 1765, everything had changed. John, who was winning prizes and famed for his joint work with George, died at the end of July 1764; then, at the end of this dreadful summer, William died too. They were buried close to their sister Elizabeth who had died in 1757, all of them gone in middle age.[25] William had made detailed provision for his wife Hannah and sister Sarah. He left to his brothers the stuff of his professional life, making special mention in his will of 'prints and books of prints and all books that treat of or relate to the art of painting'.[26] Boxes of books were to move from Shopwyck to George's house. After the social flurries of mourning, George was left alone in the panelled rooms on North Street. The family firm was gone.

He may have been thinking for some time of asking his friend Ruth Southern to be his wife, and after the loss of his brothers things happened rapidly; they were married in September 1766. Children arrived in quick succession: three daughters, Sarah, Elizabeth and Ruth. The girls brought new life to the house where the brothers had painted for so long.[27] And George brought to fruition a project that was the fulfilment and commemoration of a decade's 'landskipping': a portfolio of fifty-three etchings and engravings, published by Boydell in London as the work of 'those ingenious artists Messrs. George and John Smith of Chichester'.[28]

The period manners here are strongly marked: all is composed with the texture and charm of the contemporary Picturesque. The figures are cheerfully decorative, giving little sense of working lives, or psychological interest. Elements are selected for the aesthetic jigsaw so that moonlit ruins rise improbably behind cottages, and a lowland farmyard has for its backdrop a mountainous ravine. Yet here too are closely observed Sussex farm buildings, with fences and feeding troughs – normal things, which were at that time extraordinary in art. Here too are flights of ducks through winter skies and the wind in the leaves. Often there are two men looking out: at a full moon over a cathedral city, or at a horse coming down to drink at the river. George signed for both of them, writing their names in his clear round script, 'Geo & Jn. Smith Chichester 1767'.

Geo & Ins Smith Chichester 1767

Geo & Ins Smith Chichester 1767

George tried his hand as a poet. In *Six Pastorals* of 1770 he set summer against winter scenes as he liked to do in paintings, suggesting the narrative drama of the turning year. He made international literary shepherds like Daphnis and Argol keep company with local country boys called Will and Tom, who cool themselves in hollow-ways. And he filled his poems with birds, from timorous wheatears caught on the downs to skylarks high above. Swans, once kept flightless on the Arun with their owners' marks, were by this time free and Smith saw them pass overhead:

> Look upward, Phebe, and behold a train
> Of snow-white swans, that seek the distant main.
> Their fanning pinions please my listning fair,
> And make soft music with the yielding air.[29]

His songs ring with the joy of noticing. His lovers bid goodnight when they see 'yon teams returning from the town, / Wind in the chalky wheel-ruts o'er the down'.[30]

The best specialist printmakers in London – Elliott, Peake, Vivares – were now making editions of George's paintings. Boydell's bookshop always had in stock the prints made by William Woollett, grandmaster of English engravers, known for such closely worked detail that his thousands of burin lines melted into smooth transitions of light and shade. Prints went off to collectors in Germany, France, Switzerland and America where they influenced ideas about English scenery; George Washington would own Smith engravings by the 1790s. The French *Dictionnaire historique* would define George as an 'English Gessner', emphasising (by association with the popular Swiss painter and poet Salomon Gessner) the sweetness and charm of his style. There was a kind of late-eighteenth-century taste that doted on such sweetness, and wanted to find in landscape pictures an innocently happy country. Others valued daylit ordinariness as opposed to the 'red skies and metal-colour'd trees' of that storm-wracked sublimity machine de Loutherbourg. Smith's 'pure undissembled truth' might even be more welcome than the 'proud palaces' of Claude himself.[31]

Each year George carried new paintings up to London for exhibition at the Free Society of Artists. This remained his prime affiliation: he was not among the influential elite who broke off to found the Royal Academy in 1768.[32] He rented a room ('at Mr Perry's, opposite Southampton Street', then above a print shop in Fleet Street).[33] Up and down Smith went between Chichester and London: by horse or on the stagecoach, which left from the Dolphin inn opposite the cathedral. St Roche's Hill, dipping into the valley by Singleton and West Dean, Midhurst, Lurgashall, through the weald, Dorking, Clapham and into the capital.

George Smith, *Landscape*, 1760, engraved by William Woollett

His last London lodgings were at Mr Ustonson's, 48 Bell-Yard, Temple-Bar, an address famous to anglers as the 'Fish and Crown', supplier of fine fishing tackle. Onesimus Ustonson was the author of *The True Art of*

Angling, a book which caught the spirit of Izaak Walton's *Compleat Angler* while speaking more directly to a modern audience. George Smith, who had been peopling his ideal landscapes for three decades with fishermen sitting calmly by rivers which look like the Arun, spent the London evenings of his later life in a household dedicated to lines and floats and reels. With his love of fishing, friendship and peace, he was in a sense an inheritor of Walton whose passionately soft-spoken riposte to civil war a century earlier had been to write of his local Staffordshire river.

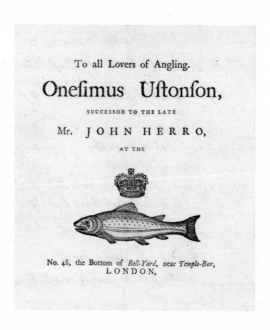

George Smith of Chichester was probably not in London in December 1770 when Joshua Reynolds delivered the third of his 'Discourses' to students at the Royal Academy, but he would have heard reports soon enough. The terms of the argument were in any case very familiar: Smith had been moving in cultural streams shaped by these debates for the last twenty years. What Reynolds articulated in 1770 more powerfully than anyone had done before was the problem with local distinctiveness.

The purpose of his lecture was to define the 'grand style' that raised art beyond imitation of nature to a state of 'intellectual dignity'. The work of the artist, he suggested, is a continuous labour of contemplation and comparison. He must study many objects of a certain kind until he grasps which parts of these objects are 'blemishes and defects', 'accidentals' and what is essential. By training himself to recognise the 'deficiencies, excrescences' of things, the artist 'makes out an abstract idea of their forms more perfect than any one original'. Let the 'central forms' shine and all marginal things, eccentric things, fall away. Discover, among infinite variation, the general truth.[34]

The study of physical forms became an ambitious quest for nature's best self. It was profoundly optimistic, this reaching for ideals, and it was humanist, seeking perfection on earth. Seen from another angle, it was a terrible suppression of individuality and natural variety, a condemnation of all that differentiated one person — or place, or tree, or sky — from another. Those who knew him commented on the soft Devon accent with which Reynolds spoke; he always kept up contact with the West Country community from which he came. Yet the aim of his art, and the ability he praised in the artists he most valued, was to paint without accent, to rise above local affiliation. 'The whole beauty and grandeur of the art', Reynolds remarked in 1770, 'consists, in my opinion, in being able to get above all singular forms, local customs, particularities, and details of every kind.'[35]

Reynolds acknowledged the value in humble genres, even still life and flower pieces. (He did not mention topographical drawing, which was not to be counted as an art at all.) He thought it would be absurd for a flower-painter to attempt the intellectual heights of the grand manner; this lowly kind of artist might be left to pursue 'minute discriminations'. That had been William Smith's life: the fur of a peach, the weave of a basket. Landscape was a borderline case and Reynolds left the question moot. Was the subject of landscape serious enough to repay the painter's philosophical investigation?[36]

George Smith had been responding, all his painting life, to his particular Sussex surroundings, and also to the elevated aesthetics of ideal form. He had sketched local oak trees and then shown the most elegant shape oaks might achieve. He had taken a Dutch route to depicting rural villages and country people, but in his local work there was always an element of fantasy, collage, capriccio.

George made his will in 1774, probably ill already. His eldest daughter was not yet ten, and he was going to be leaving them all without a father – as he had himself been left. The children would have their mother, Ruth, but he was anxious that there should be men to look after their legal and financial affairs. Having named three guardians in his will, he added a codicil with two more.[37] The friends he chose give us a glimpse of the strong local network he retained to the end of his life. Except for the painter James Lambert in Lewes, they were all linked to the Eastgate Baptist chapel. And they were tradespeople. William Woolridge was a brewer, John Chaldecot a goldsmith. Stephen Austen was a maltster with premises in Rumboldswick on the edge of the city, where he had grown up as the son of a wheelwright and continued his father's trade before diverting into malt.[38] Though George Smith was among the most admired painters of his time, he did not live in a separate sphere of elite culture and conversation. Landscape painting was his trade, as malting, brewing, victualling, cutlering were the trades of his friends.

The illness dragged on in a way that must have wracked the whole family. There was, at least, a sympathetic doctor to attend him: Thomas Sanden, a young friend, was just back from university in Edinburgh. He would be Chichester's most respected doctor for the next forty years and would remember the calm resignation with which this early patient bore 'months of great pain and languor'.[39] In September 1776 George was buried near his brothers and sisters in the Litten, the large burying ground at the East Gate. Ruth's life as a widow is hard to guess at from the few traces of evidence. She stayed at the North Street house, where a 1784 census found her living with two daughters, one maid and one female lodger. She occasionally subscribed to publications, keeping up the household library.[40]

In the twentieth century the burying ground was cleared, the graves stacked against a wall and tarmac laid down for a car park. Then, when work started in 2014 on a development of houses and shops, the stones were shifted again, across the road this time and into the gardens to join the war memorial. Whoever was in charge wanted them out of the way close to the wall. There's no room to walk between the lines and read the words. The inscriptions are gone for the most part anyhow. A helpful sign explains where they came from and refers to the Smith brothers, 'celebrated local artists'.[41] My father bought one of the new houses on the cleared site of the old burying ground. When I visit we look out together towards St Pancras through triple-glazed sash windows that catch a faint echo of Georgian Chichester.

15. MOOSE

Experiments with habitat

Gilbert White, the Hampshire naturalist, travelled to Goodwood in September 1768, not to admire the picture-hung halls but to see a moose from Canada. He expected to find a living animal and was 'greatly disappointed' on arrival to be told that it had died the previous morning. Still, having waited through weeks of summer rain, ridden over from Selborne on the first dry day and arranged to stay with his friends near Chichester that evening, he 'proceeded to examine this rare quadruped'. 'I found it in an old green-house, slung under the belly and chin with ropes, and in a standing posture; but, though it had been dead for so short a time, it was in so putrid a state that the stench was hardly supportable.' It was a sultry day, which probably didn't help.[1] Working in the thick of the smell for as long as he could bear, he did his best to make observations, measuring the height in hands (as he would a horse), trying to see from the length of the legs how the creature had moved while alive, studying the 'vast and lopping' ears, the huge nostrils, and an outsized upper lip that might indicate a habit of browsing on trees. The Goodwood animal-keeper told him a bit about the moose's behaviour and how it had 'seemed to enjoy itself best in the extreme frost of the former winter'. White wrote up his notes in a letter to Thomas Pennant, who was nearly ready to publish a *Synopsis of Quadrupeds*. 'I should have been glad to have examined the teeth, tongue, lips, hoofs, etc., minutely; but the putrefaction precluded all further curiosity.'[2]

There had been non-native animals at Goodwood since the 1720s when the second Duke of Richmond established an ambitious menagerie in his vast park. In 1728 this lightly wooded chalk downland was inhabited by not only sheep and wheatears but (according to the Duke's records) '5 wolves, 2 tygerrs, 1 lyon, 2 lepers [leopards], 1 sived cat, a tyger cat, 3 foxes, a Jack all, 2 Greenland dogs, 3 vulturs, 2 eagles . . . 3 bears, 1 large monkey, a woman tygerr, 3 Racoons, 3 small monkeys, armadilla, 1 pecaverre and 7 caseawarris'.[3] The mason Henry Smart, working on the estate, would have known these animals. Lisbon Peckham the wine merchant, or Mrs Collins and her little boy William, could have come out from Chichester, past the turn to Boxgrove, through the hunting chases and into the High Wood to enjoy the novel sight of a camel – or an ostrich. Certainly many of their neighbours enjoyed excursions to see the sights in the pleasure grounds, peering between the bars of the tiger cage or holding back in fright.

This was one of the European zoological collections built in the eighteenth century by aristocrats who had the space to accommodate them and the enormous wealth necessary to fund the shipping of animals from across the globe. Exotic beasts were a show of influence as well as cash, since collectors needed to know the right people and were often in competition for rare specimens brought back from expeditions. A menagerie was a collage of the explored world, its pieces cut out from remote places and pasted in exotic juxtaposition in a duke's country garden. Most collections also functioned as museums and laboratories, their owners keen to further the cause of zoology by welcoming natural historians.

It was a major logistical undertaking to source and keep these animals. For the Goodwood stewards on menagerie duty, the to-do list was endless. A cart was needed to carry a lion. A tiger was at the Tower of London awaiting collection.[4] A baboon was en route by boat from Deptford to Chichester. Agents negotiated handling fees for a bear, 'a very fierce one', to be brought from Jamaica and a beautiful civet cat from Barbados, where the Duke's friend Thomas Robinson was governor.[5] Male and female pairings were sought in the hope they might breed and raise a generation of native Sussex monkeys, or bears, or racoons. But the zoo was not often self-sustaining in this way, and the Duke's purchases kept pace with the rate at which his animals died. Henry Foster, the head keeper, was at the sharp end of this haphazard imperial experiment, faced with ailing creatures on a daily basis and enormous food bills. By 1730 he was all but pleading with the Duke. 'Here is no more Roome of entertainment nor vitles enough to get for them to eat.'[6] On the evidence of their poor health, the animals were less entertained than the crowds who came to see them, sometimes several hundred on a sunny Sunday.

Iron enclosures could not do much to approximate prairie, jungle and tundra on the Sussex hillside, and there does not seem to have been any systematic attempt to recreate the beasts' natural habitats. The second Duke was, however, interested in the expanding horizons of gardening as well as zoology, and was collecting the world's plants as enthusiastically, if less sensationally, as he was importing bears. 'No man living loves propagation (in an honest way) more than I do', he told his horticultural friend and mentor Peter Collinson.[7] 'Be quick' he urged when Collinson was buying cedars of Lebanon on his behalf; he wouldn't have rival aristocrats taking the trees he most wanted for Goodwood.[8] His planting in the 'Wilderness' was particularly focused on American specimens. One knowledgeable visitor to Goodwood noted 'four hundred different American trees and shrubs'.[9] Richmond was possessed by paintings and reports of the flowering trees to be found in Carolina. 'I must have them', he wrote of magnolias he couldn't really afford.[10] He wanted tulip trees, junipers, pines from across the North American forests, many of the seeds for which were gathered by the great Pennsylvania botanist John Bartram and brought over by Collinson. The nursing of young trees from seed requires a strong sense of the future. The Duke would know his firs and spruces only as saplings, though he listened keenly to descriptions of America and envisaged a microcosm of New World flora unfurling in the High Wood; the chalk grassland would be thick with American pine needles.

Here too in this garden of global curiosities was the classical temple he had built to house the most precious stone yet to emerge from local earth, the first piece of irrefutable evidence that Chichester had been a

Roman city: a tablet found by builders digging a cellar on the corner of St Martin's Lane and North Street in 1723. It was clearly inscribed – NEPTUNO ET MINERVAE TEMPLUM – and had been paid for by the Roman guild of smiths ('collegium fabrorum') who had presented it in the temple at least thirteen hundred years earlier. Now it had been presented to the Duke and he installed it in the High Wood. Old World and New World met in these grounds; living things and ancient artefacts from different empires were arranged for best effect. The natural topography of the downland needed these kinds of improvement, the Duke thought, but once he had planted trees on 'a very bleak hill' and erected a Palladian banqueting lodge in front of them, he could enjoy the view across miles of country to Chichester cathedral and out to sea, feeling this might be his favourite spot of all.[11]

Close to this favoured place, set into the hillside, was a doorway under a rough stone arch reminiscent of a natural cave. The frontage gave away little of the secret within. The interior was decorated with the most intricate shellwork imaginable. Except for the floor studded with horses' teeth, every inch was set with shells. Pearlescent oysters glinted within dark borders of mussel; ribbed bivalves were braided in swags above sheeny conches. Made over a period of seven years in the 1740s, it was the creation of the Duchess, Sarah Lennox, and her daughters – though much of the construction appears to have been the work of unnamed craftspeople. This Goodwood grotto was among the earliest and most elaborate of the shell houses that were to become prized features of rococo gardens, most of them made by women. Though it was primarily a virtuosic exercise in ornamental aesthetics, it was also a conchological museum. The Governor of Barbados made a collection of West Indian specimens and shipped them to the Duchess. Clams and winkles from nearby Sussex beaches provided patterned borders and backgrounds for shells sent from across the world. The beachcombings of the Empire were glued into position here, transformed into shell urns in shell alcoves with shell flowers heraldically studding the vaulted shell roof overhead.[12]

At the heart of the Duke's garden was 'the Dell', formerly a quarry and reminiscent of an amphitheatre, planted with exotic trees which in time would provide deep shade. Various structures were set into its grassy sides and into the flint walls that enclosed this enchanted and disturbing Xanadu. The Duke wanted a hermit's cell, and he had a mock ruined abbey installed to provide an atmosphere of melancholy and studiousness for the hermit and his visitors. George Smith, the Duke's local protégé, arrived to paint the Hermitage in an eerie, claustrophobic picture, with a bent monk edging his way between flint walls. The landscape tricks and exotic collections of the Dell were a long way from the spreading oaks and resting fishermen that were George Smith's more usual choice of subject.

The abbey marked the entrance to the most sensational feature of the Dell (and in this Richmond was well ahead of Francis Dashwood who didn't start on the Hellfire Caves at West Wycombe until 1748): lucky or unlucky guests could enter a tunnel leading below ground into a range of catacombs, some walled with flints so as to appear a mysterious natural formation in the downland. It's thought that animals were brought into these underground passages to be encountered face to face by visitors, howls and roars echoing in flint-lined caverns and muffled by the softness of chalk.[13]

The Duke died in 1750, suddenly and still young. There was a pause in estate developments while his teenage heir went off on a scientifically oriented Grand Tour and then, seeking the best education Europe could provide in the new branches of knowledge, he studied botany in Leiden. His mentors from this time would remain colleagues in the pursuit of knowledge. The third Duke never revived the menagerie on its previous scale, but he continued the family interest in natural history and made concerted attempts to naturalise imported species at Goodwood.

He was especially interested in the fauna of Canada, or New France, or Province of Quebec as it was renamed in 1763 after the long bloody war to secure the territory for Britain. He was not going to cross the Atlantic to study the wildlife of northern forests to either side of the St Lawrence or the vast country stretching towards the Great Lakes and Ontario, but he aspired to have the quadrupeds of Canada brought to him in Sussex. He would provide an environment in which they might be studied by British scientists, and attempt to breed them. His interest was fostered by a personal connection. In 1766, when he saw that there might be a vacancy for a new Governor of Quebec, he proposed Guy Carleton, whose insight and military knowledge impressed him and who had overseen the provisioning of the British army in Quebec.[14] Carleton rapidly established himself in Canada, where he needed to reconcile the interests of the long-established French Canadians and the new British merchants, negotiate with complex alliances of the indigenous nations and improve defences in expectation of further French claims to the territory.[15] Nonetheless, he found time to arrange presents for his sponsors in England. He sent a young female moose to King George and another to the Duke of Richmond (females because they were marginally easier to transport than the male of this giant species, second only to the elephant in size). These were not quite the first American moose in England (two had been sent as gifts to Queen Anne), but no living naturalist in the country had seen one before.

There's some doubt over whether the Duke took receipt of his first moose in 1766 or 67, and whether two females (cow-moose) arrived together or in succession.[16] There was certainly a female caribou as well in Carleton's first consignment from Canada. The Duke observed that his moose and the caribou were 'remarkably attached and affectionate'. He told the Marquis of Rockingham that he thought the cow-moose had 'died of grief for the loss of her companion a Miss Caribou who came over with her'.[17] By Michaelmas 1768 both of the Goodwood moose (or, in French Canadian, 'orignals') were gone. Gilbert White saw only a body. This did not auger well for the future domestication of moose in Sussex. Persuading himself that his moose had died of loneliness rather than for lack of appropriate habitat, the Duke remained undeterred.

Carleton took leave of absence from Canada in 1770, and in advance of sailing for England he sought to procure another moose from the indigenous hunters who traded in moose meat and skins. He wanted the animal itself, alive and strong, not the pelt of it. For all their expertise, the trappers had a fight to capture a moose in good condition. It's not clear where in Quebec this took place and the trappers might have been from any of the Algonquian or Iroquoian First Nations of the region. According to the anatomist William Hunter, who probably had the story from Carleton, they set upon a pair of month-old moose twins and their mother. The mother escaped with one juvenile; the other young bull was 'catched by the dogs of the Indians, and thereby had one ear a good deal torn, and was otherwise so hurt, that for some time it was doubtful whether or not it would live. It was fed with milk for some time; then the milk was thicked with flower, Rice, &c, & at length it fed upon herbage and leaves of trees.'[18] It had lost an eye, and there was no restoring that with milk and nurture.[19]

This was the early life of the animal that was then transported down-river to the port at Quebec City, shipped across the Atlantic (with General Carleton in a cabin above), and ceremonially presented to the Duke in September 1770, by which time it was just past a year old. Naturalists lost no time in going to visit, shown by the keeper into the 'wild woody place of about 4 acres walled in' where the moose was kept. William Hunter took detailed notes on the mane, shoulder humps, 'stilt-like' legs and the caruncle hanging at his neck. 'He knew his keeper, and there was a very sincere and mutual friendship between them: but he was so little shy of strangers, that he would follow anybody who would shew him a piece of bread or an Apple.' Hunter stood there in Sussex proffering apples in his hand. What did this animal eat in Canada? Not bread and apples. Like Gilbert White before him, seeing that the large lip and upward-tilted posture would be suited to browsing trees, Hunter deduced that 'he is a beast of the woods, and disqualified for being an inhabitant of this or any other populous and well cultivated country in which woods will be always both too small and too valuable to admit of such inhabitants'. Nor could England offer the climate it needed. It was autumn, but the moose was hot. 'His keeper had been instructed to throw a Pale-full of water over him now & then to cool him.' Hunter's phrasing suggests that he watched this in action: 'He appeared to be pleased with it, and always shook himself after it exactly as a horse does when wet or dirty.'[20] The horse comparison made it sound as if the moose could be kept happy with the odd splash from a bucket, though Hunter suspected its more serious need for water, its capacity for swimming and aquatic feeding, its perfect suitedness to the vast lakes and forests of sub-Arctic Canada.

Wanting an anatomically precise picture that he could show to other scientists, Hunter commissioned the finest animal painter in Britain, George Stubbs. The resulting image is among the more extraordinary productions of eighteenth-century Sussex. The moose stands poised with furred ears alert, large eye gleaming, absent eye hidden from view. The antlers are only small protruding horns as yet, but Stubbs shows the antlers of a full-grown male on the ground, indicating what this yearling will grow on its head.[21] The artist gave the moose a setting, making for him a rocky prominence, with a mountain rising steeply behind, a sharp cool light breaking dramatically through dark clouds, and in the distance the shimmer of

water. It was an imagined homeland for a displaced creature, not much like the woods of Quebec Province, which Stubbs had never seen, but a patchwork dream of Canada superimposed on the English park.[22]

While the bull-moose stood for its portrait, the Duke tried to arrange a mate for it. 'My young gentleman is rather too young to breed from this year,' he wrote to Rockingham who had a female moose (kept in the garden at Grosvenor House in London), 'but I think it would nevertheless be right that the two young Americans should be together'.[23] He thought they would both be 'much at their ease' in his 'wild woody' garden. It's not clear whether this envisaged courtship took place, but the project to establish a moose population in Britain continued. General Carleton (who pursued a courtship of his own before returning across the Atlantic) arranged more imports, and a second male, more mature at two years old, reached Goodwood in October 1773. The naturalist Joseph Banks (back from his own even longer journey – to Australia and New Zealand on *The Endeavour*) went to see the new arrival in Sussex. So did Hunter, who took the Stubbs painting along for comparison and asked Stubbs to draw this moose too.

Hunter's interest went beyond the close study of an unfamiliar creature and beyond the possibility of domestication; there was something more at stake. Other naturalists had supposed that the American moose must belong to the same species as the animals that had apparently once lived in Ireland and whose enormous antlers were occasionally discovered in peat bogs. Hunter thought otherwise; that was why he needed Stubbs to paint the full-grown antlers so carefully. By the time he inspected the second Goodwood bull-moose, Hunter was certain that this was a different creature to the unknown 'Irish elk' which had once roamed Ireland with antlers twelve feet wide.[24] North America had yielded no animal capable of growing such antlers and none had been encountered elsewhere in the world; he was satisfied that the Irish elk was extinct, and he was right: the antlers from the peat bogs belonged to *Megaloceros giganteus*, which ranged across Eurasia and died out around ten thousand years ago.

In 1773 the idea of extinction was heretical. It ran counter to the logic of divine creation. Accordingly, there *had* to be a living descendant of the Irish elk; it was probably the moose eating apples by the flint wall in Goodwood Park, and to claim otherwise was too radical an act to be risked until every piece of evidence was in place.[25] As things stood, there was still a remote possibility that another species or sub-species might be discovered somewhere in Canada.

Hunter put aside his work on the moose and turned back to finishing his study of the human uterus. Gilbert White rode into Sussex that winter and stayed with his friend near Chichester, but he did not visit Goodwood. Instead he watched 'rooks, larks, stone-chats, kites, gulls, some fieldfares, some hawks' over the downs near Steyning and noted that at Houghton the Arun was flooding right over the clapper bridge.[26]

Eric Ravilious reread Gilbert White's *Natural History of Selborne* in 1936. One hundred and fifty years after publication, White's book was a classic, revered for its pellucid prose and close, questioning observation of creatures' characters and habits. Ravilious was commissioned to make woodcuts for a new edition and he was struck by the description of the moose. It wasn't an obvious subject for an illustration; it certainly wasn't part of the natural flora and fauna of White's intricately observed Hampshire and Sussex chalklands. But the moose hung there in his imagination, startlingly strange, and he began to draw out the scene.

I've known this engraving since I first encountered Ravilious' work, and because it's so memorably odd it comes to mind whenever I think of Gilbert White. All his day-in day-out observations of garden plants, swallows, bees, cold frames, thermometers are faintly coloured, or imprinted, by association with this image of the moose; the bizarre, sensational and out-of-place seems to tell on the homely and habitual until all such categories are thrown awry.

Ravilious shows the wild creature, now lifeless, tightly contained within a framework of polite gardening. He takes the opposite approach to Stubbs, who painted in a rocky background across which the moose might turn and run. Ravilious could never resist a greenhouse: he had long been attracted to the combination of complicated geometries and well-tended plants. He often introduced something a little eerie into his views of potted geraniums and ranked tomatoes: there might be a hosepipe coiled suspiciously snake-like on the floor, complicating the neatness. Now here was a grand, comical, tragic thing to find in a greenhouse: a lifeless moose slung from the rafters. White is safely outside, though about to hold his breath against the stench and go inside with the tape measure. For the moment the moose is firmly sealed into its rhomboid specimen case, like one of Damien Hirst's sheep or calves suspended in formaldehyde tanks – except the tank is definitely still a greenhouse, there's a lawn roller leaning against it, the trees have a pruned look, and everything in Ravilious' pattern-making evokes a tightly arranged domestic world. He wasn't very interested in the anatomical facts it seems: he's put a big pair of antlers on the moose, though White clearly states that he saw a female. He probably just liked the shape of them.

16. DESOLATE PARADISE

William Cowper at Eartham,
Charlotte Smith on the hills

Three miles of downland stretch between Goodwood and the small flint village of Eartham, where there are signs of another, much more modest, eighteenth-century landscape. The serpentine walks are lost in the shadows of overhanging trees that have been growing since the 1760s. Yew hedges that were once clipped to shape now throw out limbs across the path, and the undergrowth has risen to meet them. There's a gap in the planting where a 'hermitage' used to stand. The woods curve in an unmistakeable 'line of beauty' around the sloping lawn, framing a vista back to Eartham House. It's all still there in outline: a vision of an ideal landscape as it was conceived by the poet and patron William Hayley, and as it was known by the visitors who came along the narrow rutted lane to the village, up Hayley's drive and into this chalky garden.[1]

Hayley grew up in Chichester, at what is now 7 North Pallant. He was a child looking up at the stone ostriches next door. His father bought land outside the city, in Eartham, and built a small villa that the family used each summer. The schoolboy who explored the hills would remember the place with passion and a longing to return. In 1774, when he inherited the Eartham property at the age of twenty-seven, he was in little doubt about what he wanted to do. He left London to create a rural home for his family and a haven for poets who – he was sure, and he was mostly right – would be glad to court their muses under his patronage.[2]

It's not clear how much of a say his wife Eliza had in the matter, but Hayley anticipated with satisfaction how she would appear as a ministering angel among the villagers (right again). He imagined the happiness of their future children, running free in the clear Sussex air. There was a problem with his eyes: he thought it was the east wind that had triggered ophthalmia and filled them with blood. He felt weakened and punished, but he focused his hopes on Sussex. Writing of himself in the third person as he usually did, he made his wish:

> Perchance long banish'd from his failing eyes,
> Th'heroic muse will come with all her fire;
> Yes! In thy shades her sacred form will rise,
> And strike to liberty the lofty lyre![3]

It was a political vision, art allied to the democratic cause of 'liberty'. At Eartham he would make a green arcadia in which to be a poet. He would pour his energy and wealth into his 'native spot', hopeful always of the muse rising in the shade of his trees.

It was not so much Hayley who drew me to Eartham as the people who came to stay with him, and two guests in particular, William Cowper and Charlotte Smith. Cowper was the most celebrated English poet of the late eighteenth century. There is no one else, except perhaps John Bunyan, who was once so important to readers and is now so little known. Part of what mattered so much about Cowper was the attention he paid to the creatures, plants and paths of his immediate surroundings, and the way he linked the near with the far. His long poem *The Task*, published in 1785, articulated the goodness of habitual, homely things; it was a tribute to 'Domestic Happiness, thou only bliss of paradise that has survived the fall!'[4] But its glimpses of bliss are precarious, constantly threatened by gulfs of loss and desolation.

Cowper lived a life of retreat in Buckinghamshire, first in the market town of Olney and then up the road in the village of Weston Underwood. Seclusion was the way he found to cope, though sometimes he barely coped, with mental agonies that made each day a struggle. For twenty-seven years, Cowper did not go more than a few miles from home. Except for one extraordinary occasion. In the summer of 1792, he went away for six weeks, and the place he went to was Eartham.

Hayley first wrote to Cowper on seeing it announced in the press that they were engaged on 'rival' editions of Milton.[5] Their exchanges must have been stimulating because both wanted the conversation to continue. It was optimistic of Hayley to suggest a trip to Sussex. Cowper's 'local attachment' was a bond that held him as if by a chain, he explained, 'an invisible, uncontroulable agency' keeping him at home.[6] He was now sixty-one and there was little reason to suspect that the chains of attachment could be broken. Hayley promised not only literary company and support, but good air for Cowper's beloved and ailing partner Mary Unwin. In his anxiety for Mary, he was willing to try almost anything – even a trip to 'the other side of London, nobody knows where, a hundred and twenty miles off'.[7] 'Nobody knows where': Sussex was often a blank in the minds of even well-informed people from other regions.

On 1 August they set out, accompanied by Cowper's cousin Johnny Johnson, his two married servants and his spaniel, Beau. They made the journey over three days with overnight stops at Barnet and Ripley. All went well except for 'some terrors' that Cowper felt 'at passing over the Sussex hills by moon-light'.[8] He was 'a little daunted', he admitted, by their 'tremendous height'.[9] Mary was unperturbed, Cowper's terrors passed, and to his astonished relief the whole party arrived safely at Hayley's door.

Since the 1950s Eartham House has been the home of Great Ballard School. The building as it stands today is really an Edwardian mansion, but a portion of it is Hayley's: the upstairs library has its three big windows looking onto the 'airy hill'. The wide lawn, right up to the house, has the feel of both designed landscape and open chalk down. Hayley's paradise, I think, was both a generic model garden featuring hermitage, secluded seats, serpentine walks (the eighteenth-century requirements for any designed landscape) – and a particular place, distinct from anywhere else, following the natural contours of Eartham Hill. In naming one of his 'walks' for Otway, he was affirming, like Collins, the literary history of his native county. He vowed that in his gardens the arts of Sussex would be revived. I climbed the 'Mount' and looked out at the garden's most dramatic view: the spire of Chichester, the flat of the Solent, the lozenge cloud of the Isle of Wight. The trees once framed the expanse of Chichester harbour like the Claude paintings that Walpole and George Smith thought it resembled.

Hayley's own ways of writing about the Sussex he loved were lavishly conventional: encomiums to 'tranquil shades' and 'dear retreats'.[10] In his memoirs he described the joy of returning home from travels in Lincolnshire and Derbyshire, yet never said what was different about Eartham.[11] To be generic was part of the point: rather than observe the local particularity of his native spot, he wanted to match it with exemplary scenery. By contrast, Cowper was searchingly precise as he tried to understand the effect that different places had upon him. At first his response to Sussex was determined by his hopes for Mary. He liked the air because it seemed to be helping her; plus the chalk drained better than the Buckinghamshire clay, which was helpful for the wheelchair.[12] But Cowper's sense of Eartham changed as he realised that his restless melancholy had come with him.[13] 'Gloominess of mind . . . cleaves to me even here.' He did not add, though he could never forget it, Satan's cry of pain as he approaches Eden in *Paradise Lost*: 'which way I fly is Hell; myself am Hell'.[14]

As his own spirits wavered he responded to what he perceived as sadness in the landscape. He kept calling Eartham 'delightful': 'more beautiful scenery I have never beheld'. But he was looking forward to home:

> The Genius of that place [Weston] suits me better; it has an air of snug
> concealment in which a disposition like mine feels itself peculiarly
> gratified; whereas here I see from ev'ry window woods like forests and
> hills like mountains, a wildness in short that rather encreases my natural
> melancholy.[15]

The area was certainly not 'wild' in the sense of being untouched by human hands. The hills were intensively grazed by sheep. Even the particular green of the close-cropped turf was the result of this long pastoral use. Close by, there were lime-burners in the woods and fishermen at the river. The turning sails of Halnaker windmill were visible from the house; below them, just out of sight, carters lugged grain and flour sacks to and fro. It was no comfort to Cowper. 'Within doors all was hospitality and kindness but the scenery *would* have its effect, and though delightful in the extreme to those who had spirits to bear it, was too gloomy for me.'[16] He hadn't the strength to feel what the place seemed to demand.

For Hayley it was the fulfilment of a dream to have Cowper among the company in his 'tranquil shades'. The gathering was a large one for a modest house (and involved Hayley sleeping in the library). As well as Cowper's party from Olney there was James Hurdis, whose poetry celebrated the natural history and working year of the parish of Burwash in the east of the county. The painter George Romney had been coming to work at Eartham each summer since Hayley's first years there, appreciating the peace away from his clients. The novelist and poet Charlotte Smith was well known to Hayley too; keen to meet the author of *The Task*, she came to stay. Assembled on the Mount this remarkable group looked out towards the sea.

They adopted a routine of work and leisure. Cowper, Hayley and Smith went off to write (or, in Cowper's case, feel unable to write) from eight to twelve every morning. Then lunch, a walk and more writing. After an early dinner Hayley and Cowper worked on translating an Italian play about Satan (*Adamo* by Giovanni Andreini). After this, a game of quoits or more walking (these were long summer evenings), and reading until a late supper. Hayley was working on a biography of Milton, and Cowper had brought his translations of Milton's Latin

The gathering on the 'Mount' at Eartham, as imagined by the illustrator
William Harvey in the 1830s. Cowper is equipped with writing slope, and
Beau at his feet. Hayley and his son Thomas Alphonso are front left; James
Hurdis and Romney are behind Cowper. Charlotte Smith and John Johnson are
standing. Chichester is visible on the right.

and Italian poems to discuss; Romney was planning his illustrations for *Paradise Lost*. 'You may imagine we were deep in that poet.'[17] The most productive of them all was Charlotte Smith, whose life usually allowed her little time for cultural company and quoits. She was writing for money to support her family, working every hour she could manage. In those few August weeks, among people who felt no such pressures, she wrote the first volume of her fifth novel *The Old Manor House* at such speed that she had a new chapter to read aloud each evening in the library. The chapters were never in need of correction, Romney noted. He was frankly amazed. 'I think her a woman of astonishing powers.'[18]

Smith's novel was a romance of illicit loves in a manor long past its prime 'in one of the most southern counties of England'. It was also about the whole nation's idea of itself. Was Britain in thrall to the inherited systems established by the aristocracy in former ages, or might there be another kind of future? It was set in the 1770s, in the years of the American Revolution. The hero, Orlando, joins the army and crosses the Atlantic in the cause of Britain's colonial rule. But even before he arrives, he wonders why America should not be self-determining. It occurs to him that young British people are brought up 'to look with contempt on the inhabitants of every other part of the globe'. They keep doing it out of habit. What if they looked and thought for themselves? By the time he returns from his experiences in the 'wilds of America' and comes ashore near Worthing with a mere few coins in his pocket, he has different ideas about the world.[19]

Smith's narrative of recent revolutionary history was shaped by the cataclysmic events of the present as they unfolded that summer of 1792 in France. Everyone playing quoits in the downland garden was imaginatively half in Paris. From the Mount they looked over the Channel, knowing that these were decisive weeks for the lyres of liberty and for all Europe. Conversation at Eartham circled the possibilities for democracy and justice in the emerging French republic and the immense difficulty of achieving the transition. The reading and editing of Milton was republican work, interpreting the great poet of the English Commonwealth for a new generation, hopeful that his prophetic voice might still inspire political change.[20] But the news that reached them by late August was appalling. In a great insurrection, revolutionaries had massacred the army guarding the Tuileries Palace. The Royal Family was in prison, threatened with murder. The reports were of blood in the streets, corpses, people in flight. This did not sound like liberty.

⁓

Cowper arranged his departure for mid-September. He was keen to get away from the cold. Hayley, so effusive in his prose and manner, was ascetic in his domestic habits. He liked to be up at four, opening windows around the house. But the cold was also a perceived coldness in the character of Sussex. Once safely home, Cowper evoked the chill by describing the landscape: 'we shiver'd constantly with cold during the last 5 weeks' (they were only there for six). 'Two degrees farther South might have been expected to be proportionately warmer, but the aspect of the country is bleak and wild and the land lofty.'[21]

A few months later, when the summer's laughter was far behind them and Mary Unwin's health took a turn for the worse, Cowper thought of the downs with instinctual horror. His cousin suggested they might go to Eartham where Hayley would support them. He reported Cowper's very definite response:

he told me yesterday that the melancholy wildness of the scenes about Eartham is more than he can bear – the extensive prospects that present nothing to the view but uncultivated Hills, rising beyond Hills, and the vallies are so uninhabited that you see no signs of life look where you will – nothing but one vast and desolate country, much like that where Don Juan Fernandez uttered his mournful soliloquy.[22]

The comparison to the Juan Fernandez Islands in the South Pacific is extraordinary. A Sussex village is being likened to the uninhabited shore on which Alexander Selkirk was washed up and where he survived alone, his story providing the inspiration for *Robinson Crusoe*. Cowper had imagined Juan Fernandez in an earlier poem, and tried to affirm that 'There is mercy in ev'ry place'.[23] But still he was writing about being stranded far out from all help. In his own great sadness, Cowper could not stand the thought of the exposed Sussex slopes. He needed the 'snug concealment' of Weston. Hayley had turned a Sussex plot into a version of eighteenth-century arcadia but in Cowper's mind it had become a place of dread.

For Charlotte Smith this stretch of downland was a beloved native country, yet she felt herself to be an exile in it. She had spent her early girlhood at Bignor Park. It was at that time an Elizabethan manor house with later additions of Gothic turrets, set in its own parkland slightly apart from the village centres of Bignor and Sutton though in sight of the same wooded scarp of Bignor Hill.[24] At school in Chichester, she attended art lessons several times a week at George Smith's house on North Street and developed a particular love of close botanical drawing. Though the family moved to London, school holidays were back at Bignor, with long days by the streams that ran, as they still run, through the fields to join the Arun. In her adult poetry of the 1780s and 90s, the Arun is the river of a childhood paradise forever taken from her. She might walk again along the riverbanks, and she often did; but it was always with a sense of what was lost.

Charlotte was married young – she was fifteen – to a West India merchant and gambler called Benjamin Smith. It was a disaster from the first and went on for twenty miserable years that saw Charlotte raising nine children without support, protecting herself and her family from Benjamin's abuse, staying with him for a time in debtors' prison and working relentlessly to earn enough for them all to survive. The spectres of creditors and jailors were regularly at her shoulder, as too were images of the other life she might have led – as a gentlewoman in the landscapes she wanted to write about, free to work at her own pace as a poet and political thinker. She published as 'Charlotte Smith of Bignor Park, in Sussex'. But the house was not hers. It passed to her younger brother Nicholas. Though she often stayed there or sent the children, her own addresses were elsewhere: a London apartment above the merchant docks, a farm in Hampshire and, once she had separated from Benjamin, a series of borrowed or rented houses in Sussex: Woolbeding, Brighton and my own first village, Storrington (which she didn't like at all).

In her *Elegiac Sonnets* of 1784 (printed by Dennett Jaques in Chichester), and in the expanded edition of 1786, which included a new group of poems located in the Sussex landscape, she wrote of the 'hills beloved' and the river valley that were her inspiration. 'To the River Arun' was a gift to the river and a conversation with it. 'On thy wild banks, by frequent torrents worn / No glittering fanes or marble domes appear.' It was not Rome with its Pantheon; it was not Oxford (celebrated by Collins' friend Thomas Warton for 'bright domes' and 'fanes sublime').[25] It offered other kinds of education among the birch, oak and hazel of its banks.

Another sonnet to the Arun made a contrast with the Thames. 'Be the proud Thames of trade the busy mart! / Arun! To thee will other praise belong.' There was a good deal of trade cargo on the Arun in the 1780s, and many minds focused on making the river a busier, more efficient commercial route. Major schemes were underway to increase capacity and provide a navigable water route through to London. In the year of Smith's poem, the Arun Navigation Company was engineering complex new locks and canals to take shipping north from Pallingham. But the Arun was also the stream of Smith's pastoral vision, where lovers and mourners could sit quietly on the 'willow'd shore'.[26] Smith's melancholy is inseparable from her delight in the regenerative natural life of these places, 'Where o'er the rocks the mantling bindwith flaunts'. Sorrow's 'lonely haunts' are bound in rhyme with the flaunting dance of bindwith, the native clematis of chalk country.[27]

Smith had inherited no property, and was trapped in a long legal battle over a bequest from her father-in-law to her children. In her sonnets she placed the emphasis on a legacy that could not be argued over by lawyers in Chancery, or spent by Benjamin against her will. It was bequeathed to her in poetry and in the landscape: Otway's 'plaintive strain' and Collins' 'deeper tone' were carried on the 'classic stream'.[28]

Smith's poems in turn suggested a local inheritance to those who read them. It was probably through the *Elegiac Sonnets* that Ann Gittins in Norfolk first encountered Collins' odes in 1786 and started to perceive a literary community of Arun writers across time. Gittins may not have felt much connection with Smith, whose radicalism was at odds with her own declared politics, but she started to write of her remembered places.[29] Readers of a younger generation, too, were finding in Smith a startlingly emotional connection with landscape. Wordsworth, just after graduation in 1791, equipped himself with a letter of introduction, keen to meet the author. Later, when he was celebrated as a poet of nature and place, he made a guarded tribute to Smith, 'a lady to whom English verse is under greater obligations than are likely to be either acknowledged or remembered'. She wrote with a 'true feeling for rural nature', he thought, 'at a time when nature was not much regarded by English poets'.[30]

Returning from the summer at Eartham to her lodgings in Brighton, Smith saw the émigrés from France who were arriving destitute on English shores after secret crossings in small boats: clergy families and minor nobility, people who embodied the *ancien régime* and had fled for their lives. They climbed onto the shingle with nothing. That winter, desperate people were to be met with on the city streets and on the downs.

The despotic turn in the character of the revolution was deeply distressing to her. Wanting to act, she contacted an acquaintance whom she knew to have influence in Paris. 'It seems to me wrong for the Nation [France] to exile and abandon these Unhappy Men', she wrote, adding that there were also 'a very great number of Women and Children'. She stated her case clearly: 'They should suffer the loss of a very great part of their property and all their power. But they should still be considered as Men & Frenchmen . . . They should still have a plate of Bouile at home if they will take it & not be turned out indiscriminately to perish in foreign countries.'[31]

Smith the prominent radical writer found herself offering accommodation, and probably also bowls of bouillon, to fallen noblemen. She was surrounded by considerable 'confusion of tongue'. 'I must write in company,' she explained in February 1793, 'as the Emigrants . . . find some consolation in the society my small book room affords them of an evening.'[32] Her lodgings were already full of family – two grown-up daughters, an adult son not yet employed, a ten-year-old daughter, a boy of eight (her youngest) and fifteen-year-old Lionel when he came home from boarding school. The books in the book room, one of the great pleasures of her life, had been that very month seized by bailiffs when she couldn't pay her rent; she was, as usual, frantically trying to raise money to keep her precarious household together. But if the furniture was about to be carted off, the room could still be a welcoming place for the 'very agreeable men'.[33] She seems never to have regretted opening her door. In her letters she expressed only delight when her daughter Augusta fell in love with a young *chevalier* from Normandy called Alexandre de Foville. Smith welcomed their deepening relationship as a precious source of happiness in times that were breeding fear and violence.[34]

She set the first part of her long poem *The Emigrants* on the hills above Brighton in November 1792, and the second near the Arun in April 1793, by which time the French Convention under Robespierre had declared war on Britain. Urging rational co-operation rather than murder, she raged at the unleashing of 'wild disastrous Anarchy'.[35] She was writing to the moment, boldly voicing her politics in those febrile days.

Thinking of France, she was thinking also of her own native spot. 'Memory come!' she calls, situating herself or her poetic persona on high ground above the river – 'which I see / Make its irriguous course thro' yonder meads.' If only she could be borne back to 'those hours of simple joy' spent playing by the river as a girl, 'unconscious then of future ill'. Looking into the valley, she is a child again, paddling:

> . . . I have stood,
> And meditated how to venture best
> Into the shallow current, to procure
> The willow herb of glowing purple spikes,
> Or flags . . .

The child is neighbour to the living flora and fauna she walks among, 'Startling the timid reed-bird from her nest, / As with aquatic flowers I wove the wreath' to welcome May.[36] Sussex as she sees it now is still beautiful, but personal struggle and the suffering of others stand between her and those old pleasures. Her experience is the lens in which her beloved downland now appears – not the Claude glass used by her old teacher George Smith of Chichester, but a darker mirror. In a remarkable yoking of personal memory, present politics and social critique, she puts the image of a paddling girl in Sussex at the heart of her long poem about the French Revolution.

It is April, but what are 'lively verdure or the bursting blooms / To those who shrink from horrors such as war spreads o'er the affrighted

world?' She insists that 'here' does not exist apart from 'there'. She re-
fuses to stand safe and separate. This is the political force of the poem,
this folding together of places and people. 'In neighbouring countries,'
she knows, there are 'scenes that make / The sick heart shudder.' Smith's
son Charles joined one of the new regiments formed that month and left
almost immediately for France, taking up what she would call 'this trade
of Death'. The violence is a travesty of spring, as if it has leached into the
very ground. The flowers of the downs could not bring joy when 'neighbouring' flowers are bloodied. 'Violets, lurking in their turfy beds /
Beneath the flowering thorn, are stained with blood.'[37]

She looks from others' points of view, letting empathy shape her
response to the fields spread 'even as a map' before her: the commons
and 'winding brooks', the hills where she breathes 'fresh odours of the
mountain turf'.[38] Rural work here is not, she knows, a happily pastoral
alternative to war. The labourer in 'yon low hut' is not free to revel in
the scents of the turf if his health has failed and he cannot earn his bread:

> Then, thro' his patch'd and straw-stuffed casement, peeps
> The squalid figure of extremest Want.[39]

This figure of Want looks in at the window, but we seem to see the
casement from the other side too, the labourer's face looking out at us
through a window half stuffed against the cold: a Sussex neighbour taking in the view.

Smith dedicated her poem to Cowper, 'having read *The Task* almost
incessantly from its first publication'. She celebrated his power of giving
'to the most familiar objects dignity and effect'; she set alongside this his
defence of liberty and his foretelling of revolution in France.[40] She, too,
was finding literary form for the deep ties of connection between 'familiar objects' and the passionately hoped-for liberty of nations.

17. A MARBLE HEAD

A fresh wind blew in along the coast. At Bosham the head was propped up among stones in the vicarage garden, watching the grass with worn eyes. Part of the jaw was lost on one side, battered in a bar brawl by a smaller giant punching from below, but the head's expression was still one of composure. There was salt in the air this close to the sea. Hammering and rumbling came in gusts from the harbour.

The eyes grew worn with looking, though they never saw a thing. Blindly, they receded. One spring, when the frosts were gone, they were not eyes any more but hollows.

A gardener scythed the lawn at the end of August and tied in an old rose to the wall. A blackbird picked about in the leaf litter under the great round cranium. One of the local robins stood on the jutting brow sometimes, pausing with a worm looped through its beak.

Very occasionally, people came and pointed. Canes were waved; gods and rulers were mentioned. Two men arrived in early summer (it was Whitsun 1782) and sounded excited. One of them, his name was Grimm, set to work straight away with paints and paper. The head sat for its portrait, which wasn't a good likeness. The painter's gift was for buildings and their settings. Heads weren't a speciality. In the morning Mr Grimm would sit in the field behind the church and paint the whole scene with the flat coastal land open to the sky, the vicarage sheltered by trees, the masts of boats in the harbour rising higher than the roofs.[1]

The vicarage windows were boarded up and the gardener stopped scything. He only came when he let in the occasional curious visitor through the warping gate or promised to check the sheds for a lost house cat.

One enthusiastic gentleman stood telling a lady all about it. 'Woden!' he announced, in a mystical voice. He explained about the Saxons and the gods they brought from Germany to Sussex. People were quite wrong, he said, to think this was Bevis of Hampton, the giant who stepped from the Isle of Wight to Southampton. A breeze moved the branches of the apple tree, and the lady watched the shadows on the strange cratered stone. The surface looked doughy and then crystalline. She recalled the Saxon shapes she knew in local churches: round, open arches, deep embrasures, plain tub fonts. She did not think the giant head was Saxon, but she let her companion carry on.

Bosham Parsonage by James Rouse, from his *Beauties and Antiquities of the County of Sussex*, 1825

Emerging from a brief tour of the darkened house, a travelling antiquary declared the parsonage a wretched sight. It was 1823 or thereabouts.

Freed from the low rooms, straightening himself, he wondered that a clergyman had ever been persuaded to live in such a place. Attending to the head by the shrubbery, he exclaimed at the contrast in scale. Here was a giant to stand tall in the world, not to crouch in dank rooms. But the carving was rudely done, he could see: a primitive Saxon god. He thought of Sussex densely forested, wild, wolf-prowled, and a few wooden huts in the clearings, from which people came to gather round the Woden they had made as tall as the beech trees. He would make a drawing of this head, he thought, next to the splendid votive altar dug up last year in North Street. Quite a contrast: the perfect double cube of the Roman altar and this lumpen god about to fall forward onto his nose. But the altar was inscribed to the *genius loci*, and perhaps this head was a genius of the woods, a spirit of the place as the Saxons understood it.

The gardener was taken by surprise once, forgetting the old god was there. Struck still as if he had seen a ghost, and it was the middle of the day.

A woman stayed a long time by herself. Moving her hands over the marble, she had the concentration of a blind woman learning a face by touch. Where was it from? An Italian quarry, she thought. Dimples showed the place of a long-ago mouth that had never smiled. There was nothing behind the mouth except marble. It was indecent to be so close to this dead-weight lump with a few pockmarks suggestive of human life. It was never meant to be touched or looked in the eye. She could visualise how high it had been, this head which belonged to a matching body standing tall against the sky. She thought of the huge marble figure glistening in the harbour, blandly monstrous, not a person but a presence, looming over the ships as they came round the quay, and over the sunburnt men rolling barrels on the cobbles towards the warehouses.

The head lolled in the garden and the shrubbery advanced around it.

A major removal operation was put into action. The head was taken from the abandoned vicarage, transported to the centre of Chichester and manoeuvred into the bishop's garden to sit in a niche by the wall. The garden was open on summer afternoons and people strolled in twos and threes under the specimen trees. The head looked over the roses of 1910 and 1912. A moon, a meteor, a snowball petrified, a solid ghost.

A woman reading late one night came upon a passage in Pliny that made her think of it. The ruins of a Colossus, he related, lay upon the ground at Rhodes where people would go to see the broken pieces. Pliny seemed to have gone himself and was awestruck. You could hardly stretch your arms around the giant's thumb, he said. She considered the thumb of a sun-god. Was there once a Colossus of Chichester harbour, she wondered. She shifted the marble lump to the quayside in her mind and filled in the water, which was deep, and the salt marshes low and glinting, the flapping of canvas, the restless tapping of ropes against mastheads in the breeze. She saw groups of men talking and tried to think what they were saying. She raised the marble emperor to his full height at the harbour entrance. He was oppressively large, dominating the view. The coopers and traders on the dockside all looked subordinate; even the sea looked under thumb. She let go of the picture and turned the page.

The head was carried to the new museum and fixed upright on a smart black plinth with a view of an excavated bathhouse. It was at eye level with the visitors who came by, though their heads were half its size. A sign suggested that this was the Emperor Trajan and showed another carving of Trajan for comparison. School parties filed through from the ticket desk with clipboards and lists of things to look for. 'You're weird', said one girl to Trajan, unnerved by the lump of stone that was so living and so dead.[2]

PART III

18. AN OPEN GATE
William Blake at Felpham

At Felpham, on the coast west of Littlehampton, a high tide flooded up over the beach and ran into the sea meadows, finding its way over the grass. The white smock mill was turned away from the strength of the wind. In late spring, a bathing machine was pulled down onto the shingle. The Martin brothers pushed out their boat each morning. Travelling labourers came in late summer for the corn harvest, bent in the fields until night.

> So Milton's shadow fell
> Precipitant, loud thund'ring into the Sea of Time & Space.[1]

A comet, a meteor, a lightning strike, a descending angel, an arrow fired from heaven into the map of England: the author of *Paradise Lost*, nearly one hundred and forty years dead, came down from eternity onto a garden path. Milton's shadow fell into the garden of the cottage that William Blake and his wife, Catherine, were renting at Felpham. In all the sea of space, it was to this spot of earth that Milton came, imagined into being by England's most revolutionary living poet, summoned in to land as by a lighthouse or lightning rod. In all the sea of time, it happened during the three years Blake spent at Felpham between 1800 and 1803. It was the vision of a moment, cutting across the recurring cycles of the seasons, the windmill turning, the cattle brought onto the meadows and away again. Yet it was a moment, for Blake, in which all that continuing life of the world was shot through with new potential.

In his epic poem *Milton*, mostly written though not published in the Felpham years, Blake related the arrival of his blazing visitor:

> Then first I saw him in the Zenith as a falling star

Descending perpendicular, swift as the swallow or swift:
And on my left foot falling on the tarsus, enter'd there.[2]

This is what literary inspiration and inheritance felt like, looked like, really *was* for Blake: a spirit coming into his body, stirring and strengthening him for action. Like the dove of the Holy Ghost hurtling from the upper regions of Renaissance altarpieces into a room of quietly talking saints, or like the conversion of St Paul as Michelangelo painted it, with a yellow beam shining down from heaven so brightly that crowds are blinded, the scale is both cosmic and very intimate. At its centre is a communication between a spirit and an individual. The event resounds through space, but its point of focus is specific. Milton's shadow zeroes in: to Europe, to southern Britain, to Felpham, to a cottage garden, to a man standing at his door.

Like many readers in love with a poem, Blake feels he is the one to whom the writer is talking. But no one else inhabits the mind of the author in order to narrate a second coming. After a century walking about in eternity, looking down on the strife and inertia of men, Milton thought it necessary to return to earth. He must go in the form of his 'shadow' self, all beings in the 'vegetable world' existing as shadows of their whole cosmic selves. Milton's Satan landed in Eden and whispered into Eve's ear; Blake's Milton lands in a Sussex garden. 'My Path became a solid fire', writes Blake, and, with quiet solemnity, 'Milton silent came down on my Path'.[3]

These events are both ethereal and intensely physical. Swallows and swifts raced so high and fast in the summer air that they were less like bodies than a flickering of energy, and it is to those birds that the visitor is compared. Milton's shadow-self falls, like the shadow of a sundial gnomon falling across the arc of time. But the path is solid, and the place is real.

The communion is penetrative: the spirit enters into Blake who then carries it within him in a kind of pregnancy, even as the impregnation is working the other way: Blake appropriating Milton, taking up residence. The entry into the foot is as quick and smooth as Satan's pouring of words into Eve's ear, but the tarsus of the left foot is an altogether stranger point of entry. Saul was far from his native Tarsus when he was knocked to the ground by the light of God on the road to Damascus. Blake connects himself with that distant miracle, bringing it into his garden as he receives Milton into his ankle. He, too, falls to the ground. He pictures himself terror-struck, outstretched on the path; then a lark flies up above 'Felpham's Vale', and the poem carries us soaring northwards towards the weald, over the Surrey hills where the thyme is flowering, and towards London, across country where the wine-presses stand ready for the final harvest of the human vine.

Blake came to Felpham because he was invited there and offered work by William Hayley. After many years at Eartham, Hayley had moved away from his landscaped arcadia in the downs. The death of his son in 1800 had made the house too painful a place to stay. He was renovating his 'marine villa' in Felpham. A keen sea-bather, he had been coming here since boyhood; now he added a turret library to his house and made a permanent seaside home. The architecture was exuberant, or at least distinctive, in its melding of ideas for a hermitage, a Gothic folly, a gentry residence, a poet's study, and seaside retreat. But it was a melancholy time.

Hayley's response to this desolation was to bring artists into his life. He knew Blake a little, and invited him to Felpham. Blake visited in July 1800, at a time when he too was in trouble, struggling for the rent on his Lambeth house, and chafing against political, social and financial tensions that had closed in around him. He had already written some of his greatest poetry, but he was known to the public only as a talented engraver, illustrating other people's books – and for being, people said, a madman who went about naked and talked of visions. Hayley's promises of well-paid employment and creative community were attractive and a first breath of the sea air stirred his interest in leaving the smog of his native city. There was a cottage, owned by the landlord of the Fox inn, that seemed ideal.[4]

Construing the move as an escape from darkness into light, Blake described his destination in an ecstatic song:

> Away to Sweet Felpham, for Heaven is there;
> The Ladder of Angels descends thro' the air
> On the Turret its spiral does softly descend
> Thro' the village then winds, at my Cot it does end.[5]

It was a vision and a wish. He did not worry with the details of roads and directions: the topography that mattered, more vertical than horizontal, was that which joined heaven and earth. Another traveller to Felpham might have studied 'The Road from London to Chichester' unfolding as a scroll in the pages of an atlas. Hambleton – Brick kilns – Common – Chiddingfold – Enter Sussex: a ribbon paid out from old home to new. Blake's focus was on the roads, or scrolls, that reached upward to the sky, and down from the sky to earth.

He had once etched a tiny image of a ladder propped against the moon. 'I want! I want!' it was called. It was gloriously simple: one just had to make a ladder long enough, and keep the moon still for a moment. It was ridiculous, a child's dream, and yet we must keep making cosmonauts of our minds. At Felpham, Blake would not need a builder's ladder at full extension. Heavenly steps would be lowered down to that chosen spot, touching the material world first at Hayley's turret (which acts as observatory and anteroom) and then joining the looping village lane along to Blake's cottage. His watercolour of *Jacob's Dream* (which appears to date from just after the Felpham period) may give some indication of what he saw in the Sussex sky: an architecture of soft stateliness, a graceful staircase sweeping up through the stars, women and children embracing, reading and making music.[6] (PLATE) There was no tradition in art or in theology of understanding Jacob's ladder as a spiral stair. This was a spiral made by Blake, and by the turret, and by the winding lane of Felpham village.

The journey down to Sussex from London was not so weightlessly elegant as the steps of the angels, or the swifts he watched in the September sky: Blake's luggage included a dauntingly heavy roller press. But his language leapt with responsiveness to light and air. He felt a new life opening. 'I met a plow on my first going out at my gate', he reported, '& the Plowboy said to the Plowman "Father, The Gate is Open."' He treasured up the words as an omen, a signal of his starting out. 'Heaven opens here on all sides her Golden Gates.'[7]

The cottage was smaller than the Blakes' house in Lambeth, and on the north side the thatch came right down to the ground floor with tiny windows wedged under it.[8] But the front windows could be opened to the sea air and the view was not 'obstructed by vapours' as in London. 'If I should ever build a Palace it would be only My Cottage Enlarged' wrote Blake in the first throes of enthusiasm.[9] Mr Grinder, the landlord, had several cottages that he had whitewashed and 'furbished', hopeful of a nascent market in seaside rentals. He did not know, when he had new rugs put down, that he was carpeting the stairs for angels.

There was a small garden in front, and then a field for common grazing, then cornfields and the beach. Blake had never seen the sea until visiting Felpham, and now he lived a two-minute walk from the sight of infinity. A quarter of a mile down the village lane and he was on the pebbles, feet sliding down into uncountable stones, each one dense with its private curves and chatter-marks.

The low fields were an open stage under the skies. 'Voices of celestial inhabitants are more distinctly heard and their forms more distinctly seen', Blake confirmed after a few weeks' experience. He set down his 'first Vision of Light' in seventy-eight lines of glowing simplicity and concentration, rhymed like a nursery song, falling like a beam across the page:

> On the yellow sands sitting
> The Sun was Emitting
> His Glorious beams
> From Heaven's high Streams.[10]

Felpham appeared jewelled. Motes of dust caught the sun; even the cottage thatch was gold. In the streams of light it was clear to Blake that all these things, 'each grain of sand / Every stone in the land', have a distinct existence, their own life, as each human has life. 'I each particle gazed / Astonish'd, Amazed; / For each was a Man / Human-form'd.' These were verses 'such as Felpham produces by me'. It was a strange formulation, suggestive of the place as the poet, talking through Blake. A man is said to produce a child 'by' a woman; here it is Blake and Felpham that are fertile.[11]

~

Felpham was a farming village in 1800, surrounded by good arable land and grazing marshes. The fields, not yet enclosed, were carefully marked out into parcels and occupied by different farmers: Mill Field, Owlee Common Fields, Water Lane Common; Wish Field over near Flansham Brooks and 'the Common called Punch Gaston'.[12] There were crops of barley, peas and beans, but mostly wheat. The yield was large enough to warrant two windmills for the grinding of flour: the tarred Black Mill and its large white sibling, only recently erected. Its presence signalled the urgent effort to keep Sussex fed as the war with France went on and on, requiring soldiers to be stationed near the coast.

An increasing number of visitors were drawn by sea-bathing, 'courting Neptune for an Embrace' as Blake put it with a floridness caught from Hayley.[13] Bathing machines with their big cartwheels and wooden steps stood waiting on the shore. Sir Richard Hotham had been developing hotels and pleasure gardens at next-door Bognor until his death in 1799 and seaside buildings were still going up fast. So there was plenty of work for masons and glaziers, several of whom rented cottages in Felpham. The lime kilns at the end of Limmer Lane probably supplied the builders with mortar as well as the farmers with fertiliser.[14] But the village was still small and the old local families remained: Cosenses, Hollises, Chapmans.[15]

Four bells rang out the service times and tolled the burials. 'Brianus Eldredge me fecit', said one, like the bells at South Stoke and Slindon, all made at the same foundry. Below, in the Norman nave, altered in every century since the twelfth, the Squibb and Boiling and Cosens and Grinder and Sparkes families gathered and dispersed. There were arguments about a bulky new box pew that had been installed at the front and now obscured the view for others. People asked why the old, open benches couldn't be good enough for everyone, with the poppies carved on the bench-ends each the same. James and Elizabeth Chapman brought their baby daughter to the font. Richard and Maria Hollis brought a daughter and a son.[16] They stood and saw the creased pink heads held over the square stone bowl, the vicar's hand under the soft necks.

These people knew every square yard of Felpham, and would have described it in many different ways. Those who fed themselves from cottage gardens knew how the soil drained and where the frost lingered. William Beecham, a blacksmith who was building up the forging business he would run at Felpham for the next thirty years, knew the characters of local horses and their owners. To the fishermen and drowners (who controlled the flooding and draining of the water meadows) the intricate lettering of water running through the land was clearly legible. Drainage

streams had to be dredged each season. The large stream called Alding-
bourne Rife, which carried much of the water away from the levels, had
to be cleared and monitored, the sluices at its mouth opened at the right
times. William Blake saw something else. He saw Milton meeting Urizen, the bearded god of reason and control, 'on the shores of Arnon &
by the streams of the brooks'.[17] The giant figures moved over the water
and the marsh. Urizen baptised Milton with the cold water of the Jordan.
Blake saw figures towering over the land, fighting for the future, while
the water trickled in its streams through Felpham Brooks.

My father drove me over from Chichester, around the edge of Butlins,
and we parked in the hush of hedge and tarmac on Links Avenue. We
walked to where the road narrows. The old village buildings stand close
onto the lane, and the bungalows between them recede behind conifers,
claiming their privacy. The Blakes' cottage is end-on to the road so that
you see the gabled chimney wall pointing upward. It was white-rendered
when they knew it, though now the render has been stripped to reveal
coursed cobble flints. The best cobbles for walling are the size you can
comfortably hold in the hand; each stone relates to the next and each
course has a rhythm.

A quarter-of-a-mile's housing has filled in the old cornfields between
the cottage and the water: what is now called Blake's Road runs through
an estate laid out in the 1920s and 30s with low-rise marine-view apart-
ments and private lawns. It is an effort to imagine the clear view from the
cottage windows, though the proximity of the coast is still palpable and
we didn't need the sign pointing with its arrow 'To the Sea'.

On the front we stood looking out to the grey horizon. Flags on the
promenade were flapping frenetically and ice-cream spoons skittering
near the kiosk. People from the sailing club were waiting to launch a small
boat and a little crowd was gathering to watch, dogs leaping at cagouled

owners chatting against the wind. On the shingle I looked at the infinite shapes and colours into which flints are worn until eventually they are sand. The dark silica that began in chalk moulds lives its open-air years on the beach, turns brown, white, grey, rolls and rolls in its company of billions, and is at last a grain of sand. Black to yellow, black to gold.

Blake looked back at his windows from the shore. He made a water-colour drawing of the view, sketching with exactitude the bulk of the windmill, Hayley's turret, and his own bright house picked out in a shaft of sun. The painting expressed his sense of being chosen to see the beams of heaven. It also showed something very ordinary: the clarity with which your own home stands out from the rest. The Squibbs and Cosenses of Felpham, looking inland from the sea, would have marked out their houses. Each had the lit-up cottage that brought the others into focus.

The place near the White Mill where Blake stood has long gone un-derwater, along with Middleton Church a mile or so east, which was already deserted in the 1780s when Charlotte Smith imagined bones from the graveyard whitening in the waves, 'with shells and sea-weed mingled'.[18] But the mood in Felpham was not elegiac in the early 1800s. The bathing machines were ready for the bathers. The tides were meas-ured and managed. Wooden groynes parcelled out the beach, and the pebbles piled against the groynes.

As I sifted stones on the beach, a childhood memory returned of sitting for whole afternoons with friends in the lay-by at the top of our driveway, manning the stall on which we had arrayed a selection of shining stones. They were brought from Worthing or Rustington, a few at a time smug-gled home after a shopping trip, carried inland to un-cobbled Storrington where they gleamed as a hoard of mysterious finds. Each one was a rarity that only we had spotted. We wetted them to deepen the colours and show up marbling or strata. We waited for people we could amaze. The road was potholed and led nowhere, so there were no passing converts to at-tract, but we kept on dipping the stones in water, turning them like gems, and when they dried to pale opacity dipping them again.

With the tide going out, Blake came to the shining pebbles newly cleaned, and saw the sand exposed for a short while. It was probably in 1802 that he wrote his 'Auguries of Innocence' in a notebook. 'To see a World in a Grain of Sand,' he began, 'And a Heaven in a Wild Flower, / Hold Infinity in the palm of your hand, / And Eternity in an hour.'[19]

Blake's printing equipment was installed downstairs, the room dominated by the copperplate-rolling press. Bending over sheets of copper, he wrote or drew with an acid-resistant 'stopping-out varnish' and then dipped the plate into acid that ate away at everything in between. The words were islands in the acidic sea, cliffs eroded on all sides. Edward Marshall had once engraved the shapes of figures into brass to be laid down in churches, including the figures of the Bartelott family at Stopham; he scored his pictures into the metal. Blake did the inverse. The copper words stood out, delicate and intact. Very gently, they were inked with a leather-wadded dauber, the finest possible coating of ink, a black dab on the raised words. Pad, pad, pad: soft leather moving over the wild words that invoked giants and fires. Often it was Catherine Blake who did this. Then she, or he, laid paper over the plate and propelled it through the press by the turning of a heavy 'star-wheel'. The star turned, the heavens wheeled, words were pressed onto paper.

Outside in the fields were the tools that furrowed and pressed the earth. At ploughing time ox-drawn blades scored into the soil. The old was turned over for the planting of the new. It looked to William Blake like a revolutionary process. He noted the harrow and roller left under his window and imagined forms of cosmic farming. When the words of *Milton* started to come, they recalled the agricultural language of the

Bible, from the harrowing of hell to the pressing of souls, and also the daily work of rural Sussex. Blake heard 'the Harrow & heavy thundering Roller upon the mountains'.[20] He thought of the ultimate harvest that would take place at the end of the world as it was foretold in Revelation. Ox-teams crossed the fields of his mind's eye for a final gathering-in and, with necessary violence, harrowed the earth to a finer tilth in preparation for the next season of the universe.

Day after day Blake commuted along the lane to the house of his employer. Theirs was a creative collaboration, or so Hayley felt, though he made it clear to gentry friends that he was in charge, and had brought the promising artist from London to work with him. Among the first commissions were decorative panels for the turret library. Blake worked intensively on eighteen portraits that were to form a frieze of literary genius, predella-shaped panels running round the top of the room so that the heads of great writers would look out from above the bookcases. He spoke of meeting Homer and Dante and Spenser as 'majestic shadows, gray but luminous' on the shore. So he made portraits of those shadows with whom he walked on the shingle. 'Gray but luminous', they appear in the paintings both god-like and delicate, surrounded by painted stars and skies so that one has the impression of heads appearing from clouds, or moons, or dreams.

Once these were complete, new tasks multiplied. Hayley was an insatiable writer of high rhetoric, rarely content unless his pen was dashing across paper. Eager for visual embellishments of his compositions, he invented projects more rapidly than the artist at his side could possibly accomplish them. Plates for his ballad 'Little Tom the Sailor', plates for his biography of the poet William Cowper in four volumes, plates for a poem on women's tempers and a whole book of ballads about animals. In the upstairs library Blake worked through the evenings, designing and engraving images of utmost intricacy, as if he might compress infinity into images barely larger than his palm.

'Miniature is become a Goddess in my Eyes' said Blake, bending before the goddess through long days of delicate watercolour stippling when Hayley asked for miniature portraits of friends, jewel-like cameos to be held close in hands and pockets.[21] But Blake was a more radical miniaturist than he could express in these portraits. In poetry that came to him in off-duty moments of the night he was imagining giants as fossils, stretching and waking, growing as large as whole cliff-faces or hills. As for infinity: it might be the shape and size of a uterus. 'The nature of a Female Space is this: it shrinks the Organs / Of Life till they become Finite & Itself seems Infinite.' It might be in the 'unfathom'd caverns' of the ear, or folded into the corridors and chambers of the brain, lodged under the egg-like skull. He was thinking of the earth as a 'Mundane Egg', small as a hen's egg or a woman's ovum.[22] Thus he shrank all the 'vegetable world' into a fragile ovoid to be gathered warm from the hay, all cottages, trees, cities condensed in its yolk.

In March 1801 parish officials throughout England were responsible for providing information for the first national census. Enumerators went door to door around the village, recording how many people were there on Tuesday 10th: 306 people (including children) spread between 71 inhabited houses.[23] Notes were made of the number employed in various occupations. Agriculture. Trade or manufacture. Other. The vicar of Felpham went through the church registers and added up the births and deaths over the last hundred years, information requested of every parish in an effort to understand how rapidly the population was increasing.

Blake was a number. Catherine another. Their cottage one dwelling to be added to seventy. The King was in his counting house, counting out his nation. The clerks were copying out the records, as clerks had once copied out the surveyors' returns in the register of Domesday (Falcheham 1086: 73 households, meadow, woodland, fishery, church). Parliament was anxious to get a grasp on the situation. Population growth across the country as a whole was thought to have reached frightening rapidity by 1800. There were panicked forecasts of suppressed wages, mass overcrowding and food shortage.

> Seventy-nine: Elizabeth Chapman.
> Eighty: Joseph Cosens.
> Eighty-one: William Hayley.
> Three hundred and four: William Blake.
> Three hundred and five: Catherine Blake.

Blake's art suggests forms of thought opposed to the workings of a census, opposed to listing and surveying and totalling. The census-taker might be a version of Blake's Newton with his skewering compasses, constraining the universe with his calculations. Nobody was simply 'one' for Blake. Blake's female spirits or 'emanations' could be drawn out from them like Eve from Adam's rib: the emanation of Los, or Inspiration, was Enitharnon, the spirit of music. Ololon, misunderstood by Milton himself, was the six-fold composite of his three wives and three daughters. The figures of Blake's world were self-multiplying and self-dividing. Four-fold, eight-fold: the ancient language of folding (old English *feald*, Old German *fealt*, Old Norse *faldr*) had a physicality about it that any printer and publisher would understand.

> Three hundred and seven: the giant Albion, comprised of four zoas:
>   Tharmas (instinct and strength), Urizen (Reason), Luvah (Passion),
>   Los (Inspiration).
> Three hundred and eleven: the 'Starry Seven' appear as seven angels,
>   blowing their trumpets into the ear of Albion to wake him, though

at the second coming they will fold together in the one figure
   of Jesus.
Eight million and eight: the number of the Sons of Ozoth, 'fiery
   glowing' in the optic nerve.
Infinity: 'And every Space smaller than a Globule of Man's blood
   opens / Into Eternity'.[24]

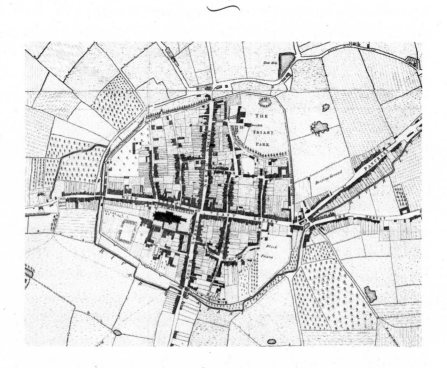

It was a good seven miles into Chichester if you wanted anything from
the shops or the tradesmen. William and Catherine walked it, and carried
their purchases home again. Or Blake borrowed Bruno, the horse that
had belonged to Hayley's son, and rode through the lanes at a trot,
towards the spire, into the stalls and traffic around the East Gate. What
was his Chichester? Did he talk with the tanners outside the leather
sheds or the boys paid to mind penned sheep in the streets, or make visits
in the Pallant?

He was not quite part of the Chichester scene described by Hayley's friend John Marsh, the resident musician whose prolific and evocative diary gives day-by-day news of who played at the subscription concerts, and who would replace the cathedral organist, and which books should be purchased by the Library Society. If you want the news from Chichester on almost any day from the 1790s to the 1820s, read Marsh. His journal is a capacious portrait of social and cultural life in a provincial city with a firm identity of its own. Marsh lived at Hayley's old childhood home in the Pallant, next door to the ostriches. There he would write out songs, glees, voluntaries, at least one new symphony each year. There he would sit in the evening with the white parlour cat on his knee, reading aloud to 'Mrs Marsh', his wife Elizabeth. He nursed a white kitten in order that Mr Blake should have it. But 'Blake the engraver' was an artisan on the edge of the concert-going, book-buying, cathedral-running social world.[25]

From Marsh's house we can walk through the city with Blake and Hayley. We know the building at 21 East Street: the house where William Collins grew up. Since Collins' time it had been for many years a printers' shop. A succession of printers had worked at Number 21, each establishing a reputation, training apprentices and passing the business on. Here Dennett Jaques printed Charlotte Smith's *Elegiac Sonnets*. Now Joseph Seagrave was well established as Chichester's printer, and Blake and Hayley called in to see him. Regional publishing was expanding rapidly, and Seagrave was part of this new landscape.[26] His presses were busy with handbills, adverts, concert programmes and especially local papers (*The County Mirror* and the new *Sussex Chronicle*) of the sort that were growing in number and circulation as regional journalism expanded all over the country. Alongside all this, he was increasingly printing books.

Generous, anxious, melancholic, unconventional, Seagrave was not always a firm businessman but he inspired loyalty. He and his partner, Mary Shepherd, lived by their principles, declining to marry and braving the disapproval they attracted. There was a vein of resilient radicalism in them both. In the rooms at Number 21 where William Collins had begun to love poetry, Joseph Seagrave liaised with the startlingly skilled engraver, Mr Blake.

Seagrave printed Hayley's book of animal ballads, with Blake's minutely crafted illustrations, and (a large task for a small press) he undertook to print the biography of Cowper. Hayley's London publisher Joseph Johnson, one of the most admired and influential men in bookselling, was loath to allow an important publication like this to be produced by a provincial printer in Chichester. There would be delays and mistakes, he thought. But Hayley's insistence on using Seagrave was a vote of confidence in a friend, and also in local production. 'There does not exist a man, in his line of life, who has a more just and delicate sense of professional probity.'[27] Blake agreed with him. It was a tug against the 'London model' of a centralised metropolitan literature, an affirmation of diverse vitality and expertise.

Blake went much further in his thinking about the life of the cathedral town he had come to know. In his long poem *Jerusalem*, composed at least in part at Felpham, the shape and history of Chichester are legible in Blake's vision of a reborn Albion and a holy city rebuilt.[28] He knew the story of St Wilfrid arriving at Selsey in 681, building a church and converting Sussex to Christianity. He knew that, after the flooding of Selsey, the bishop's seat was moved to Chichester, and he would have seen the Tudor artist Lambert Barnard's large painting in the cathedral of Wilfrid on the shore.[29] 'Selsey, true friend!' cries Los in *Jerusalem*, imagining the inundation as a flood of despair but telling how an 'Emanation'

> rose above
> The flood and was nam'd Chichester, lovely mild & gentle! Lo!
> Her lambs bleat to the sea-fowls' cry, lamenting still for Albion.[30]

In these stretching, compressing lines, he not only catches Chichester's pastoral-marine identity between the downs and the sea, and fills our minds with the call of seabirds, long associated with both freedom and desolation, but he connects the city with the pagan and early Christian past that spoke to him of pre-modern energy. Other towns and cities then follow: Winchester, Gloucester, Exeter, Salisbury, 'benevolent Bath'.

Chichester retains very strongly its Roman plan: an approximately circular wall with gates at the cardinal points and four streets meeting in the middle. You are always moving north, south, east or west, inward or outward. The new holy city Blake prophesied was called Golgonooza, and it had four gates. 'Every part of the city is fourfold; and every inhabitant, fourfold.' 'Travellers to Eternity pass inward to Golgonooza.'[31] In Blake's system of folded microcosms, the human body is a city with four gates: the gate of the genitals, of the heart, of the head (or the eyes) and of the tongue. The city – in turn – is a body, and the city is a mind, an inner landscape. Los walks around the walls night and day, beating out rhythms of time and thought, pacing, pacing.

At Felpham in summer Blake watched the larks flying up over the corn-fields, finding no limits. They commuted vertically, as Blake did in imagination, 'mounting upon the wings of light into the Great Expanse', where they seemed to dissolve into pure sound.[32] In the first 'Vision of Light' Blake had described the eye-opening spaciousness of the open sea: 'My Eyes more & more / Like a Sea without shore / Continue Expanding'.[33] But the sea did have a shore, and even if you stood on a clear day looking apparently into infinity you were looking towards a French coast that was enemy territory. The presence of soldiers billeted all along the Channel was a daily reminder of the situation. When a peace deal was brokered in autumn 1801, Blake's hopes flew out across the water towards the pictures he might now go and see in Paris; all Europe would be open again, reigned over by 'literature and the arts'. Worlds opened out in the turret library, where Hayley taught Blake Greek in the evenings – and then (when the student mastered that with alacrity) Latin,

French and Hebrew.[34] A winter of late-night study and the shopkeeper's son could talk with Homer and Virgil in their own languages.

In March 1802, two days after the signing of the Treaty of Amiens, Catherine Bridger gave birth to a son and called him Horatio Nelson. He was christened at Felpham church in July. Sarah Hudson from Arundel gripped the pen and made her mark the day she married James, Duke of Felpham, at the end of August. James and Elizabeth Chapman, back with another child, took their son William up to the font during the service on Christmas Day.[35] Blake watched strands of seaweed to gauge the coming weather.[36]

The peace was uncertain; space seemed to close in again. The soldiers were still at the Fox. The cottage was palpably damp, which was lowering for them both but disastrous for Catherine who was hampered by rheumatism.[37] Milton may have entered Blake's foot, but the damp was entering Catherine's knees and swelling her joints. Unable to walk without pain, she was physically trapped, though she continued to work the press and to colour prints, contributing, as she had done all her married life, to the making of art. 'My sweet shadow of delight', William called her in *Milton*, bidding heavenly spirits help her in the cottage 'for she is sick with fatigue'.[38] Frustration mounted as Hayley demanded more and more work. Unhappy ambivalence swayed into anger. The Blakes soothed themselves by resolving to return to London where they could work 'unannoy'd' by the overbearing patron.[39] Hayley was capable of being Los, the spirit of inspiration. And yet ('O God protect me from my friends'), Hayley was also a Satanic figure, tethering and damaging creativity.

But: 'There is a Moment in each Day that Satan cannot find'.[40] Blake sought the moments when he could be free, held them, magnified them and wrote. The poetry came, he said, twenty or thirty lines at a time, 'without Premeditation & even against my Will'. He was working from 'immediate Dictation'. 'I dare not pretend to be any other than a secretary; the authors are in eternity.'[41]

Britain declared war again in May and Napoleon swore to 'leap the ditch'.
Was he giant enough – like the giants of Blake's art – to step across the
Channel at a stride? As defences were stepped up, there was more counting of troops, boats, mills, village bread ovens (eighty-three).[42] And
then, for Blake, the doomsday atmosphere intensified. He went into the
garden and found a soldier there. He was shocked at the intruder, not
realising that the soldier had been asked in by the gardener to help with a
task. An argument broke out, and Blake was reduced to seizing the man
at the elbow and walking him forcefully back to the Fox where he was
billeted. That was the start of it.

The soldier lodged a complaint that Blake had 'damned the king of
England' and commented seditiously about fighting on Napoleon's side.
Within a few days, Blake was up before the magistrates, who ordered
him to appear at the Petworth Quarter Sessions. His name was added to
the centuries-long list of those whose lives were held in the balance at the
four quarters of the year.

Mary Owden. Petworth, Michaelmas 1643.
William Blake. Petworth, Michaelmas 1803.

The presiding Justice, the Duke of Richmond, knew nothing about him
and was exercising no favours. The Earl of Egremont recognised that
this was his friend Hayley's resident artist, but he did not intervene.
Blake was to be put on trial.[43]

He left Felpham as a man accused. He had arrived stretching his limbs
and his spirit in miles of fresh air. Hayley's demands had closed in as a sore
constraint, but now there was a real threat of imprisonment. Two lots of
bail were paid by Hayley and the generous printer Seagrave on his behalf.
The paradise of sweet airs had become a trap, its mouth open just beside
him, rayed round with accusers taunting. He returned to Chichester to
face his fate at the Guildhall just after Christmas and had no option but to

sit in silence and watch his life being batted to and fro between prosecution and defence. His lawyer called as witnesses the gardener, and Mrs Haynes who lived next door to Blake and worked at the mill. These dependable, well-known people said they had heard nothing seditious.

An eccentric artist in a small farming community can easily become an object of fear and suspicion, so it's striking that Blake had the support of Felpham people. Little evidence survives of his relationships with neighbours and we cannot know the conversations he had with the ploughmen in the lane or with the gardener who was also an ostler at the Fox. While still in Felpham he had assured London friends that 'the peaceable Villagers have always been forward in expressing their kindness for us', and he trusted them: 'Every one here is my Evidence for Peace and Good Neighbourhood.'⁴⁴ It's certain that when Blake was on trial, many country people showed themselves to be behind him. Chichester tradesmen and gentry also gathered to wish him well. John Marsh hosted breakfast in the Pallant before everyone went to the courtroom. A cheer went up in the Guildhall when Mr Blake was acquitted. He had become a local cause, though hardly a celebrity. The *Sussex Weekly Advertiser*, reporting the trial, got his name wrong.⁴⁵

Back in London he did not try to expunge Felpham from memory. Instead he worked into finished form the visions that had been granted during his 'three years slumber on the banks of the Ocean'.⁴⁶ He brought *Milton* to its apocalyptic end, foretelling the emergence of Jesus 'in Clouds of blood': 'the Four surrounded him / In the Column of Fire in Felpham's vale; then to their mouths the Four / Applied their Four Trumpets & them sounded to the Four winds.'⁴⁷ Though he was glad to have returned to his native London, the prophetic poems were umbilically attached to the place of their first making, which was in turn made mythic and universal. When he described a 'vision of the lamentation of Beulah over Ololon', he called up a sensuous succession of flowers at dawn, beginning with plants of chalk grassland and riverbank: 'first the Wild Thyme / And Meadow-sweet, downy & soft waving among the

reeds / Light springing on the air, lead the sweet Dance'. Then came pinks, jessamines, wallflowers, the plants of cottage gardens.[48]

The image of the cathedral spire in the distance never left him. It's there as late as 1821, in the woodcuts for *Pastorals of Virgil*, which include an image of the shepherd Colinet leaving a gleaming city among hills, with sixty-two miles ahead of him to London as a carved milestone tells us. It is there, too, in one of Blake's greatest paintings, the *Vision of the Last Judgement*.[49] Bodies rise and tumble, swim and fly through a composition that is both explosive and controlled in every detail. 'The Just . . . rise thro the air with their children and Families', Blake explained.[50] Green hills reach up in strange mounds, as if the downs were being pulled by their smooth shoulders. A spire points the way. After his trial in the Guildhall, this was Blake's vision of the final and just hearing. It was also the true census, the counting of souls for the only parish register that mattered.

It would be hard, and misleading, to think of Blake as a poet of local observation to be compared with Cowper or Wordsworth. We do not find him writing lines 'a few miles above Felpham' that precisely delineate the view and the day, saving up the place in memory. Topographical drawing was not, for him, the starting point for expression as it was for Thomas Girtin and John Constable and J. M. W. Turner, the contemporaries who were finding visionary possibility in landscape art. Blake was, on principle, no topographer. To map and to measure were the constraining activities of Urizen, reducing the world to material forms that are only husks of what exists.

He would not stand at trig points with the King's surveyors, yet Blake was mindful of the earth seen from heaven and looked across continents as if they were laid out in a great atlas ('Turkey, Arabia, Palestine, Persia'). He could focus in to the detail of a garden (like any modern user of Google Maps, zooming in with two fingers on a phone), but when he thought of the 'Two Gates thro' which all souls descend' he saw the whole south coast 'from Dover Cliff to Lizard Point' and the outline of northern Scotland, 'Caithness and rocky Durness'. Albion bestrides the nation with London between his knees, his right hand on Wales and his left foot (meeting and merging with Blake's own left foot) on 'the Rocks of Bognor'.[51]

If you happen to know Bognor, you stop in your tracks; the poem is suddenly at your door. The 'Rocks' are underwater now, but were prominent in the 1790s, frequented by visitors and quarrymen. (Blake's landlord Mr Grinder had run the Fox on the edge of the Rocks before moving to Felpham; the inn was painted there by Samuel Grimm in summer 1790.[52]) If you don't know Bognor, it's clear that Albion's elbow might, at its next stirring, land on you. Blake's willingness to speak of all Wales on the one hand and Bognor on the other is part of what makes his thinking about place so surprising. You wouldn't expect to find Bognor (or Windsor or Durham) in the epic poems of Milton. The reference locates Blake's personal vision, making his home by the sea the magnetic pivot point of history. But the effect is also to invoke all those thousands of other places that are personal to other people.

Provocatively thinking on planetary, national and local scales at once, there were ways in which Blake was among the most radically local of all Romantics. He was ready to countenance the existence of a world in a grain of sand, which must make a universe of a village. He would not settle for any idea of Felpham as an inconsequential backwater going on with its farming while history happened elsewhere. Protestant and dissenting Christians of many kinds felt a vivid personal relationship with a God who entered into their houses and into their hearts. Being omnipresent, He was necessarily local: a God one might find through inner exploration rather than pilgrimage to sacred places. In this theological context it was no surprise that Blake would meet divinity at home.

But there is little in British art to prepare us for the way in which Felpham became the site of cosmic eventfulness. For that we might turn back to the Netherlandish painters of the fifteenth century, to Hans Memling or Robert Campin, who move Mary from Nazareth into modern, well-furnished Netherlandish interiors, and send the angel Gabriel to find her in the bedroom or parlour. Or we might remember Brueghel's *Adoration of the Kings in the Snow*, a picture of a Flemish town preparing for another frozen night and, somewhere in the corner, huddled, hidden from view, the Magi visiting Jesus. Blake works differently, focusing on prophecy rather than a relocation of the Gospels, but there is a shared conviction about the sanctity of 'here'. Look into the crowd, look into that old stable: it might contain a miracle. What matters is here, in the midst of daily things. Look at that village on the south coast of England with its two mills and its cornfields. If you can see them, Milton and the angels are there.

19. FURTHER FIELDS
The rectory and the sugar mill

Summer 1828: in Sutton churchyard the yew tree planted by Joseph Sefton in the 1660s, after the Restoration, was growing strong. But there had been a theft at the rectory. The rector, Richard Smith, no longer had his mule. A labourer from the parish was up before the Quarter Sessions in Chichester in October. Three Sutton men said they had seen suspicious behaviour, and it was enough to convict 27-year-old Robert Smith. The gelding mule was worth about £3, and such a theft came with a major sentence. The prisoner was to be transported for seven years to one of the penal colonies in Australia or Van Diemen's Land.[1] Afterwards, if he was still alive, he would be free to make his own way.

That was the last the rector knew of this particular parishioner. With rural poverty deepening, desperation and anger endemic, the court sessions were busy. That same month transportation was the sentence handed to a man from Petworth who stole a watch, a man from Stopham who stole an ass.[2] Convicts in the 1820s were no longer sent across the Atlantic but to the newer British colonies in the southern hemisphere. It was standard. People carried in mind varyingly vivid and informed ideas of what it meant. What was it like to plough a field there and raise a crop?

Robert of Sutton was kept at Petworth House of Correction until the following spring. It was a large and terrifying jail, notorious for the industrial scale on which it enforced regimes of solitary confinement and hard labour. The governor took pride in the efficient severity with which punishment could be inflicted by means of the 'tread-wheel' on which prisoners must climb forty-six steps a minute for ten hours a day for the sheer exhaustion of it: the wheel was turning nothing.[3] Silence was compulsory, and prisoners wore masks when in contact with each other so that no communicative expression was possible. Transportation away – anywhere – from this clinically administered hell might be anticipated with relief.

Robert was taken up to London docks in March 1829 and loaded onto the convict ship *Waterloo*, converging with others from jails across England. His name is there in the list of some 180 prisoners who embarked along with a military guard.[4] Two centuries on, with transportation records digitised, we can follow him on at least the first stage of his journey. The ship was bound for Port Jackson, New South Wales. Conditions for convicts at sea were miserable but it was in no one's interests to lose potential labourers in transit and onboard deaths were kept to a minimum. There was a ship's surgeon on the *Waterloo*. All but two passengers survived the journey, and Robert Smith set foot in Australia in July.[5]

It appears that the new arrivals were taken into the Hunter Valley north of Sydney and distributed among a number of free settlers with large estates along the river. They would clear, fence and cultivate the land over hundreds of acres – which was a better fate than being assigned to the road-building and mining gangs. If he could endure it he stood a chance, after seven years, of being a free man, labouring for a wage.[6]

In Sutton the rector had other distant places to think of, or not to think of, as he passed the yew tree or crossed the steep field to Bignor. He co-owned a large estate in Barbados, where his parents had spent part of their time. His mother was of the Mapp family, and he inherited a half-share of their sugar plantation, 'Mapp's'.[7] The number of enslaved people at Mapp's in the 1820s was about 120, fewer in the register for some years due to deaths, more in others as children were born and became automatically part of the estate.[8] The attorney William Sharp, accountant and administrator in Barbados for a number of plantations, compiled financial statements summarising the profits, losses and slave population at Mapp's.

Reverend Smith's West Indian interests came to him from both sides of the family. On the paternal side there was a history of merchant and planter Smiths. His grandfather, an East India Company director, was also an investor in West Indian sugar estates. At his death in 1776 he left a complex will instructing that a number of legacies be held in trust for his grandchildren; the idea was to prevent the wealth being misused by his unreliable son Benjamin, the no-good husband of the writer Charlotte Smith. The will became the subject of one of the longest Chancery cases ever known (it is thought to have provided the model for Jarndyce v Jarndyce in *Bleak House*). It tested Charlotte Smith's energy and earning capacity to the limits as she wrote novels at the rate of a chapter a day, trying to provide for nine children who should have inherited. That's what she was doing at Eartham. The rector of Sutton was the cousin of those children: they all shared a grandfather whose legacy came to them belatedly and much reduced by lawyers' fees. Charlotte had spent much of her life fighting for the inheritance because she thought it rightfully belonged to her children and without it they faced poverty; at the same time she made her loathing for slavery clear in her writing.[9] Reverend Smith has left no record of his thinking on the subject, except that he continued to own enslaved people year after year.

There's no sign that Richard Smith ever went out to see Mapp's, and no way of knowing how he visualised his largest farm, so profoundly different from the Sussex glebe fields. This other farm extended over about 250 inland acres in south-eastern Barbados. The parish church was St Philip. No yew by the door, but mahoganies, and an ancient sand box tree.[10]

Reverend Smith was thirty and long established at Sutton Rectory in 1816 when reports came of a slave uprising in Barbados, particularly intense in St Philip's. The damage to each owner's property was estimated and the losses were significant, not least because high-value slaves were imprisoned and executed for their part in the insurrection. Still more concerning for estate owners was the indication of a system at breaking point, a workforce in combined revolt. The Legislature in Barbados held an inquiry, which was also an exercise in propaganda, calculated to assure owners that the system was both well controlled and morally responsible, as long as slaves were not 'indulged'. Among those who gave evidence was the manager at Mapp's, Thomas Stoute, who described the 'comfortable' conditions of enslaved people on the estate, arrangements for their food and healthcare, and his preference for only 'moderate floggings' sometimes replaced by periods of being locked up. The problem, he was sure, was that increased food rations and 'constant parties and dances on Saturday and Sunday evenings' had given slaves 'exalted ideas of their own value and consequence'. On top of these wrong-headed measures of amelioration came the Registry Bill. Slaves were told, he said (by 'evil-minded and mischievous persons') that it signified the British Crown's intention to emancipate them. When plantation owners showed no sign of enacting any such emancipation, enslaved people sought to claim their freedom for themselves.[11]

Stoute gave a version of events designed both to prove the danger of leniency on the part of managers and to discredit anti-slavery campaigners as purveyors of false hope, confusing slaves, leading them to action for which they would suffer. The rector of the parish neighbouring St Philip's had, he said, talked with condemned rebels and found them penitent. This clergyman of Barbados, counterpart of Richard Smith in Sutton, questioned chained captives in prison, including a man named Dainty from Mapp's. Dainty regretted his rebellion 'against a good owner'. He wished he had listened to his wife's warnings against involvement; he begged that his children, who he would not see again, might be brought up 'in such a manner that they might never be reproached with their father's having been hanged'. So the rector reported.[12] These are the colonial clergyman's words, of course, not Dainty's. We cannot hear Dainty as he goes to his torturous death, leaving his children to the life of slavery he has himself endured and which, in the desperate effort of one April day, he tried to rise against.

⁓

Voices for the 'West India Interest' continued to sound loudly in defence of the system through the 1820s. Like other modestly sized port towns, Chichester and its environs had long had a small but influential community of absentee planter families. John Duer, for instance, one of the best-known local proprietors, was owner of Big Duers plantation in Antigua, inherited from his father and brother. The estate was managed on the ground by men from Chichester families. James Brown, son of a gunmaker on Tower Street, had been in charge until his death at Christmas 1824; according to the local paper, he was knocked from his horse and murdered by 'a negro, named Cambridge', rushing at him from the sugar cane.[13] A few column inches of Chichester news: good fat stock at market, regiments embarking for India, new guesthouses for those visiting the delights of Worthing, gin smuggling, murder in Antigua, early nesting of blackbirds on the downs.

Plantation owners would sometimes have servants brought over from their West Indian estates to work in their Sussex households. Very little evidence survives to tell us anything about their lives in the area. By searching parish registers, though, and piecing together scarce references, archivists are beginning to trace some of the Black inhabitants of Chichester in the eighteenth and early nineteenth centuries. Charles Douglass Herring was baptised in 1798 in a parish just outside the city and listed in the register as 'A Negro Servant of J. S. DOUGLASS Esq'. It's likely that he had been brought from the Grange estate in Jamaica, which was owned by James Sholto Douglass or Douglas, a prominent figure in Chichester over at least three decades – before and after his time as mayor in 1810. If Charles was a footman or groom in the house of James and his wife Sarah, he would have lived for several years between East Street and the Pallants, moments from the Swan and the stone ostriches.[14]

Chichester was where Edward Long (1734–1813) had made his home when he left Jamaica in 1769. Living in the city with his wife Mary Beckford in the early 1770s, and later in Arundel Park, he worked on his three-volume *History of Jamaica*, describing plantation landscapes in the language of the Picturesque. Views were 'adorned with the lively verdure of canes' and 'watered with rivulets'. Even among slave-owners, Long's attitudes to racial difference were extreme and he argued at length for the fundamental rightness of chattel slavery in the service of a master race.[15] His book remained a standard reference work in the 1820s. The *Bognor, Arundel and Littlehampton Guide* for 1828 directed visitors' attention to the marble monument in Slindon church commemorating the 'author of the *History of Jamaica*, a work highly esteemed'.[16] Long's memorial was one of the local cultural sights to see.

Of the relatively few sequences of West Indian landscape views in circulation, most were by artists commissioned by planter families keen to see their properties rendered in visually appealing terms. There was great political power in prints that suggested the natural harmony and rightness of enslaved labourers working hard but productively to cultivate a fertile land. Among those that the Reverend Smith and his Sussex contemporaries could have seen if they wished were the coloured aquatint views by James Hakewill, published in 1825 as *A Picturesque Tour of the Island of Jamaica*.[17] All is calm and evenly daylit; spacious views show stately homes set in green acres that might be sugar fields but look pleasantly like lawns. Palm trees take the place of European beeches or oaks in framing compositions in the classical manner. A Black figure rests by a stream; beside him, in place of the fishing rod we might expect on a pastoral riverbank, the whip he must use to drive his fellow workers. Aquatints are made with etched plates and coloured inks, but part of their popularity in the period lay in a resemblance to watercolour drawings; some of the same delicacy and glassy clarity can be achieved. So it is here, in prints that call up an echo of English landscape water-colours. Cows graze in waterside meadows that look refreshingly cool. There is no hint of the thick, humid heat that makes every step an effort. Hills rise in the distance giving an effect not so very different from that in Samuel Hieronymus Grimm's pellucid topographical views of Sussex.

James Hakewill, view of Montpelier Estate,
from *A Picturesque Tour of the Island of Jamaica*, 1824

William Clark's *Ten Views in the Island of Antigua*, published as aqua-tints in 1823, were unusual in being the work of not a touring artist but a plantation overseer still resident in Antigua. He was depicting his home and the industrial agriculture that was the business of his life, from cane planting to harvesting, the crushing out of the juice in the windmills that turned on every estate, and the boiling of the sugar.[18] He showed large teams of enslaved labourers engaged in strenuous tasks, drivers ready with whips, and white overseers watching; he depicted all this without drawing attention to violent domination. No one screams with the pain of infected skin lacerations. No one is whipped for collapsing in exhaustion.

The pictures emphasise well-managed cultivation in which hundreds of workers perform their efficiently choreographed tasks. These are landscapes in the Georgic tradition, recording and admiring productive work.

In Britain the campaign for abolition of slavery in the British colonies was so widely supported in the mid-1820s that it was clear change must come. But it had been that way for years; agreement with the West Indian legislatures still escaped the government negotiators. The public pressure on parliament was resolutely kept up, meeting after meeting, through letters, pamphlets, lectures, speeches, much of it organised at a local level in county towns. Years of campaigning in Chichester, led especially by nonconformists like the Quaker Barton and Hack families, reached a peak of public prominence in 1826 when a meeting was called in the city to adopt a petition to Parliament.

'The whole of the Clergy of the City and neighbourhood' were there in the Council Chamber with the Duke of Richmond from Goodwood presiding and professional figures stepping up to speak. It seems unlikely that Reverend Smith joined them, though other slave-owners were in attendance. The *Sussex Chronicle* reported with exclamation marks that John Duer supported the petition, but there must have been some confusion. A correction the following week stated that he did not.[19] Everyone was watching everyone else, and deciding their positions. There was no question about the views of Thomas Sanden, the doctor who had looked after George Smith the painter in his last illness long ago. He had practised in Chichester ever since and was one of the most respected men in the city, an influential voice in persuading local people to act for abolition. The Sussex signatures converged in Westminster with petitions raised in other regional towns across the country – from Colchester to Taunton. Roll-calls of petitioning towns appeared in the papers. Where there seemed to be no action in an area it was noticed and questioned by correspondents. Anti-slavery work became a prominent part of the local identity projected to the nation by provincial communities.[20]

~

Every three years in the 1820s a census was taken of enslaved men, women and children on Barbados plantations. William Sharp the attorney filed the lists for the government registers, on behalf of Reverend Smith and his co-owner. Since last count there had been fifteen births, eight deaths, he confirmed on 29 May 1829.[21] He wrote out the list of those born:

10	Rachel Grace		Black
11	Sarah Thomasin	2 years old	"
12	Easter	2 years 3 months	"
13	Betsy Kitty	1 year 5 months	"

~

It was easy to encounter information that might give nightmares to plantation owners. An 1831 lecture in Chichester was very fully reported in the *Sussex Chronicle*, detailing '*murderous* exaction of toil' and 'systematic starvation'. The audience was shown examples of West Indian whips and chains. To remain complicit with the business, the lecturer showed, was to be accessory to murder.[22] It was one of many anti-slavery events organised by the thriving Chichester Mechanics Institute, founded in 1825 along with hundreds of similar institutions in other towns. This expansion of learning (free classes, laboratories, a library, the latest pamphlets and periodicals) forged new communities of middling- and working-class men and women increasingly drawn to participate in debate, and there was no more prominent or sustained debate than that over slavery.

TOP The downs from
Pulborough Brooks.

LEFT Chalk arch at North Stoke,
supported by a carved hand.

ABOVE South wall of
St Botolph's, Hardham.

S. H. Grimm's Sussex drawings for William Burrell, made on
their Whitsun tour in 1780: the 'Mount' at Pulborough and
remains of Hardham Priory.

Reed cutter and rabbit catcher,
1930s. George Garland
photographed working people
and places in Petworth and the
Arun valley over fifty years.

Henry Doick with his sons Percy and Tom on Barge No. 64,
below Pulborough Bridge, c.1898. John Doick, bargeman of the
previous generation, spoke at the 'Arundel Roads' court case in 1851.

TOP George Smith of Chichester, *Landscape*, 1763.
Familiar places and delighted fantasies converge.

BOTTOM The writers Charlotte Smith and William Cowper,
drawn by George Romney at Eartham, 1792.

'Away to Sweet Felpham,
for Heaven is there; / The
Ladder of Angels descends
thro' the air.'
Jacob's Ladder by William
Blake, c.1799–1806.

John Constable's last painting: *Arundel Mill and Castle*, 1837.

LEFT Ivon Hitchens, *September Trees and Pond by House*, 1956.

BELOW Ivon Hitchens, *John by Jordan*, 1942.

BELOW LEFT Ivon Hitchens' studio at Greenleaves, built 1941–2.

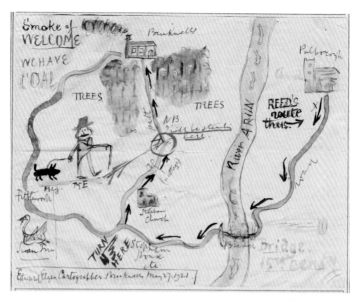

'I will be standing here': Edward Elgar's map of the route from Pulborough through Stopham to Bedham, 1921.

Adam and Eve bathing, from the early-twelfth-century fresco cycle at Hardham.

Accounts given by enslaved people themselves were arriving in book-shops, especially after 1831 when two influential volumes appeared. It was possible to read the description of Cane Grove estate on St Vincent given by Ashton Warner, an escaped former slave. He detailed the daily routine for field-gang workers, who must be up each day at four in the morning to walk the three or four miles to the cane field in time for the enforced start time. 'Before five o'clock the overseer calls over the roll; and if any of the slaves are so unfortunate as to be too late, even by a few minutes . . . the driver flogs them as they come in, with the cart-whip, or with a scourge of tamarind rods.' His wife Sally had been late and flogged in this way when pregnant with his child, and flogged again when she had a baby in arms who needed feeding. Ashton Warner es-caped to Grenada and came to England in 1830, still fraught with grief at leaving his wife and child under the tyranny of their master.[23] Mary Prince came to England in 1828 from Antigua, still enslaved, and told a version of her story, mediated by the Anti-Slavery Society. She looked around her at a nation attached to its own ideas of liberty. 'Since I have been here I have often wondered how English people can go out into the West Indies and act in such a beastly manner. But when they go . . . they forget God and all feeling of shame.'[24]

A new Governor of Barbados was appointed to oversee the island's transition from slavery to 'apprenticeship' from 1833, charged with im-plementing the government's agreed scheme in which all adults were 'freed' but bound to continue working for their former masters for six years, receiving basic board and minimal payment. The man who took on the task was Lionel Smith, son of Charlotte, cousin of the Sutton rector. Life had taken him from early days at Bignor Park in the Sussex hills, and the Brighton book-room where his mother hosted emigrants, via a twenty-year career in India, to Barbados. He knew a good deal about where he was going, his father having spent time there, his older brother Charles having died of yellow fever in Barbados years before. His job now was to enact emancipation but he had to keep the trust of the planters who so constrained what could be done. He had also to convince the enslaved population that he was working in their interests. All sides had reason to watch very closely the balancing acts of diplomacy that he undertook. The apprenticeship scheme could satisfy neither the enslaved nor the abolitionists, and would be dissolved in 1838, by which time Lionel Smith was Governor of Jamaica and able to read the Proclamation of Freedom to gathered crowds in Spanish Town.[25]

Many struggles lay ahead in the mill yards and fields of the West Indies. In Britain these places ceased to be at the forefront of debates that galvanised people in local and national ways. Former slave-holders put in their claims for government compensation, and gradually the lawyers and administrators got through the paperwork. Reverend Smith was among those who claimed for lost property and lost income. Plenty of others in the area did the same, as revealed in the twenty-first century by the painstaking work of researchers on the Legacies of British Slavery project.[26] The largest concentration of Sussex claimants was, not surprisingly, in the coastal metropolis of Brighton, with some major claims also coming from Worthing and Bognor.

The Chichester area was well represented. Some claims were small, notably those of widows and spinsters. This was a pattern repeated across the country. Theodora and Elizabeth Duer were sisters, both single women living in Chichester. For most of their adult lives they had received an annuity of £50 from the Duer plantations in Antigua. In a society that made it extremely difficult for genteel women to earn incomes of their own, they were dependent on this income without having control over the investments that produced it. They made a compensation claim and were awarded £3,306. Many times this sum was paid to the slave-holder Charles Rose Ellis, whose estate the painter Hakewill had made so reassuringly European. By the time of the settlement Ellis was living outside Chichester, at Woodend, the house where his wife had grown up, a big cottage orné under the downs with thatched roofs sloping over gable windows. Compensation went to the owners of other large local properties: Barnham Court, Funtington House (where James Douglass had lived and perhaps also his servant Charles Herring). Reverend William Holland, vicar of two central-Chichester parishes and probably resident in one of the houses in Vicars' Close where Collins lived in his last years, claimed for his holdings in Jamaica.

At Sutton rectory, the payout Smith received in 1836 was comparatively modest: a half-share of £1,259. Six hundred and thirty pounds. The price of 210 gelding mules in Sussex, or 62 enslaved people in the sugar fields of Barbados.[27]

20. NEW SOUTH DOWNS
Australian pastures

February 1829: The flock of Southdown ewes coming through the streets of Chichester was bound for Portsmouth, it was said, and then for the colony at Swan River. The *Calista* was due to sail within the week. The sheep were moving slowly, their bellies swollen wide with lambs. People looked out from shops and parlour windows. There were carts of hay, and wagons piled high with trunks and tools. A few of the people in the midst of it were pointed out as the emigrants. Later the newspaper confirmed it. 'Two families of emigrants from the interior of Sussex, all destined for the new settlement on Swan River.'[1] Swan River in Western Australia, where the swans, apparently, were black. The journey there would be at least five months. The lambing would take place at sea.

May 1829: Another month, another sailing. Farewells were said in Sullington. Indenture contracts had been agreed and twenty-three people were leaving the parish, their futures in the hands of a Colonel Latour from Bedford, who was trying his luck with a land grant at Swan River, the site to be chosen by his agent on arrival. They would serve him for seven years in exchange for basic board and lodging – and their passage across the world on the *Lotus*, sailing soon for Fremantle. It was a bid for a future, anyhow; it was a way of never seeing again the inside of the Union Workhouse.

Richard Haines had stood in Sullington and envisaged 'the prevention of poverty'; in his new poor houses, industrious labourers would earn their way to independence. Now, in the same place, hopes of improvement had run dry. They were going: William and Louisa Woods with four children under ten; the young single workers, William Grover and Charles Henshaw. Nineteen-year-old Richard Gallop and his younger brothers James and Edward all said goodbye to their father. If Australia was good, they agreed, the boys should send word and the rest of the family would try to join them.[2]

The sight of whole families leaving for the other side of the globe was still novel in western Sussex. Over the next ten years it would become a commonplace as a great tide of movement took rural working people to the British colonies. Convicts had been forcibly transported to penal camps in New South Wales since 1788 and in Van Diemen's Land for the last twenty-five years; and it went on: the jail ships setting out, carrying men like Robert Smith of Sutton, most of whom had been convicted of fairly minor crimes. But in the late 1820s and 30s, tens of thousands of citizens chose to leave Britain and try a life elsewhere – in the British province of Upper Canada, where surveyors were moving rapidly west and north, mapping the country available for settlers, ruling grid-lines through the forests and marshes grazed by the moose. Or in the southern hemisphere. The first free colony in New South Wales was advertised as open for settlers in 1829, with the British government promising good land. The farming families who saw the adverts had known years of narrowing profits. Among their workers, poverty was worsening at a disturbing pace. It was becoming impossible for a labourer to make enough to adequately feed a family. The villages of Sussex were increasingly populated by people who felt they had little to lose. If an emigrating employer were to offer work abroad, they might well go. If farmers had the courage and the capital to try a pioneering venture, they might justifiably start planning the move.

June 1829: The *Caroline* anchored in deep water six miles off Littlehampton and waited for the livestock to be loaded. Nose to tail, one hundred and fifty merinos crossed from the harbour boat onto the ship, all newly shorn and wrapped in flannel rugs made for the purpose of seeing them safely from England to Australia. The Henty family, Sussex farmers for generations, was on the move.[3]

Huge land grants were being offered at Swan River and would not be available for long. The Hentys of West Tarring had calculated that they could muster capital between them for eighty thousand acres. The money came from their banking business as well as the farm. Henty, Henty and Hopkins was doing well as a regional bank: head office in Worthing, a long-standing branch in Arundel and another just opened in Steyning. They must keep all this going, while considering the family's prospects as farmers. The Henty merino flock was famous, bred from the sheep given to George III by the King of Spain and expertly managed since then, but it was harder each year to pay the wages and troubling to see the poor in the parish getting poorer. The Hentys were big local employers but they were not especially wealthy people; their finances had been getting tighter for a decade. They had looked out over their Sussex pastures and doubled them, and doubled them again – four-fold, eight-fold. Eighty thousand.

The Hentys made their arrangements with utmost care. Thomas and Frances were to stay at Church Farm for the moment. Their eldest son, James, and two siblings were going first, taking with them a big group of local people, most indentured to serve the Hentys for five years: shepherds, stockmen, carpenters, their wives and children. The Hills family, the Sandfords, George Goble the gunsmith, the Chippers and Bushbys. They would be the pioneers. They would seek out the best land for merinos and secure their grant.

Friends and curious neighbours crowded into Littlehampton, at the mouth of the Arun, to see the great departure. Some were taking notes. It might be their turn next. Several were rowed out to the ship to see how the livestock and supplies were arranged on board. They had seen the advertisements for emigration, they had read reports from the new colony, and here was the real thing: a whole farm and its community embarking.[4] The bailiffs took a long time with the customs paperwork but at last clearance was given and the *Caroline* was ready to sail.

Relatives watched from boats as the ship moved away. The decks were piled high with fodder so that from a distance the whole vessel had the appearance of a floating haystack. Half a parish and a whole way of Sussex life was packed tight within and under it: cows and a bull, carthorses, five thoroughbreds brought from Lord Egremont's Petworth stud, pigs, rabbits, dogs, hens, plants, seeds, the precious merinos that might within a few years – if all went well – produce a vast flock grazing the downs of Western Australia. The ark of Tarring grew smaller, and disappeared.

July 1829: One night on deck in the tropics, Charles Gee, carpenter, started up a song. He took the rhythm of old Sussex shearing ballads and came up with new words.

> Now all you I leaves in England, I hope you may do well
> But allow me for one moment your fortune for to tell
> You must unto your Parish go to get small relief
> Where you will be flounced and bounced as if you were a thief.

He had lived in Arundel until this journey and was glad to be away. The party sang the chorus over and over in the moonlight:

> . . . Come join along with Henty and all his joyful crew
> For a set of better fellows in this world you never knew.[5]

November 1829: It was 106 degrees and the air was droning with mosquitoes. 'I am at present much disappointed in the appearance of the Country no good land is to be met with for 20 miles.'[6] On the sandy soil, there was little for the sheep to graze. The flock was in 'dreadful condition' after the journey, needing expert care from the shepherds James Henty had brought over from Sussex.[7] He might need to try the Van Diemen's Land colony instead, though he was not giving up on Swan River just yet. 'The country improves on closer inspection. Some of the land on the Swan is really beautiful.' For the moment he had taken a small grant in the best spot he could find. Shortly afterwards he swapped this for land upriver, about twenty miles inland from the newly founded town of Fremantle. He liked this plot better and gave it a Sussex name: Stoke Farm.[8] James had made meticulous plans for keeping his servants supplied until food could be grown, and he saw immediately how crucial this was. Colonel Latour's servants, meanwhile, were being given little but rice. Water supplies were a problem and typhus was spreading. Pressed together in small tents, lacking any other accommodation, the Sullington families were considering how to survive.

February 1830: James invested in shipments of items that would sell for a good price in the colony. Pedigree sheep were not much good here, but so many other things were wanted. Whaleboats. Shrimp nets. Huge quantities of rum. Shoes – there was no one supplying shoes. No, don't send candles through the Cape: they *melt*. But clocks would be valuable. Everybody's watches had stopped. How were pioneers meant to tell the time?[9] Customs officers at the docksides in London, the Cape and Swan River counted in and counted out the freight for Mr Henty. Coopers opened and resealed the cargo that came in wooden kegs, barrels, casks, chests, cases, baskets, boxes.

March 1830: As the summer heat dropped a little, and dysentery abated, James joined surveyors and the governor on a schooner heading south along the coast. If there was better land there, he wanted to claim it before Latour got his application in. Anchored off Cape Naturaliste he felt a flicker of recognition. This high land, he wrote, 'forms I think one end abutting into the Sea of what has hitherto been called Darlings Range, like the Downs at Brighton'.[10] They went ashore where 'plenty of natives' made them welcome and walked with them.

The people who greeted the visitors with such friendship were Nyungars. Their communities had been following the waterways and valleys of this area not just for generations but for millennia. Their patterns of seasonal movement are now thought to have been established for upwards of forty thousand years. Nyungars and Europeans walked together upriver and into the hills, the indigenous hunters knowing each creek and slope, the man from West Tarring trying to get his bearings. 'The Range is in fact not unlike our South Downs when viewed from below Birtl[e]y, although the Geological formation of them is wholly different, being composed instead of Chalk of hard Granite.'[11] The schooner turned back to Port Leschenault and a surveying party went by boat up the Collie. At last, in the 'rich & good' valleys, and on the 'fair upland' wooded with wild pear, James felt some cause for hope. He put his faith in the place, though he had known it for only a few days. After Easter, he registered a grant of 69,000 acres and began to move over his labourers and sheep.[12]

March 1831: James was getting impatient with his parents. Did they not *think* before they packed books and letters in a trunk together with pickles? Why was his mother sending homemade pickles anyway? Preserves kept in a Sussex larder were one thing, but you couldn't expect them to last through the tropics. 'They fermented, blew the corks out, and spoilt everything', he reported, with never a trace of sentiment. The pickles had exploded all over the letters. Now he couldn't read any of the messages and didn't know when the family planned to come over.[13]

April 1831: The decision was made. The first months on the Collie had not gone well. 'I have deceived myself too long', he told his brother.[14] He must try Van Diemen's Land. It might take him six months to sell off all his trading stock, but as soon as possible he would move. He wouldn't take all the servants with him though. The men with large families were too expensive to keep on. Charles Gee was restless and wanting his independence anyway. The Gees and a few others would stay at Swan River and find new employment.

Early May 1831: Louisa Charman and her brothers wrote home to Sussex with an update. They were all much happier and better off without being indentured to the colonel and they were finding work on their own. The settlement at Fremantle was 'young as yet, but it is now as large as Storrington, and vessels keep coming in every week from all places'. Apart from the fleas, the animals weren't hurting anyone. 'There is kangaroos all the same as deer in the park.' Louisa probably had the Parham deer in mind. The 'natives comes down to Fremantle every day for food to eat'.[15] She did not understand how the expanding colony, even if only the size of Storrington, had already separated the local clans of Whadjuk people from their established hunting grounds and fisheries.[16]

Late May 1831: Charlotte Carter from Worthing had arrived – to James' surprise – on the *Atwick*, and now they were married. 'She is quite well and cheerfully submits to the discomforts our little colony entails upon us.'[17] James could think more happily about the future. Reports from Van Diemen's Land were good: 'the settlers there are in the highest spirits with the result of the last year's sale of wool'. The Sussex Hentys should join them at Launceston. Even Charles, the only brother showing no interest in emigrating, should stop wasting his time in Arundel, James scoffed, and come south to make something of himself.

September 1831: Thomas had applied for government permission to exchange the Henty acres in Western Australia for a grant in Van Diemen's Land. They were still waiting to hear, but either way Thomas would take the rest of the family out to join his pioneer sons. The old West Tarring house next to the church, with its dormers in the steep roof, its familiar flint garden walls, was to be given up at Michaelmas. Its contents would be auctioned, along with all the property on the farm. Mr Lassetter, the Worthing auctioneer, would run the sale over three days on the premises.

300 volumes of books
Blue and white china

Washing, brewing and dairy utensils
About 50 elm trees
2 bay saddle mares, 1 useful cob and pony chaise . . . 100 pure
merino ewes, and 30 very superior merino rams
Iron and other water troughs, oak cribs, wattles, ladders . . .[18]

The Henty family home in West Tarring, by James Rouse, 1822

October 1832: Thomas Gallop went to the baker in Storrington and
dictated a letter to his sons, to be carried on the ship *Isabella*. 'If you do
not like it come home', he said. 'I should be glad to have you all here.'
Their 'broken down colonel', he had heard, was in the King's Bench
Prison. Were they finding their way on their own? He advised them not
to 'interrupt' the indigenous people. 'Recollect that you are intruders in
their country.' Thomas listed their dates of birth – useful information
for free settlers.[19]

April 1833: The Hentys were established in Launceston, trading, banking, training racehorses from Petworth. Even the most reluctant brother,
Charles, had left his office in the bank at Arundel for the last time, and was
now organising the Australasian arm of the Henty financial business. But
the dream that had brought the family across the world was of land, of
wide-open sheep runs, of well-fed shepherds and stockmen. The younger

brothers, Edward and Francis, followed every chance that might lead
there. Across great distances, back and forth over the Bass Strait to the
Australian coast opposite, they went in pursuit of places as yet unmapped
in which to make their lives as agriculturalists. Edward dug a piece of turf
from hills above the coast of New South Wales and carried it back to his
father, believing he might have found the place for the family to farm. A
square of turf, a pot of soil: father and son looked and looked.

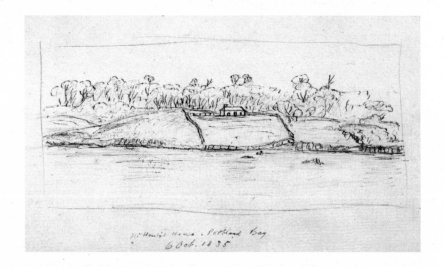

December 1834: Edward had brought the first materials for a settlement
over to Portland Bay and was getting a wood-framed cabin fixed up as
well as huts for shepherds. This new colony had no official licence yet
but it was ready for the merinos. Before Christmas, Edward set off to
see more of the land around him. He was imagining the stock on these
pastures. 'Sheep or cattle's sides would soon shake with fat with a taste
of the grass here.' Climbing a particularly tall gum tree he took in a view
over 'open hills and *very* extensive marshes'.[20]

As they explored further inland, past what they called the North
Downs, Edward and Francis found more rich pasture. But because it
put them so far from established colonies, their applications to settle
this land were repeatedly refused. The negotiations and representations

would go on for years, James negotiating in London on the family's behalf. Determinedly, they pressed on as squatters, encouraged by hints that they might eventually be deemed by the colonial office to be rightful occupants.

Edward Henty's telescope

September 1837: Five Henty brothers, all together, were riding inland and they knew where they were going. They had been told about beautiful country seventy miles from Portland, in the valley of the Wannon river. Stephen had been ahead to see it. The others had brought supplies across from Launceston on the family schooner *The Thistle* that had carried them so many thousands of miles. James had brought his little son with him: a boy just one year old. They wanted him to see with his own young eyes a land for future Hentys.

As an old man visiting England, the little boy would tell the story. After days cutting through woods, they emerged into the country that had been described to them. His father and uncles galloped their horses for joy and threw their caps into the air. 'Here is Sussex', they said. 'Sussex without inhabitants, Sussex all our own.' They rode over wooded and grassy plains, and then suddenly they were at a height, with a view, like the heights and views they knew on the high chalkland above Worthing. It was 'as if you all at once found yourself at the summit of High Down Hill'. They called the place Merino Downs.[21]

Afterwards: The expanses of country occupied by the Hentys – from the high sheep runs and the Wannon Valley to stretches of the coast around Portland – were, as they understood it, in the gift of the British government. But they met daily the people who had other and prior claims to these coasts and hills. The Hentys didn't call it a war in their letters, but on the ground they were fighting a sporadic battle of conquest against Gunditjmara clans driven to defend themselves and the lands they had always known.

The place where they first pitched their tents in 1837 remained the centre of the Henty enterprise in New South Wales. Francis and his wife Mary Ann lived, farmed and bred sheep at Merino Downs for the rest of their lives, replacing their first sod hut with a timber-framed house in the 1840s, cultivating a garden (native gum trees along the driveway; hedges of English hawthorn at the boundaries), and bringing up their children.[22]

The former servants who remained at Swan River met with widely varying fortunes. Charles Gee had sung heartily on the voyage out of the plentiful provisions that awaited, but he couldn't make enough as a carpenter and needed state support. By 1838 he was in court for theft and sentenced to the prison on Rottnest Island, off Fremantle. By the same time, the Gallops from Sullington were managers of a large farm. They heard from home that their father was sick and being ordered into the workhouse. They were able to send enough money for their sister to emigrate and advised her what to bring.[23]

In the 1930s a discovery was made in an Australian garden. A stone bowl was found to be an old church font, and it was identified as the font from Tarring in Sussex. The local paper in Portland carried the story and photographs were taken of the battered-looking relic, which had been outside through many seasons. The pedestal was deeply cracked; the octagonal bowl was grown over with lichens and filled with earth for use as a planter.[24] This was the medieval sandstone font to which Thomas and Frances brought their children to be baptised at Tarring in the first years of the nineteenth century. It had been removed from Tarring, transported to the docks, and shipped across the world.

It seems to have been James Henty's sons Thomas and Henry who arranged the move in 1882. More than fifty years after their departure, the family retained a close sense of connection to the village and the church, arranging for James to be commemorated there with a memorial window and sponsoring an elaborate scheme of mosaic decoration by William Butterfield. Thomas spent time in Tarring, and while there he saw the old font bowl in the rectory garden. It had been displaced from St Andrew's, probably during the thorough-going 1853 refurbishment that rendered eroded medieval fittings surplus to requirements. The original medieval base was left intact in the church and a new font constructed above it in Caen stone with gleaming Purbeck marble shafts. But outside, in the garden, lay the ancient octagonal bowl. Thomas Henty asked for the gift of it. He arranged for its transport to Melbourne. It was a token of old Sussex faith and family setting out to a young city.[25]

Among the family photographs are many pictures of Henty life at Merino Downs. For instance the one in which Francis and Mary Ann's three daughters are playing croquet in the garden in 1870. One woman is preparing for her next swing of the mallet; her sisters are perched on the post-and-rail fence. They face the camera and the croquet lawn in the enclosed garden. But when they turn they'll be looking into the huge view that opens beyond the eucalyptus tree, where the land drops away to the wide waters of Henty Creek. The downs rise on the far side of the river, and in the big open sky above, cockatoos are flying.[26]

21. THE FAT OF THE LAND
From Sussex to Canada

At Felpham the white windmill by the sea was turned into the breeze. Summer visitors to Bognor, seeking a change from the hotel and the pleasure grounds, could walk there along the field path. Mr Dally's 1828 *Bognor Guide*, packed with antiquarian investigations and suggested excursions, warned that the stiles were an impediment to ladies but described the rewards of this short ramble. 'On the left, a rich inland country, dotted with farmhouses and cottages, bounded by the downs, the intervening space pleasing to the eye with its rich and variegated hues.' Dally, a local solicitor, loved the 'wide spreading trees', the quiet cattle, 'the distant murmurs of the tide', the waving corn that was the product of Felpham's 'peculiarly rich' soil. It was a vision of tranquillity expressed by an attentive resident who had searched many sources to supply the place with a history. He listed plants to look out for (sea spinach, sea crane's bill, golden samphire) on the foreshore and marshes.[1]

But there was trouble in the view not immediately apparent to the eye of the rambler. In April 1832 eight adults and twelve children took their last look at Felpham before setting off for Portsmouth, where they would board a ship for Canada. In May, twenty-five left from the neighbouring parish of South Bersted. Three years later, a further forty-four people from Felpham followed. At Cocking, under the scarp, where chalk springs run into streams and pools, ten people said their goodbyes in 1836. Then sixteen left neighbouring Heyshott. Like the Swan River emigrants from Sullington and Tarring, they were leaving everything they knew for places they could barely visualise, but now they were not going in fives and tens but in hundreds. Over a few years in the mid-1830s, nearly sixteen hundred people from western Sussex left behind everything that was familiar, and joined ships bound for the British province of Upper Canada.[2] It meant that in the villages around Petworth and down through the Arun valley, emigration became part of everybody's life. If you weren't thinking of going, you probably knew someone who was. The intensely known network of parish lanes and fields was now contrasted in imagination with a much wider world.

Canada was already home to thousands of Scottish and Irish immigrants, as well as loyalists who had gone north to British-held land after the American Revolution. The policy of Governor John Colborne was to welcome as many British and Irish settlers as would come. They came: in just the three years 1829–31, 62,000 arrived at the Port of Quebec from Ireland, 10,500 from Scotland and 21,000 from England and Wales.[3] But many of these people were arriving penniless, vulnerable to disease, lacking the boat fare to get them up the St Lawrence, let alone build farms from scratch. Colborne saw that future migrants must have financial and practical assistance if they were not to die of cholera in the shanties expanding outward from the docksides at Quebec and Montreal, or die of starvation in the wilderness before they could harvest a crop. He greeted the plans of the Petworth Emigration Committee with interest.[4]

Lord Egremont of Petworth was proposing to pay the costs of any labourers on his estates who wished to go. He would subsidise anyone from the parishes in which he held lands, if parish poor relief committees made significant contributions too. The project was organised by Thomas Sockett, the vicar of Petworth and Egremont's right-hand man in many ambitious enterprises. Sockett's energetic work towards the alleviation of rural poverty may have owed some of its conviction to his own narrow escape from cottage poverty as a boy in the 1790s.[5] Like most tax-payers in Sussex he was also motivated by the huge sums he was paying out in poor relief: 'these labourers have eaten me up'. By the 1830s he believed that emigration offered the best prospects for those who had no adequate livelihood in England. Liaising with MPs and Colonial Office staff, winning round gentry and farmers, he pushed through a large-scale plan offering assisted emigration to local people. When he advertised for takers in April 1832, the responses were so numerous that he had to charter a second ship.

Twenty-eight: Richard Neal from Sutton, bricklayer.
Twenty-nine: Edward and Catharine Boxall from Coldwaltham.
Thirty-one: James and Avis Napper from Pulborough with three children.
Thirty-six: Martin and Fanny Martin from Felpham with six children.
Forty-four: George and Ann Hills from Sullington with six children.
Fifty-two: John Luff, fifteen years old, an orphan roadmender from Bury.[6]

George Hills wrote home in August 1832. 'Dear father and mother, we left you almost broken-hearted, but you may be satisfied that we have bettered our condition by coming here.' After the long journey upriver (the boat pulled through the rapids in places by ten yoke of oxen), they had stopped in Ancaster and were settling in. George was full of relief at being able, at last, to earn an adequate wage, 'but my wife don't seem to be quite so well contented yet'. They had found a job for their ten-year-old son, also George, working with a saddler from Horsham. (I think about that boy of ten who knew Sullington Warren as I did too when I was ten, tripping on tree-roots rising through the sand, pausing on the ridge of the heath.) 'We have all had the fever ague', wrote Elias Elliott from Fort George on the Niagara in September, five months after departure from Sutton. After what sound like appalling difficulties, he was rallying. 'I am getting quite right again and I feel happy that I ever took the resolution to leave my native home.'[7]

Martin Martin had spent several years as landlord at the Fox in Felpham after the departure of William Blake and the Grinder family, but he couldn't make enough to support his wife Fanny and the children – four girls and two boys. By September 1832 he was working as a joiner in Guelph and sounding confident. When he wrote back to friends in Felpham, he was buoyant about everything, from Montreal ('very fast improving') to Hamilton ('flourishing'), and his own prospects of buying land. After his years behind the bar at the Fox he can't have been easily shocked on the subject of drink, but he was certainly impressed by the consumption of whiskey at logging parties: he reckoned five gallons was about standard for an afternoon. It was a business letter, and pioneering was a man's subject: was that why he said 'I' instead of 'we' and never mentioned Fanny or the children? Perhaps there was another reason lost in time.[8]

The emigrants were encouraged to describe their new lives in letters sent back to England, dictating messages if they could not write themselves. They knew these reports of their progress, or otherwise, would be passed from house to house and perhaps even printed.[9] Little wonder the writing tends to be formal and factual, and not to dwell on troubles. The letters are, all the same, as the editors of a revelatory modern edition say, 'a remarkable source for a class of people who left few written records'.[10]

All the time I had been going through wills and inventories and court records, I had hoped for clues as to how working people inhabited their places and looked at their surroundings. Always the outward facts swarmed in the midst of great silences. Then I found the emigrant letters and read them in astonishment. Here were men and women describing the country around them. But it was a different country altogether. I had been hoping to understand a bit about what working-class people made of the places in which I grew up. Instead, I heard them describing the St Lawrence river and the forests of Ontario. There was the shock of confronting what I had known without really grasping it: the desperate poverty that disfigured the lives of working people in these Sussex villages. Then there was the effort to imagine what Canada looked and felt like to those who had known only a few parishes around Petworth. Their responses to the 'new country' revealed much about what had mattered to them in the old, so that I found myself reading backwards from pioneer townships more than three thousand miles away to life in the places left behind.

⁓

Rotund and flushed after an Easter lunch provided by my great-aunt and -uncle in their warm, low, firelit, picture-hung Sutton cottage, I wandered up the village lane thinking of those who had left many Easters ago. George Carver, Joseph Leggett, Elias Elliott, Richard Neal. These were people whose families had lived in the village for as long as anyone knew. (John Legatt of Sutton was defending himself in 1646 for felling Petworth trees; those who stood as surety for him at the Quarter Sessions were his Sutton neighbour Richard Carver and his brother Joseph Legatt.) The Leggetts and Carvers of the 1830s went away to start again.[11] At Niagara, Elias Elliott crammed onto his sheet what he wanted them to know back home: he was well, and Joseph was well, and he wished to be remembered to the Charmans, and to James Francis and Mary White.

Richard Neal, a builder, was not so happy at Dundas on Lake Ontario. 'I do not like this country so well as England', he admitted. His reasons are hard to interpret. 'The men are not so strong as they are in England, nor the meat is not so good, but very cheap.' He took solace in the thought of return. 'I can come back when I like, if it pleases God.'[12] It was a useful thing to tell himself. He stayed on, and his skills as a bricklayer were much in demand as pioneer settlements grew into cities. Neal's Flemish-bond brickwork is apparently still to be seen in buildings around Dundas.[13] There's plenty of Flemish bond in Sutton now I look for it, though I've no idea whether Neal built any of the houses or barns along the lane. He would have known the White Horse, at the corner where the road forks off to Bignor. It has brick dressings around its sashes, a modillion cornice, and tiny gallets of ironstone pushed, decoratively and usefully, into the mortar around every block. Dot dot dot, like stitching or beading. As I stood looking, a roar of laughter came through the open windows.

I crossed the meadow dropping steeply down to the chalk stream and up to Bignor. The Elliotts and Leggetts knew this as Greenfield, farmed in strips on the open-field system. Mill Copse opposite was carefully managed for coppicing. In Bignor they knew the fifteenth-century house that stands prominently on a bend with its patchwork bays of herringbone brick and flintwork. They knew the path over to 'Pavement Field' on the hillside where Roman mosaics had been discovered during ploughing in 1811. They knew the thatched buildings like large cottages that still shelter Medusa riding on a dolphin, gladiators wielding tridents, a bleak figure of winter holding a single bare branch.

In the autumn of 1832 Mr and Mrs Scutt of Bignor heard news of their daughter. The letter came from her husband Thomas. 'We are in a land of disappointment.' Sarah and her baby Harriet had been very ill on the journey upriver from York. They had died within a few days of each other; scarlet fever, the doctor said. Thomas had given their two-year-old daughter, a motherless toddler, to 'a gentleman by the name of Chapman, a carpenter'. He said nothing of how he was himself – only that he had work, and whiskey.[14]

The Scutts watched as other families in the village received news of sons and daughters overcoming initial hardships and establishing themselves. James and Sarah Carver heard from their son George, who was in London near Lake Erie and sounded pleased. He had taken a hundred acres, but was biding his time before starting to clear them, saving up the high wages he could earn as an employee. He felt more respected as a labouring man in Canada than he had ever been in Sussex. 'The servant is made equal with his master', he wrote. Employers in Ontario, he found, 'will not get their servants . . . to sit down at a second table to eat their crumbs'.[15] When he settled in Delaware, he wrote again on the same theme, glad not to have farmers 'blustering and swearing' over him, glad to be living on his own terms.[16] His anger at the social order in his native country flared out from his letters. He had found a place where things were done differently, and it deepened his rage at the injustices that had driven him away.

How had it got so bad in England that a young man like George Carver felt compelled to leave? Agricultural labourers had always lived precariously. Every record of the Manor Courts and Quarter Sessions shows that working people were sometimes driven, by desperation, to take dire risks in order to bring home a rabbit or a little firewood. Open the Quarter Sessions rolls at any page, say April 1821: a succession of Amberley labourers charged with stealing bundles of wood; two months' solitary confinement for a Singleton labourer (his sight gone in one eye) who stole clover hulls worth two pence.[17] What happened in the 1820s and 30s was the worsening of already strained circumstances. The surge of continental trade after the wars with France brought in over-supplies of wheat that pushed down the price of home-grown crops, on top of which a run of disappointing harvests made it hard to compete. And there were more fundamental changes. The new agricultural machinery, especially for threshing, reduced the human labour required for arable so that hands were laid off at farm after farm.

The practice of many centuries in Sussex had been for workers, particularly unmarried men, to live with their employers. Their remuneration came largely in the form of board and lodging.[18] Though rife with its own difficulties, this arrangement gave labourers stable places within the community of the farm. Eating at the same table, responding together to the demands of life indoors and out, the different classes were closely knitted. As the value of labour started to fall, the commitment of farmers to their live-in employees faltered. They took on day-labourers as needed. The trajectory was from year-round interdependence under the same roof to a gig economy without even the advantages of choosing one's hours: when there was work available, you did it. On the farms of the South Downs 'living in' persisted, but changes were widely noticed.[19] What George Carver complained of was a symptom of the widening gap between farmers and workmen. He had clearly been fed under the same roof as his employers, but he sat at a 'second table', feeling inferior and disregarded. The farmhouse kitchen was not for him a scene of warmth and reward after a day's exertions.

Lord Egremont offered charity to the poor around Petworth, for instance an annual 'Bounty of Clothes' given to those deemed most in need. The Leggetts and Carvers of Sutton were sometimes given 'bounty' and sometimes not; these were not bountiful times. In any case, no one wanted to be dependent on handouts. The south was particularly hard hit by unemployment, there being so little industry or urban work available in a country dominated by agricultural estates, and it was in the south that protest took hold. The Swing Riots began in August 1830 with the burning of threshing machines in Kent. It was the time of harvest-home, but celebrations that year were strained. In market squares and on country roads, workers gathered to demand fairer wages, year-round work and better conditions. In mid-November, following what appeared to be the peaceful disbanding of an angry crowd near Goodwood, fires burnt in the countryside around Chichester. Hayricks went up in flames and threshing machines were smashed.[20] In the harbour village of Bosham, while the marble head of a remote emperor lay silent, rioters hammered at doors, demanding money, beer, hammers, candles.[21] There were stories of men pulled from their beds and coerced into joining the gangs. 'I was compelled to follow the party or have my brains knocked out', one labourer recounted.[22] Others joined out of deep grievance and desperation. Police back-up was called in from London as groups gathered to march on Arundel; every man in the crowd knew that he could hang for the company he kept that day. Some were indeed taken to the gibbet, though most convicted Swing rioters were sentenced to hard labour, or transportation. A number of them followed Robert Smith of Sutton to the penal colonies of New South Wales.[23]

The tensions warned of a rural society at breaking point, but the reforms arriving from Westminster offered little relief to those who were living from hiring fair to hiring fair. Under the Poor Law Amendment Act, there was no child allowance or relief for able-bodied adults except those actually resident in the poorhouses, which were now emphatically termed workhouses and regarded with unmitigated dread.[24] There were many sides to the arguments that rebounded from government offices to the vestries where worried parish councils met. Sockett and Egremont in Petworth were both disturbed by the stringent enforcement of the new regime. They pushed hard for the parish funding that would buy new lives for Sussex labourers abroad.

⁓

I walked the few miles from Pulborough station over to Nutbourne, past the Rising Sun, past a school-friend's house, past the turn to the vineyard on the greensand ridge with the whole valley opening below. Lower Nash Farm, Upper Nash House: in the sunlit lane I stood looking up the driveways. Stephen Goatcher and his wife Elizabeth Burchill lived here in the early nineteenth century, in a farmhouse that no longer exists, though a thatched cottage, stables and cart shed remain. They were reasonably prosperous people, the kind of farmers who had work to offer labourers; but they saw the poor relief taxes narrowing their profits. Goatcher, who was drafted in as a special constable during the riots, knew that all was not well in rural Britain.

When he was invited by Sockett to sail on an emigrant boat as an overseer, Goatcher agreed. He was to travel on the *Eveline*, one of the two ships chartered in April 1832; his job was to see two hundred and fifty emigrants safely across the Atlantic, help them find employment, and report back to the Emigration Committee. As to his own future, he wasn't sure: he was going to try setting up in Canada. Elizabeth was staying behind to manage Nash Farm with her brother William. Did she imagine she would follow later, or was she glad, now, of some limited independence?

A letter came in the late summer, dated 6 July. 'Dear Wife,' she read. Stephen had seen Niagara Falls, 'the most wonderful sight that ever my eyes beheld', and the governor had received him royally at York (which would later be Toronto). The wheat looked good, and he was intending to buy land. He could see already that no one in Canada would want to work on the roads 'as they do in your country', since there was good farm work for all. 'Your country': he was distancing himself.[25] By January he had cleared fourteen acres and set up a dairy. He was hoping old friends from Pulborough might go and work with him. If they'd bring out a malt mill they would grow barley together. There were Sussex people around him, but he missed those at home. Dear Wife: 'remember me to Mr Challen, Comper, Jupp, Clement, Parry, brothers, and sisters, tell them I should be glad to smoke a pipe with them'.[26]

At Graffham, to the west of Petworth over Lavington Common, Mrs Boxall received a long-awaited letter from her son Edward and his wife Catharine who had gone out on Goatcher's ship. Like other former soldiers who had served in the Napoleonic wars, Edward had been granted a hundred acres of land. They sounded well. 'We can make our own sugar and soap, and starch, and I buy the deer's fat of the Indians, to make my own candles', Catharine said. She was baking her own bread in an iron pot and had found a good way to use the black squirrels in a pudding. Hummingbirds were the most beautiful in the world, she said. There were wolves they could hear in the night.[27]

April, the beginning. 'Thanne do folk longen to go on pilgrimage', wrote Chaucer. The emigrant ships left in April – each April for six years. April, the best time of the year for travelling, in the 1830s as in the 1380s. April, the time for starting over. Leases in England ran from one Lady Day to the next, so anyone moving house would make the change at the end of March, and be ready to sow. For those headed to Canada, spring departures gave the chance of a fair crossing and safe passage up the difficult St Lawrence river. On arrival, at midsummer, there would be harvest work available for them on established farms.

Some people couldn't wait to get away. There were reformers for whom a new society was in reach. There were explorers wanting a look at the world. There were the young and bold. Edward Heming was a man with prospects. He had grown up in Chichester cathedral close, son of a canon there, but he wanted to farm, and knew his money would go further in Canada. He was twenty-two and anxious to build a life for himself. Arriving in Guelph, he bought the best land he could find, and employed Sussex labourers who had all travelled in the same party to help him transform it. He got a crop sown immediately and brought in a first harvest with a breathless flourish: 'I have hardly known which way to turn myself. I have bought 134 more acres of land, with 30 in crop, and a loghouse to put Chase [his servant] into. I have now 367 acres in all.'[28] He would not have done that if he'd stayed with his mother in Bognor.

The very poor had fewer choices. For people breaking deep attachments to their homes, April became a cruel month. If they could not feed their children, they felt they must apply to go. The hedges were budding, currant bushes scented and bright-leaved, a faint haze of green in fields of seedlings coming through, soil softening, and it was just then that the adverts went out: those thinking of departure had three weeks to decide and prepare. It's surprisingly rare to hear anyone wondering whether it might be a safer, less drastic, more reversible step to seek work in the industrial centres of the Midlands and the north. A huge migration was going on within the bounds of Britain, hundreds of thousands moving from rural to urban employment, and yet Sussex labourers and gentry farmers travelled 3,500 miles to Ontario rather than try Birmingham or Derby or Sheffield. For many of these native country people, equipped with rural skills, lakes and woods on the other side of the world felt closer than the manufactories or mining towns of Britain.[29]

They were told very little about the people native to Canada, the people who knew the rhythm of the seasons, the routes between hunting grounds, the power of the river currents in the land they were going to.

They were advised to maintain friendly, business-like relations with the aboriginals working in or trading with the settler townships. Correspondents mentioned Indians who lived among them, selling venison or helping with manual work or delivering the post (all forms of interaction encouraged by the colonial policy of 'amalgamation') but none of the Sussex writers showed awareness of the established ways of life that the farmhand or postman had left behind.[30] They didn't mention the movement of people onto reservations as their traditional lands were surveyed and pegged out for white settlements. 'The Indians are very civil but [do] not love work: they more love hunting', wrote one Petworth man who hadn't grasped that in losing their hunting grounds, his

James Pattison Cockburn, *The Road between Kingston and York*, c.1830

neighbours had lost their work, their livelihood and their sacred plac-es.[31] Between these groups of dislocated people, committed to different kinds of life on the land, there were gulfs in understanding. Occasion-ally there were connections. Thomas Adsett had news of a friend 'now married to an Indian woman, a black': 'she has two hundred acres of land and a grist mill'.[32]

What would spring be like in Canada? Martin Doyle's *Hints to Emi-grants*, which was liberally circulated in Petworth and surrounding parishes, evoked scenes of luscious plenitude. There would be wild pi-geons, and no fines for shooting them; 'everyone may help himself without scruple'. There would be salmon from the lakes for dinner. In summer, at the water's edge, fireflies would glitter, the air bursting into 'atoms of green fire'. Fruits waited plumply for them in Eden: 'melons and grapes growing wild in the woods; peaches, nectarines, plums'.[33] Those were the images to hang on to when steeling oneself to say goodbye. 'Take your fa-ther and your households, and come unto me: and I will give you the good of the land of Egypt, and ye shall eat the fat of the land.' That promise of Genesis was prodded and rolled in the imaginations of people who saw too little fat now that few labourers could afford even a pig in the yard. After two years away, George Carver announced the fulfilment of the dream: 'Here you may live on the fat of the land', he wrote triumphantly to Sutton.[34] But there was no knowing who would make it that far.

Travellers in the backwoods would come upon abandoned cabins in the wilderness, unnamed memorials to settlers who had left, or giv-en up, or died. The governor called them, sadly, 'little monuments of the failure of human expectations'.[35] Tremendous skill was required of immigrants simply to survive on a new plot, eat something every day and go to bed at night. The bed for instance: choose suitable logs, saw planks, measure, shave, plane, craft tight-fitting joints. Doyle's *Hints on Emigration* made it all sound so easy: 'The bark of the bass tree, woven or laced across his bedstead, will support his mattrass, and that mattrass need consist of nothing more expensive than the boughs of the spruce fir, or dry beach leaves; a buffalo skin will answer for quilt and blankets.' He insisted that in a land of abundant natural resources, only laziness or bad planning or drunkenness could explain a family's failure to prosper. 'The desponding have no business [in Canada] where all is energy of mind and body.'[36]

It was the age, and the place, of self-reliance. Expectations were high, observers quick to judge, and it was not surprising, given the rhetoric of success hard-won through tireless industry, that many pioneers waited before writing their first letter. They waited until they had something positive to say, even if that meant months of anxiety for those left behind.[37] The writing was often a communal process, with relatives and neighbours pitching in and the best scribe shaping the sentences. Few thought to unravel their interior lives when what was needed was a group update.[38] Good and bad news was weighed in the scales, strong emotions carefully levelled out. James Rapson, a fluent and vivid writer, filled his page with appealing news about ambitious gardening (cucumbers and melons) before forcing himself to say what must be said. 'I will now tell you who is dead', and he gave a list. The names of Sarah Adsett and her baby came towards the end of a long roll-call. He used an image from his gardening. 'So the Lord hath thinned us out.'[39]

The letters brimmed with other kinds of lists, inventories of new-made lives. There were lists of tools used, seeds sown, foods eaten, catalogues of prices for all necessary goods. 'Here is wild deer and turkeys, pheasants, partridges and rabbits: and anybody may kill them', wrote Edward Boxall.[40] If he saw a rabbit and needed food, he could shoot it: there was no law by which he could be hung for such an act.

Progress on a new homestead was routinely summed up with a stock-taking. It might be a pig, three chickens and hopes of a cow in the spring, or a more extensive tally: Edward Heming reported '1 yoke of cattle, 10 pigs, 1 cow and calf, 1 pony, Neptune and another dog, 1 cat, 30 fowls'.[41] A list could express plenitude or ingenuity, as when the bravura list-makers James and Harriet Cooper from Tillington explained

their success as Canadian gingerbread-makers. They had been struggling with their bakery near Petworth when they heard news from
Ruth Waldon in Canada, who was doing well selling 'sugar goods' as
fast as she could bake them. They travelled out with gingerbread moulds
in their luggage. Within a few years they were itemising what they could
make with the syrupy sap of the abundant maple trees on their Ontario farm: 'sugar, treacle or molasses, beer, cider, vinegar and ink', thirty
gallons of molasses in 1838.[42] Hannah Tilley made another kind of list.
She and her family were doing well in Nelson, but she missed Petworth
and her emotion went into the simple act of naming as she asked to be
remembered to Mr and Mrs Price, and Mrs Burgess and Granny Boxall,
'and indeed all Petworth if I could mention them'; in imagination, she
was going through the streets, round the houses, into the stores, greeting
'Mrs Nevett, the Tailor, and Mrs Bridger at the shop . . . and I could remember fifty more names if time and paper would allow me'.[43]

⌒

When the Sussex Canadians launched into formal 'accounts of the country', they usually began with the soil that would define their farming.
'Black loam', reported Goatcher as he passed through the Ontario backwoods on his way to Kettle Creek; his Pulborough farm was on similarly
fertile soil of greensand and loam. People who had been employed back
home in the aching labour of stone-picking, gathering flints one by one
from ploughed fields that seemed to grow more stones as they worked,
looked in amazement at the smooth earth. 'I have not seen a flint stone
since I have been in Canada', Ruth Waldon told her old friends near
Petworth. There was no need of the heavy nailed shoes worn in flinty
Sussex fields, for 'here is no stones to wear them'.[44]

   The Sussex labourers and their families didn't involve themselves in
the language of literary and artistic landscape appreciation. They didn't
call their log cabins humble cots, or refer to the forests as 'sublime'.

Though they may well have felt combined terror and excitement at travelling into the wilderness, no one among the working-class letter-writers thought it relevant or worthwhile to dwell on those emotions.[45] Nonetheless, a sense of beauty in their surroundings was clearly important to many who went out on the Petworth scheme, whether they perceived it in a strong tree or varied soil, or the clemency of a temperate summer. Or it might be 'a beautiful spring of water like your orchard water at Milton', as Charlotte Willard told her sister near Dorking, its beauty inseparable from its provision of clean, life-sustaining water.[46]

Land was described by what grew in it – and what might grow. James Parker hoped his father in Pulborough would send 'crookhorn' or field peas. 'Bring me a little crop grass seed,' Edward Boxall asked friends he thought might come over, 'swede turnip, and stone turnip seed, mangel wurzel seed, carrot and onion seed and all kinds of working tools'.[47] There were flower gardens among all the vegetables: *Amaranthus* seeds arrived and flowered handsomely in Waterloo Township, their purple plumes or 'prince's feathers' waving as tall and extravagantly as those of their parent plants in Sussex, and indeed their long-ago ancestors in Mexico and Guatemala. Livestock, too, was sent from England. It took time to establish pasture on land where there had never been grass, but by 1835 Edward Heming was ready to receive a consignment of Southdown sheep. They were brought over from the flock at Sullington. They had grazed the slopes above Storrington and now they would graze and fertilise Heming's land near Guelph.

Comparisons had many uses. Martin Martin told friends in Felpham that York was 'quite equal to Chichester' for shopping and seeing tradesmen.[48] The streets of the newly built capital of Upper Canada were overlaid in his mind with the ancient streets leading north, south, east, west from the market cross by the cathedral. The Niagara peninsula, considered most comparable to England, was settled already and land there was expensive. Pioneers discussed keenly the relative merits of other regions. As they moved upcountry, deciding where to concentrate

King Street, Toronto, by John George Howard, 1835

their efforts, many swung between wonder at sights that were like nothing they had ever seen and relief in finding places that felt more familiar
in scale, or social arrangement, or natural environment. They wanted
new lives; they wanted to reconstruct the old home; they wanted to forget the old home: all these things in shifting combinations. James Rapson
thought the Galt township in Dumfries (where a group of Petworth people settled) was 'the most like Lodsworth of any in the Province as I have
been in'. He was making it more so, with his well-tended English garden.
The thousands of miles stretched and folded in on themselves. The children, he said, were often running out to see if their Sussex grandparents
were coming. 'Here comes Grandfather!' they would say, as if he had
just come along the road from Petworth.[49]

William Phillips couldn't help remembering, though it made him re-
gretful. 'Here is fine orchards, but the fruit is not half so good as with
you.' He had been a shoemaker, living on the Drove estate at the edge
of Singleton, below Levin Down. Canada was not yet his country, and
he was not yet one of 'them': 'As for their gardens, there is no variety
in them, as they plant very little but French beans and potatoes.'[50] His
appreciation for home gardens came out in his way of missing them.

The agricultural reformer William Cobbett, researching his influential book *Rural Rides*, had particularly noticed the gardens in Sussex

downland villages. Those near Singleton, he wrote, were 'some of the very best that I have seen in England'. He probably passed by Phillips' own.[51] There may have been serious unhappiness beneath Phillips' hints of dislocation. What's certain is that he returned to Singleton. Several years later, he tried again, earning his passage out in 1837. It cost him dearly to go back to Sussex after his first attempt at emigration, but a few years in England confirmed the impossibility of his leading a decent life there. The poor were only getting poorer. 'The lane goes along through some of the finest farms in the world', William Cobbett had observed a decade earlier, on the road that goes past Singleton. He had good reports of the landowners and found no evidence of misery; 'I have seen no wretchedness in Sussex.'[52] Yet now the men who cultivated those fine farms were starving.

The papers Phillips read, and which he asked to be sent over to him in Canada, suggest how politically alert and informed he was. He looked especially for the *Twopenny Dispatch*, the most widely circulated of the radical working-class papers, and *The Champion*, which was run by Cobbett's activist sons and published news that most affected workers.[53] During 1837 *The Champion* printed some of the evidence given to the Poor Law Committee about the effects of the new legislation. Had the reforms helped to resolve the crisis of poverty? From across the country came stories of desperation. If Phillips was reading, he would have noted the testimonies from Chichester. A grocer in East Street was selling a sixth of the bacon he used to sell: workers could not afford meat. A draper reported that his former customers could not now buy his clothing, and it was customary for children to go about in Chichester without shoes.[54] William Phillips the shoemaker had seen enough. By the time those reports were published, he was landing in Quebec.

In Petworth, Elizabeth Hooker was sad and tired. She was in her sixties, still living within a few miles of the place she was born. Her children were grown up and had families of their own, but she could not take much comfort as she looked around her. It was April, a year since her son Richard and his family had left, a year since they lost their eldest daughter to a fever on the journey over. They were now out in the country, fifteen miles from the nearest store in Delaware. It had been a hard twelve months for everyone. Elizabeth wrote them a plaintively chatty letter, which survives in manuscript so that we can see and hear the rhythms of her emphatic language as she described the winter just passed in Sussex: 'A very Severe Winter More So then Ever Was known since the Memory of Mn for it kild All the furs bushes on the Commons And in the farmers feilds Except on the South Side of the Hills Witch I Never Remember Seeing the furs All Dead I Hope that you Have Not Had it Colder in Canada.'[55]

The woody, prickly furze is a tough plant, well suited to survival on open heaths in the face of the wind. When the furze dies, things are bad. The image of the exposed and blasted bushes set the tone for Elizabeth's letter. In every household there was someone ill. Children were succumbing to whooping cough and typhoid. Workers had been laid off from the big house after the death of Lord Egremont (in late 1837, after seven decades in charge at Petworth). Her daughter Martha had moved to the lodge house, probably to look after the estate poultry, but her other daughter Sarah was in trouble; there was no work for her husband Charles, formerly a gamekeeper on the estate. 'They Have Been in view of A Place several times But it is All A Blank.' There was still family living up at Colhook Common. Her son William was too ill to work and seemed unlikely to live much longer. Their neighbour Jane Baker, 'poor old creature', 'she was a planting of potatoes hop[p]ing about as usual'.[56]

Another year, another April: 1839. William was still unwell, but could walk about and read his Bible and go to his mother in Petworth – probably at the house in North Street where the census enumerators found her in 1841. Elizabeth herself was 'much as usual': 'I bless the Lord I can get about and do my work middling'. Richard and Fanny wrote that they were settled in a cottage with fowl and pigs. They held out a prospect of return: they had heard that wages in England were getting better. But

Elizabeth didn't expect to see her family reunited in this life. When she spoke of 'getting home' she meant home to heaven, where they would meet. The emigrants had braved wildernesses, but to their mother in Petworth life itself seemed a 'dreary wilderness'. She missed Richard and Fanny, she missed her grandchildren, and she sent her love to the 'little Stranger', the new grandson she had never seen, now nearly one. She imagined the older children learning to write: was there a school for them in Delaware? Perhaps in the next letter from Canada, the children might add a message of their own.[57]

Two years on from his second arrival in Canada, William Phillips felt he had made the right decision. But he was still trying to find the right place to set down roots. He intended to go north from Galt to Woodstock where he knew many Sussex families were living. He would find familiar people – and he mentioned another reason for going, one which sounds so simple we might hardly notice that it carries mysteries of the human heart within it. 'I like the country up there.'[58]

A wolf started up in the night, a long way away. It was somewhere south, beyond the river. There it was again. Fanny Martin, awake for hours with a throbbing pain at the base of her neck, thought of the sound rising up between the trees. The dogs would be on their feet, bristling, eyes fixed on the door. Martin shifted next to her, breathing loudly, not hearing. Another wolf, closer, and the two calling to each other. The sound was liquid and cold, flooding over the Guelph Road towards Elora, through the cedars and maples that stood in its stream, around the stump trees in the new cornfield, shaking the pea seedlings in the garden with their tendrils just beginning to catch on the poles. Silence, except for Martin, and a creaking from where the girls slept on the other side of the wooden wall: the tremendous silence of their house afloat on the darkness. Then pad, pad, and Esther appearing, tiny and pale. She saw her mother and father there, both sleeping. She must not mind the night. She slipped back into bed, proud to be the lone custodian, the listener for them all.

Fanny took herself back to Felpham and tried counting the waves. It didn't often get her to sleep but was worth a try. Fifty-seven, fifty-eight falling in the dark on the shingle. It only worked if you took no notice of the suds in the sand, or the seaweed rising on the swell. The brothers were out: she could see their boat in the distance, a tiny lamp moving over the water. Mr Blake had told her to watch for angels. Sometimes they live in stones, he said, long ago when she was young, and you'll see the impress where they have been. He said it quite plainly, she remembered, as if he were telling her which mushrooms you could eat: it was a thing she ought to know and look out for. Sometimes a road opens from the hillside into heaven, he said once, and only a few people will ever see it. She was Esther's age, seven or eight years old, stone-picking all the daylight hours in winter, crouched in the furrows with chapped hands stinging in the cold. After that the time went more quickly because she was always watching in case the angels came.

In Sussex, Elizabeth Burchill drove her cart fast over the causeway from Coldwaltham into Pulborough. There was moon enough to see the ruts and the patches of chalk where the ditches were filled. She wouldn't meet anyone at this time. Fixing her eyes on the straight stretch of road ahead, flicking the reins, she told herself she was on the road running right through Adelaide Township, on and on towards Lake Huron. The road they said was so grand and long. She was going west to see the land in the backwoods where you could pay off fifty acres in one harvest. She wanted to try out the feeling. There was more of a bend at Hardham than she remembered – trees flashed up from the verge, the cart lurched. Then, for a few moments more before the lights came into view, she let herself imagine an immense land around her, waiting. She would hold black loam that had never been ploughed. There would be magnificent trees on her land, which she would save from the axe, and the corn would grow up around them.

At Graffham, Mrs Boxall pushed open the upstairs window and listened. The Canada folk said they had wolves. And they had a bird that called 'whip poor Will' over and over. She tried making the sound, wondering if she had it right. Poor Will. Why must he be whipped? Whip poor Will, she whispered, and listened. A tawny in the copse. The sound made the night feel very large. It fell over the woods and hills, a great sheet falling, folding. No female? Yes, there she was, high and sudden, and the answer came, unhurried, a soft sheet lifting on the cool air and falling over the fields. There were plenty of owls, they said, in Canada.

22. A HISTORIAN'S BOOKS

I had been looking online at a series of tithe maps that showed all the field names in Sutton and Bignor as they were in the 1830s when working families left them behind for Canada. A credit line on the database revealed that Elizabeth helped to transcribe and digitise them twenty years ago. I told Caroline. We wished we could tell her mother, but Elizabeth was further away now than four thousand miles. There was no kind of letter that could travel the distance.

⌒

I was still reading the maroon-bound journals inherited from Elizabeth, the books that used to live by the window in the crowded front room at Pulborough. The bookplates pasted into the first hundred issues of the *Sussex Archaeological Collections* told me that this series had belonged to another woman, Helena Hall. She must have bought, or been given, the Victorian volumes, and collected the rest year by year through her lifetime until 1967. I had a moment's vision of myself and Elizabeth and Helena Hall – all standing next to each other with our books. I thought I must try to find out who this Sussex scholar was, though the first clues were somewhat forbidding. The bookplate showed a barefoot monk standing with an open volume under high Gothic arches. Did Helena Hall think of her historical researches as continuing the tradition of a tonsured monk in a flag-stoned cloister? It was a curious image for a modern woman, and it led me into an unexpected life.

In 1892, when she was nineteen and had finished at boarding school in Tunbridge Wells, Helena Hall went to be a nursemaid with the Gill family in Brighton. She had a ten-year-old Eric in her care. It was only a brief stay, while Mrs Gill was coping with newborn twins, but Eric took to her immediately. The future artist was already addicted to drawing, and showed his fondness for Helena by drawing her pictures of 'boats and trains and railway tunnels'. He would remember her always as 'darling Heddie'.[1]

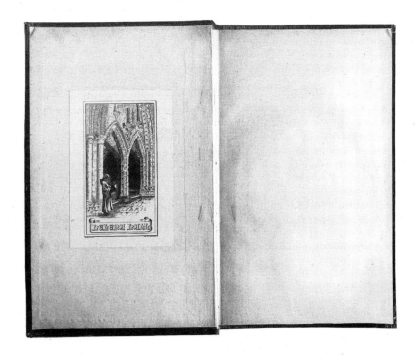

By the turn of the century, Hall was in London. She was among the first students of the lettering specialist Edward Johnston when he started to teach at the Central School of Arts and Craft; Eric Gill (still in touch) took Johnston's classes shortly afterwards, fascinated by the history and the modern possibilities of calligraphy, letter-carving and typefaces.[2] Hall studied heraldry at the College of Arms, made items in embroidered silk, and worked as a designer for the publishing firm Gordon Gill in Bond Street. It was this firm which printed the book-plate. She drew the monk and the arches herself, at Westminster Abbey in 1900. The Ex Libris Society praised the design in its journal, but thought it might not meet with approval as a bookplate for ladies.[3] Too solemn, was it, awkward in not separating women's reading from male scholarship? But Hall was serious about antiquarianism, and particularly about its relationship with crafts.

To be sure of an income, though, she set up another kind of enterprise. By 1911 (it's a census year, so we can trace her) she was living in a large house in Hyde Park Gate, Kensington, and, rather surprisingly, running it as a hotel, with nine staff in her employment.[4] On the night of 2 April there were nine guests staying. Hall wrote their names on the census sheet and had to ask them for the information required: years married, children living, children lost. She listed the staff and then herself, the twentieth person at this busy address:

Twenty – Helena Invicta Hall, Head, 37, single, Hotel Keeper Proprietor

She had made a mistake, listing the oldest male guest as the head of the household. Was it her default assumption that 'Head' on a government form must mean a man? Or had the colonel (Lt Colonel Alfred Warden, retired) moved in and in some way taken over? The correction was made; this was Helena Hall's household and business. And this was the house she was renting from Virginia Stephen (soon to be Woolf) and her siblings.

It was 22 Hyde Park Gate. I stared at the census sheet, making sure of it. The Sussex books that had taken me so far from my work as a literary critic, so far from modernist fiction, had brought me back to the high stuccoed house with its large dark rooms where Virginia Woolf spent the first twenty-two years of her life. She had left it in 1904, after the death of her father, to set up a new home in Bloomsbury. But she and her siblings still owned the old family house, and rented it out.[5]

The census of 1911 found Virginia Stephen resident in Fitzroy Square, where she was re-working the drafts of her first novel. From her letters, though, I think she was temporarily somewhere else that day. At the start of the year she had decided to make part of her life in Sussex and rented a house in the village of Firle, outside Lewes. 'It's right underneath the downs', she told friends in excitement.[6] The income from Hyde Park Gate was part of what made it possible. 'Little Talland House' was decorated and furnished by the spring, and Virginia went down by train on 1 April to spend her first proper stretch of time there. Friends came to visit but she was mostly alone in the deep country quiet of snowy days and found that she was happy. 'I read furiously and write and walk. It's a very satisfactory life, and much more exciting, even than talking. As for the country, I never imagined anything so beautiful.' 'I frequently have to stop and say "Good God!"'[7] It was the beginning of a relationship with the Sussex countryside that would go on now for the rest of her life. For three decades it brought her intense pleasure that could never finally be summed up, for all the words she had at her command.

In 1911 Hyde Park Gate remained vividly present in her mind. At intervals over the years she would write about it, remembering every detail of those rooms, the shape of them emptied out when the family and servants left, the marks on the walls. For now, Helena Hall was there. Helena Hall and her guests and her books – my books – were there, all leaving marks of their own.

~

After the Great War, Hall left London for Lindfield in mid-Sussex, a former ironworking village in the weald. It was the village where the Henslow brothers grew up in the 1550s, one of them leaving to run the theatres of Shakespeare's Southwark, the other staying in Sussex and organising the supply of timber to the forges. Lindfield in the twentieth century had a busy, practical high street known for its lime trees and medieval buildings. She had brothers still in the area. They had all grown up on the coast, at Shoreham and Lancing, where the dramatically elevated Gothic chapel of Lancing College commands the downs and tends to provoke strong feelings about ecclesiastical architecture in anyone living nearby. In Lindfield in the 1920s Hall found a place she would love and write about for the next forty years.

One of Helena's brothers, William Hamilton Hall, was an active member of the Sussex Archaeological Society; his own research focused on the cataloguing of early wills, in all about thirteen thousand medieval and early modern documents.[8] Helena joined the Society in 1929 (by which time about 30 per cent of members were women) though she never published in the journal.[9] Her interests in art, design and especially vernacular craft suggested other kinds of project and she embarked on a survey of ornamental ironwork. She toured every Sussex parish by bicycle, gained entrance to the churches, examined the iron fittings, and made a carefully drawn record of the blacksmith's art: the scrolling door hinges, the grilles, the gates.[10]

When war came again, she turned her historian's eye on the present. The journal she kept at length almost daily in Lindfield stretched to thirty-four notebooks as she combined local observations with international news. She monitored the world from her air-raid-warning posts.

> 25 September 1940. There is one German plane we call DI, meaning District Inspector. It comes regularly every night, drops its eggs, usually 2, about midnight and then departs.

> 14 March 1944. At our Post this evening Mr Parsons held a wardens' meeting pointing out the routine of procedure when a bomb dropped . . . A short alert 12.05 to 1.25. Russians are driving on and have opened a new offensive.[11]

At eighty she published a life of the scientist, Quaker and activist William Allen (1770–1843) who established a model farm at Lindfield in the early nineteenth century. Hall was drawn to her subject by the local connection, but Allen led her into the wider culture and politics of his time. She followed the abolition campaigns in which he played a leading part, and the strong Quaker networks that sustained them. There was his research as a chemist to get a grasp on and the growth of his business at Plough Court Pharmacy in London (later Allen & Hanburys, famous to Hall's generation for its blackcurrant pastilles). She followed Allen's move to Lindfield in 1824, his rapid establishment of a school oriented to the teaching of practical skills, his thinking about how to alleviate the poverty of the rural poor in mid-Sussex and across Britain.[12] Labourers were migrating in huge numbers, but what if there were to be what Allen called 'colonies at home'? People would have the resources to support themselves like pioneers, but in their own regions.[13] Hoping to demonstrate the potential of such a scheme, he built twenty-five cottages to house the working families of Lindfield's new 'colony'. He imagined a New World in southern England, and the place became known as 'America'. Helena Hall had known those cottages, still standing in the 1930s, and she had seen them demolished in 1944, the end of an experiment. Her book put that experiment on record.

She turned next to a book-length history of Lindfield and work on *A Dictionary of the Sussex Dialect*, reviving and expanding the dictionary published in the late nineteenth century. She added explanatory notes on obsolete tools, charcoal-burning, hop-drying and especially ironworking. Dialect was the language of a different class from hers. She didn't have the acute ear of George Forrester Scott, for example, an earlier Lindfield writer whose 1898 *Idlehurst* caught the voices of the weald. But she understood that regional phrases often expressed precise practical knowledge of craftsmanship, materials, methods and conditions, things she valued and wanted to study seriously. She put in helpful drawings, the pen-and-ink runes of her Sussex language book.

Chucle. Clucket. Cotteril.

Grisset: An oval iron dish for melting the fat into which rushes are dipped to make Grisset rush lights, or for making candles.

Hox: to cut the sinew of a rabbit's leg and put the other foot through, in order to hang it up.[14]

Hox, a word familiar for centuries to the warreners at East Dean and South Stoke.

Helena Hall is the woman whose books are now on my shelves, the minor character passing in the background of Eric Gill's life, looking out for a time from the same windows as Virginia Stephen. She was the author of a few volumes of specialist local interest, who pursued her historical research energetically over nine decades, who cycled to Pulborough, Boxgrove and Arundel, and made drawings in sketchbooks, which years later burnt to white ashes in a fire at Brighton Museum.[15]

23. MILL AND CASTLE
John Constable exploring

In the bedroom he was given at the palatial Petworth House in September 1834, John Constable laid out objects of fascination and beauty: flowers and feathers he had picked up on early-morning walks through the park, and on the excursions he took almost daily for two weeks into the surrounding hills and fields. His friend C. R. Leslie was also staying at Petworth, and peered in surprise at the items on the dressing table where other guests might array their silver combs and snuffboxes. Constable's toilette involved 'pieces of bark with lichens and mosses adhering to them which he had brought home for the sake of their beautiful tints'.[1] He was in one of the most exquisitely decorated houses in England. He had the freedom of all the rooms that had dazzled Turner with their enfilade perspectives and high, gleaming windows onto a boundless park where mist rose at the heels of spectral deer. J. M. W. Turner, almost exactly his contemporary, had long been celebrated and hosted by Lord Egremont, whose patronage of the arts was as famous as his schemes for assisting emigration and for agricultural improvement. Constable thought the house very fine, but he wanted to be heading towards the river and the water meadows, studying the trees and verges on the way.[2]

It had taken time to get Constable to the house at all. When Leslie encouraged him to visit Lord Egremont's picture gallery the answer came back that 'the great were not made for me, nor I for the great'. 'My limited and abstracted art is to be found under every hedge, and in every lane, and therefore nobody thinks it worth picking up; but I have my admirers, each of whom I consider a host.'[3] There was defensiveness and conviction in this explanation. Constable was in his mid-fifties, and firm in his commitment to the flowers under the hedge and the rough common heath. He valued those who 'hosted' him with their understanding, and not necessarily with grand company and wines. As it happened, the new friend who hosted his first stay in this part of Sussex made him welcome with beer.

George Constable, no relation, was the owner of a large brewery in Arundel. He devoted his spare time to landscape painting, and spent his profits on a growing collection of pictures. He had London lodgings near John Constable's family, and it was a domestic kind of fondness that grew up between them, the brewer encouraging the painter's son in his geological interests and giving him fossils. Father and son were both delighted with the specimens. The brewer and his wife, Frances, had a large family of their own, their eldest boy about the same age as Constable's. They persuaded the painter and his son to come and stay. Seventeen-year-old John went on ahead, taking a seat in the stagecoach on 5 July 1834. His father followed a few days later, travelling south for a summer fortnight in the old port town on the Arun. It would be one of the happiest periods of the painter's later life, a relief and a brightening in the long 'season of Sadness' that had closed in with the loss of his wife Maria six years before.

His grief, and the worry of being a single parent to seven children, ran through everything. He was working intensively despite fragile health. He had been going over sketchbooks from long ago, working up oils from Suffolk drawings rich in association, fraught with memory, sending paint flickering and crackling across the canvases layer after layer. But that summer in Arundel he was receptive to new subjects. The countryside lifted him more than he had expected.

George showed him the villages upriver from Arundel. They drove over to Bignor, where Constable promptly found the millpond and waterwheel and started to draw. They visited Bignor Park, which Constable knew about from the sonnets of Charlotte Smith; the house had been rebuilt since her time there but he could see Smith's 'hills beloved'. They walked along the wide meander of the river through the water meadows between North and South Stoke, edged on one side by ash and beech covering the hillside of Arundel Park, the gurgling flatlands stretching away on the other side towards Camp Hill in the distance, and here they had something extraordinary to inspect.[4]

For as long as anyone could remember, a solid wooden footbridge had run across one of the drainage streams. Workmen deepening the drain in April had dug into the banks and found that the bridge was in fact part of an enormous object, thirty-five feet long, most of it buried. Gradually, an ancient canoe emerged from the mud, a log-boat formed of an oak trunk, halved and hollowed. There it was, within sight of the river where punts and barges still carried cargo up and down this tidal stretch: a boat from the remote past, a boat that carried earlier people on the high stream.

Constable made a sketch, added precise measurements (careful anti-quarian that he was), and noted the location a hundred yards from the Arun. He thought, or he was told, that it was pre-Roman. He got the

reference books out (Edward King's 1799 *Munimenta Antiqua*; Samuel Rush Meyrick's 1815 *Costume of the Original Inhabitants of the British Islands*, with illustrations) and found descriptions of similarly excavated log-boats. 'The ancient Britons in the very early periods of their history', he wrote below his drawing, quoting Meyrick, 'used a kind of boat by them called CWCH, which seems to have been formed out of a single tree like the Indian canoes.' This boat at North Stoke, Constable concluded, was 'at least 1800 years old'.[5]

Modern dating shows it to be younger than that: somewhere between AD 1030 and 1250, not the work of ancient Britons but early medieval.[6] But Constable was right in thinking the method and design much older: the Britons had used canoes like this. Country people had carried on making these sturdy vessels for generations, long after the Romans left, long after the Normans came. If the North Stoke canoe was used on the river in the twelfth century, it was paddled by people who saw South Stoke and Hardham churches when they were newly built and painted. The boat was well preserved in the wetland bog, stopped in time by the lack of oxygen. Unearthed, it was already decomposing. It was wrapped in straw until it could be transported to the British Museum later in the summer. Constable, following its progress, would report on its safe arrival there and recommend the use of linseed oil for preservation rather than the broth of mutton fat proposed by an expert on timber rot.[7] Whichever course was taken, the boat was apparently 'quite gone to decay' by 1860.[8] There was enough of it left in the 1890s for it to be displayed under the colonnade at the entrance when Helena Hall was a regular visitor. It spent the twentieth century in store, though in 2003 it was brought out for a clean.

Constable sat by the stream to make a detailed drawing of the fen landscape from which this boat had risen. His years on the Stour showed him what to look for on the Arun. With the simplest graphite pencil, he caught infinite variations of texture and movement in the low grassland edged by hills, a working landscape dug and sculpted to control the water.

Conversation at Arundel in the evenings roamed over antiquarian discoveries, pictures and modern technology. George Constable caught young John's imagination with talk of scientific advances (would he like an electricity machine for experiments at home?) and for these keen geologists there were many discoveries to be made in the landscape. They took their fossil-hunting hammers into the quarries – probably at Amberley and at the Black Rabbit near South Stoke where the hillside had been carved open in the early 1700s. 'John is enjoying himself exceedingly', reported a pleased father, seeing his son's enthusiasm and sharp eye: 'The chalk cliffs afford him many fragments of oyster shells and other matters that fell from the table of Adam in all probability.'[9]

Oysters of Arundel:
oysters coming in by boat to the harbour, half a hundred due to the
    water bailiff for each cargo
oysters in the taverns shucked and slurped and cooked in pies
oyster shells heaped out the back for burying, dropped shells crushed
    on kitchen floors

> Adam at his table on the slope of the down, Eve pouring the wine and
> turning a trout in the pan, a dozen oysters knocked back in salty gulps

> And what the Constable household didn't yet fully understand: ancient molluscs in the warm Sussex sea, and shells falling through millions of years.

~

From the lower gate of the castle, where I used to sell the ice creams, I crossed to the river and watched a few pleasure boats being moored or mended. Here on the wharves in 1834, wooden kegs and stoneware bottles of beer from the Constable brewery were loaded.

I had been asking around for hints about George Constable's home address and then found an estate agent's particulars for a big late-Georgian house on Maltravers Street, near the top of the steep town. It was advertised as having a place in the history of art: 'Painter John Constable stayed here.' I searched the street for the house in the picture with its fan-shaped window above the door.[10] Red brick, modillion cornice, five sashes: it looked right as the home of a prosperous businessman in the 1830s. I stood across the road, looking and not looking into the front room where, on 16 July 1834, one of the most original painters in Britain sat down to write a letter. He told Leslie about his pleasure in the countryside. 'The meadows are lovely, so is the delightfull river, and the old houses are rich beyond all things of the sort.' He could hardly ignore the castle, 'the chief ornament of this place', dominating every view of Arundel for miles around. But Constable's eye was elsewhere: 'all here sinks to insignificance in comparison with the woods, and hills'.[11]

'I never saw such beauty in *natural landscape* before. I wish it may influence what I do in the future.'[12] He had no desire to be an 'English Claude' like George Smith, who had sketched before him on the banks of the Arun. Smith had tried to make the scenery fit contemporary artistic tastes. Constable thought the place set its own standards of beauty.

He thought it falsely imitative to adopt the compositions of Claude or Ruisdael. Real artists might learn from other painters, but they must look at the world for themselves.[13] Constable looked. Just the evening before, he had left the talkative party in the house on Maltravers Street and gone out walking in the summer night, finding his own way. 'By chance I stumbled on an old barn situated amid trees of immense size like this', he wrote, and drew the scene there on the page.[14]

At Petworth in September, having surrendered himself to the great house at last, Constable used the late-summer days and Egremont's carriage to see as much of the country as he could. He studied old barns and labourers' cottages. A woman in one remote farmhouse said human bones had been pulled from the well; people suspected something dreadful had happened there. 'Wicked Hammond's house' she called it.[15] Wordsworth might have made a ballad from such a hint of local life; Constable made a drawing.

The very soil fascinated him. On Fittleworth Common he collected sand and different kinds of earth, bringing specimens back to add to the dressing table. The range of colours from one small patch of ground amazed him, and he liked the contrasts with the green furze of the heath.[16] He was going to carry all the bottles of soil back to London.

As Constable studied the sands of Fittleworth that September of 1834, Edward Henty was bringing soil samples from Portland across the Bass Strait. And in the townships of Ontario, emigrants from Petworth were testing the ground, working out what they could grow.

'John Constable walked past on the lane', said my friend Jonathan. He was looking meditatively towards the window in the low sitting room of the estate cottage he rents from the current Lord Egremont, another supporter of painters. I followed his gaze, as if to catch sight of Constable before he was gone. It was September, and the lane was invisible behind leafy tents of runner beans in the garden. 'He must have come down here to the water meadows.' We went out to follow him, past the turn into the deep sandstone burrow of the hollow way that was once the main road to London. Jonathan listed the smuggled goods that used to be stored at the lonely cottage on the corner before they were sold on. From the shadows we turned out onto the brooks under a dazzling sky. With red Sussex Cattle coming steadily behind us, and Jonathan reminding me that he herded cows as a boy, we made an ambling tour of meadows that will be underwater by midwinter. A wood on the left, dense and secretive: 'We never knew who lived there, but someone did.' A disused stone barn, which Jonathan has been drawing, and next to it a hedge, 'loved by yellowhammers, linnets, reed buntings'. A stone culvert carrying a drainage stream: '*Under* the river and out the other side. Think of the work. That's eighteenth-century engineering.' We looked appreciatively across acres of land flooded and dried, recognisable in every detail from the drawing Constable made on Friday 12 September 1834.

After the holiday, letters went back and forth all year between Arundel and London. The brewer, becoming known as a good amateur artist, was commissioned by a local woman to paint scenes she loved. Miss Boniface was due to leave for Van Diemen's Land and 'wanted to take with her a few memorandums of her native home'.[17] Landscape paintings could be souvenirs, treasured by the many people on the move. Susan Boniface was setting out to marry a man she hadn't seen for four years, though she and Charles Henty had begun a courtship before he went to join his family in Launceston. Charles had run the bank in Arundel. He knew the local places Susan cared about and had been reluctant to leave them. Four years apart they made the journey from Arundel to Van Diemen's Land, and their reunion was said to be a happy one. If George Constable's pictures survived the voyage (though Miss Boniface's ship was struck by lightning not once but twice in the Indian Ocean), they were presumably hung in the Henty home in Launceston, views of the Arun countryside transposed across the world.

John Constable wanted to see more of the Arun for himself. 'Panting for a little fresh air', he wrote to ask if another family holiday might be possible: 'I long to be among your *willows* again, in your walks and hangers, among your books and antiquities'.[18] Everyone was pleased to be reunited in July 1835. Constable got plenty of fresh air while painting Littlehampton windmill in a gale. And he saw things that spoke to his restlessly melancholy mind. He walked on the eerie coast at Middleton, next to Felpham, where the churchyard burials, deeply eroded, were being exhumed by every tide. Charlotte Smith had set the most desperately sorrowful of her sonnets here, where great waves tore the village dead from their 'grassy tombs'. 'Lo! their bones whiten in the frequent wave!' exclaims the speaker, but still she envies them their 'gloomy rest'. Fifty years on, the church itself was almost lost to the water. Like the unearthed boat, like the ravaged tower in Constable's paintings of Hadleigh Castle, like the painter himself when he reached for images of self-expression, it was a moribund last survivor. It was 'time-mangled matter', yet clinging on. He drew Middleton church on the brink, and the impress left behind where a skeleton had been washed out from the chalk. We are met with a shadow and left to imagine the bones whitening in the waves. 'See Charlotte Smith's sonnet', Constable wrote on the back, along with the place and the date.[19]

A particular view in Arundel held Constable's attention on this visit. He walked out from the town to the old brick watermill on Swanbourne Lake. Seen from here, the castle grew like an outcrop from the wooded hill. He knew the site was ancient. The Arundel antiquarian Mark Tierney, whose history of the town Constable consulted, turned rhapsodic about Swanbourne; he ended his book with a long, loving description of the lake and the mill, 'in whose presence the lapse of centuries will easily be forgotten'. 'The mind, hastening back to the age of the Confessor, will . . . fancy itself beside the mill which was at work nearly eight hundred years ago.'[20] Constable was not much concerned with Edward the Confessor; it was the history of practical life that moved him. Through the winter of 1836–7 he would take himself back to these sketches, and back in imagination to that spot by the Arun, to work on a large oil painting.

In *Arundel Mill and Castle* he celebrated, as he always had, the vernacular brick and wood of a working place, moss-grown and dripping, chimneys smoking, wheels turning (PLATE). He put in boys fishing; he let trees dominate it all. The painted surface intensified as he worked over and over it; the summer hours pool and swell like water behind the millpond sluice. If the distant turrets made Constable think of Claude's *Enchanted Castle*, he knew that a watermill harbours its own kind of enchantment. The painting was all but finished when Constable died suddenly one night in March 1837. He had often borne in mind Wordsworth's idea about artists striving to make permanent 'one brief moment caught from fleeting time'. In his last picture, brevity and permanence meet. The pink-flushed sky will change, the boys will go, but for a moment they are ageless.

Such scenes were not quiet idylls outside time, as Constable knew. This millpond had been drained in the civil war while prisoners gasped for water. Now, in the 1830s, too many Arundel boys were doomed by poverty to labour at stone-picking rather than fish by this stream. The mill would be demolished in 1844 to make way for a pump house and a big new dairy in Jacobean style. The pool was ornamentally reworked for the enjoyment of visitors to the Duke of Norfolk's park.

George Constable did something bizarre in the 1840s. He made a series of imitation Constables, took them to a dealer, and passed them off as the work of his friend. They were scenes on the Arun: he said he'd watched them being made on those summer visits years before. Fakery: just what John Constable detested. The dealer wasn't fooled; for one thing the paint was hardly dry. But through other dealers poor fakes did get onto the market. Leslie was shocked by the discovery and couldn't understand how the art-loving brewer could have sunk to such a fraud. No answer has emerged.[21]

The brewer remained a much-respected figure in Arundel, and became something of a local hero in 1851. The Duke of Norfolk planned to close or 'stop up' the lane that ran under the castle walls to Swanbourne and on under Offham Hanger to the Black Rabbit and then to South Stoke. He wanted the public access pushed out further from his park. A new road was promised in its place, out on the brooks and running between fences. George Constable took on the fight and raised an appeal against the court's decision to allow the change. It was an expensive, risky and time-consuming business, not likely to succeed against an opposition of giant wealth and power.[22]

The case was heard at Epiphany Quarter Sessions, and the transcript is a portrait of a community. The Arundel baker, grocer and auctioneer were all called as witnesses to describe which paths they used and why. George Constable argued that the new road would flood and would be unhealthily exposed to fogs, and he emphasised something else: the pleasure people took in walking on the existing path, 'sheltered by the natural formation' of the wooded hanger above them, and with 'scenery of great beauty and interest' around them.[23]

Many witnesses were tenants of the Duke and depended on his favour; little wonder few were willing to raise objections to his plans, though they may independently have liked the thought of a good modern road. But a succession of people spoke about why they valued the old route and wanted to keep it. John Doick said only that it was two minutes quicker. Richard Collis, an Arun bargeman who lived on his barge, liked the shelter in rough weather, and used the route in summer too, when it was 'as fine a road as there is any where'. Another bargeman, John Strudwick from Pulborough, had been using the lane by the millpond for sixty-five years. He could remember when there was a rabbit warren at Pugh Dean and then after the rabbits there were houses there, and people coming to and fro on the path.[24]

One by one, these people were asked to say how they walked through Arundel and what they thought about it. They are people whose responses to landscape are rarely attested but who were out in it through their working lives, making fine daily judgements about practicalities and pleasures. They appeared for a few moments in court, and we can set their words alongside the celebrated oil painting in which the artist John Constable expressed some of what he felt about the 'beauty and interest' of the ponds and hangers visible from the lane.

The jury listened and returned its verdict. The existing road was 'not unnecessary'. It was used and valued. George Constable had won his appeal. The paths by the castle have changed since then but we can still walk under the wooded hangers, past the site of the old mill, peering into the bright blue chalk-spring waters of Swanbourne before going over to South Stoke and back again.

24. NEW TIMETABLES
A doctor's view

'Let the reader imagine a plain of chalk . . . extended over a part of France, and continued without interruption to the north of England. Let him then suppose that, looking from the Alton-Hills, he sees the chalk, with its accompanying strata rent asunder.' The writer of these words had visualised it happening: a giant shuddering and breaking, massive plates of chalk moving apart, and at the same time 'a flood of water, powerful beyond comprehension', pouring over and into the broken surface, sweeping the 'whole contents of what is now the weald excavation before it, into the North Sea'. This was the cataclysm, he thought, by which the chalk of all southern England and France was heaved into new form and the weald left bare, its chalk layers washed away and its clay beds exposed. Again he asked the reader to countenance it. 'Or let "a change come o'er the spirit of his dream / That is not all a dream."'[1]

PROFILE OF THE WEALD DENUDATION.

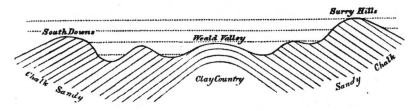

Dr Peter Martin was in his early forties when he published his *Geological Memoir on a Part of Western Sussex* in 1828. It was concerned with the area he had known all his life – stretching down to the coast and up to the weald but centring on the Arun parishes around Pulborough. He was one of the geological writers bringing a new kind of local knowledge to people such as Mr Constable of Arundel, who could take boys out for an afternoon tap-tapping for fossils in chalk pits. He was offering a radically altered landscape vision, penetrating under the surface, perceiving hills not as fixed but as dynamic formations with histories that exceeded his contemporaries' strangest notions. With his 'dream / That is not all a dream' he remembered Byron's poem 'Darkness', an apocalyptic glimpse of a moment when the sun is extinguished and the earth hangs dark in space, 'a lump of death – a chaos of hard clay'. Peter Martin was thinking on the same scales of cosmic transformation, but where Byron dreamt of the whole icy earth swinging blindly 'in the moonless air', Martin brought his geological thinking to bear on his home stretch of southern England. Riding between his patients, or taking visitors out in a chaise, the doctor looked out across epochs of time. He knew of more than oysters that had fallen from the table of Adam and settled in the chalk cliffs: he knew of ancient forests, fish and crustaceans, crocodiles and quadrupeds.

He was following very closely the work of another Sussex doctor and geologist. Gideon Mantell was based on the other side of the county, in Lewes, and was making Sussex one of the focal points for international research into the development of life on earth. His 1822 *Fossils of the South Downs* mapped out the deep pre-history of Sussex for the first time, and it was in Mantell's vivid turn of phrase that readers met the idea of a tropical environment inhabited by turtles and crocodiles, waving with palm trees. Mantell had studied the chalk of the eastern downs and he drew on the knowledge of correspondents to cover the western part of Sussex including the Arun valley. From his brother he had intelligence about Parham Park, where the sand beds beneath Lord de la Zouche's cedars contained a marine cemetery of echino-spatangus (sea potato), *Rostellaria parkinsoni* (Cretaceous gastropods), cucullea (bivalve clams) and mytilus (mussels). Under the Elizabethan gardens, under the passing feet in buckled heels and workmen's boots: trillions of shells. From John Drewett at Peppering (the farm across the river from South Stoke) he heard of a larger species in ancient Sussex. The 'bones and several grinders of elephants' had been found; Mr Drewett brought a grinder tooth over to Mantell for him to see.[2]

Peter Martin wrote to offer his services. 'If I can be useful to you in this neighbourhood by procuring specimens of minerals or fossils . . . I shall be happy to be so', he assured Mantell, adding a diagram of the rock strata at Pulborough. In signing off he mentioned the 'curious disruptions and disturbances' in the sandstone at Parham, which was a way of saying 'come and look!' And Mantell did: he was shown over Parham and Pulborough by his host. After a cautious start, Martin and Mantell became collegial correspondents, and then loyal friends. In books that appeared through the 1830s and 40s Mantell made frequent reference to Martin's identification of new species. 'Among those for which I am indebted to his liberality are *Mya mandibula*, *Trigonia spinosa*, *Nucula impressa*, *Mytilus edentulousm* . . .'[3]

Mantell's real focus was further north, in the weald, where the oldest rocks were exposed. There, the chalk that once covered the whole area from North Downs to South had worn away and left open for inspection the world of a hundred million years ago. In Tilgate Forest his wife Mary Ann had found teeth that eluded identification. Ribs and vertebrae followed, supposed by Mantell to belong to something that 'exceeded in magnitude every animal of the lizard tribe hitherto discovered'. Years of effort and argument later, in 1833, he was able to write about 'the Iguanodon of Tilgate Forest'. What Mantell was describing was an unknown class of animal. The word dinosaur was not yet coined.[4]

The dramatic story of geology in Sussex, and in early-nineteenth-century Europe all told, lay with Mantell and it lay in wealden rock millions of years older than the downland chalk. As I read my way into the revelatory papers of the 1830s, the history of science said, 'Over there! There's the man who changed our knowledge of time and the planet.' But

John Martin, *The Country of the Iguanodon*, which was engraved for Mantell's *Wonders of Geology*, 1838. An iguanodon is being attacked by a megalosaurus and a crocodile, in a tropical landscape based on fossil remains in Tilgate Forest, in the north of Sussex.

I was stubbornly turning back to Pulborough and the Arun. I carried on in the company of Mantell's friend, the country doctor and part-time geologist of Pulborough, one of the thousands of nineteenth-century provincial figures who were widely respected in their professional milieus, featured in the *Dictionary of National Biography* at the end of the century and then rarely heard of again.[5]

Peter Martin would discover no new dinosaur. His local greensand area was less geologically sensational, giving little access to the Jurassic strata. Though he was elected to the Geological Society in 1833 and continued to present new research, Martin remained a minor figure in the burgeoning world of the new sciences. The problem was largely that his central theory was wrong. He believed that the weald had been denuded of its chalk in a great cataclysm, and he sought clues to this story of decisive upheaval even as his contemporaries abandoned theories of cataclysm and tried to understand much more extended processes of change. His name would not be remembered. But in Pulborough he kept up with the development of European geology and palaeontology. He answered carefully the enquiries of those who consulted him about the Arun area he knew better than anyone.

He applied all his geological thinking to places within reach of Pulborough as he went on his rounds or took weekend walks, observing every local quarry, well-hole and cutting that he could. The brickyard at Stopham was particularly rich in marine life. Adam's oysters – and snails and sponges and crabs – in dizzying numbers.

ammonites dentatus
coprolite
a new species of carduin
panopoea plicata.[6]

Dr Martin could take a census of ancient inhabitants.

His *Memoir* offered a 'district survey' of rocks. He noted how, on certain deep-cut roads, you could see the earth change: 'The transition of the malm into the galt clay can nowhere be better observed than in the hollow-way leading from Sutton to Bignor.'[7] The lane that the Sefton brothers had taken so many times in the restless years of the mid-seventeenth century, and the Sutton emigrants had left forever when they went to Canada – that lane told Dr Martin of turbulence in a much deeper past.

He took readers on a tour of the Arun that projected the river back thousands – or could it be millions? – of years. The sturdy stone bridges so prominent in the water bailiff's history of the High Stream were motes in the eye once Martin conjured the 'early ages' when the river at Stopham ran through a wooded ravine, and giant oaks fell into the flood to be carbonised and preserved until the present time. 'The Arun receives the Rother . . . and being opposed in their direct course by the outlying galt of Hardham . . . they run round by Pulborough and Wiggonholt.'[8] The bailiff's river nymphs had long departed and the waters behave as the rock directs. The practical man with local knowledge was nonetheless thinking in literary terms about how to express a great subject: the story of rock and water, flora and fauna, on a part of the earth's surface. He was reading Byron and he was reading the fossils of Sussex.

～

Peter Martin had grown up in Pulborough. He moved back after medical school in Edinburgh to practise in partnership with his father, who had been treating the ailing bodies of the Arun valley since the 1770s. With his wife Mary he had four children and theirs was a literary, scholarly, enterprising family. Dr Martin found time, whenever he could, for concerted study of poetry and history, as well as geology.

The family house was on Lower Street. The front looks straight onto the road (in the twenty-first century the traffic is continuous and goods lorries rattle the sash windows) but the back is another place altogether, facing the wild brooks and with a garden sloping to the river. The property was part of Puddle Wharf when his father bought it in 1789; it acquired the more gentrified name of Templemead when a small Doric temple was installed close to the water's edge. With a chessboard set into the floor for summer evening games, the temple established the garden as a place of picturesque delight, friendship and conversation. A pedestal paid tribute to a friend of the family who played chess here when Peter was a boy – the foreign secretary and abolitionist (and gambler and rogue) Charles James Fox.[9] Pulborough and the world, classicism and local knowledge, contemplation, politics and liberty were all mixed up in the riverside house and garden.

Peter's father was still reading widely and writing forceful letters in his eighties, by which time he was pursuing an active retirement in Paris. He could sit in the Jardin des Plantes and write to his doctor son, who was listening to the chests of the next generation of Pulborough patients and running his own large household. The 1841 census records eleven people living at Templemead: Peter and Mary, Peter's 'assistant surgeon', three daughters between ten and eighteen years old, a son, and four servants all in their teens or early twenties.

Their neighbours were mostly tradespeople and their families: a brewer, grocer and blacksmith. There was the bargemaster John Doick, one of the men called to speak at the 'Arundel Roads' appeal.[10] He lived with his daughter Mary, a schoolmistress, and the pupils she was schooling; the Doick barge business operated from the Pulborough wharves. There were still heavy goods coming in and out next to the Doric temple of Templemead: chalk being barrowed over gangplanks onto waiting carts, white chalk marks on every surface. A large stone kiln on Old Wharf burnt chalk to produce the powdery lime that would be mixed with sand for mortar or carted by the hundredweight to be spread on fields as a fertiliser. Over the wall from Templemead, workers fed the kilns with layers of charcoal and chalk; they raked out the lime, their eyes and lips hot and swollen with the alkaline dust.[11] Beyond that was the malt house, with its own landing stage for the barley coming in by river.

Times were not easy for any of these people. They were working for survival, watching as acquaintances left for the colonies. They had customers and clients who could not afford to pay the bills. At the large house next door to the Martins, the front windows were blocked up to reduce the liability for window tax. Further along, one of the smartest houses, with modillions and cornices that spoke of money to spare, had been built from the outset with three of its big front sashes missing.[12]

Nothing in Pulborough made so strong an impression on me when I was young as those blind frontages. I imagined the claustrophobic dimness of the rooms within, and tried to fathom the desperation that would lead people to close up their lives like this. It was often the rooms used by servants that were stopped up first, and in the case of rented properties landlords might block tenants' windows to keep the charges down. In extreme cases, the tax made involuntary anchorites of the very poor. It was doctors who saw the worst effects of it on patients and campaigned for a repeal. But the tall windows of Dr Martin's home looked south to the midday sun and the big sky over the wild brooks.

While Mantell's iguanodon forced the world's geologists to reconfigure their thinking, Peter Martin kept deepening his knowledge of his part of the world in successive ages. Fixed in Pulborough by his work and family, he came to know his village as an extraordinary range of places including warm seas, rocky ravines and lush plains. Grappling with the shape of the whole region, he refused to relinquish his theory of a cataclysm that broke open the plains of chalk. 'All wrong', they heckled at the Chichester Philosophical and Literary Society; at the Geological Society in London they lost his submission for the journal ('a large roll of papers, with six sections of the Ordnance Map', he specified in exasperation). He reasoned and persisted through the 1840s; he marked up new maps.[13]

Mantell did not accept the 'cataclysm' theory, but as they grew older the doctor-geologists still enjoyed talking and swapping specimens. 'My old friend Mr Martin of Pulborough dined and spent the evening with me', Mantell recorded in November 1848, by which time he was frail and pained, all too conscious of his own ageing bones.[14] Fame had brought him no riches and he was in a precarious state. He spent his later years in London and Martin made holiday visits to see him. They got to know each other's family, exchanging confidences and worrying aloud about their children.[15]

Peter Martin was pursuing many other kinds of research alongside geology in the 1840s and 50s. He was conscious of his marginal status in the world of the gentlemen's journals, but it didn't put him off. His self-consciousness, and unabated enthusiasm, showed when he explained in the *Gardeners' Chronicle* why he preferred to contribute anonymously. Being 'unknown to fame' his name would 'convey no definite sense of intellectual superiority'; he preferred in any case to 'remain private'.[16] A local scholar, he felt out of the stream, but he also found that there was room for voices like his in the chronicles and quarterlies of Victorian intellectual life.

He had plenty to say. Ambitious gardening was going on by the river at Templemead, and Martin wrote about hollies, bay trees, soft fruits. He observed the skill of his neighbours in tending their orchards. To a connoisseurial riff on the perfect ripeness of medlar pears, 'bletting' and *espèce de pourriture*, he added his observation that 'the common people of Sussex call it drocksiness' and 'apply it to pears especially'. It was a reminder that 'common' local growers are connoisseurs as much as anyone.[17]

His archaeological research was much more substantial. He had been observing the tumps and barrows of the area all his life, comparing their shapes, reading all the available literature. The earthworks high on the downs gave ample evidence of ancient-British presence, but Martin was sure the Britons had lived in the valleys too – including in the sandy, marshy lands of pre-Roman Pulborough, Nutbourne and West Chiltington.[18] As a young doctor he knew Edmund Cartwright, the most prominent historian of Sussex (as well as clergyman, poet, inventor of the power loom); together one summer they made 'cross sections' of the mounds on Nutbourne Common. Fifteen years later, long after Cartwright's death, 'a labourer, who remembered the circumstance', found a ring of stones around one barrow and told Martin about it. The mystery of the mound had stayed in the labourer's mind all that time. They excavated together, revealing a substantial circular wall in the sandy earth.

The labourer wasn't named, of course, when Martin lectured on the subject in Chichester, proposing that the wall was the foundation of a Celtic hut, or another two decades later when Martin published the Nutbourne discoveries, with illustrations, in the new journal that was creating great excitement about local antiquities: the *Sussex Archaeological Collections*. Forty years after his first dig at Nutbourne, Peter Martin was more confident than ever about its ancient-British history. He had identified settlement enclosures on Hurston Warren outside Storrington and neighbouring Winterfield. His native landscape, he was sure now, 'gave shelter to, and was the hunting ground of, the British savage'.[19] He imagined the forests through which those predecessors roamed, and the sandy clearings where they made the 'rude cottages' he thought so primitive.

Barrow and Foundation of Wall.

In a future century he couldn't guess at, my father and I walked to the end of Monkmead Lane, along the short stretch with no pavement where you dodge between conifer-shadowed driveways, and climbed the stile into the open common. Boggy at the bottom, the path dries as it rises; rabbit burrows pit the sandy ground. Over to Nutbourne, past the house my parents bought when they first came to Sussex, one in a row of cottages at the top of the hill. My father told me all the news from 1978 – about the water-treatment works, the farmer's field behind the house, the arrival of my mother's high-spec typewriter, and working from home during the 'three-day weeks'. The house was cold, with its ironstone walls, though the view was almost worth it. One winter the pipes burst and the whole place flooded, leaving my parents with a deep aversion to old cottages. I was born three years later in a new-build bungalow with a damp-proof course. As for the mound it was long gone, flattened to form a cricket pitch in the 1850s. I was taken to play on the recreation ground beside it, swinging, I suppose, on top of the Britons.

Dr Martin turned from Pulborough's 'primitive inhabitants' to those who brought 'the arts of Rome'. Again, it was people working out in the fields who provided pivotal clues. Farmers showed him where strange lines of barrenness appeared between crops, and he assembled from such hints, written with a kind of invisible ink on the land, a map of Roman Pulborough. Local workmen talked of using material from the Roman road for modern repairs.[20] An old woman had found third-century coins buried by a spring at Red Ford Farm. From the back windows of the house he could see where Stane Street crossed straight over the brooks, and he set to writing part of its history. His last paper was called 'Some Recollections of a Part of the Stane Street Causeway'. 'Recollections' meant observations, but in this case the word carried a sense of personal memory: Martin had known this road all his life.

From the Templemead riverbank he could also see the proposed route of a dramatically new kind of road. The railway-construction gangs moved into the area in 1857, building at astonishing speed the line from Horsham to a new station at Pulborough. By late 1859 trains were running on the Mid-Sussex Railway that would place the village little more than two hours from Victoria, and put an end to the river and canals as the highway for cargo between London and the sea.

Down trains from Victoria:

5.45

9.50

1.50

3.50

5.45 arriving 8.17.[21]

Next in sight for the railway company was a route south to Arundel. This involved the huge engineering project of embanking a track over the marshes through Hardham to Amberley and negotiating the wide meander of the river at South Stoke. Dr Martin worked rapidly on the Roman remains in the knowledge that railway labourers would soon be throwing the earth of the valley into new shapes like a geological force. The navvies and overseers were always up against the clock, answerable to investors, and you couldn't ask them to look out for urns. In his mid-seventies, still anxious to glean everything he could about the history of the landscape in which he had spent his life, he rushed to investigate the ancient past exposed by the railway of the future. He died in 1860, before the navvies reached the brooks.

Dr Martin would not have been surprised by what a visiting archaeologist found in spring 1863 while the ground was being dug for the new embankment. The antiquary was 'obliged to work by moonlight with a hammer' before construction continued each morning.[22] The site was just across the road from the church at Hardham and its paintings. Even in the rush, there was no mistaking the Roman cemetery. Mr Dawkins sifted through the disturbed soil, trying to understand, at speed and in the dark, the shape of the graves. In each he found an oak chest and urn. Several graves still contained the sandals of their occupants, leather and laces preserved in the bog conditions of the wild brooks.

The extended line through the Arun valley and right down to the sea at Littlehampton opened in August 1863. Five trains a day up, five trains a day down: rumbling and steaming fast over the Hardham meadows, past Amberley Castle, and across the flood plains, so close to the little group of grey buildings under the trees at South Stoke that you catch your breath.[23]

25. A TEACHER'S HISTORY

I was going back compulsively and Caroline wasn't going back at all. I think she was protecting her sense of home, and didn't need to disturb the memories by visiting. I rang from the Chequers at the top of the hill in Pulborough, an old coaching inn run as a lovely small hotel. Nothing made me happier than walking up from the train station past the church to the Chequers, and opening the window in a room looking over the Glebe Field towards the distant ridge of Rackham and Amberley Mount. That afternoon I had walked to Hardham and on past the ruins of the priory to Coldwaltham. I had spotted the old OPEN sign hung round the side of the fourteenth-century house that used to be a restaurant. We spent our evenings and Sundays waitressing there, delivering coq au vin and jambalaya to customers in the low-beamed room, inventing complex washing-up rituals until the CLOSED sign was finally hung on the gate.

Did she know about the 'Blue Books' I asked. No, she couldn't think of anything particularly blue. Lissette at the Chequers had mentioned them to me. There was all sorts of local history in the Blue Books, she said. She had them somewhere but hadn't seen them for years. It was slightly unsettling. If there was a series of useful books about Pulborough, I should have come upon them by now. Lissette stood thinking, paused among the breakfast pots and pans, handsome in her black dress and workman's boots, more Whitechapel than rural B&B. She would hunt them out and let me know.

Three A4 booklets bound in light blue, spines too thin for a title, text typed on a typewriter and copied. They would have been easy to pass over. Each followed a Pulborough road: the Roman road out of town, or Rectory Lane on the hill (including the Chequers), or — the subject of the first booklet, produced in 1986 – *A Brief Guide to Lower Street*. They were jointly written by a small group of local people, including Elizabeth Garrett. I skimmed the first volume for useful facts and then realised it was not a utilitarian 'guide' or anthology of archive snippets, but something intricately coherent: 'an imaginary walk along Lower Street as it was in the days before the First World War'.[1]

Later I took the walk with them, slowly, on the flint-surfaced road with its horse-and-cart traffic. A new doctor had come to Templemead after Dr Martin, seeing patients through the 1880s and 90s; his daughter now lived in the house. We passed the dairy next door, the new houses built on Carpenter's Meadow, the big shop on the corner of Barnhouse Lane, almost a department store ('Grocers, wine merchants, drapers, outfitters, furniture dealers and retail ironmongers'). No building was overlooked, however unremarkable; each had its present and its history. At every one we met the current (1914) occupants, and looked back to their predecessors. There wasn't much mention of sources, or gaps, or purposes, but the politics were in the doing: in the discipline of stopping at each door. Attention was given evenly to the big houses, the barns, the condemned cottage behind the boot shop where an old woman was refusing to leave.

Elizabeth had a little girl of four years old. She took Caroline to nursery and got in a few hours at the Record Office. She was coming to know Pulborough as she had known Soho – its backyards and old disputes, its inner fabric, not all visible from the street. Fewer pole-dancing clubs making planning applications, but she liked it.

Before I could report on the Blue Books to Caroline, there was an eruption of wailing upstairs, loud even on my end of the phoneline. Henry was in bed but not asleep. Caroline rang back an hour later. Did your parents have a trick for getting you to sleep, she asked. I said they needed one; I tormented them. And yours? 'They had me naming the shops and houses along Lower Street. That sent me off. I still do it sometimes. Though I suppose the shops have changed.'

PART IV

26. JUST COUNTRY

Ford Madox Ford's rhomboid of green

For several years after the death of my mother, my father went for a walk each day. Allowing for a few minor variants, like a diversion made to a postbox, it was almost always the same walk. I joined him when I was back home for a few days, but most of the time he had the walk to himself and it formed the basis of evening reports on the telephone. I answered emails or cleared up the sitting room while I was listening. I didn't understand the repetition of the same route each day, but I greatly admired my father's capacity to find satisfaction in it. He would note a poppy in bud, and find the next day that the flower had opened. He did not seek more than that. In the face of extreme difficulty he had not flinched, and now he required no further eventfulness.

Now, long after he sold the house on West Chiltington Common, left that walk and moved to Chichester, I can think my way through the shadowed gate onto the golf course, over grey sand paths between gorse, across the fairway to where a new fence was always being put up around the stables and a small dog was throwing itself in perpetuity against a mesh of chicken wire. The path runs past a half-hidden pond to Poohsticks Bridge where we threw in our twigs, then there's a stile onto the upward slope of a meadow, guarded in this corner by a chestnut that has been holding onto a slender thread of life since it caught canker fifteen years ago. After the overhung lanes and driveways, the meadow is upliftingly expansive; towards its green horizon you walk to meet the sky. As a teenager I associated this spaciousness with an imagined America; once, coming over the brow, I said 'New England' and the name stuck. The stile at the top of New England brings us over a little sandstone cliff, down with a slither into a gulley and another kind of place, enclosed and inhabited. A water garden, sunken and secret, lilies opening silently on a pool fed by streams. A grassy bank on the right where bluebells succeed daffodils. My father would report the progress of spring according to that bank.

In London one evening I mentioned my return visits to Sussex. It was a way of explaining myself. 'What are you doing?' 'Well I keep going to look at the downs.' I gave the requested co-ordinates: Pulborough, Storrington, at which the biographer of Ford Madox Ford nodded. 'That's where he lived after the war.' Was it? Disparate planets collided. Ford's 1915 novel *The Good Soldier* had been one of my set books at A level, so that for several years I knew much of it by heart. It suggested to me a remote world of emotional sophistication among people I was never likely to meet. French was spoken fluently and adultery silently signalled. I looked on from a distance, impressed. Yet certain things shook me with their nearness. This was my first encounter with a narrator whose way of ordering or disordering his story is as much the subject of the novel as anything that happens. I learnt that in trying to fathom the pattern of events, 'one goes back, one goes forward'. Also that it is not always possible to say what is important and what's not. I understood, too, that the veering between ordinariness and melodrama was not crazy stylisation but a kind of truth. The characters were 'just good people' going about their business; at the same time they were dancing to the furthest stars or they were shrieking in agony.

Twenty years later I pulled out my Ford books and ordered more. *The Good Soldier* was written mostly at Winchelsea on the Kent coast, I discovered, where Ford felt the claustrophobia of respectable small-town surveillance, and partly at his lover Violet Hunt's rented cottage on the Selsey peninsula south of Chichester.[1] When war was declared, he revised his draft to make the most fateful events occur on 4 August. The effect was to make every 4 August complicit in 4 August 1914, each Edwardian summer anticipating the catastrophe. It was that, or else the outbreak of war sent a shudder backwards, so that dates once unremarked stood forward in a sinister parade.

Ford joined the Welch Regiment as an infantry officer that autumn and spent the next two years at a series of training camps in England and Wales before going to France, his battalion responsible for transport logistics just behind the front line. At Bécourt Wood in July 1916 he was caught in a shell explosion, which, improbably, he survived. For three weeks, lying in casualty clearing stations and then in hospital at Corby, he had no memory. But the past did gradually come back to him. He returned to service in France and Belgium, evaded direct hits for two years, came back to England alive, and moved to a cottage called Red Ford near Storrington.

For some time I wasn't sure where it was. I rented a room on Hurston Warren, in a house that had its own stories to tell, and walked the unfamiliar paths on the far side of New England. Nothing corresponded with the two-up two-down cottage described by Ford in his letters. Then I saw that the large house by the bluebell bank harboured between its modern extensions remnants of an older core. I checked the stream at the bottom of the garden. The water was a bright rusty orange-red.

It was Ford's new partner, the young Australian painter Stella Bowen, who heard about the farmer with a house to let, went down from London in March 1919 and looked it over with an optimistic eye. Neither knew the Arun area, though Ford had made a journey across the wild brooks at least once before.[2] The place on offer was an old farm labourer's cottage, 'built of old red brick and old red tiles, all greened over with mossy stains', as Stella described it later in her memoir of this period, 'and it was tucked under a little red sandstone cliff'.[3] She considered the rats and lack of all amenities, also the cheap rent and seclusion, and took the lease. The name, of course, delighted Ford. He always set store by omens: repeated dates, magnetic places. Red Ford, he could believe, was his longed-for sanctuary.[4] Stella was to stay in London through the spring and join him in Sussex later. Ford went alone on the train from Victoria to Pulborough on 3 April, got a lift to Hurston with his few supplies, entered the decrepit house for the first time, and made a fire in the hearth.

He ate 'fried chicken and beans and oranges' and kept off the drink, he told Stella in the first of his daily letters, but that first night was a nadir, a lonely reckoning in the darkness of a broken building, sunken in a hollow, unable to explore this new place which was not yet home but from whose raw materials he must try to make one.[5] He let a note of distress into his letter, and though by day two he was reassuring Stella that the cottage was perfect, the long evening he spent enclosed by country darkness, turned in upon a post-war self he did not know, came to stand in his private mythology as a meeting with destiny.[6] He could not tell Stella how desperately he looked into his stewpot that night for signs of fate, but he wrote about it much later. Too tired to peel the shallots that were to accompany his mutton (not chicken, in this account), he made a deal with himself and the vegetables. 'If the skin came off the shallots I was to make a further effort. If not, I was to let go.'[7] He put them into the boiling crock and watched them in the meagre light of the fire.

If in fact he cooked fried chicken and beans, there would have been a spitting pan of fat rather than a stewpot. Perhaps the shallots belonged to the second night or the third, or it may have been at some other time altogether that they appealed to him as messengers of the gods or barographs of the soul. His pact with them was a moment of self-surrender, an exhausted delegation of choice. There was in it a Keatsian idea of fading away with the nightingale into the forest: the 'Ode to a Nightingale' moves under his account of the evening. It was not to Keats, however, that he referred directly for the dream of dissolving, but to a 'peasant frame of mind'. 'The peasant can say: Enough and fade . . . and lie down in the shadow of a rick . . . and so pass away.'[8] Having made it through the war to peace, he was now half willing to lie down and die. He could die because he had arrived at the place he had aimed at: a nook of English country. That was also, he knew, a reason to live.

He was forty-five. He was an enormous man, with trousers stretched to their limit and a strong sense of his own physical comedy (fondly expressed in exotically unflattering images of himself as a bear, a great auk, an obese cockatoo). He had sustained lung damage in France, probably from slight mustard gas exposure that left him wheezing 'like a machine gun'.[9] In photographs, his mouth is usually open beneath his small moustache in a way that suggests respiratory effort. He had no money and must write in order to live, but he could not reclaim the mind he had when he wrote *The Good Soldier*. He pictured himself as an 'extinct volcano' and drafted a novel (not published) about an author who falls into obscurity.[10] At Red Ford he needed to work out whether his propulsive force was really gone. Though the fighting was over, the negotiation with memory and injury was just beginning. He was also a pursued man; Violet Hunt, the beautiful and punishing woman with whom he had lived before the war, would not let him go and was vowing to corner him, flushing him out of whatever retreat he made. His home must therefore be a defensive position in an ongoing private war so tormenting that the other war had been almost – and sometimes he was certain of it – a relief.[11]

Ford and Stella lived in West Sussex for three and a half years, first at Red Ford and then in a more weatherproof cottage about ten miles away, high and hidden on Bedham Hill near Fittleworth. It is not a period much discussed by admirers of Ford – not like the Edwardian years in Winchelsea when he was a close friend of Henry James and collaborated with Joseph Conrad, or his time at the centre of literary life in Paris. They left Fittleworth for the south of France at the end of 1922: the land of the troubadours, with its arid hillsides and shuttered houses, constituted Ford's ideal place beyond all others. But it was in Sussex that he faced the task of 'reconstruction' – not the officially sponsored post-war reconstruction of house-building and industry but the re-making of himself as a thinker, lover and writer. Years later, he was still writing himself back into his Sussex garden. The last volume of his Great War tetralogy *Parade's End* is set in a green fold of English country, where an injured soldier, so exhausted that he has given up all speech and movement, lies mute on a bed with long grass growing up all around him.

Through April and May, as Ford prepared the scene for their country life, he and Stella wrote daily to each other, Ford reporting on refurbishments and progress in the garden, Stella advising on paint colours and recounting her hunts around London for the household items he requested with his usual specificity. '*Don't* forget the egg boxes. Two: to hold six each. URGENT. Also: return that rush basket. I have *heaps* of garden stuff etc, ready for you! I love you.'[12] Ford walked over to the postbox on Wiggonholt Common, the paths soft with sand and conifer needles, the bracken beginning to unfurl its summer fronds. The sheets of their love letters are packed with discussion of solid objects like bedsteads and flooring, practical things that could be relied upon. There are few such objects in the world of *The Good Soldier*, where silver-nickel bread baskets are passed across starched tablecloths in the hotels of Europe. There was to be no alloy plating in Sussex, where baskets were made of willow or rushes. Yet there was no forgetting what the war, he said, had revealed: 'that beneath Ordered Life itself was stretched the merest film with, beneath it, the abysses of Chaos'.[13]

The nearest shop ('the size of a rabbit hutch but it produces *everything*') was at Cootham on the edge of Storrington, a two-mile walk on a deep, damp path opening onto paddocks and then a glimpse of the downs at Parham.[14] You couldn't carry much home at a time. Pulborough in the other direction, with its railway station and helpful stores, was a mile over the sandy common and then two along the road, so there was every reason to be as self-sufficient as possible.

Ford set about repairing the house with desperate energy, as if he were fighting for life with every log he sawed. The most ambitious project was the construction of a kitchen. In a labourer's cottage like this, the fireplace in the main room was the place for cooking and certainly there was always a pot on Ford's sitting-room fire: sometimes animal feed, more often a stock, simmering all day and night so that everything smelt of it. Ford was serious about food, however, and intended more than one-pot meals. With improvised carpentry, he made a lean-to extension ('cock-eyed', said Stella: the joints weren't quite right) and installed an 'old Sussex stove'.[15] Since Ford was extravagant and perfectionist in his way of living the simple life, some very fine cooking would occur here.

Just as he had hoped when he imagined a Sussex home, there was a 'monthly rose' on the wall ('I knew there was never a labourer's cottage in Kent or Sussex without one').[16] A scented jasmine was making good progress towards the bedroom. The box hedge under the windows 'must have taken *centuries* to grow', he rejoiced, and the hawthorn boundary ('twenty feet high and quite solid as a quickset should be') was 'the product of the care and attention of generations'.[17] The lives of those past gardeners were close to poverty, as he knew. The pre-war tenant, he was told, 'was here for 40 years – and then went into the Union Workhouse', that fragment of rural biography evoking a life profoundly different from Ford's restless moving and reinvention.[18] Ford didn't know the tenant's name, but we can see it now on the census returns. George Heyler, farm labourer, sixty-six in 1911. He and his wife Ann had three grown-up children living with them in the small cottage (one a carter, one a general servant), all needing to be fed from pots in the fireplace where Ford watched his shallots. And in the end they couldn't do it.[19]

The cottage was blessed with fresh water; there was a spring under the oak tree, which supplied a 'dipping-hole'. It had been in use for longer than perhaps even Ford imagined. Before the man who trimmed the box hedge for forty years and died in the workhouse, there was another predecessor at Red Ford, and a remarkable event.

'An aged widow named Shepherd' was cleaning and deepening the dipping-hole in September 1855, hoping to renew her supply of water in the dry summer season. As she dug, part of the bank collapsed and a decayed elm tree fell down with it. 'In the earth thus loosened' (the story is told by one of the founders of the *Sussex Archaeological Society*, who went over from Lewes to see the place), 'a large number of Roman coins were found'. In his study at Templemead Dr Martin of Pulborough wrote about this new evidence of Roman life near Stane Street. There were eighteen hundred coins, all brass, arranged as if packed in a box that had rotted away, and the faces shone out when they were cleaned by staff at the British Museum: Claudius Gothicus, Tetricus senior and junior, Constantius I and II.[20] The rarer ones are still in the museum. Nobody knows who buried them in the fourth century, 'probably in haste and in a time of danger', choosing the spring as a landmark that would survive even if roads and buildings were destroyed. Fifteen hundred years later, after the Great War of 1914–18, the water was still bubbling from the ground and Ford had found his sanctuary after a time of danger. The water supply looked murky and needed cleaning out. He proudly conducted some engineering. 'Redford Reservoir!' he christened his new waterworks: 'three crystal clear springs running into it straight from the rocks; a concrete dam, a filter bed, a pipe under which pails stand to be filled!'[21]

Ford's plumbing skills had limits, but he was genuinely expert in the garden. He started planting the morning after his arrival, hired a boy called Joseph Burton to help dig the long-abandoned beds, and had all the summer crops established by the end of the month: French beans, broad beans, peas, salsify, carrots, radishes, kohlrabi, sorrel, beetroot, tomatoes, marrows, maize. Since there was no money to buy food if the vegetables failed, the future depended on his seedlings. He defended them against all invaders, slug-hunting with a candle in the evenings. He made time, too, for flower-gardening, posting off the first mignons to

Stella as tokens of love and invitation. When she arrived, there must be sweet peas next to the door. Alongside the wild creatures of the garden – the nightingale in the tree over the house, the frogs that were abundant in this damp place by the stream, the enormous spiders, the fleas (these were the limit for Stella, who gave firm instructions for fumigation) – he assembled an assortment of animals (dogs, cat, goat, pig), each named and made part of the household.

The slug-hunts turned from warfare to reverie as he stood in the dusk. He had written, long ago in *The Heart of the Country*, about 'the little shocks and emotions' that come to country people digging potatoes in the evening.[22] He respected in his neighbours and in himself those depths of feeling that rose through the meditative rhythms of manual labour. He would work naked sometimes, if Joseph was not around, a large Adam making an Eden. The madness and rage of war stood at the edge of consciousness, as if it were the other side of a hedge in which, if he stayed quiet, he could hear the sparrows hopping. 'I'm nearly as much in love with the place as I am with you', he told Stella. On a warm night with a new moon he went onto the top of the downs and lay there until after midnight. By late May he was replete with all but Stella: 'Darling! Walking in the garden in the cool of the evening – like God! – it suddenly seemed as if there was nothing left to do but just wait for you.'[23]

Country books were among the literature Ford most admired. He revered the writer-naturalist W. H. Hudson, whom he associated with a saintly closeness to nature. Years ago, before the war, he had begun an essay on Hudson with an image of St Francis among the birds. 'Don't we see him? – walking, silent, in a tranquil garden towards evening, peering up at the families of swifts.'[24] That was Ford too, in Sussex. He wanted to go silently in the garden and listen for the movement of wings in the hedge. The qualities of the birdwatcher (self-effacement, acute observation) seemed to him admirable qualities for life and for prose. Gilbert White was another hero. It's hard to think of two English writers more unalike than the naturalist of Selborne and the modern impressionist Ford Madox Ford who, at his most equivocal and volatile, could only fantasise about directness. At Red Ford he wanted to observe nature steadily and slowly. It was one of the ideal lives he would give to Christopher Tietjens in *Parade's End*: to walk like Gilbert White in the garden, or like George Herbert, 'a contemplative parson farming his own tithe-fields (with a Greek testament under his arm)'.[25] Herbert's nook of bright green is intensely imagined by Christopher, a standard he holds on to. But he cannot remember the name of the place; like peace itself, the word 'Bemerton' eludes him.

All through the first summer in Sussex, Ford came in each evening from the garden and worked at a new book to be called, he thought, 'English Country'. First in a series of articles for the *New Statesman*, and then in the book that would actually be called *No Enemy*, Ford tried to articulate what the war had done to his sense of landscape. He wrote about the intensity with which, in France, a particular vision of 'country' had come into his mind and taken hold. From the moment when German troops crossed the Belgian border 'near a place called Gemmenich' on 4 August at six in the morning, 'aspects of the earth no longer existed for me'. Every green field of the world was tense with premonition. 'There were no nooks, no little, sweet corners; there were no assured homes, countries, provinces, kingdoms or races. All the earth held its breath and waited.'[26]

In 1916, on the transport line behind the Somme, Ford had written a poem with a ballad rhythm reminiscent of Housman. It was about the present ('Dust and corpses in the thistles / Where the gas-shells burst like snow') and about the mind's recourse to the past: 'But I'm with you up at Wyndcroft, / Over Tintern on the Wye.'[27] Ford knew well the history of Romantic recourse to sustaining landscapes exemplified by Wordsworth's return to Tintern. What the Great War did to landscape and to the mind, however, put in jeopardy all storehouses of remembered country. Ford had a notion of blood leeching like a toxin into rivers and seeping across all the earth. Living things 'might at any moment be resolved into a scarlet viscosity'.[28]

Many soldiers from southern England noticed the topographical similarity when they arrived at the camps behind the front lines. Some felt it as a comfort, like a familiar hand. 'I am sitting warm in the sun on a heap of chalk', Edward Thomas told his wife Helen when his unit moved to dug-outs in a disused chalk pit near Arras; a copse of young hazel and birch with chalk showing between the stems reminded him very specifically of Hampshire.[29] Ford probed his own feelings about that beauty. 'The sun has a peculiar quality in the sky over downlands,' he wrote, 'as if chalk dust in the air whitened the rays.'[30] He was thinking of himself as a boy on the hills behind Folkestone, and remembering his vision of light and white as he looked over the country of war. Now the English chalk was overlaid with many kinds of memory – a child running in the wind, planes glittering in the sun above soft hills, chalk dust from an explosion forming a low white cloud over the turf.

For much of the war Ford had moved through places with a kind of numbness. It was a necessary disregard: officers were not there to admire scenery but to plot its defensive potential, map viewpoints and identify targets. Landscape, to which Ford had responded all his life with the rapture of a lover, was hidden from him, transmuted into so many critical points on a chart. The purely utilitarian looking was a form of self-protection too, restricting emotion and memory. Except that on several occasions 'the veil lifted'.[31] There were just a few that he could name. A moment of clarity had come on chalk downland behind the Somme. He was looking out from an officers' camp to where shells were falling over the shoulder of the next hill. 'It came like one of those visions that one's eyes, when tired, will see just before one falls asleep.' There appeared a 'rhomboid of deeper, brighter green', brighter than the green of the fields around him, 'a green that was really alive'. It wavered like the projection from a magic lantern, and resolved into an image of 'just country', accompanied by the feeling of birds watching from the hedges. 'You see the idea – sanctuary!' 'Possibly that little vision of English country, coming then, was really a prayer.'[32] Sitting in the cottage in the hollow near Storrington, he wanted to understand that vision. He took himself on the march to the railhead at Méricourt-Ribemont, and then up the hillside towards the officers' camp, moving slowly in recollection along the bare downland road, wheat on the left and oats on the right: yes, he remembered which way around the crops were growing.

The green rhomboid showed itself one other time, a little differently, on Mont Vidaigne looking towards Ypres. In the story of that day as he told it in 1919–20, Ford was waiting alone on the hill for many hours. Shells were falling through bright autumn air – 'little white balls! Beautiful!' – and such was their beauty from this distance that his 'soul exalted'. Then, in the dusk, he was possessed by an intense longing for an old and sheltered place. It seemed to be there before him: 'the secure nook at the end of a little valley, the small cottage whose chimneys just showed over the fruit trees'.[33]

In their suddenness and intensity, these experiences Ford described in 1919 are similar to what Joyce would call 'epiphanies' and Woolf would call 'moments of being', when the 'cotton-wool' of practical daily life clears to expose some underlying order of things. Ford was feeling his way towards a language for such revelations. He likened the quality of his perception to the extreme clarity one finds 'in the little paintings of Van Eyck on the Chasse de Ste. Ursule at Brûges' – paintings which shine out with detail, giving individual emphasis to every strand of a saint's hair and every fold in a fluttering flag beneath intense blue sky.[34] St Ursula's painted shrine is known now to be by Hans Memling, but it doesn't change the force of Ford's comparison. Like his Pre-Raphaelite grandfather, he felt the heightened vision in these early northern paintings. His passing allusion suggests a richly associative layering of scenes: the Netherlands of Van Eyck and Memling in all its sanctity and domesticity casting its light on the Belgium seen by Ford in wartime, when Bruges was occupied and those bridges smashed, all seen with the mind's eye from Sussex.

The 'English Country' articles were presented as straight recollection, as 'straight' as a looping, backtracking account of remembered impressions could be. For the book version, *No Enemy: A Tale of Reconstruction*, he invented a character with the French name Gringoire, a demobbed soldier and writer like himself. He had his narrator listen to this veteran Gringoire talking on through the evenings about the war, and about the meaning of countryside. He was splitting himself between the soldier-writer and the listening 'compiler'. We feel all the time that this is really one person, who is his own audience. The many listeners and soliloquists in Ford's writing hold the night at bay with their talk, soothing themselves and each other with their voices. Gringoire goes on narrating to the friendly editor, who recounts it all with the hint of a disciple saving up the words of the master (the master who is 'Gallophile, Veteran, Gardener . . . Poet').[35] Conversation, the most valuable salve Ford knew, replaces lonely writing with the reassuring sociability of being heard.

No Enemy is both a simple and an elusive title. The urbane courtiers in Shakespeare's *As You Like It* retreat to the Forest of Arden where, under the greenwood tree, they will 'see no enemy / But winter and rough weather'. In his Sussex Arden, Ford faced no external enemy except wind and rain (and Violet Hunt). But after military action came the rough weather within. It was a simple story that he was telling about a soldier who survived the war and found the place he had longed for; it was also elusive, slipping every tie. Ford was projecting his current circumstances back onto the green rhomboid glimpsed near the Somme, so that his new Sussex life became the precise answer to the longings conceived there. He was explaining to himself as well as to his readers how a cottage with a kitchen garden had been all he wanted, and why now, if he were to speak more grandly, he thought life in such places might be the salvation of Europe.

After a summer that both Ford and Stella would remember as halcyon, they looked for a house in the area that they could buy. Coopers Cottage was about ten miles away; it was just the kind of old Sussex smallholding they wanted, and had a view that made the decision for them. The only trouble was a sitting tenant who had the right to live and die there: they would have to wait. They settled in for winter at Red Ford.

They didn't go around visiting historic towns or requesting tours of manor houses or even walking far on the downs. There wasn't the time: the garden, the poultry, the animals, the long walks to buy what they needed, the guests who came most weekends and chiefly Ford's writing (which demanded exertion from both of them) took all the hours of the day. Valentine in *Parade's End* reflects that though Gilbert White's village Selborne is only thirty miles away, they had never had a chance to go there, what with 'pigs, hens, pea-sticking, sales, sellings, mending all-wool under-garments'. There would never be time to go to 'Selborne, nor Arundel, nor Carcassonne'.[36] Nor George Herbert's parish, Bemerton. These unvisited places were important to Ford as imaginative concepts: he needed to be too busy, too absorbed, ever to reach them.

He wanted to know his home by working the soil. Boasting of the rural knowledge he had accrued through years in Hythe and Winchelsea, he liked to show his familiarity with the regional particularities of south-eastern labourers. Then again, he wasn't going to conflate Romney Marsh with the Arun. 'West Sussex to a Kent-minded man is as foreign in speech and habits as is China', he remarked, and there was a boast in that too, an assertion of his ability to tell the difference.[37] That was the kind of extreme localism he advocated, and which he cultivated in tandem with his international life.

'Just country', Ford kept repeating. 'Just a house.' He looked with reverence at his own house though the roof was still leaky and the rooms tiny. He would write about this years later in *It Was the Nightingale*, still trying to explain the force of his emotion at Red Ford: 'We had seen Ploegsteert, where it had been revealed that men's dwellings were thin shells that could be crushed as walnuts are crushed.'[38] When he rebuilt a ceiling, or set to making stools from old floor planks, he worked with the conviction of someone restoring solidity to the world.

These feelings grew stronger still when Stella found that she was pregnant. Ford's poem from that spring, 'A House', is closely related to children's tales of domestic objects coming to life. It is a night poem, borrowing from the late-watching meditations of Coleridge's 'Frost at Midnight', whispering while a household sleeps. With its tick-tock rhymes, it's a lullaby for a child, though shaped by the longings of a troubled man. 'I resemble / The drawing of a child / That draws just a house', says the House. The tree speaks, then the nightingale in the tree, the clocks indoors, and 'the unborn son of the house': as the clocks tick on, the house counts out the lives of generations who have lived in it. 'Is . . . was . . . is . . . was . . .'[39] It is partly Red Ford and partly an anticipation of Coopers Cottage, where they now had possession and were directing proceedings as old pipes were patched and a new dormer let into the roof.

In the poem Ford enters his future house like a spirit, listening for its voice. 'There were floods, out far and wide', says the House, with all its windows 'blazing across the tide'. That is a feeling that comes from the Arun valley, where the floods rise each winter and a lit window is safety glimpsed. Making illustrations for the poem, Stella showed windows from outside, reflected in water, and the writer at the window, working within.[40] Ford's house is a precarious ark only just resisting a tide that is also the flow of worry and bills. In an epilogue that catches up the tone of Coleridge's 'all seasons shall be sweet to thee', we seem to watch all the old hardworking houses of England through the years – through 'seasons dark and holy', through 'great winds and drought' until the tiles blow loose and the steps wear down.

Both Ford and Stella were highly specific about the qualities of 'just a house': it must be old, unshowy, vernacular, eloquent of continuous life. Coopers was a fine seventeenth-century cottage, built of stone with half-timbering above. The inglenook was the kind you could walk into: room enough to look into a pot and read one's fate. There could be no fading away under a hayrick for either of them now. They worked at the renovations all summer, moved in the pigs, ducks, goats and chickens, a heavily pregnant Stella hauled the furniture onto the dog-cart in September, and Esther Julia was born at the end of November.[41]

Coopers was, as Stella put it, 'extravagantly beautiful and quite inaccessible'.[42] There is no village centre to Bedham: the name describes a lane winding several miles over a wooded hill, with paths dropping down to cottages at intervals along it. There was a stone chapel that doubled as a tiny school (where Ford was co-opted into presenting the prizes and other duties of a local celebrity). Vitally, there was a postbox. The lane would bring you eventually to Fittleworth village, which had a branch-line station connecting to Pulborough and then to London. The Swan inn by the river was a favoured spot for visiting painters, who paid their weekend's bed and board with pictures. The pub became a local gallery of landscape art, its walls hung with views of haystacks and medieval stone bridges. For some of the artists who came, there was reconstructionary power in these glimpses of rural peace, different as they were from the hybrid, refracted visions for which Ford was trying to find literary form.[43]

Ford and Stella had ten acres of their own on which to build up a smallholding, and beyond that was 'the common', intricately known and regulated through centuries. The area is called The Mens, from 'ge-maennes' meaning common property; all the cottages came with customary rights to collect underwood and graze animals.[44] A stretch of the hillside is ancient woodland, with wild service trees, spindles and huge beeches. On the south slope, water emerges from the sandstone and splashes down into the stream below; it looks like it might have special powers and was for a long time treated as such by locals who held aching limbs hopefully under the waterfall.[45]

Edward Elgar and his wife, Alice, had moved to Bedham in 1917, renting a cottage called Brinkwells from the artist Rex Vicat Cole and hoping that the whole area might have curative powers for an ailing composer. So it had proved. Elgar marked his scores variously 'Bedham' or 'Brinkwells', as if giving an address, or the signature of a co-composer, to music that came with a fluency he had thought was lost. He felt he was working with the woods as he listened to the movement of sound through beech canopies, over damp, sandy woodland floors, into sudden declivities and streams. 'Wood magic, con sordino' he gave as the notation for his Violin Sonata in summer 1918.[46] When Elgar sent his friend W. H. Reed a map to guide him from Pulborough (PLATE), he drew in the landmarks of his world with delight, colouring the stone bridge ('15th centy.') with yellow ink, adding fish in the river and the painted Swan inn sign at Fittleworth, sketching himself and his dog coming along the lane.[47] These were directions into Ford's world too.

By the time of Ford and Stella's arrival in summer 1920, Elgar had suffered the loss of Alice to cancer and was struggling through the loneliness of grief. Still, he looked over the hedge at Coopers and hailed the new resident, who was feeding the pigs.[48]

Word went round in Fittleworth that Stella was not Mrs Ford. Some people minded, but mis-managed sows on the common were more likely to cause offence. Guests arrived from London, bedraggled by the journey. Ezra Pound eyed the scene dubiously, baffled that a genius should spend his time in so remote a place, with pigs. Much less welcome, friends of Violet Hunt came to spy on the ménage and report back. These visitors turned off the lane and made their way down a steep path through an orchard to the cottage sunk below the crest of the hill. Barking dogs raced round them, the chickens flapped out of the way. Stella was at the kitchen door, feeding the baby with a bottle of milk she'd squeezed from the goat, or she was handing the baby to the local girl Lucy, who would clean out the fire while Stella mixed the chicken feed and changed their straw, or lugged the cauldron of pig food through the mud. The labourer Mr Standing ('heavy, badger-like, with his old dialect that was just half Anglo-Saxon and half forgotten French words') was mending hurdle fences or loading manure onto the barrow for the fruit beds.[49] Ford was forking out furze animal bedding, or he was at a desk on the upstairs landing, writing fast at his new novel, *The Marsden Case*. He would be down in a moment, he often called out. Stella did the rounds outside in the dusk, settling the animals for the night; she kept the dinner hot and poured the visitors more wine. She was, she said astutely, a 'shock-absorber'.[50]

As at Red Ford, they were in love with the look of Coopers. 'Come and look at the moon', they would call to each other, 'come outside and see how the whitewash glows in the dusk.'[51] They would hang lanterns in the apple trees and eat outside with the smell of tobacco plants and the song of nightingales above them. Where Elgar wandered deep into the woods, absorbing atmospheres, yielding himself to the place, allowing himself to be haunted by the distorted forms of ancient trees, Ford and Stella had their minds on what they could make from their own domestic plot.

All his adult life Ford had set store by the culture of smallholding. He paid attention to the way it was done in France, where a *jardin* traditionally included seriously managed vegetable plots and fruit trees. Cottage economy was for Ford a philosophical foundation and moral framework. He would refer sometimes to life itself as a 'small-holding of time': we are granted an acreage, and we tend it (as Voltaire advised) as best we can.[52] It was literal tending of the land that he talked about most often: planting, sowing, hedging, feeding, cooking with care and without waste: these he considered the highest forms of cultivation. 'The country is good', he wrote to Herbert Read, 'when one has discovered various hollownesses – those of the plaster pillars of the state and the papier maché hearts of men.'[53] For a writer intensely responsive to falseness, who wrote with perfect pitch the languages of deceit, the processes of growing and cooking were charged with meaning.

He was both self-mocking and serious when he explained his plant-ing routines: 'I always seed while the moon is waxing; I never begin a planting on a 13th, but always on a 9th, an 18th or a 27th.'[54] It was a fastidious kind of paganism: 'If there is a wishing well in the neighbour-hood I fetch a bottleful of it to start my first watering of the spring.' The ceremonies of his garden were as elaborate as the coded choreography of Edwardian high society. In *The Good Soldier* he was acute and partic-ular about both kinds of ritual, but the procedures of planting he could carry out in better faith.

Ford in his garden was a large child among four-legged friends, a bon viveur, a scientist, perfectionist, philosopher, an eager, overreach-ing agriculturalist with major aspirations. It's hard to tell how seriously he was working on his breeding of disease-free potatoes. Likewise with his pig-rearing. He aspired to national prizes and imagined his black-bristled Anna and Anita in triumph.[55] But these 'monstrous quadrupeds', who reg-ularly broke out onto the common or set off down the lane to Fittleworth village where a male pig lived next to the police station, were better at escapades than medals. It was Stella who sorted out the scrapes. It was Stella, pushing Julie's buggy up the hill, who saw Anna hurtling heavily towards her, gave chase and managed eventually to pen her into the roadside by means of the pram.[56] John Dowell, the narrator of *The Good Soldier*, remembers laughing at a cow pitched upside down into a stream. Four feet in the air, that cow lies ridiculously in the current of the novel, both farcical and desperate in ways that reflect back onto Dowell himself. There was some of that extraordinarily mobile tone in the way Ford related the many animal adventures of his Sussex life. Ford's infant comedy could flip over into a dark sense of ignoble fate.

At Bedham in the summer of 1922, Ford read *Ulysses*. He was part of a network of avant-garde thinkers across Europe and America who were encountering the book, but he read it, too, as a countryman. Considering the indecencies of which Joyce was accused, he observed that 'the great proportion of the food we eat and of the food eaten by the beasts that we eat is dung; we are resolved eventually into festering masses of pollution for the delectation of worms'.[57] This was the smallholder speaking, who forked the manure from the stables, who was proud to deal daily with things hidden 'from the usual contemplation of urban peoples'. There he was, the large man breathing loudly in his reading chair, the enormous book in his hands, while apples ripened in the orchard outside and the pigs shifted heavily in their sties.

⌒

The cottage today is still recognisably theirs, though its years as a small farm are long past. The big orchard on the wide slope is gone. Well-garaged cars stand in place of the dog-cart. There have been keen gardeners in recent times, though not in Ford's style. What he set aside as hay meadow has been arranged into terraces. For subsequent residents on Bedham Hill, life's ideal has not been the old mare in the open stable and black sows moving their great weight across the common. It has been a carefully tended ornamental garden: specimen ferns backed by rhododendrons, a fine-leaved maple by a pool. The dormer built in 1920 by a carpenter from across the common is still so straight as to make the rest of the house look slanted (an effect that Stella said made them feel seasick). The big stone inglenook still has its bread oven and the iron pot hanger that held the 'immense cauldron' of pig food over the fire. 'The original builders knew what they were doing', the current owners tell me, explaining how the prevailing weather from the south blows straight over the top of them. At night, I'm told, the lights of the towns appear gradually under the stars; from up here, Billingshurst is a delicate glimmer. The house is tucked into the hill, safely sheltered, yet feasting on a view that is a revelation.[58]

I stood looking out from Ford and Stella's cottage across the weald to the North Downs, letting my eyes adjust to the scale, picking out details in the grey-green ocean of semi-wooded land. Up the drive and over the lane, the land to the south stretches away across the wild brooks to the white lamp of Amberley chalk pits and the trees on Chanctonbury Ring.

Stella said they could almost live on a good view.[59] The work of getting up and down the unavoidable hill (on foot, pushing a pram or in the dog-cart) suggests what they were both willing to do for the vision laid out before them, 'a view, as it were, from which one could see the kingdoms of the earth'.[60] The young inheritor in *Parade's End* stands with four counties running out below his feet, 'to the horizon!', as if he stood on the lip of a waterfall with life streaming out beneath him.[61]

Perspective was Ford's business. In his fiction he was continuously shifting viewpoints, considering the situation from over here, and right up there. His people want to know whether it is safer to hole oneself up or to lie out in the open. His wartime hilltop visions had a biblical quality in his mind, as if the devil were showing him the misleading glory of the world. On the downs above Méricourt-Ribemont, he saw a dreadful thing at a distance that made it look beautiful. He saw shells falling on a ravaged country and his 'soul exalted', so Gringoire says in *No Enemy*: a confession, a warning. As a shelter from such distances, the green nook had appeared to him and pursued him until at last he sat in it at Red Ford: 'the closed up end of a valley; closed up by trees – willows, silver birches, oaks, and Scotch pines; deep among banks; with a little stream, just a trickle, level with the grass of the bottom'.[62] Then, rising with the shallot skins, he moved to a house that, though hidden in the woods and under the slope of the orchard, offered from its windows a view of the kind that can be a daily challenge and exaltation.

Ford, Stella and Julie (nearly two) left for France in the autumn of 1922. Ford was troubled by his lungs, winters at Bedham were grindingly hard work, and the offer of a cottage in Villefranche was too tempting to decline. They had to sell the animals, but they intended to return after the winter and start up their Sussex life again. Ford ordered two hundred Darwin tulips for the garden, choosing not one-season dazzlers but the kind that will naturalise and last for years. He was imagining future springs.[63] But he never came back. At Saint-Jean-Cap-Ferrat he began *Parade's End*, the tetralogy that would endure as one of the greatest novels to examine the effects of war on the human mind, and worked at it rapidly through the mid-1920s in a series of small houses and hotel rooms across Provence.

At a little deal table installed by the dormer window of a hotel in Villeneuve-lès-Avignon, he worked on the fourth part, *Last Post*, through the summer of 1927. He thought his way back to Bedham and lay down in the orchard. At the centre of the novel, Mark Tietjens lies mute and unmoving on a bed in a field of grass. Though the scenario is bizarre, the tone of narration implies it is quite understandable that a man who has come through the war should lie still for years on an outdoor bed under a roof of thatch held up by six oak-sapling trunks. The bed is a bier in advance, or a tomb topped with a still-living effigy, or a divin in a rustic loggia, or a manger in which a newly peaceful life is swaddled. If Mark fell silent at the Armistice, when he seems to have had a stroke, he has been here for years. In the strange workings of this novel, it seems possible. Ford leaves the case history indeterminate. Mark may be paralysed, or he may have chosen not to move, as part of his withdrawal from life. His muteness may be a rational choice, a deliberate withholding, or a symptom of physical and psychological conditions. For all the idiosyncrasy of his situation, here on an outdoor bed on a hill, and for all the precision of his thoughts, Mark is a representative figure. He is a version of the unknown soldier, though this is a man who worked in government and was never in khaki. He is a figure between death and life, exhausted and silent as so many people were. He is also an example of the governing class that, having failed, must now silence itself. He is a shape, a vessel, a blank, a void.

Things happen around the still centre of Mark, though all the time we are aware of his silent body and the movement of his mind. Ford, who wrestled every day with the writing of words, imagined the renunciation of language. And in the form of Mark's wife, Marie-Leonie, he fantasised a French gardener, cook and housekeeper applying her considerable energies to the pressing of cider and the growing of beans. The topography of *Last Post* follows precisely that of Coopers Cottage high on Bedham Hill. Thinking with Mark, Ford stretched himself out. He had strung a hammock between two trees in the hedge at Red Ford, and then in the orchard at Cooper's. He and Stella lay swinging in it. Here was a deathbed as a kind of hammock. Was this a pleasant way to go?

Christopher Tietjens, the central character of the previous *Parade's End* novels, is nowhere to be found. 'Where is he?' 'Christopher?' It transpires that he has flown up Yorkshire to stop the felling of an ancient tree at his childhood home, though he is too late to save it – he can only bring back a lump of it like a piece of the Cross. The large figure of Christopher is replaced in the centre of *Last Post* by the prone body of his brother Mark. Like Woolf's post-war novel *Jacob's Room* (which begins with Jacob's family calling for him on the beach), the book echoes with people trying to find someone who has gone.

Christopher is alive, however, as Ford found himself to be alive in Sussex. His partner, Valentine, is soon to bear their child, and they have established a smallholding where they will practise a discerning frugality. After labyrinths of deceit, the growing of potatoes; after stucco facades, a whitewashed cottage; after finery, a skilled economy. Hot, uncomfortable and anxious in her pregnancy, Valentine cannot grasp what is being said but knows that the marigolds in the jug need more water. Mark dies outside shortly afterwards, with the grass 'infinitely green' around him. Ford sailed alone for America in September 1927, finishing the novel on the journey. He sent the first copy back to Stella, who knew their 'long intimacy' was at an end. The novel was a memorial to their time together, and she let him go.[64]

27. TANK TRACKS
A few miles of a world war

The view from my bedroom window, upstairs in our house on West Chiltington Common, did not suggest the kingdoms of the earth. It was a more modest corner of the world. I looked onto a shiny laurel hedge and the gravel driveway, and across the road the Scots pines in Monkmead Wood. Many waking hours each day I spent in that room, for the best part of six years from the age of thirteen to eighteen, poised at a little wooden dressing table labelling diagrams for biology or condensing the Russian Revolution onto revision cards. Every feeling I had as a teenager came home to be examined and written out in that room, with the pine trees through the window.

The woods were both known and unknown, a little eerie when I crossed the lane and took the slippery green-shadowed path along the stream. Wanting it to feel like countryside, I edited out the concrete slabs seamed together by moss and the rusting rivets anchoring the occasional crisp packet between fallen branches. But the fragments of dead-end tracks were always there, jutting up through leaf litter or wrapped with bramble. 'From the war', my father said. The neighbours' gardener said one afternoon that there was a Canadian tank in the lake. This was the lake, or what the map called a fishpond, that we looked over from our sitting room, watching its calm surface reflect the light of every season. I thought of rusted iron in the depths, lethally sharp in its corroded state, and a gun pointing into liquid darkness.

Twenty years later I tried to find out what tanks were doing on Monkmead Lane and who used the concrete roads in the wood. I didn't realise that my knowledge of Britain in World War II was so inadequate until I came to ask 'who was here?' And that other simple-sounding question liable to take us to the brink of what can be known: 'what did they see?'

⌒

Nine-year-old James Roffey from Camberwell was billeted in the cramped quarters of Mr Burchell's shop opposite Pulborough station. If you were a child it was principally a sweet shop (glass jars lined the shelves, much depleted by rationing but each sweet consequently prized), while adults wanted cigarettes or a cup of tea in the adjoining tea room, where wireless announcements were turned up for everyone to hear and all events discussed. Sometimes James was in the back room listening, half watching everyone through the curved glass of the sweet-jars, or he was cleaning out the chicken runs, but often he was out walking, sent off to amuse himself in the fields because there was so little space for a boy indoors.

In the first months of evacuation he had formed a strong attachment to the patch of countryside in which he had been arbitrarily deposited. Under the blue autumn skies of 1939, he had spent hours by the river, 'leaning on the stone walls of the bridges of the Arun, watching the shoals of fish swimming in the crystal clear water'.[1] Not just bridges but stone bridges: Roffey's late-life account of this time is bright with precise places and sensations. The first 'holiday' phase gave way to the lonely and disorienting necessity of getting used to long-term life away from his parents, but the shock and sorrow did not diminish the boy's desire to learn everything he could about where he was. Usually he went out with his brother, billeted nearby, and their friend Brian. They knew the high spots for a good view and the sheltered spots for a cold afternoon. Up at Park Farm they watched the milking of the cows and the rapid ferocity of ferrets sent into rabbit burrows. When sheaves were lifted from a hayrick, they watched the farm-workers gather round to catch the rats leaping out from the bottom of the pile. All this was mixed up with intense excitement about military operations. Close watch was kept on the installation of tank-traps, roadblocks and machine-gun posts; a premium was placed on any intelligence from the soldiers who were increasingly to be found at every corner.

In Roffey's memoir the boys are always watching from the margins, outsiders not quite trusted to take part. Suspicious attitudes to evacuees ('dirty' 'lousy' 'thieving') were a problem throughout the 'receiving' areas, and children could be the most forthright in their tribal cruelty. At school in Pulborough, local boys made their resentment clear: resentment of the incomers crowding their homes and lessons, taking parents' attention, talking differently, getting the answers right in class. Anger and defensiveness were chalked up on the walls. 'Vaccies go home.'[2] The vaccies longed to go home and couldn't. They had to find places in the landscape that would temporarily hold them, even as they were told they did not belong.

The Burchells' nearly grown-up daughter Gwen befriended the boys, and showed them, as James would remember gratefully all his life, such insiderly rural secrets as 'where the best blackberries could be found and how to tell the difference between mushrooms and toadstools'.[3] Like many young boys James was lit up by trains and boats and how things work, and he was learning how the lines of the past can be visible just under the surface of the present – in a reed-grown inlet upriver from Pulborough, for example, which was once a busy quay. Mr Burchell saw James' interest in the river and shared his knowledge, for instance about the old canal and the barges that went through to Stopham. 'Apparently when he was a very young man he had worked as a labourer helping to build the London to Arundel railway.'[4] Mr Burchell couldn't have been working as early as 1863, but was perhaps involved in later development of the line. As for James the evacuee in 1939, his ideas of history and engineering, and of the seasons and work and pleasure, were all becoming rural.

⌣

The 'coastal crust' of Hampshire, Sussex and Kent was the obvious landing ground for invasion; the whole south-east area, reaching back from the sea into the downs, was prepared as a battleground. The beaches, closed off to civilians, were not for deckchairs now but for gun emplacements. Explosives were laid under the shingle at Climping and Bognor; the world was still there in a grain of sand at Felpham, though beneath it was a device that could shatter your legs. All the scaffolding poles of the south were amassed and assembled at the edge of the waves, concrete tank obstacles hauled into place, and barbed wire rolled across it all for mile after mile.

If invading forces landed at Littlehampton and broke through the coastal defences, they would try to take control of the Arun, and crucially of Stane Street, which would be a key route for panzer convoys moving inland. The water bailiff's tour of the river was reprised, yard by yard, with minds focused on attack and defence. The bailiff had written out the history of each bridge and who was responsible for repairing it; now, in classified documents, plans were made for blocking them with dragons'-teeth tank traps, and for emergency repair if they were bombed. All through the valley, gun emplacements were discretely sited, low and grey, their openings framing panoramic views across the fields for the purpose of turning the gun barrel

towards the target. A gunner's squint window, angled into the enemy. Pulborough, with its ancient defensive position, the 'burgh' raised over the lowlands, became a fortified village on the designated 'stop line'.

⌒

The Luftwaffe photograph for target A14, Littlehampton, showed the mouth of the Arun at high tide (Mündung des River Arun bei Hochwasser) and the wide meanders of the river. The caption pointed out salient features like Ford Airport. A pilot might look down and identify Arundel – 'mit markantem Schloß über dem Flußtal, dahinter der bewaldete Anstieg der South Downs' – with its distinctive castle over the river and the downs rising behind.[5]

In the mid-1930s John Piper had written about the landscape features revealed by aerial photography. The new technology was exposing archaeological traces not visible from the ground: faint shadows and crop marks of ancient Britain were rising to the surface, the past exposed in contemporary dark rooms. Aesthetically, too, it was thrilling to see the ground rearranged as a vast pattern of lines and shapes, no longer a matter of foregrounds and distances with the horizon in control. But reconnaissance pictures, hastily taken at height, were the opposite of abstract artworks. Here was the Arun 'as the hawk sees it or the helmeted airman', and seen with a purpose in mind.[6]

Great efforts were made to render aerial views as unreadable or misleading as possible. In addition to the blackout came decoy airfields, designed to lure bombs intended for real airfields. RAF Tangmere therefore gained a double several miles to the north. In a field at Gumber Farm on the old Roman road, recruits billeted in damp bell tents moved painted plywood Hurricanes across the grass.[7] This 'K-site', designed for daylight, soon became a 'Q-site', meant to breed confusion in the dark. It's thought that the line of Stane Street was used to plot out the false landing strip to be lit with flares: a Roman road dressed by night as a modern runway. The moving lights of imaginary planes were the will-o'-the-wisps of this countryside, but Luftwaffe pilots knew their falsity: the decoy site was already labelled on German maps. The crypt-like entrance to the control bunker still stands up from the Gumber grass.

Abb 1   Littlehampton (10 000 Einw.) an der durch Leitdämme eingefaßten Mündung des R i v e r A r u n bei Hochwasser, von den beiden Buhnen in Verlängerung der Leitdämme ragt nur die westliche aus dem Wasser heraus Flugplatz Ford (a), Eisenbahnkreuzung (b), A r u n d e l (c) mit markantem Schloß über dem Flußtal, dahinter der bewaldete Anstieg der South Downs

Lorna Wishart and Laurie Lee lay in the woods outside Arundel while the sky buzzed and pulsed. It was 'hot and green and dusty' under the trees on 18 August 1940. They were supposed to have split up when Lorna returned to her husband and moved back to live at Marsh Farm in the tiny village of Binsted, but neither was inclined to take the promise too solemnly. Lee had come down to stay, and they spent their time together, as they often did, walking along the river and back through the ancient Binsted woods. They felt detached, separate from the war, 'otherwise intent', as Lee put it in his diary. Another raid came over. 'The sky was full, cut, slashed and shattered with noise.'[8] Lee dodged through the trees to the roadside and lay watching in a ditch. When the planes had gone, they went out onto Ford Lane, which led down to the aerodrome, and saw a blaze roaring in the distance.

What they had just heard was one of the fiercest air battles of the war, and this would be remembered as 'The Hardest Day'. Luftwaffe forces had been concentrated on an effort to disable British air power by attacking bases in three waves of bombing from lunchtime until evening. The second wave of planes took off from Normandy at 1.45 p.m. and within fifteen minutes were picked up by Poling radar station north-west of Littlehampton. Hurricanes and Spitfires from Tangmere and Westhampnett were in the air moments later, and in an hour of spiralling dogfights and fatal crashes on each side the planned destruction of RAF Fighter Command was prevented. But no one could stop the bombs that fell onto the Royal Navy airfield at Ford where mechanics were working in the hangars, or the bomb that went straight into the main oil store and unleashed an inferno.

None of which I had any idea about when, once a month on a Sunday, we went to the market held on the old concrete runway at Ford. I'd take my mother's hand or my father's as we decided whether to go clockwise or anticlockwise around the rows of stalls with their striped awnings flapping and plastic bags straining in the wind, and banked up J-cloths and mops, T-shirts, big bags of broken biscuits the memory of which comes back to me as a defining feature of childhood: no madeleines in our house, but the accidental taste of lemon puffs flavoured by gingernut. All that haphazard life going on where young pilots and engineers had died, biscuits carried by a pleased little girl going home from a flat concrete field on which the future of Europe had tilted.

~

Mr Burchell at the Pulborough sweet shop showed his evacuee boy how to read the local weather signs, and James took it all on board. Out in the fields he knew what to look for. How clearly could he see the downs? If everything looked sharp, if he could see the individual sheep grazing, that was a sign of storms in the air. He knew that the familiar sounds were subject to subtle changes. 'If you could hear the clacketty-clack of approaching trains even before you could see them, that was another portent of heavy rain.'[9]

James paid attention to hedges and field-gates until each had its own character and nothing about the area felt alien. There were eerie places though. On Steppey Lane he and his brother went quickly past the ruined barn that people said was haunted. It was unnervingly quiet on the sunken track that had once, they were told, linked up with Stane Street; 'for a short while we became Roman soldiers'. At the pillbox on the path up to the old castle mound, where Samuel Grimm had once painted the earthworks in watercolour, they looked through the opening, over the brooks where the modern enemy would come.[10]

Laurie Lee got off the bus at Pulborough on 12 October 1940, determined to stay more than a weekend. He had had enough of the GPO film unit, mocking up military sounds for public information films, and enough of the nightly raids on London. He wanted Lorna. Wondering where he could hole up without being immediately located by anyone official, he was told about an eccentric woman with a commune near Storrington and he gave it a try.[11]

The Sanctuary was past its heyday, but it was still run by Vera Pragnell on the basis of offering a home to all who needed it. As a young woman in 1922 she had bought fifty acres of pine-wooded heathland just beyond the village and within view of Chanctonbury Ring. There was a cottage which she lived in herself, always keeping a 'tramp room' open for wayfarers, as well as a small chapel. Devout in her Christian faith (though she made a point of not imposing her religion on anyone else and particularly welcomed communists), she set a large wooden

cross on the hillside and issued a general invitation. She shouted out
at Hyde Park Corner for people to come and live simply and openly.[12]

Those who answered the invitation lived in tents and caravans at first,
and as the community stabilised Pragnell assigned individual parcels of
land – not unlike the land issued as part of the 'American' experiment
in Lindfield, or in the pioneer territories of America itself, though not
many of Pragnell's guests were interested in steady commitment to self-
sufficiency. Harry Byngham, who called himself Dion after Dionysus,
took up residence in 1931, advocating nudity, eugenic selection of healthy
bodies, and performing priapic rites by the moon.[13] The shared elements
of life at The Sanctuary were eroded in time by settlers fencing off private
homes and selling the plots they had been given. As the community ideal
slipped away, Vera's husband began to develop areas of residential
housing. In 1940 there was no longer an experimental society, but there
was still room for a wanderer looking for somewhere to stay.

Laurie Lee chose a large green caravan instead of the proffered cottage. Lorna drove over from Binsted; they lit the oil lamps and drew the
curtains. For the next few months, Lorna came most mornings to the
caravan. They walked, they cooked, and spent a long time making love.
'Bed & sherry & sunlit gloom and smooth pools of eyes in the darkness',
wrote Lee: 'Late afternoon crept up like a thief behind our backs' – late
afternoon when she must leave. Another day, in another stretch of time
stolen from war, living hidden and unsummoned: 'We felt secure in the
warm shadows of the van. In a nightdress fragrant with sandalwood, her
nakedness was transparent in purple light.'[14]

~

Stopham church was full to capacity for a memorial service; there were
mourners gathered on the green outside. The dead man was the rector
himself – the rector of Hardham and Stopham together, killed the week
before. Reverend William Masefield had been on the road near Stopham

Bridge when a German plane came in low and strafing. The details of the story vary between accounts, but most suggest that the firing was aimed at a group of children and that Masefield ran over to get them into the roadside ditch. As he shielded them, he was shot. He had 'died in battle', the Bishop of Chichester told the congregation.[15]

There was sunshine on the last Sunday of November 1940. The promenade at Bognor was closed off, but 'there were seats on the opposite pavement and the wind was soft and sun-warmed'. Moved by this mercifully uneventful scene, a local reporter thought it worth an item in the *Gazette*: 'a steady stream of strollers passed to and fro in the roadway, finding enjoyment in chatting about anything but war – homely things, family matters'.[16] The troops charged with coastal defence this winter were Canadian brigades on three-week rotation, a long way from 'homely things'. There were soldiers again in Felpham, as there had been in Blake's time – though military relations with residents were better now. Servicemen were energetically befriended and asked in for tea.

After dark came the aerial orchestration of engines. 'One of ours.' 'One of theirs.' The searchlight unit at Barns Farm below Sullington Hill lit its lamps; tunnels of light soared up over the chalk, fingering the air with giant hands, finding and following the metal glint of a target. Some nights the smell of burning blew on the wind: burning gorse, burning heather.[17] By daylight the bomb craters were assessed, their distance from nearby houses measured in blessed inches and yards.

In Storrington, the Home Guard had taken over the monastery, the Premonstratensian white canons having moved out for the duration. The cloister was lined with sandbags and became a small-bore practice range.[18] High in her niche, Our Lady shuddered and kept a not-quite-smile on her painted lips. The report of gunshots rattled through the village.

The West Chiltington Home Guard was led by Mr Kerr from Monkmead House, who had his men clearing land around the lake. Beside Monkmead Wood, a small factory began production. It took over a workshop that had been used by Reginald Fairfax Wells while his firm was building cottages on the surrounding heathland. Carpenters, brick-layers, thatchers had come and gone. 'Wells Cottages' now sat deep in their gardens along Sunset, Spinney and Monkmead Lanes, crafted in a revived vernacular emphasising the dream of rural peacefulness – available with modern amenities laid on. New owners were settled in and brasses shone over brick inglenooks. But at the workshop the doors slid open on another scene. Eustace and Partners, office furniture suppliers bombed out of London, were making bespoke containers for ammunition.[19] Grenade cases, waterproof mortar boxes, crates for rifle cartridges, all made to the shape of the explosives that would fill them. And when they were empty again, somewhere – in France or North Africa or Malaya – the wood could be used on a camp fire.

'Wells' cottages and Monkmead Wood just before the war

Ron Callon, one of thirty evacuees at Parham House, was entrusted with everyone's ration coupons and sent off to the sweet shop. It was satisfying to stand at the counter while the big order was measured out. Pear drops, dolly mixtures, stripey bull's eyes. He carried them all home to

Parham. It was still hardly believable that his home was a country house. He turned in past the lodge, walking towards the lovely grey house and the smooth down behind it. The whirr of a plane drew closer, suddenly very close and loud. He had heard about the Stopham rector and the children. The black cross was coming straight for him. Then he was in the ditch, the wet coming through his clothes, pear drops disappearing into the mud, and he was still alive.[20]

From the day of his arrival at Parham, Ron had felt he was in paradise, and he was conscious of wanting to save up in memory every scrap of experience. He was one of the Peckham children popularly supposed to be dirty, noisy and oblivious to the natural world but his heart raced with exhilaration when he ran through the park. 'The forest and copse areas became our adventure playgrounds and we were overjoyed when it was suggested that we plant our own forest', he remembered, telling the stories of his Parham life over and over in later years.[21] They each planted a tree and a sign was put up to mark the place. 'Peckham Grove' still stands in what is now a mature wood. It was all there in the two-word name: the tight terraced houses, the buses, the pie-and-eel shops, all brought into the parkland where children firmed the earth around their trees.

The young woman in charge of hosting them was the daughter of the house, Veronica Pearson, who had done much of her own growing up at Parham. She wanted the evacuees to feel the spirit of the place as she had felt it, and to open the possibilities of the rural world to them. She was better equipped and supported than most other evacuee hosts – who found themselves struggling to manage the extra laundry and cooking on top of long working days. Veronica had an opportunity and took it. On long walks she taught the children to recognise bird calls and animal tracks. They stayed up late on a spring evening, and she took them out into the grounds, along the drive that seemed eerie to Ron in the darkness, 'listening to the hooting of the night owls, the barking of foxes and the swishing of leaves'. At the end of the drive, Veronica gathered and hushed them. 'After a few minutes the melodious song of the nightingale began and we listened, enthralled and mesmerised by this beautiful sound filling the air.' In subsequent years he owed to the memory of that short time what Wordsworth called 'sensations sweet, / Felt in the blood, and felt along the heart'. In his old age, Ron had perfect recall of the nightingale excursion and could recover its feelings. 'A calmness descends upon me.'[22]

Sections of the Canadian army had been arriving in Britain since December 1939, most going to the battle school at Aldershot in Hampshire. Through 1941 the whole Canadian corps moved into Sussex – about three-quarters of a million men. With much of the British army abroad, the defence of the south-east was now largely in the hands of the Canadian 2nd Division. Sussex became a vast training ground for those who would carry out future operations in France.[23]

Queen's Own Rifles Regimental Diary:

3 March 1942 0700 hours:	100 men under Lt EA Dunlop, RW Sawyer and NR Pilcher left for Pulborough area to work on camp site under RCE direction. Work is principally laying 2500 feet of pipe, digging drainage ditches and weeping tiles.
12 March 1942 0700:	Party of 100 went to Pulborough continuing work on new camp.
16 March 1942 0700:	Working party of 300 men went to new camp at Pulborough.
30 April 1942 1145:	Battalion reached Pulborough Camp map ref 490403. Chichester & Worthing 1 inch sheet.
1315:	Hot lunch served.[24]

At Templemead, Dr Martin's old house in Pulborough, army tents filled the garden down to the river. Two miles along the road, trucks rolled onto West Chiltington Common. Canadian engineers designed and installed a camp stretching across Monkmead Wood as far as the Wells cottages with the thickly thatched eaves. Areas of pine and birch were cleared – for a parade ground and wash house and Nissen-hut barracks – but not too much: tree cover was useful. A water tower was erected and rough plumbing rapidly instated. Tanks were driven onto hard standings. A new landscape came into being below the Scots pines; it was to be home and workplace for about 750 soldiers at a time.[25] A century after labourers left the area for Canada, unable to survive at home, Canadians had arrived to defend it.

They sent home letters with their highly censored news, and their impressions of England. 'A real genuine old castle one of the first I've seen', wrote Gerald Smedley Andrews after driving past Arundel: he didn't mind or didn't notice that it was mostly Victorian. He noticed the landscape though: 'very beautiful'.[26] Both in pre-war life as a British Columbia Forest Service surveyor, and now in the development of new aerial photography techniques to improve topographical mapping, landscape was his business. On days off, it was also his pleasure. In letters he reported spring walks, and summer cycling on quiet country roads.

⁓

Jomo Kenyatta watered and tied in the tomatoes at Linfield's farm north of Storrington, later known as Chesswood's. Much of the site was given over to glasshouses now that tomatoes and other fruit could not be imported, though out in the fields there were also acres of vegetable crops to be tended and harvested. Hundreds of local people and women from the Land Army were employed to do the work. Kenyatta stepped in with the heavy jobs, like carrying the loaded crates through the fields to the waiting tractors.[27]

He had been living in London for most of the 1930s, petitioning the British government about the rights of his people, the Kikuyu, in East Africa. Colonial settlers had taken Kikuyu land, refusing to recognise the claim of those who already inhabited and cultivated it. Kikuyu farmers had been evicted from thousands of acres and were now living dispossessed and in poverty. The colonial government meanwhile persisted in treating Kikuyu customs as expressions of savagery that must be overcome. Kenyatta's approach centred on reconciliation of traditional tribal and Western ideas through sustained dialogue and education. Studying anthropology with Bronisław Malinowski at the London School of Economics, he wrote a graduate thesis that applied ethnographic methods to his own people, setting out Kikuyu customs of leadership, generational exchange, religion, family life, land ownership and much else, building a portrait of an intricately developed and regulated society. He published his work in 1938 as *Facing Mount Kenya*, with an author photograph that showed him as a tribal leader testing the point of a spear.

'Anthropology begins at home', wrote Malinowski in his preface; but

the question of 'home' for Kenyatta was extremely complex.[28] He was a representative of the Kikuyu, embodying his people in the West, but he had been away from Africa for ten years, and with the outbreak of war could not freely return. He needed somewhere to settle and Storrington was the place he found. Roy Armstrong, head of extramural education at Southampton University, a man with wide interests and strong commitment to progressive education, was offering rooms in his large house on Bracken Lane – on high, sandy, wooded ground close to The Sanctuary.[29]

Kenyatta worked first at a plant nursery in nearby Ashington, then stayed at Linfield's all through the war. He was happy there, he said, and found good friends among other workers. 'He was a real gentleman', said Gwen Smith, remembering her time on the farm as a girl and vividly describing the freezing-cold packing rooms with iron washing tanks. She went home each evening to her mother in a little turning called The Birches in West Chiltington, and she knew that Kenyatta meanwhile led another kind of life. 'He was very clever', she said, adding that he gave lectures after work.[30]

Kenyatta's long project of educating the English about Africa continued in Sussex village halls and meeting rooms, in public talks and Workers' Educational Association classes, and lectures for troops in the camps across the downs. His reputation as a showman and storyteller went ahead of him. There was always a big turnout, though it hardly dispelled his frustrated sense of being 'a general separated by 5,000 miles from his troops'.[31] His interests ranged across colonised peoples; at the White Hart by the river in Arundel (opposite the old Constable brewery) he lectured on the prospects for Indian independence. But always he returned to the histories and cultures of Kenya. He was speaking for his people, and yet in order to do so he had left their place. Could the educated traveller also remain a representative tribesman?[32] Letters went back and forth from Storrington to Nairobi, most of them opened by MI5 who had under close observation this market gardener who had never made a secret of his desire to overthrow British colonial rule.[33]

'What does Europe want with Africa?' he asked one wartime evening at the Arts and Crafts manor house Little Thakeham (I used to love
passing the lane to it), where stone-mullion windows look out onto intricate gardens, shallow stone steps dropping to rose borders and lily
pool. Laurie Lee listened in the audience, faintly bored, but anticipating
interesting evenings with his new friend playing Duke Ellington records
and flamenco at the caravan or at the house on Bracken Lane.[34] Then Lee
turned back to his poems: simultaneously luxuriant and urgent evoca-
tions of Lorna's body in the lamplight, or in the woods, or in the reeds by
the river while the bombers came overhead. And Kenyatta returned to
the draft of a novel, and to a short book mixing history and legend: *My
People of Kikuyu and The Life of Chief Wangombe*.[35]

He was thinking about Kenya, but he was also attentive to the Sussex
landscape, bringing to it his own knowledge and ways of seeing. In the
countryside around the house, glimmering under or behind the heath
and birchwood, he felt the shapes of his native places in rural Ichaweri.
He cleared bracken to make a garden and for the next few years kept up
a productive vegetable plot on the model of East African farms, 'a miniature *shamba* in the west Sussex heath'.[36] In the humdrum routines of
wartime, his imagination was leaping. 'He was able to address the toma-
to plants as though they were a Soviet meeting', one of his biographers
reports; 'he could stalk a fox in the heathland as though it were a leopard
in the bush'. Taking up a fireside poker one Christmas at Storrington he
mimed for friends 'a Masai stalking and killing a lion with a vividness
that took their breath away'.[37]

He was a man in waiting, but while he waited he lived the fullest kind of
Storrington life he could invent for himself. He became close to a woman
who was working as a governess in Ashington and giving adult education
classes. He would walk over to see her in lunchbreaks, and they were married at the registry office in Storrington: Mr Jomo Kenyatta, whose other
wife and two children were in Kenya, and Miss Edna Grace Clarke, who
didn't know about his African family and was soon pregnant with a son.[38]

He chose a birch as a sacred tree ('through which he claimed to communicate with the spirits of his people', Armstrong's daughter remembered).[39] The Kikuyu, he explained in *Facing Mount Kenya*, 'selects huge trees, generally *Mogumo* or *motamayo* and *Mokoyo* trees, which symbolise the mountains . . . These sacred trees are regarded in the same manner as most Christians regard churches – as the "House of God".'[40]

At our Storrington bungalow in the 1980s, a mile or so away, we would tell the direction of the wind by the strength of the mushroom smell; northerlies 'from Chesswood's' brought thick compost draughts over the patio and round into the kitchen. 'The wind's from Chesswood's': it generally meant a cold day too. I imagined miles of mushrooms in their tunnels, pushing up through the dark. I don't know whether people in the 1940s told the weather by the smell in Storrington; mushrooms were out of favour, deemed too low in food value to be supported by the Ministry of Food. But there were several purpose-built mushroom sheds at Thakeham, thatched buildings from 1913, which couldn't be used for anything else and were kept in cultivation. Kenyatta turned the compost, and young Gwen Smith wondered who was buying mushrooms at £1 for a pound.[41]

⁓

'ASPRO steadies the nerves and brings sweet sleep' said the adverts. 'Drink delicious Ovaltine for nerve-strength and vitality.'[42] Warship Week in March 1942 brought parades in Chichester and processions in Arundel. Royal Navy divers entertained crowds at Bognor. Canadian servicemen played fundraising baseball games on grounds more used to cricket. At South Stoke in the bend of the Arun, a mother received news and the local paper reported it: 'one of her twin sons, John Ernest Denyer, is missing and believed a prisoner of war following the fighting in Malaya. The other twin, Leonard Daniel Denyer, is a prisoner in Germany.'[43]

With war-work to organise, Helena Hall in Lindfield had little opportunity to follow research queries through the maroon volumes of the

Sussex Archaeological Collections. But she was writing history nonetheless, making time each day to record events in her journal. She set the military progress of the war side by side with details of evening shifts in the canteen and her patrols as an ARP warden. Night watches became more pleasant as the weather warmed. War brought strange enchantments to the place she loved. 'The searchlights between 12.30 and 1.30 were very beautiful, criss-crossing the sky.' 'They caught a plane and I watched its silvery flight across the sky. It was fairylike.'[44] It was all going on above her and her books, my books. She and her ARP colleagues made a census of the parish. If a house were bombed, they should know who to search for in the rubble. She went house to house around her air-raid sector and wrote 135 names.

Bren gun carriers waited in the rhododendrons. By the summer it seemed to locals that every bit of Sussex woodland was inhabited by Americans or Canadians, who poured out from the trees into the midst of village life, setting up roadblocks, mining bridges, erecting concrete gun emplacements, boring gun-slits in flint garden walls, and issuing invitations to a party. They had hired the guide hut in Storrington and brought in a dance band. Or they were giving speedboat rides to schoolgirls from their Pulborough base, flying upstream by motor power.[45] Under the willows on the banks at Stopham or leaning over the old stone bridge, children watched in admiration.

A Canadian bugle band played the same tune every day 'for so long that everyone in the village was whistling it', or trying not to. Loudspeakers were hung in the trees at the West Chiltington camp, playing dance music in the evenings.[46] Big band and swing under the pines, amplified in the night air, audible across the golf course where saxophone riffs fell muffled into grey sand, audible in the cottages along Monkmead and Spinney Lanes after the cocktail glasses had been brought in from the gardens and the small bedroom windows pulled to under the eaves.

In a mock battle to test stop-line defences, tanks advanced over the causeway from Hardham into Pulborough to be met by bags of chalk dust thrown in place of grenades. Soldiers white with chalk (comically white, ghostly white) counted themselves as injured or dead. James Roffey, watching at a distance, saw the 'O' in the sign for the Dreadnought Garage swivelled round to reveal a pre-cut hole and the barrel of a gun pushed through.[47]

In August 1942 more than five thousand men went from billets in southern England into the active combat they had trained for. Those left behind waited for news, and horror spread through the camps when it came on the evening of the 19th. The raid on Dieppe had gone badly wrong. Soldiers had surged onto the beaches and become trapped, unable to get past long stretches of sea-wall and gun positions. The South Saskatchewan Regiment and Cameron Highlanders were machine-gunned near Pourville; the Royal Regiment of Canada was devastated – half killed, half captured – during a few desperate hours on the steep-shelving shingle beneath the while chalk cliffs at Puys.[48] Of the Canadian soldiers who had gone from Sussex woods, farms and towns towards Dieppe in that August dawn, more than half were lost.

'Where is everybody?' asked a young recruit from Ontario who was still in training and newly posted to the camp at Middleton near Felpham. A storeman was in the empty store. 'They never came back, Sir.'[49]

When the Parham estate was requisitioned in summer 1942, the evacuees were moved on. Ron Callon was sent to a series of hosts who varied between insensitive and abusive. With a concentration so intense that it became a kind of spell, he imagined his way back into paradise. In a bare room, trapped, angry, sore from beatings, he focused his mind on a beautiful stone house beneath a green slope of down and held it there.[50]

Parham was going on without him. The Royal Canadian Engineers drove truck by truck over the cattle grid and through the park, approaching the grey stone house in its valley. A cedar of Lebanon held out its arms. Sappers at the mine school learnt to lay and detonate devices. In the swimming pool, engineers practised the underwater repair of bridges, their skills preparing them for a future second front in France, though the bridges of Sussex might yet be blown apart.[51] Veronica Pearson welcomed the soldiers as she had welcomed the evacuees. She kept an exercise book in which she listed their names and a few notes – who had a dog, or had left photographs behind. 'Repaired our basketwork chairs and was an American Indian', she noted for one soldier; did he tell her about the long traditions of Native American basketwork, and did he get the rushes from the wild brooks?[52]

⁓

All summer Ivon Hitchens kept painting in the hastily cleared and planted garden around his newly built studio near Lavington Common. He painted his wife, Mollie, as a bright odalisque, orange and yellow under the sun, and he painted the flash of a blue door glimpsed through a tunnel of dancing greens.

They had left London in the Blitz, after a near miss when a bomb fell so close to their live-in studio that the building was damaged in the blast. They moved with their baby down to a plot of Sussex scrubland they had bought before the war. A wooden caravan, purchased from a woman in nearby Heyshott, had already been towed by carthorses to a clearing in the rhododendrons. This holiday caravan became the Hitchenses' wartime home. It was a squashed, damp place for a young family, miles from all conveniences, but it was a piece of luck to have it.[53]

There was a scaled-down bay window, which gave a helpful ledge on the inside from which the dining table folded out – the tiny surface which was also kitchen table, drawing table, worktop on which to do everything that family life required. In the corner above the smaller-than-double bed was a ledge on which a Moses basket fitted snugly. John spent the sleeping hours of his first years on this shelf. Across the room, his mother cooked on the stove or manoeuvred pans into a bowl perched on a fold-down ledge under the tap. The tap was a luxury, though it wasn't joined to an external pipe. Ivon or Mollie collected water from the well at a neighbouring farm and carried it across to refill the little cistern above the caravan sink, which would hold a bucketful at a time.[54]

They were building a house. The studio was finished first, and doubled as a bedroom. There was everything to do – buckets, builders, baby – but Hitchens painted with unbridled exuberance. *Nude in Summer*: deep orange curve of back and thighs, both in and out of doors, a suggestion of windows thrown open and curtains swept aside, orange blots of California poppies weightless in the air. Green of grass and green of cushions, unseen breasts touching this green. *Figures in Sunlight*: Mollie a shimmer of pink against white, John moving at her side, a birch tree borrowing their fleshy colour for a thin, vertical life of its own. Foliage flourishing around them, leaf patterns brushed in with a delighted looping calligraphy reminiscent of Matisse. An inheritor of the Fauves had come to Petworth.

On Michaelmas Day 1942 people in Petworth looked up to see a German plane flying low over the Pound Street chimney pots.[55] James Roffey heard the explosion five miles away in Pulborough. The target may have been Petworth House, or the military camp in the grounds, but its cargo fell on Petworth Boys' School. Twenty-eight children were killed as well as the headmaster, a teacher and a laundry worker. It was the end of morning break time on a rainy day. The children had not gone into the playground because it was wet, and were gathered in the classrooms. Some were drinking their milk – in the regulation third-of-a-pint bottles supplied to all junior schools. 'It was a normal morning break', remembered Terry Lucas, who was ten: 'some of us [were], certainly I was, drinking a third of a pint of milk through a straw'.[56] Peter and Ronald Penfold, twins, were killed. One class of older boys had been at a carpentry lesson the other side of town, and the timetable had spared their lives. A few boys from far afield had skipped school because it was so dreary walking the four or five miles in the wet. Men of the Canadian 7th Anti-Tank Regiment brought the coffins in a slow convoy through the town, people gathering along the pavements as the army trucks became hearses.[57]

James Roffey went walking to fend off the homesickness. He was drawn to Old Place, the ancient house beyond Pulborough railway bridge. It had been a fine manor in the 1500s, but for centuries the buildings had been ageing quietly, livestock nudging at the softly eroded stone of arched heraldic doorways. It was not alone in parkland but companionably there on the lane by the watermill, the large millpond lapping right up to its outhouses. Children displaced from their London homes felt its welcome as much as any antiquarian. James Roffey sat on the low stone wall by the pond, watching the water-boatmen walking over the surface.[58]

Often in the afternoons he went with Gwen to check the chickens and collect the eggs. There was a special basket for this purpose, a deep wicker one, and Gwen had a trick that impressed James. 'She could swing the wicker basket over her head without any of the eggs falling out.' One afternoon, sent out alone to do the chickens, James swung the basket up over his head – and the eggs went smashing to the ground.[59]

Anthony and Barbara Bertram at Bignor Manor Farmhouse were running a convalescent home for French soldiers, so the neighbours were told. There were many comings and goings through the narrow lanes to the village, and the French guests were often seen out walking. They would go to the pub in Sutton, sometimes daily, for afternoons of darts and company. Once, an energetic patient was keen for gardening work and went round scything grass in Sutton gardens, carrying bundles of it back as bedding for the Bertrams' goat.

They were not convalescents but agents in French resistance networks.[60] Anthony Bertram, an art historian (and friend of Paul Nash, who had often stayed at Bignor), was working for the Secret Intelligence Service as chief 'Conducting Officer' for French agents moving into and out of the field. He arranged for spies to be flown from Tangmere in Lysander aircraft and put down without discovery in Nazi-held France, and for others to board the same plane during a three-minute touch-down, cross the Channel and proceed from Tangmere to debriefing meetings and appropriately warm hospitality in London. Moonlight was essential for the flights; the pilots needed to find their way, without radio contact, across France and towards small ad-hoc landing fields. So these precarious operations were planned for the two weeks each month around the full moon: passengers and pilots, as well as their drivers and Conducting Officers, must be ready to use any night of fine weather in that interval. Anthony's wife Barbara was employed to receive, feed, accommodate and entertain them all as guests at Bignor, hosting them sometimes for a few hours of darkness before morning departure, sometimes for a week until conditions were right for the flight to France.

She told the story many times after the war, paying tribute to the agents and describing her round-the-clock efforts to have the right number of camp beds made in the right rooms, and enough food ready for when it was needed. 'We lived entirely by the moon.' In the 'dark period' agents might come to rest and work, or trainee radio operators might practise with their transmitters in the attic before using the equipment under intense pressure in enemy territory.[61] The neighbours understood, of course, that there was secret work going on in Bignor, and knew not to ask. The keen gardener who scythed the Sutton grass after days of work in Barbara's vegetable beds was Pierre Delaye, who had escaped a Gestapo prison and been re-arrested in the USSR, endured a gulag, and returned to work for the resistance. He left Sussex by Lysander after the gardening and was dead before the summer vegetables were ready, shot in Loyettes while trying to finish a radio transmission.[62]

Through moon weeks and dark weeks Barbara set to with the catering, supplementing rations with produce from the chickens, ducks, geese, bees. Like the late-night reception meals that everyone was too tired to enjoy, and like the gifts of wine and perfume brought over by French visitors who could ill afford the extra luggage, it was all part of a pattern of support offered and received.[63] The Bertrams themselves became near-mythic figures for those who passed through their home. And the place – the gabled farmhouse with brick floors, surprisingly furnished in bare modernist style, the village with a Roman villa in its back garden and the chalk stream feeding the mill. The place, too, made its mark. It was a place without a name, since the agents could not be told where they were. So the house was in 'a village' and the nearest shops were in the 'small town'. Barbara Bertram said that this vigilant un-naming of her familiar territory was among the hardest aspects of her job.[64] But the anonymous village lived distinctly in visitors' minds. Country walks were less popular than darts as the chosen activity of French agents, but Christian Pineau and Stéphane Hessel were among those who liked being outside on the downs in their few days of calm before returning to their perilous work.

Marie-Madeleine Fourcade, leader of the Alliance resistance network, flew over at last in July 1943, after refusing for months to leave France. She had squeezed herself through the bars of a Gestapo prison cell with not a millimetre to spare; she had been in danger almost continually for three years. Coming in on the plane, 'we saw the cliffs of England, and then a great sweep of searchlights, a flood of beacons, a festival of lights', she remembered, and then came the deep dark of the blackout, an evening's drinking in the smoky fug of the Tangmere mess, and a car taking her through country lanes to what she thought would be an army billet.[65] 'The cottage that came into view, buried in a garden, flower-filled, looked like something from the nursery-rhymes of my childhood.' It was three or four o'clock in the morning, she was exhausted, but it was a ritual that guests must have a meal of 'reception pie' before going to bed. 'We finished breakfast to the first pink flush of sunrise', and there were not many hours' sleep before leaving for London.[66]

By the August moon she returned to the Bertrams' house to meet her colleagues who were coming over: Ferdinand Rodriguez and Léon Faye, the latter her deputy and her lover. They had a precious month together in London, but she was back in Sussex in September for their departure. Fourcade was haunted by a nightmare. She had dreamt of Faye and Rodriguez climbing down from a Lysander into a field of heather and the Gestapo closing in. On the drive to Bignor, the heather appeared to her as a terrible premonition connected with the dream. 'The rolling, wooded English countryside flashed before my eyes, the sunset creating a dazzling scene with its own pink hues mingling with the pale purple of thousands of heather bushes.'[67] She was certain of disaster for her friends, and could not find a way to stop them going. She waited in the lounge at the Bertrams' house. 'I sat for hours listening to Barbara's knitting

needles clicking away in time with the ticking of the clock.'[68] After abort-
ed flights and delays, the landing was made. One of those waiting for the
plane near Bouillancy, while Fourcade waited in the nameless English
village and Barbara steadily knitted, was a double agent. Faye was arrested soon after, imprisoned, tortured and eventually shot in January
1945. Barbara prepared for the next guests.[69]

~

After school on a grey afternoon, after feeding the hens, after being told
to make themselves scarce, a brother and sister wandered over to the
mound outside Pulborough, where all that remains of the castle motte
is grown over with trees. They did handstands on the rough slope, their
palms imprinted with twigs and stones. When the wind got up they
went round to the gun emplacement on the side of the hill just below
the thicket of trees and sat in that for a bit. They weren't manned, these
small concrete forts all through the valley that looked out over the river
and the railway. John was glad to be there in case anything happened. If
the Home Guard wasn't going to keep watch, he'd do it. Lynn started
a chalk picture on the inside wall while the wind whisked around a few
dead leaves and a fir cone. John carried on looking through the large
opening. The view stood in its big rectangular frame. It wasn't like the
pillboxes that gave you just a slit to look through. He adjusted his position to get everything he wanted in the picture. When an 'up' train went
through, he couldn't hear it, the sound obscured by the wind.

Ammunition trains came down in the night. In the goods yard at Pulborough Canadian soldiers worked to load up armoured lorries, their
shaded lamps moving in the darkness.[70] Further down the line, Home
Guard volunteers kept watch on some of the vulnerably remote stretches
of track, at the tunnel near North Stoke for example. A train right out on
the lonely wild brooks was a target for sabotage. Each man sank into the
night thoughts of his line-side vigil, breathing the damp darkness down

on the water meadows. Losing sleep after a day's work, listening: a young barn owl, the low trickle of water among reeds, the flurry of a coot. Quiet. The report of a gun from somewhere over Wepham Down.

⌒

Men from Number 3 Troop of the Number 10 (Inter-Allied) Commando, known as Jewish Troop or X-Troop, scanned the cliff face in the quarry behind the Black Rabbit pub at Offham, cut away by generations of quarrymen. Shells fallen from the table of Adam, in all probability. Over this hill lay the place where warreners once surveyed the rabbits of Pugh Dean from a watch house. *Coneyman will catch you.*

X-Troop was here in order to practise being elsewhere. Each soldier had been specially selected for highly classified missions. Many were Jews who had evaded Nazi capture and joined the Allied fight. There were German, Polish and French-speakers among them, whose knowledge of Europe would be used in the coming months. Beside the Arun they rehearsed for the opening of the Second Front. All were living under new identities and gathered at the Black Rabbit carrying vividly imagined fictional pasts, details ready for interrogation, overlaid on the histories that had brought them here. Freddy Gray was and was not Manfred Gans, a young German from a Jewish family in Borken who had come to England for a summer in 1938 and was told by his parents, before they were arrested, that he must not come home.

The road from Arundel to Littlehampton became the route of regular endurance marches. The speed was unforgiving: thirty-nine minutes for the five miles while carrying packs and munitions, though it was not much after the Welsh training march from Harlech to the top of Snowdon and back. The troop captain surveyed the valley with its exposed marshes, its strategic roads and railways, its camouflaging copses and downland viewpoints on all sides. It didn't provide the mountainous challenges of his native Wales, but this countryside, he thought, studying it as an assault course, offered ample opportunity for 'compass work, fieldcraft and infiltration'.[71] When dropped into France these soldiers would need to get their bearings wherever they landed, undertake complex surveillance and get messages back to Britain. 'Night-work' was timed for the weeks with no moon. In the unbroken darkness of a blacked-out landscape the men found their way through downland hangers and across flooded marshes.[72]

The plan for leaving France after a reconnaissance mission was that they should reach a designated stretch of coast with steep chalk cliffs, wait for naval transport to be ready below, and abseil down. They had practised with mountaineering ropes but the equipment would be too heavy to carry around through the whole operation in France. On the chalk cliffs of England they practised with different ropes. The captain and another Welshman, Treffor Matthews, experimented at the Black Rabbit, demonstrating a thin nylon variety. When Matthews was still near the top, with a drop of about ninety feet below him, the nylon gave way. Extraordinarily, he survived the fall, but he would be in hospital for many months and his days in the Troop were over. Manfred Gans, injured from rope burns on another descent, watched it all. He and his colleagues, facing again the white cliffs of the Black Rabbit quarry, read the wall of chalk for weak points and possible footholds, knowing that a slip could be disastrous.[73]

⁓

Through the warm days of April 1944, the largest invasion force ever mustered gathered in southern England: about two million troops in all. At Barns Farm on the edge of Storrington every inch of space accommodated French-Canadian regiments. At Monkmead, Parham, Singleton and Boxgrove, camps overflowed into surrounding fields. In the tented city of Petworth Park, the 27th Armoured Brigade worked on the waterproofing of amphibious Sherman tanks.[74] Men from the East Riding

Yeomanry thought they could have done worse with the surroundings. It wasn't Yorkshire, but it was good.[75]

At the end of the month, troops were ordered down into marshalling areas close to ports, and onto ships. Each battalion was briefed for a beach landing, and given its own objectives in the giant machine of the invasion. Eighteen-year-old Richard Harris and his colleagues in the 1st Suffolk Regiment boarded an Infantry Landing Ship on 3 May and 'sailed all night, somewhere in the direction of France', expecting with the dawn to be running across French sand into German fire.[76] When the great moment came they were lowered into assault craft and made towards shore, following the passage made by mine-sweepers, surrounded on every side by flotillas of other laden craft, the air studded with barrage balloons. In the morning light, they waded onto the beach between Littlehampton and Bognor.

Operation Fabius was a full-scale rehearsal for the Normandy landings, with six exercises unfolding concurrently along the south coast.[77] The troops at Littlehampton on 4 May did not know the geography of the planned attack; they did not know that the shoreline stretching round to Felpham and Bognor stood in for the coast between Saint-Aubin-sur-Mer and Ouistreham, where 25,000 British 3rd Division soldiers would need to land and from which armoured columns would move inland, through country lanes and villages, to take Caen. But they were learning to invade Sussex so that in France they would have a sense of recognition. Locations had been selected for the similar movement of tides, the shelving of beaches, the quality of sand, the height or the absence of cliffs, the shape of river mouths. Landscapes were layered onto other landscapes, and never have so many lives depended on the accuracy of that tracing-paper match.

Sherman Crabs nosed up the beach, sandstorms rising behind as rotating chains lashed out from giant rollers, detonating explosives in their path. Churchill tanks came behind, steel bridges held vertically in their jaws. Infantrymen streamed down the rungs from landing craft into the water, where, in William Blake's time and after, swimmers had stepped with pleasurable caution from bathing huts into the sea. Soldiers knee-deep wading to shore; an incoming tide of men laden with kit bags and guns.[78] On this shore Blake had seen visions of heaven and the 'majestic shadows' of creative spirits. On the downs behind him, he saw local farmers engaged in what looked to him like the work of a cosmic revolution, 'the Harrow and heavy thundering roller upon the mountains'. Now the tanks were thundering rollers heading for the hills. The chains of the mine flails scoured the sands, harrowing the shore.

Each battalion had its destination. The 27th Armoured Division formed a tank column proceeding inland to Arundel with No. 6 Commando on foot. Bicycling troops followed the River Arun (or French River Orne) past the Black Rabbit and on to Offham and South Stoke where the railway crosses the marshes.[79] They secured the routes into and out of Arundel, as they would need to secure Caen.

In the strange mirror of war, Arundel and Caen stood reflecting each other. The two towns were fortified with the same stone: Arundel Castle keep was built with Caen stone in the 1130s, a show of Norman strength and distinction. Tanks stood at the gate where I would sell ice creams all summer half a century later. Those tanks would go on to help liberate France, but for now they went into the downs, rolling through the chalk lanes and up onto Kithurst Hill.

James Roffey was getting to know his family again in Camberwell and learning the city's rhythms. He missed the tasks of the rural year so much that an allotment was found for him: a square of London that might be his countryside. Like many returning evacuees, he was not encouraged to talk about his other life, in his other place. But he was never quite at home again. He would return for a time after leaving school, working on a farm in Pulborough; later, in his married life, he found a landscape in Nottinghamshire that seemed to carry Sussex in it: 'in the distance is a range of low hills with a clump of trees that could almost be a copy of Chanctonbury Ring'.[80]

Nurses in Goodwood Park, 1944

On 26 May the camps were sealed. The pillar boxes had their mouths closed up. Days of waiting: cards, boxing, football, the burning of possessions that could not be taken to war, last treats in the NAAFI camp canteens. Wages were now paid in francs.[81]

At Goodwood the specimen trees collected and planted by the second Duke of Richmond in the 1740s were in full midsummer leaf. Army nurses explored the sunny parkland on breaks between shifts, knowing that these few days of peaceful routine were a prelude. Goodwood House had been a hospital since 1940; the ballroom was equipped as a surgical theatre, and iron beds ranked in close file around the damask walls of the drawing rooms, a few marks and shadows hinting at where the Lely portraits and Smith of Chichester landscapes had hung. Bedbound servicemen considered hour by hour the possibility of being wheeled outside, a joke, a cigarette, the unimaginable future, the glints of shifting daylight on the chandeliers suspended above them.[82]

Supplies were delivered and sorted: tents, generators, lights, drips, drugs. Laundry for an invasion: sheets by the thousand, pressed, paired, folded and folded again to be unfurled and spread in different worlds. There were picnics on the lawns as the nurses waited, and walks into the groves that George Smith had long ago painted as Arcadia.[83]

Few people in Sussex slept through the night of 5–6 June. The air thundered with the engines of an airborne invasion force taking off from bases around Chichester: Ford, Tangmere, Appledram, Funtington, Selsey, Merston, Shoreham. Everyone knew that the next stage had begun. In the morning Flora MacDonald Brown went out for a walk with a few nursing colleagues, heading up the hill behind the house. 'It was a beautiful, glorious sunny day, and as we lay on the grass we heard and then saw some planes approaching.' Then she saw there were gliders attached to each plane, and she understood that the gliders would be cut loose over France: 'left to drift down to a very uncertain landing'.[84]

She followed those advance-guard glider pilots in imagination, conjuring to herself the places they would fall. What she envisaged, with her army experience, was probably closer to the truth than any scene I can imagine eight decades later, though I can hit the search key and scan assault details that were classified in 1944. I can see that gliders passing over Sussex later that day would be over Utah beach just before 9 pm and cut loose above landing zones near Sainte-Mère-Eglise.[85] I can see that by the end of the month the nurses of Flora Brown's unit were on their way to France. Several loads of equipment fell into the sea from trucks negotiating the mulberry harbours, but not all the linen was drowned or scattered. Thousands of sheets folded at Goodwood would be unfolded outside Bayeux.[86]

28. THE PINE TREE
Journeys from Poland

Canadian soldiers masterminded local celebrations in May 1945. Up on the downs where they had rehearsed manoeuvres for years, they cut a big white V in the turf, poured in their lethal flame-throwing oil and set it alight. Victory blazed above Storrington. Leftover ammunition was repurposed for a spontaneous firework party that night, flashing and raining through the spring sky. At Parham, Veronica Pearson climbed out onto the roof to watch.[1] The 3rd Battalion Canadian Engineers stayed on through the next few months, clearing mines, moving tanks, making safe the vast infrastructure of heavily defended West Sussex. The Monkmead camp was wound up. If there was ever a tank driven into the large fishpond beside Monkmead Lane, the lake just beyond the fence from our garden, perhaps it was then.

If I try to visualise it, one world is superimposed upon another. We are sitting by the lake on the springy band of grass below the patio. I'm adjusting the angle of a frayed 1970s sunlounger patterned with faded orange flowers. My mother is upright in the other lounger, reading the paper. Over the low fence, on the bank between the willow and the loosestrife, two drakes and a mallard (there were always two drakes and a mallard) are doing their impression of being asleep. From nowhere, through the afternoon, comes the moving steel mountain of a Sherman. Ducks scuffle into flight. Caterpillar tracks turn like waterwheels, grinding turf into mud. The weight tips and tilts. The chassis plunges and the shock runs in waves across the lake. The gun and turret sink steadily, like a submarine. The water closes over the gap. My mother is still reading the paper. Across the road, there's no sound from the woods.

By 1946 the Nissen huts were being reopened and new homes established with expert resourcefulness. At Monkmead, the army base with the concrete roads and water tower was transformed into a Polish village. Clean curtains were hung at the hut windows and tables laid for dinner. Infants could be left in a crèche while mothers went out to find farm or domestic work, returning in darkness to confront endless tasks of household cleaning without hot water, making and repairing clothes, arguing precarious stoves into life. One of the huts (or *beczki* in Polish, also the word for barrel) became a chapel where Mass was said by the camp's Polish priest. A fluctuating population of around five hundred people lived here during 1946–8. They were all connected with the vast Polish 2nd Corps, the Anders Army; they were the wives, sisters and children of those who had mobilised in Siberia, served in the Middle East, and fought the long, bloody campaign for Monte Cassino. By extraordinarily gruelling journeys, they had come to this patch of Sussex ground.

Between the silver birches, a remarkable institution was up and running: the Ignacy Paderewski School for Girls.[2] Through the winter of 1946–7, still the coldest on record in England, 165 young women slept in barrack dorms and attended lessons. A core group of these students had a shared history at the hands of the Nazis. They had trained and fought in the Warsaw resistance and been captured in the ruins of their city; they had been taken as prisoners of war, and survived long enough to see the arrival of liberating Polish forces.

In any moment of thaw, meltwater dripped through joins in the corrugated iron roofs or came in round the windows. The Monkmead camp was not an easy place to learn algebra, yet these maths classes were welcome and hard-won. The conditions bothered the three government inspectors who visited the West Chiltington school in January 1947 (and who also went a few miles through the downs to Petworth Park, where a similar school had been established for boys). According to the report they filed to the Committee for the Education of Poles in Great Britain, huts were heated only three or four days a week and hot

The Polish school in Monkmead Woods, 1946–7

water was available on one or two days. It was 'almost impossible' to wash clothes. As for lessons: 'the books available for instruction are very few and seemed very out of date'.[3] Given the years elapsed since anyone here had been to a Polish library or bookshop, this was not surprising. The inspectors couldn't follow the classes in Polish so found it hard to judge the teaching. Language was a worry: since the teachers hadn't yet had a chance to learn English, the girls were not getting the English-language education that might equip them for their new country. The curriculum was centred on Polish university entrance exams, but it was clear that most of the students needed to prepare for jobs or tertiary education in Britain. The inspectors didn't know individual stories, but they understood that many had been subjected to years of forced labour and untold violence. Their report emphasised the discipline and willingness of the students, and the necessity of offering better facilities without delay.

In photographs taken that winter, young women and their teachers smile in the snow, exuding a spirit of energy and friendship that looks, in these grainy shots from eighty years ago, absolutely unvanquished. Among them, grinning with laughter, is Tosia Jaroszyńska, who had her twentieth birthday at West Chiltington in December 1946. Most of a lifetime later, as part of an oral history project for the Warsaw Rising Museum, she talked about what had preceded her arrival in England.[4] As a young teenager in the first years of the occupation, she went to a vocational school near the family's home in the Wola district of Warsaw, one of the few Polish institutions allowed to open under the German regime. Only courses in basic practical skills were permitted. Classes were in German; education conducted in Polish was punishable by death. Tosia and her contemporaries were being trained for the manual work they would do as Slavic servants to the Aryan master race, before being eliminated altogether.

When an older friend introduced Tosia to the underground movement, she began another kind of learning. She took her oath of allegiance to the resistance in 1943, and studied nursing in the intricately organised secret system of training, mentoring and examining. When the Uprising came in August 1944 she was ready. She remembered the 'fantastic' moment of running into the street from her waiting position to join the long-planned action ('I zdecydowałam się i to było fantastyczne'). She recalled her pride as her battalion took German prisoners. Then came the tense nights leading up to the bombing of the Main Post Office. She remembered the casualties in the wreckage of the building, and the hungry, dangerous weeks that ensued until she and a group of fellow fighters were taken captive.[5]

In describing her time as a prisoner of war, Tosia had little to say of fear or pain, though she dwelt a moment on the memory of collapsing on a straw bed after a march of 125 miles from Warsaw south to Ożarów, carrying a backpack and wearing the ill-fitting boots she had taken from a wounded German soldier during the insurrection. 'It was only seven months of captivity', she said, as if it were nothing to worry about. When the Polish 2nd Corps liberated Stalag VI-C Oberlangen in April 1945 and cooked up a decent soup for the freed prisoners, she was too malnourished to digest it.[6]

Tosia and others from Oberlangen travelled south with the Polish army towards Italy. The convoy stopped in Bavaria to open the prison camp at Murnau where thousands of Polish professionals, including teachers and university lecturers, had been held. A school was established there and then: a Polish school in southern Bavaria attended in those first months by about a hundred students. It was there that Tosia picked up again the education that had been closed off in her girlhood. In Murnau she learnt Latin, though she felt very behind.[7] Himmler had intended a life in which she would write no more than her name.

The school group was taken to Italy under the protection of the Polish 2nd Corps and settled in the large camp at Trani on the Adriatic. This, too, had to be temporary. With the 2nd Corps about to be disbanded and partly reconvened in Britain as the Resettlement Corps, it was hoped that the school, which had been formed and fostered by that army community, might be re-established in England. Tosia liked the idea of going to England. Her thoughts were not of 'home'; she had not known a safe and free home since being a girl of twelve or thirteen. What she wanted now was to see the world. Her family was really the group of young women with whom she had spent the war – women like Zofia Burzycka. Zofia too had been to the inadequate vocational school in Warsaw (where she learnt tailoring), fought with the insurgents, endured the marches and camps, and was now in Trani, wondering what might come next.[8]

School staff: Maria Felinska, Marjory Wood, Jadwiga Żmigrodzka, Bogna Domańska and Romana Sochocka, 1947

Only soldiers and their dependants were being accepted by the British government, and the school, therefore, was not allowed. It was a blow. Quiet negotiations began in Trani. The 5th Rifle Division was about to travel to England, and the commander arranged for those as yet unmarried to take 'fiancés'. The school group set out together. The official who took down their details on arrival started to raise questions about what was patently a scheme. 'What is this, an entire transport of brides?'

It was exactly that. Tosia had never met her groom and never would, but the plan got the whole school to Sussex. Tosia could at last change out of the wounded German's boots, though she would never forget how she came by them in the confusion of a Warsaw street, the soldier calling out as he was stretchered away: 'mein Schuhe, mein Schuhe, mein Schuhe'.[9]

Some of the West Chiltington teachers had been there in the same streets, playing leading roles in the resistance. Bogna Domańska, who sat on the step of a hut at Monkmead in 1946 and smiled with her colleagues for a staff photo, worked with the Council for Aid to Jews, trying to equip Jewish families with money and intelligence that could help them escape Nazi Poland. The job put her in harm's way, as she very well knew. Bundles of cash would be brought to her in hollowed-out logs; neighbours began to ask why she needed so much wood.[10] Often she could not save those she wanted to support. As preparations for the Uprising intensified, she became director of communications for the Kiliński battalion, the unit Tosia joined as a nurse.

In the aftermath, she was held at Oflag IX-C Molsdorf with other female Polish army leaders, though not with Jadwiga Żmigrodzka, the teacher sitting next to her on the steps at Monkmead, who was at the much larger camp XI-B Fallingbostel. Two photographs from a life: in one, Jadwiga holds up her prison number for identification and closes her eyes; in the other, under the West Chiltington pines, she wears a woollen suit and tie, and smiles from her seat on the step. She stayed in England, made her career as a teacher and lived in Horsham until her death in 1988.[11] Just behind her in the staff picture stands the headmistress, Maria Felinska. She went to live in Leicestershire after her time at the Ignacy Paderewski School and carried out research as a marine biologist.[12] Specialising in single-celled organisms, she worked at the Plymouth Laboratory in the 1960s and published analyses of ciliate species never previously described.

In the upstairs room across the road from the woods, I studied for my A levels in 1999. I wore grooves in the carpet with my blue plastic swivel chair and covered the wall above my dressing-table desk with colour-coded sheets of equations and diagrams. I tried out answer after answer to the questions on past History exam papers. 'Why did appeasement fail?'; 'How similar were Nazi and Soviet conceptions of "homeland"?'

The younger children at Monkmead were taken into West Chiltington village for a Christmas party, with 'an excellent tea' laid on by local Sussex women and (according to the *West Sussex Gazette*) 'enjoyed by all'.[13] There was a big tree, a Punch and Judy show and a visit from Father Christmas. 'The Polish Band sent a detachment to play and this greatly added to the success of the entertainment.' Clearly there were efforts on every side. In Pulborough on a January night, 'Polish National Costume Dances' shared the stage with the Astoria Dance Band at a subscription dance in aid of the Polish Relief Fund.[14]

'This camp is rapidly settling down to a reasonably happy atmosphere,' wrote the British officer-in-charge at Monkmead, 'morale is improving noticeably week by week.'[15] But the *Worthing Herald* reporter found that the wood was 'a frozen waste'. 'Life is not easy for the people in this "foreign village".' Concentrated in those few words were both concern and an overwhelming sense of difference. The article described this 'little bit of England that is no longer England' with mixed tones of bafflement, worry and respect. The writer could see that the Polish women were 'doing everything possible to fit themselves for life in this country' but did not, apparently, take much notice of their advanced maths, alacrity with language and scholarly ambition. Readers were assured that, though some may imagine the Poles to be a burden on a weakened country, they would be 'particularly useful as domestic servants'.[16]

There were difficult politics underlying such uncertain responses to the Polish exiles. In 1947 it was deemed better not to ask strangers about their personal stories; everyone had suffered, everyone had lost. Among the British public it was not widely understood that between one and two million civilians had been forcibly deported from Kresy, the large eastern region of Poland annexed to the USSR in 1939.[17] A million times, over and over, the voices in the night, the journeys barely survived, the slave labour and starvation. Russia was a crucial ally against Nazism, and partly for that reason the scale of Soviet atrocity against the Polish was not clearly acknowledged in Britain. Criticism of the USSR was firmly discouraged, and those Poles who reached England after the war were left to wonder at the high regard in which it seemed to be held.[18] They had every reason to consider the agreement at Yalta a dire betrayal, after which it could only be incumbent upon Britain to welcome displaced Poles, providing for all who wished the means to stay and prosper.

The Ignacy Paderewski School at West Chiltington moved on. Girls were applying for admission from camps all over Britain, and in autumn 1947 the school transferred to larger premises at Stowell Park in Gloucestershire. Nissen huts again, better waterproofed this time and with more hot water. It would continue there until all the girls displaced by war had successfully finished their courses in 1954.

The community at Monkmead changed as new groups arrived or departed. For many this was only another in a long series of transit camps. Sixteen-year-old Franciszek Herzog was just passing through, after eight years in which he had coped with extremes of loss, rescue, friendship and loneliness. His father, an army officer, had been taken away early in the war, and was not one of those few who reappeared.[19] The rest of the family had been rounded up in the mass deportation of April 1940 and delivered to the 'Red Sickle' farm in Kazakhstan. As a boy of nine, Franek made a few roubles by catching and skinning prairie dogs for their pelts:

250 dogs, he thought, in the second summer on the steppe. His mother died soon after the haunted, sickly Christmas of 1941, indicating to her boys that without her they would be able to leave the village and join the army. The brothers managed to get by train to Tashkent, and then to the assembly point at Kermine where the eldest left to join the navy, and then to Ashgabat near the Persian border, where Franek joined crowds of orphans waiting to be stewarded to safety by the Anders Army.[20]

He was driven through the desert in a convoy with other children and guardians assigned to them, stopping on the way for an Easter Mass celebrated by a Polish priest using the back of a truck for an altar. They were making for India, and there, at last, he and thousands of other Polish children found refuge.[21] Franek would remember a plump orange waiting on each child's bed. (Someone had taken his orange; someone else agreed to share.) He lived first in Bandra, and then in the orphanage built for Polish refugees in the grounds of the maharaja Jam Saheb's hilltop palace in Gujarat. Here the children had plentiful food, medical care and a school routine. They chased peacocks on the lawns, running barefoot between the cacti and acacia trees and, after classes, racing down to the wide Balachadi beach and into the sea.[22] Many would continue all their lives to refer to the Gujarat orphanage as a paradise.[23] Franek was more circumspect, remembering the grief and difficulty, but also the friendships. He concentrated on Scouts. 'We did not bother much about the future . . . We had to organise our Scout camp for the first time in tents.'[24]

The future was in another country. Franek sailed from Bombay in November 1947 with 970 other Poles, docked at Liverpool, and spent a miserable few weeks at Daglingworth.[25] There, in the heart of the honeyed Cotswolds, he shivered for a week in summer clothes he had brought from India. He had been issued with a coat by the time he was moved to West Chiltington. Neither the weather nor the welcome was so warm in England as in India, at least not at first in that straitened post-war winter. He bedded down in the leaky hut under the pine trees remembering sunlight and acacias. Letters went back and forth to his brothers who were trying to get school-leaving qualifications in Scotland. ('It looks a bit like Southern Poland in the mountain region', his brother Tadek explained soon after arriving in Perthshire, thinking of the Podkarpackie province with its upland lakes and ancient woods. But in Scotland it was harder to enjoy the hills when there were signs staked along the roads reading 'Go Home Poles'.[26]) They travelled down to be with Franek at Christmas – a family reunion of sorts at West Chiltington, on the sixth anniversary of their mother's death in Siberia.[27] Franek moved on to a school in Norfolk, and moved again when the school transferred to Beccles. He would take his O levels at Bottisham in 1951, and go on to become an electrical engineer.

In sixth-form History we compared Soviet propaganda documents. Elizabeth, Mrs G, wiped her glasses, which were always getting tangled and were a running joke. Bit by bit she prompted our questioning of the sources reproduced on the worksheets. 'Remember NOP: nature, origin, purpose.' 'Who might benefit from a photograph of a miner receiving a medal from Stalin? Do we know what the miner himself thinks?' In my bedroom on Monkmead Lane I went over more worksheets. I walked round the woods in the breaks between revision. Anxious, distracted, I tripped once or twice on the corners of concrete blocks hidden under soft rotting depths of birch leaves and bracken. Nature, origin, purpose.

The women of Monkmead Polish village gradually joined demobbed men and set up family homes – more Nissen huts – in camps across the country that became semi-permanent 'Polish housing estates'. The nearest was in Petworth Park. About a hundred families began from scratch, yet again, this time on the north bank of Petworth's ornamental lake.

Children who grew up in that camp over the next decade called up their memories in later life and shared photographs from family albums. In the pictures they are all immaculately turned out, holding a new toy or standing proudly by a tricycle. The adults had been cut off from everything known and loved in Poland, and the recent past contained experiences that shook every notion of humanity. Yet this community made surroundings in which the young could have childhoods, and the children themselves made this new English-Polish world their own.

'As youngsters in the camp we were one big family', said Stasha Starzec, who was brought there as a girl in 1952. They were 'in and out of each other's homes' or 'playing in the wide open spaces of the Park'.[28] Zygmunt Krawczyk was a year-old baby when his family came to Petworth. His father had been in the Polish army when it retreated from Poland into Russia, and then, like tens of thousands of compatriots, he had travelled through the Middle East and North Africa and fought at Monte Cassino. In Italy, after the war, he met Rosalia, freed at last from years of enforced work on an Austrian farm. Their two boys would grow up at Petworth, riding tricycles around the concrete perimeter road, inventing excuses to avoid cold showers, swimming in Lower Lake (still known locally as Polish Lake), leaning back dizzily on a swing tied to an English oak tree, watching the English-Polish-Sussex sky bob and dip above them.[29]

Children went to the girls' and boys' schools in Petworth, but there were further lessons when they got home covering things not on the English curriculum: Mr Cisek (remembered with fond respect) taught Polish history and organised costumed performances of Polish plays. Vegetable-growing was a priority. The expanses of chicken wire were not a remnant of military security but a necessary precaution when trying to grow produce in a deer park. Whatever foods were in short supply, there was an unending, unrationed stock of pickled cucumbers and sauerkraut kept in big barrels. Mushrooms too: Stasha Starzec remembered the mushrooms that grew up on the hill by the folly. 'We picked as many as we could carry and brought them back for Mum to sort. She knew which were poisonous and after a while so did we. Some were cut up and threaded onto string and dried over the range for use later in soup and goulash' – mushroom knowledge brought from the forests of central Poland and Kresy.[30]

In the 1750s Capability Brown's workmen had laboured with tons of earth and miles of waterpipe to create a pastoral ideal in which nature proffered its fruits without effort. It turned out to be a congenial environment for the Polish residents whose lives were far from any eighteenth-century conception of ease. As Turner had done in the 1820s, they settled themselves on the bank of Lower Lake for fishing – and remembered the pike proudly brought home for tea. As Constable had done in the 1830s, the children took joy in the oaks and cedars and birds.

It's striking how prominently the landscape features in these Petworth recollections. The children would squeeze past the perimeter fence and make off over the grassy hills. Lydia Stefanska recalled 'lying in the grass looking up at the sky, listening to the bird song and soaking in the warmth. I thought it was heaven on earth.' Feeling her way back, she tried to remember exactly how the surroundings had looked to her. Going out on mushrooming expeditions, 'we seemed to walk for miles through woodland covered with huge scarlet, white and purple rhododendron bushes and I distinctly remember thinking how beautiful it all was'.[31] For the children, these were the first and defining landscapes. For their parents, the heaths and chalk hills and the Petworth parkland were layered over memories of farms left behind, lakes, roads, Białowieża forest, the squares of Lida and Warsaw.

All traces of the Polish estate at Petworth have been cleared away now, but Zygmunt Krawczyk knows how to find the place where he grew up. 'I can still pinpoint the tree which held our homemade swing', he says. It is an oak tree, with marks on a branch where the rope of the swing made deep grooves in the wood.

The Monkmead camp had several more years of use after the school moved away. Women continued to be sent to the Polish village there. As late as March 1948 there were new arrivals, including Maria Bassara who had sailed from Haifa on the Cunard liner *Franconia* along with troops leaving at the end of the British mandate there. A silent Pathé film records the scene on the dockside as soldiers carry the eternally packed and unpacked kitbags through driving rain. Civilian women queue to board, taking the hands of uncertain children as they go up the gangplank; Maria Bassara may be there in the picture. Her destination was written on the ship's passenger list: 'W. Chiltington Camp Sussex.'[32] What happened next I do not know.

Patched and re-equipped, part of the site became a military base again, this time for several remaining sections of the Polish army. Among those stationed there in 1948 was Tadeusz Dudzicki, a young man just past twenty who had not known a home since his boyhood. He told part of his story to the *West Sussex Gazette* in 2013, when he was a retired architect living in Kent.[33] His father 'disappeared' in 1939 and the remaining family were arrested the following spring at their house in the city of Lida. It happened in tandem with the arrest of households across eastern Poland, on the night of 13 April 1940. Twelve-year-old Tadeusz said goodbye to the dog, and packed his school bag with an atlas.[34] He left with his mother and sister. They endured two years of penury in Kazakhstan before the news of the Polish-Soviet alliance and 'amnesty' came through, reaching them in Południno.

They made their way towards Uzbekistan. For a brief time in the sprawling assembly camp at Kermine, Tadeusz was reunited with his father, who had also been released and was now in charge of the Polish hospital where exhausted refugees were crowding in hope of medical care. For Tadeusz, war and journeys lay ahead, crossing page after page of the atlas. He joined the 7th Infantry Division of the Anders Army, which would have to do instead of a school.[35] With the army he travelled through Iran, Iraq and into Egypt, and eventually came to Britain at the end of the war.

As he remembered it, the summer of 1948 under the pine trees was one of the best summers of his life. 'It was something beautiful', he said. 'The smell of the flowers, roses, trees, and greenery everywhere.' 'There were beautiful houses on the left-hand side', he remembered, as you came from Storrington. 'It was the first time I saw people cutting grass, because nobody cut grass in Egypt or Iraq.'[36]

There is always, still, somebody cutting the grass if you walk down Monkmead Lane on a summer evening now. It is a land of Flymos and Qualcasts. The names of houses are engraved in slices of varnished wood and lodged in small rockeries planted with heathers or alyssum. Wide gates swing across gravel driveways. The hedges are laurel and conifer or, more recently, as tastes lean towards naturalism, hawthorn and beech. There is plenty of tarmac, but also wide verges and trees arching across the road that give the impression, just about, of 'greenery everywhere'. I would not have thought that the upkeep of rural-suburban gardens would make much impression on men who had escaped Siberia and lived in army camps across the Middle East. That was a failure of imagination. The lawns and trees were vividly beautiful to the wanderer who had been a long time in the desert.

Tadeusz had always had strong feelings for his surroundings. The memoir he wrote in late life dwelt on the places of his childhood, imaginatively re-inhabiting them, calling up with sensuous exactitude the flower beds in the garden of the family's Lidsian home. He listed the shops in the market square and the buildings he had walked past on the way to school – before that life and that city disappeared in ruins.[37]

At Monkmead he waited to go back to these places, and in the meantime contented himself with Sussex. It was here that the family came together again. In one of the war's miracles of survival and reconnection, Tadeusz's father travelled to England and worked as a paramedic based at the Monkmead camp. Tadeusz's mother and sister, both nurses, joined them in Sussex and found work at the large Polish hospital that had taken over the searchlight battery at Barns Farm, in the fields below Sullington Hill.[38] To and fro they went along the few miles from Storrington to West Chiltington, past the Wells cottages and lawns on Monkmead Lane. From different hells across the globe they convened in this square of Sussex ground.

Mr Dudzicki's recollections were prompted in 2013 by seeing a modern photograph of Monkmead Wood. It showed the sandy lane at the entrance where dog-walkers now park their cars, and three or four mature pines including an especially large one so familiar to me that I had never properly looked at it. Dudzicki's familiarity with that tree was of a different and a deeper kind. His recognition, after seven decades, was immediate. 'My God, I remember that tree', he said when he saw the picture: 'that's it, that's it, about ten paces to the right was our Nissen hut, where I slept.'[39]

29. AN OPEN WINDOW

I went back. I took the train to Pulborough, and walked the last few miles. The pine tree that Mr Dudzicki knew was standing firm. Across the road was the house that used to be home. It had taken me a long time to get there. I had been to William Blake's gate and Dr Martin's door, but not to the door I used to open each day. I didn't feel any need to go inside; a look up the driveway was enough.

I stood on the apron of grass by Monkmead Lane. The conifer hedges were smoothly trimmed and the paintwork was bright. We turned out of this drive in the car each day on the way to school, my father straining to see if anything was coming round the bend, me delving through stuffed bags of ring binders to find a locker key on a luminous plastic coil, or finishing a bowl of cereal and promising not to let the dregs of milk spill in the footwell. Grass, tarmac, gravel, a wooden sign with the names of the houses that share the drive.

We moved here when I was thirteen, transferring our lives from the bungalow on the edge of Storrington to this house that seemed excitingly grand by comparison. I had lobbied for ancient cottages, and got nowhere; I was ready to work with a few mock-Tudor beams. West Chiltington Common wasn't a common in 1994: it was tree-lined roads and carefully mown verges. My friends lived behind several of the nearby hedges, there was a helpful shop we could walk to, a little courtyard wall by the kitchen deflected a tennis ball at interesting angles for whole afternoons, and best of all I liked reading in the 1970s wood-ceilinged sitting room with patio doors. The doors faced onto the lake (the lake with the tank in its depths), and the lake was the defining presence of the house. It belonged to the neighbours, but that was fine: we could look at it, and look we did. I had a glimpse of it now, through a gap in the hedge.

On warm nights we took our desserts outside (Arctic roll or Viennetta) and sat watching the sky flush and lighten to the blue of a spring morning before darkness fell. At the same time each evening through the summer a skein of Canada geese flew in from the wild brooks – the honking audible from the moment they left Pulborough. Each evening someone said, 'You can set your watch by it.' I know now that *Branta canadensis* was first brought to England in the late 1600s and displayed in stately parks in the eighteenth century. It took to its new habitats better than the moose, and multiplied. At Monkmead in the 1990s there were usually several goose families nesting by the lake and hundreds of others would come in each night to sleep on the water for safety. Anyone awake at dawn would find them floating in the pink light.[1]

My mother was increasingly confined to home with multiple sclerosis. She had known her future; that's partly why we moved to a house with space for a wheelchair to turn. It's why my parents rejected small, high cottage windows and chose glazed sliding doors. The use of her body was ebbing from her. Each week some ordinary task presented itself as newly impossible. Every few months another finger refused to move until her hand lay clawed in her lap. Through it all, she looked at the lake. The view through the patio windows was what she saw of the world. No naturalist, she longed for shops and streets and for driving fast on open roads, but geese were what she had instead. Geese and the first dimpling of rain on the mercury surface of the water. And the crested grebe looking round, disappearing, challenging us to hold our breath until it reappeared.

That, too, is part of the history of this place, I thought, standing on the verge. If Thoreau had had no choice but to sit by Walden pond, I'm not sure he would have liked it so much. If walking and digging and the possibility of going somewhere else entirely had all been taken away from him, I think he might have come to hate that wood. But we didn't know about *Walden*. With a courage that now astonishes me, my mother reassured us that there was always something on the lake for her to watch.

I could see my bedroom window: varnished wood frame, double-glazed but with diamond-pane effect. It was open. It faces the other way from the lake, across to the pine trees, and those trees looked a little different now that I knew who else had seen them. Hundreds of Canadian troops had camped under them, not sure if they would see the woods of Ontario or British Columbia again. Teachers and students had made their school in freezing Nissen huts. Tosia Jaroszyńska and Maria Felinska had been here, and Tadeusz Dudzicki, for whom the pines meant freedom.

My mother was reading Simon Schama's *History of Britain* in her last year. She left it part-way through the third volume, and it sat on the coffee table for a long time afterwards. I can't remember now where she was up to. The rise of Churchill, I think. I wonder if I can add another kind of history, connected but closer. I wonder if, on this unremarkable spot, I can run back through time. It's not an obviously historical place at all. A 1970s house on a 1920s lane: not such a promising place to be a traveller in time. It's not like the churches and stone farmhouses that wear the centuries in their stones. But oh yes it has a history.

Before the tanks of 1940 there was a rural dreamland here, built in the aftermath of the Great War, cottages reimagined, with electricity wired in. Plots were laid out along the old paths over the common: from Monkmead you could turn into Heather Lane, Westward Lane, Sunset Lane. Buyers came eagerly to this thatched estate and expressed their hopes in house names. Ye Sylva Lyning. Roamers' Roost.[2] Brick inglenooks, low armchairs, small-paned windows opening under thatched eaves. The ready-aged houses were set in large lawns, with some of the old trees retained for instant maturity. Front gardens for flower borders; room for chickens and a pig at the back. Around them, acres of wooded heath. Sand martins arrived in the spring, making busy colonies in the old sandpits. On June evenings there might come the sudden stream of a nightingale's song. The people here listened and didn't forget.[3]

Before the Great War, on the small estate then known as Munckmead, about fifty acres, Edward King had a substantial house built. It was made

to look as if it had been there for centuries; the architect re-used materials from an old brewhouse, vernacular and weathered. Here was the
latest in Arts and Crafts, collaging pieces of the past.[4]

The village of West Chiltington was several miles away, through a
deep-sunken hollow way that was for much of the year impassable. But
a few people lived on what remained of the common. Elsie Cattell grew
up in the 1910s in a cottage here with eight siblings. Her grandmother,
she remembered, would read and write letters for the Roma families who
had the common as a long-term 'stopping place' or in Romani 'atchin
tan'. She remembered the woodsmoke from the campfires, and she knew
that many of those men and women were buried nearby.[5]

Here, before a Parliamentary enclosure award in 1868 allowed the
common to be divided up, the heath and woodland was unfenced.
Local residents with grazing rights put cows and pigs on the land.
Furze-cutters piled the gorse onto wagons. Some Roma groups lived
continuously on the common; others drew up their vardos along
Common Hill in the winter.

Here for many years in the early nineteenth century, the big sweeps
of a smock windmill turned, grinding the corn and barley of West Chiltington.[6] There can never have been enough wind in the clearing on the
common by the lake, too low a site for a mill – but there it is on the
earliest Ordnance Survey map, published in 1813.[7] A windmill on what

would be our garden. The grindstones turned where we ate our Arctic roll. Carts of flour pulled out from the driveway. As Napoleon rode conquering across Europe and Africa, the mill by the lake ground the corn. A man called Charlwood Hammond was miller in 1800, when he had four bushels of flour stolen.[8] Only when things go wrong do these names get into the records.

From its flying viewpoint the Ordnance map sees the lanes and the stream that feeds the lake; the common is a blank apart from these. But people on the ground knew every bank, bump and tree. Here, in 1609, a group of local men traced out the boundaries of the land they cultivated in common, marking it off from the other sort of common, the 'lord's waste'. They had decided to enclose their open fields so that each tenant had his own ground to use as he wished. They noted landmarks along the way, measuring the distances between them. This perambulation was reported to a meeting of the manorial court in West Chiltington, and written up in the court rolls.

> Viz – ffrom the hedge of Richard Searle adjoyninge to the high way against the comon of Sr Thomas Bishopp on the east, from thence southward to the watercourse, and from the watercourse to a thorne where Jo: Duppa gent for a memoriall of the bounder did sett I.D. on ye ground —[9]

News of these men walking from the stream to the thorn (I know the stream, but not the thorn) comes to us from an estate steward named John Rowe, who had responsibility for Lord Abergavenny's manors from 1597 to 1622. He was steward of West Chiltington and neighbouring Nutbourne in Shakespeare's time. During his last years in the job, he wrote down all he knew of the customary laws of these manors, checking his knowledge against written sources and foraging through court, estate and parish records to clarify what remained obscure.

John Rowe sounds to me like the water bailiff of the river. Both were ordering and narrating long research into the places where they had spent their lives; they had become antiquarians out of practical need and also out of pleasure. They were working for nobility, committed to the service of duke or lord, but their subject as historians was not primarily the lives of nobles: it was the tenants, the commoners, the running of fisheries and farms.

Rowe was driven to distraction by the aberrant customs of Nutbourne, where my parents had their first Sussex home. 'I thinke will hardlye be found in any other manor of this realme the like confusion, except it be in the adjoyning manor of Chiltington.' The customs of the two places were entangled, and the whole lot was a mess, 'fitter for the reverend Judges of this kingdome upon mature del:bacon [deliberation] to resolve than for mine insufficiency to determine'.[10] Rowe did what he could, writing out the names of reeves, tenants and freeholders, and checking the status of commons 'lately inclosed' by the tenants themselves.[11]

The presence of Robert Johnson, the rector, was particularly noted in the manor records. He was eighty-three when he accompanied the younger tenants around the boundaries, and he had lived all his eight decades in Chiltington. The elderly were the authorities as far as custom was concerned. They were the witnesses to what had been done over time. Folded in with the court papers was the statement given a few years earlier by Robert Barnard, then aged eighty-two, formally written up in Latin by a clerk. Robert confirmed what he had seen 'with his own eyes to be true' about the common as he had known it in the reigns of Henry VIII, Edward VI and Mary. John Rowe copied this into his book beside the report of the perambulation in which the old rector joined the next generation in walking the bounds.

The little scene comes through time, and in it the land is sharp as an etching, sharp as the thorn that stands out so prominently to these men who know every yard of ground. Or every 'paulle', pole: that's the unit they measure in. Forty poles make a furlong, eight furlongs a mile (the Roman unit of a thousand steps). Step by step they agree the boundary along the bank of the stream that still runs through on its way to the Arun. They follow the path along 'Monckton Meade', the earliest reference I have found for my road. I recognise their names: Bisshop of Parham, Duppa, Searle and Goble (we used to live next door to a family of Gobles). They feel so close I could run to catch up with them, and they are immensely far away. As a woman, I would not have joined them in this little bit of local business or any other. This land was not mine to measure. I was not elected reeve; I did not agree upon enclosures. In seventeenth-century West Chiltington, property and associated customary rights descended by default to the youngest son.[12] I am glad, though, to see for a moment through the eyes of these farming men. Here is John Duppa setting his 'I.D.' upon the ground, his initials painted on wood perhaps, or carved into an upright post like the 'dole stones' used to mark boundaries in water meadows.[13] John Rowe the steward copied the perambulation into his book of 1622. A line made by people walking long ago:

> — from thence to a tolte, berge, or hillocke being 29 paules southward
> from ye thorne, and from the bearge directly westward to a bancke,
> and so alonge the bancke to a great bounderstone lying on the east
> end of Monckton meade, and from thence directly northward to the
> middle of the high way —[14]

I go with them to the highway, where they turn back towards the village and I take the road to the station and my train.

30. SHADOW AND BLAZE
Ivon Hitchens at the blue door

September Trees and Pond by House, 1956 (PLATE): the sunset is a lake of coral red pouring across the ground towards us, along a path neatly edged as if it were a channel dug to catch a sun which now overflows its bounds. Pink, orange, red, the light rushes forward but is kept back by rough strokes of vegetation and scrubbed out by the cerulean of September afternoons. The double doors from the studio make a blue block at the side, set in the salmon-pink wall. Ivon Hitchens often put his easel outside the doors, on the patch of grass that was more a woodland clearing than a lawn. He had looked out from this spot most days for sixteen years, and he was here again.

Under the splashing freedom there is geometry. The canvas is a double square, a shape that brings attention to itself because it offers two centres, a diptych without a hinge, squares continually merging and pulling away from each other. Hitchens defines at least five distinct areas across its width, as if we are looking in many directions – which is what we do instinctively all the time. The curtain of trees leads rippling into the distance. Leaf-shapes are scored with a brush-end into the thickness of paint: late-summer skaters on sheets of colour. The first of winter comes to woodlands on September evenings. There's a chill in the grey-greens, weight in the sky, and the coral might cool into the dawn glow of Turner's *Frosty Morning*. But there's also a carnival spirit here, a seizing of riches. Another twenty years in this place and Hitchens would still be bringing the harvest in.

He lived in a brightly painted, exuberantly stylish modernist house hidden in a dark wood. That was the kind of complication in which Hitchens excelled. He decided what he wanted to do and pursued it for forty years, making paintings at the meeting point of landscape and abstraction. I had known his address since I first became interested in painting. Almost every Hitchens picture carries a label on the backboard: *Green-leaves, Lavington Common*. Again and again I had seen it in catalogues: one of the most productive places in modern art.

Hitchens didn't think a tree was any less interesting for being in the same spot every day. He went into the woods, pushing a wheelbarrow loaded with easel and brushes, equipped with sandwiches for later, and he began the work of responding to the tones, rhythms, shallows and depths of the living landscape. There was an element of the visionary discipline that kept Cézanne looking at Mont Sainte-Victoire, and Monet seeing all life when he looked into his lily pond.[1]

He was frequently referred to as the outstanding British landscape painter of the twentieth century, and his name was also frequently met with a blank. 'Ivon Hitchens I have certainly heard of,' Elizabeth Bishop pondered in Brazil in 1954, 'but I can't seem to recall any particular pictures.'[2] For his part, he might have loved her banana-leaved tropical terrace, but would never have left his wood to see it. The next generation of abstract artists in Britain navigated by his work as a central fact in the history of painting. Hitchens wanted to be recognised and was: his Venice Biennale show toured to Munich and Paris. There was a Tate retrospective in 1963, and another in 1979 at the Royal Academy (where he had repeatedly declined to become an Academician). He didn't live to see David Bowie buying a series of his most involving water pictures, but wouldn't have been surprised. His wide landscapes make spaces larger; you might think of buying one instead of building an extension. A friend of mine had a Hitchens painting in his small Oxford sitting room and when his active life was constrained by illness he feasted on the greens of that picture as if it physically expanded his horizon.

I had never consciously taken the overhung turning that goes to Lavington Common. I imagined it was like other places between Petworth
and Duncton, abundantly grassy, well gardened, with a deep lane edged
in old man's beard becoming a steep track up the down. An exploratory
walk in early spring suggested my error. 'Relax and unwind' suggested
the National Trust, which now owns part of the common. I felt differently: I was on my mettle, skin prickling.

The sand path led out across heathland where a few pines and birches
stood like lightning conductors above woody heather and a rust swell of
matted bracken. There would be adders stirring from their hibernation
between roots and fronds. This is one of Britain's richest ecologies and
most ancient landscapes, habitat for lizards, insects and fungi, a rare late
survivor of England's former heath: alien, absorbing and to me profoundly unhomely.

A few minutes along the lane was another world again, not exposed
to the sky like the common but secluded and shadowed. The light itself seemed green where it came filtering through leaves. There were
glimpses of grass framed by rhododendron trunks, and a sense of water
somewhere between reeds. Sand, pine needles and leaf moulds cushioned the ground.

Hitchens felt a connection with the sandy places of his boyhood: 'at
a very early age I went to live among the silver birches and bracken and
heather of Surrey, so that this area of Sussex has seemed homelike and
familiar from the start'.[3] He had known both sand and chalk: sand at
home with his parents and chalk at Bedales School in the downs. As a
young painter he was drawn to the countryside between Petworth and
Midhurst, where a pinewood on acid greensand might suddenly give
way to open downs. These places mattered to his artist father too. Before his death in 1942, Alfred Hitchens visited the Swan at Fittleworth
when he could. From there, he walked into the woods and made pastel
drawings that would be long remembered by his son.[4]

The plot that Ivon and Mollie purchased near Lavington Common had been a fir plantation before the Great War, when the trees were felled. By the 1940s it had reverted to scrub, with rhododendrons spreading and birches gaining height. Trees were cleared for the building, but not too many: this was always to be a woodland home.

At first family life was squeezed into the caravan and studio. But no cramp or constriction got into Hitchens' pictures of mother and child. They had a galvanised bath they called Jordan, in which John had his regular baptism in the open air with soap and sponge. *John by Jordan* became a series: blue bandy legs wobbling, or an orange silhouette broaching the violet lozenge of the tub (PLATE). Piero della Francesca had painted the baptism of Christ in the holy river; Hitchens (who studied all his life the paintings of quattrocento Italy) painted his son's metal tub in the back garden.

The house that was appearing from the building site, made in partnership with Mollie, was Hitchens' largest work of art and one that would grow over the years. The whole structure emanated confidence. Hitchens had always loved millhouses beside streams and wanted his tall studio building to give that effect, echoing with its high gable ends the distinctive shape of Dutch and East Anglian mansard roofs (PLATE). He remembered too the large bungalow-villas he had seen as a boy in New Zealand, where single-storey was not only for retirement, and now he thought about how spaces could open in lateral succession.

Rooms were added one at a time through the 1940s. After the studio came a designated 'telephone room', then a glasshouse. When Ivon's mother came to live at Greenleaves, an extension was added for her. As money allowed, rooms were built to accommodate the rest of the family more comfortably, with space for cooking, sleeping, work and music.

Interior double doors were painted in light pink with orange panels, and suggested a home-made answer to the finest enfilades in the world to be seen across the park at Petworth. But here, as in a wood, the undergrowth kept growing up across the view: rigged-up contraptions, cushions for models, an ecology of hoarded pots and cans. Hitchens would pose unrepentantly for a Snowdon portrait beside the 'oceans' of clutter on his desk from which relevant paperwork occasionally surfaced. Passageways, like double-parked streets, were single-file only. The whole house was a storage facility, a gallery and a work in progress.

The idea for the external painting started with the caravan, which was bright green and red at first, later pink and black. Hitchens liked the colour among the dark foliage, and wanted the house to be a vibrant painting too. The blue doors and blue bench set the key, a Wedgwood blue strengthened and freed from china delicacy. Blue gutters gurgled with rainwater, emphatically painted as if Hitchens, who loved all water-ways, thought of them as tributaries of the local streams. For the large Crittall window frames he chose a yellow between sulphur and gorse, bright enough to shine out through the woods. It was close to the yellow Derek Jarman would use for the windows of Prospect Cottage on the shingle at Dungeness, a colour at its most vibrant on grey days. This was mixed at Greenleaves with wall decorations in pale pink and cream reminiscent of sun-bleached Italian loggias, done without a flicker of rococo whimsy or nostalgia. It was a modern house for a modern painter and his family.

Smallholding of the kind Ford Madox Ford idealised was the last thing Hitchens wanted in his garden. He bought his apples and beans from the greengrocer and gave his attention to peonies and poppies. In paint he made the garden a humming jungle that called up the sounds of parrots more than woodpeckers (though woodpeckers, with their Ma-tisse colouring, were always welcome). Among the plants, there was water: dark water, reflecting water, a boat sliding between reeds on one of two small ponds. *Who's Who* asked for his hobbies. 'Streams', he answered. The *Tangled Pool* series was painted in the back garden: the pool is imagined somewhere within the 'tangle' of waterside growth, a hidden coolness behind the waving, fizzing, flaring shapes that suggest cow parsley, rushes, grasses and flags. As Hitchens painted this subject again and again in 1946–8 (ten pictures in all), he broke away from the stabilising backdrop of the house, and let the vegetation burst across the canvas.

Watercourses inside the house were much improved with the laying of pipes to carry spring water from the downs. The old system of buckets brought from the well was superseded. Now the taps produced a version of freshwater streams, with some of the same inhabitants. Shrimps occasionally tumbled into the washing-up.

Hitchens didn't drive. Like most men and women through the last millennium, his life was mostly within walking distance of the door. In the late 1970s, looking back on forty years of being 'homebound', he pondered his return in the next life. Would he be a man of radical movement? 'By then one will be expected to pilot some horrible space machine – and I'd far rather walk the downs and search out wooded glades & hollows in the chalk – watch the rabbits under thorn bushes, & see the wild rose thickets backed up by the black yews.'[5]

Inviting the young poet and painter Michael Ayrton down from London, he drew a careful map of bus stops and advised a route via 'Amberley Wild Brooks, Coates Common and Burton Lakes – a lovely bit of country'.[6] Ayrton balked at the bus challenge and took a taxi. In extravagant moods Hitchens would order a taxi himself to take them all up to the downs above Heyshott. But up here the landscape showed itself too openly. For painting, he wanted to be overgrown, secret, sunken in bracken, in a hollow where he would have to look. Walking in the area, you can feel yourself coming into Hitchens' places. They are the points at which you feel most curtained and enclosed, where you can't quite remember how you arrived or how to get away.

'In England today,' wrote Patrick Heron in the mid-1950s, 'Hitchens in West Sussex provides the most distinguished example of . . . profound personal identification of a painter with a special place, or landscape – although, in Cornwall, Peter Lanyon, much younger, has this same reverence for a particular landscape.'[7] Lanyon stood on exposed granite, submitting himself to the elements, wanting to be airborne, painting the path of the wind over the sea. Hitchens, meanwhile, submerged himself in the marginal growth of ponds. Letters went back and forth from the far edge of western Britain to the house in the thickets. Lanyon was one of many younger artists to whom Hitchens was a mentor and who championed him in turn, the most vocal being Patrick Heron himself. In his high Cornish house, Heron lifted the telephone and his voice came down the line into the telephone room among the Sussex trees.

Hitchens understood each picture to be playing out a series of 'movements', answering each other like the parts of a concerto. He told Maynard Keynes how the 'legato, indeterminate' character of one movement of *Rhododendron Glade, Spring* contrasted with the 'thin staccato accents' given by birch trees in the other.[8] Mollie was a fine pianist (they installed her grand piano at Greenleaves as soon as there was room) and Ivon listened or he painted with the radio or the gramophone playing in the studio. He was not synaesthetic (a chord was not consistently a certain colour) but music tuned his mind to spatial relationships and gave him a model for thinking about art as 'visual sound'.[9] Increasingly, he felt he could listen in to the private life of the water and trees. When shown a new picture he advised, 'one shouldn't start by thinking about it. That can come after. After you have listened to its talk.'[10] He walked in the wood like that, listening to its talk. 'I tend to like not one but two views. One says A and the other says B.' He went on, improvising: 'A is more intricate, sharply crystalline, detailed. B is softer in a way, perhaps, full of rounded shapes. Yet both are the same landscape.'[11] It was as absorbing to him as any conversation between people, or instrumental duet.

In the early 1950s Hitchens took the wood to London. Accepting a commission from the English Folk Dance and Song Society to decorate the walls of the dance hall at Cecil Sharp House, all seventy feet of them, he thought of arching boughs and clearings, dancers moving through the trees. The mural was not to distract the dancers from their steps, but when they stopped and steadied themselves, deer would appear crouching at the dado watching Arcadian pipers and painted dancers with antler masks. Nudes would lounge in the grass and a May queen emerge from thickets not of deep evergreen but of glowing yellows. Hitchens listened to horn dances, and also to Wagner; he looked out of the studio doors to where there might be mythic beings in the woods.

The real woods were lonely and he liked that, though he came to know some of the men who worked in them. On a winter day in 1956, snow thick on the ground, Hitchens found a campfire in a chestnut grove that was being felled. Alarmed, he brought water to extinguish it and waited for the culprits to return so that he could remonstrate about the danger. The two workers who came back from their lunch break were experienced woodsmen who explained how carefully they had sited the fire. Hitchens relented, amicable introductions were made. It was the beginning of a twenty-year friendship with Ted Floate, who would be regularly employed at Greenleaves, stretching canvases, pruning trees or clearing paths, building a wooden bridge near the pond. Even his name was felicitous, from the Middle English word for stream. There had been Floates around the Rother and Arun since at least the seventeenth century. Hitchens gave him a painting made in the garden, *Footbridge over a Sussex Dell*. 'It was only a little ditch really,' said Floate, 'but after he'd painted it, it looked like Cheddar Gorge.'[12] That was the magnifying quality of Hitchens' attention.

As Floate worked up trees and on the roof, Hitchens watched and sketched his dextrous movements.[13] *Day's Rest, Day's Work*, from 1960, now dominates the refectory at Sussex University. A polyptych in four parts, it has the form of an altarpiece. From the surging shapes there emerges a labourer, his figure multiplied so that we see him bending to a log and swinging his axe while also leaning protectively over wife and children (a version of the Holy Family with Joseph as carpenter or woodsman). It is a strange image for a university, where books and talk pull students away from physical work; its presence urges a connection between these different kinds of effort. It affirms the respect of an artist for a woodsman, art for craft, imagination for practical action. Floate helped Mollie with the garden for years after Ivon's death. He retired to a cottage at Whittlesey in the fens, where there was hardly room to hang all the paintings he had been given over the years and which he loved.

~

Hitchens' world was not built on sedimentary layers of time that stuck out their bones into the present. His perspectives were never, like Sutherland's, geological cross-sections through the earth. His trees, even the collapsed 'divided oak', were not witnesses of time. He did not paint the barrows and tumuli of the heath (at least six groups of them within walking distance) or the hill forts on the downs. It was life in the present moment he loved to watch. He thought that even 'romantic' painters needed to express 'present day consciousness' as shaped by relativity and radiation.[14]

His present always existed in relation to the 'grander design' of eternity. He was drawn by a strong metaphysical instinct to think, not deeply, but adventurously, about the next world. His experiments with pure abstraction in the 1930s had a religious grammar in them – *Triangle to Beyond* most explicitly, with its gesture to an exit through the painted frame. His world was full of arrows to beyond, 'little pointers . . . that we come from a greater life'.[15] Never quite able to ignore a horoscope (and he liked the wateriness of his star sign, Pisces), he stored up eclectic examples of prophecies fulfilled. William of Orange was promised great wealth and a violent death, he noted. He had himself been told by a clairvoyant that he would live in a white house surrounded by trees.[16]

He conceived of 'thought forms' left on 'inner planes'.[17] They sound like photographic plates of the mind, which might be exposed in the light of another time or an afterworld. They were certainly part of a structure 'beyond' immediate interpretation. When he painted his perspectives through trees to ponds, or along woodland rides, he felt himself to be part of a cosmic picture. The scale of that other canvas revealed itself as he attended to the living plot at his studio door.

31. A TEACHER'S RETURN

Elizabeth was one of the tens of thousands of care-home residents who had to be left unvisited month after month through the spring of 2020. In June Caroline was allowed to go in and sit at a distance, masked and unreachable but there anyway. Elizabeth may or may not have been aware of a presence that was recognisable and loving. She had stopped eating, except for sweets, and was a tiny fine-boned figure in the bed, tense and exhausted, and with shining, beautifully cut hair. In mid-July Caroline was at last able to go again and found her mother apparently comfortable, slipping in and out of sleep. If Elizabeth had in some way been waiting for Caroline, her wait had ended and she died the next day.

There was a funeral in Exeter, then the family made a cross-country journey to take Elizabeth back to Sussex. I joined them for the burial in a woodland on the downs above Petersfield — not quite her patch but you can't bury people anywhere you choose and this was close enough. Held high, the shouldered coffin advanced along the chalk path through a coppiced clearing and into the trees. The sun was streaming between beech leaves. It lit up the sunflowers and lavender on top of the coffin, tokens of Elizabeth's love of France, and her joy in explorations of the world elsewhere. The Provençal flowers, blazing yellow and blue, went riding through the green beeches.

It was my first outing beyond the Oxford ring road all year. In the car on the way down my sadness was met with a tide of relief at the moment when the motorway verges were suddenly southern after a certain roundabout, brimming with scabious, white campion, and filigree waves of wild carrot: the plants of the chalk. Then, at the first hedge, the long-armed welcome of *Clematis vitalba*, traveller's joy. I thanked the traffic queue that kept us rolling at walking pace alongside these unexpected samplings of abundance and thanked Elizabeth for the strange gift of this day. For years I had taught Faulkner's novel *As I Lay Dying* with its doomed, bungled, stinking pilgrimage honouring a mother's last wish (a black joke, perhaps, a cackling challenge) to be buried in Mississippi. Here was the very opposite, a summer journey that released us all from lockdown and brought us to the downs.

We looked into the earth: a foot of humus, and four feet of fresh-cut chalk. Elizabeth's people and places converged on that rectangle of ground – the lavender from France, sprays of English flowers brought by other teachers from school, memories from Nottingham family. Because she had grown up near Toronto and always felt partly Canadian, we had chosen a poem from Canada which I read on the hillside. 'We will drink of the long red shaft of light / That slants from the westering sun.'[1] A prairie stretched out between us and instinctively we looked to the sun, which was not setting and not red.

Afterwards, I learnt more about the family relationship with Ontario. Elizabeth's mother had been sent over as an evacuee: a little girl four thousand miles from home. As a young woman back in England she married an engineer whose firm, it transpired (a coincidence), invited him to manage a new project in Canada. Elizabeth did much of her growing up in St Catharines and then in Toronto. Decades later, in Sussex, she was still making comparisons with Ontario and in touch with friends there, continuing the exchange begun by the labouring migrants of the 1830s. 'Dear friends, I hope you will not fail in coming', Ruth

Waldon had urged from St Catharines in 1836, finding the work good, food plentiful, the children all in school. 'I wish I had come ten years before I did.' I wonder if Elizabeth knew about those letters. Probably. I wonder if she knew about the series of moose that were brought in the other direction, Quebec to Sussex, and which didn't survive the change.

Elizabeth's brother emphasised the fact that she had the whole Canadian railway network by heart. She knew the British trains too. The painted map on the wall at home in Nottinghamshire had included, he said, 'railways both open and closed', a memorial gesture to the abandoned lines of a diminished post-Beeching nation. He reeled off a reading list for me, should I want to know about the lost branch lines of Sussex. I certainly wished the branch lines of the Arun valley would be resurrected from the undergrowth, connecting the main line with the small towns, opening the whole area to people without cars. How different my own map of home would be.

We talked about Elizabeth's tiny house in Pulborough and the places packed into it. French baskets hung in bunches, strung like garlic or lavender. Books on Italian frescoes and civil engineering were double-stacked in front of the *Sussex Archaeological Collections*. About a quarter of the available floor space was occupied by a giant Welsh duodarn or court cupboard, its carved doors opening to reveal, variously, butterfly cases or Martini. In some lights it looked solidly rural and Welsh; in others it had the air of a *marchesa*'s *cassone* in a Renaissance palazzo. The dining table was also the desk on which Elizabeth trained as a teacher, marked our essays, wrote a book about our school, and gathered materials for her history of the Arun.

The duodarn and the table are both at Caroline's house in Devon now, the duodarn reliably stocked with Martini, and the table piled with estate maps, conservation reports and stray toy vehicles. Caroline checks that she has another hour before nursery pick-up and clears herself a space to work.

32. A CENSUS

On census day, 21 March 2021, I give my name and details of the house. I mark the boxes for gas central heating, no religion, no car. I sign to say that yes I am here, on a terraced street in Oxford, this cool grey Sunday in our emptied-out March. I am here at the registered address, in a place made of other places, as all our places are. In this moment of stilled time, when the nation sits for its group portrait and offers its sample day to be laid down in history, I am conscious of the register being taken in the villages and towns along the Arun and west through the downs towards Chichester.

I haven't been able to get there for a long time. Friends have phoned from high on the downs to let me hear the wind and tell me what they can see. I've watched iPhone videos in which Cissbury bounces up and down to the rhythm of footsteps and chalk paths flicker. Zoom after Zoom we've all peered through the window of our computer screens. Elbows on the windowsill that is our desks, we have all squinted and strained to see. I've phoned Chichester most days to speak to my father, who hasn't minded the pandemic much at all, and has kept walking each morning around the city walls. 'Every part of the city is fourfold; and every inhabitant, fourfold.'

Everyone is being counted. Questions for each person, questions for each household. The answers are what will survive of us. Everyone is counted in the deep-eaved Wells cottages along Monkmead Lane, three bedrooms, double garages. *Who lives here? List the names, including babies, children and lodgers.* Lucy gets bored with recorder practice and follows her mother around the house without helping as floors are swept and locomotives tipped into the toy box. Leah takes the dogs over the road for their morning run over the golf course and back through the wood. Hazy sunshine. Sunday lunches.

Everyone is counted in Storrington: in the roads near West Wantley, the post-war semis along Brown's Lane, the flats above shops along the High Street. Only the supermarket is open in Mill Square, but the people coming for their food shopping are counted. We used to shop here when it was Somerfield, and before that when it was Gateway, and before that Keyways, whose shelves I knew at increasing heights. I can stand here and take stock of time in the changing vegetable aisle. The library is closed except for collections but the requests shelf holds its treasure for readers who have ordered in advance. When I was at eye level with the counter, the librarians would have my next book waiting. Still the blue letters 'Library' beckon me across the car park to that small building with its worlds inside.

Along Church Street the people in the new retirement homes are counted, and the few couples who own parts of what used to be my school. The nuns who taught us moved away when the convent was sold twenty years ago. Are they somewhere in the country, being counted? The internet tells me more than I knew when we spent each day together; the congregation was founded in South Africa, and most of the sisters had taught or nursed in KwaZulu-Natal. Our headmistress returned to spend her last years there. This I learn from an obituary. It doesn't mention Storrington. Did our teachers ever tell us about these other homes far from Sussex? I don't think they did.

Who is staying overnight? These people are counted as visitors. There are not many visitors this distanced March — each household an island where others are forbidden to land. Everyone is counted around the four-square lanes of Bignor. Here, on history's census, were people whose papers and identities changed with the moon. Christian Pineau, Stéphane Hessel, Marie-Madeleine Fourcade, Léon Faye. 'What name will you choose while you're here?' Fourcade was asked. 'Villeneuve, I decided. That's where my father was born.'[1] A name conjured for the moment and honouring the past.

Dipping down to the mill stream I pick up the path across to Sutton. Here is the village left behind by George Carver, Joseph Leggett, Elias Elliott and Richard Neal when they sailed for Canada. Here's the lane towards Glatting Hanger. It's thick with clematis, though the old men's beards are ragged wisps after the winter. Here is my great-aunt, who must give her own name but not that of her husband, my great-uncle, who died upstairs at home in a pink dawn just after New Year. She will get into the garden this afternoon and put a mulch on his iris bed. Neighbours will come to the porch and call through to the kitchen, offering supplies. Later she will cook carefully, fighting through the hours, looking after herself for him.

It's a steep walk up Bignor Hill, but in imagination it's folded in half and half again so already I'm out from the shaded hanger turning into the wind and the view, and the wide white boot-beaten high road of the South Downs Way. The car park is full and half the cars occupied: people drive up here to sit and read – with a thermos in the glovebox and the kingdoms of the earth through the windscreen – or to snooze in muggy car warmth, or to turn up the stereo. Through the clear wall of wind, there is the sea. The glinting in the plain looks like lakes, but it's the glasshouses. Hectares of tomatoes and strawberries.

Detached, semi-detached, terraced, flat, bedsit, caravan. Down in the picker villages the rows of mobile homes await the season's labourers. Another month and it begins here: berries into boxes for eight hours a day, at which point the overtime rate kicks in and anyone who can stand it carries on. The picker villages are Ukrainian and Polish villages; the food shops are stocked with kielbasa sausages and *kołaczki* biscuits. This year there is a scramble to organise visas for seasonal labourers while the borders are otherwise closed. It's unclear whether there would be enough British workers to get the job done if migrants did not arrive. I remember with a flush of shame how useless I was as a teenage summer picker, my punnets underweight, my calves in spasm. *If a job became available now, could you start it within two weeks?*

Everyone is counted in Felpham, in the flats built on the site of Hayley's turret house, and the gabled inter-war houses behind privets.

Three hundred and four: William Blake.
Three hundred and five: Catherine Blake.

Everyone is counted in the eastern suburbs of Chichester and on the terraces around the old burying ground. And now here are the shiny Georgian doorcases in the Pallant and the ostriches guarding the art gallery. Here are the old low houses along one side of Vicars' Close and the flats above shops on North Street. Here were the Peckhams arguing about their kitchen. Mrs Collins running the hat shop. William Collins safe from struggle for a few minutes while the woman reads another chapter of the Bible by the open window. Here was George Smith getting on with the foliage in his painting of a bend in the river. Here was Ruth Smith growing old without him, taking in a lodger. My father makes his circuit of the walls, east, north, west, south quadrants, and through the Bishop's Garden where daffodils are out on the banks.

Everyone is counted in Arundel. In ones and twos and families, people are walking along Mill Road to Swanbourne, children running ahead to see the ducks. A few carry on under Offham Hanger, with the wooded chalk rising on one side and the wetlands on the other. The coming year waits in the verges: the swell of cow parsley and carrot that will rise under the double-cream saucers of elder, architectural plans for campanula's big bell towers, soft pink agrimony and burdock's spiky globes. This is the way the bargemen liked to come in the 1830s and 40s; Arundel tradesmen would walk here for pleasure on a Sunday and end up at the Black Rabbit, right on the river. The sheer cliffs of chalk show where the quarry was worked. Here, in 1943, the men of X-Troop lowered themselves over the rock face that stood in for the cliffs of Normandy, searching for footholds, willing the ropes to hold.

The tide flows in past South Stoke, the river making its horseshoe curve around the hamlet on its spur of chalk. The cows are filing into the barn for milking. Steadily they come to the top of Front Field and across the lane. Ten, twenty. Forty, fifty. Here were the Sowtons and Styants, moving their stock between the meadows. Here was Ann Gittins learning her lessons and noticing the breeze on the hills at dawn. Here are the rectory windows she knew, facing out to the river.

The tide flows in under Houghton Bridge and through the wild brooks. The inhabitants of the river are on the move: it is close season, what the water bailiff called Fence Month, when the fish 'claim free passage' through the river from their winter 'garrisons' to summer breeding grounds. No fishing net or weir may stop them. Swans are finding nest sites. There's no census of swans on the Arun now, no swan-roll kept as a directory; but local people know which pairs are settling where.

Here, four hundred years ago, the bailiff signed off his account of the river and its customs, wishing 'peace and privilege to Fish, Fowl, and Fisher-men'. 'Having travelled many Bridges, passed many Ferries, waded some Fords and Shallows', he made an ending. He was conscious of having come a long way, and yet of hardly leaving home. He put 'his little Barque into the Dock that never indeed durst venture far abroad'.[2]

There is no one at St Mary's, Stopham, keeping company the brass men and women who lie under the carpet, though outside the village moves with the lockdown rhythms of circular walks and front-path conversations. The leaf buds are breaking on the Stopham estate vines: Pinot Gris, Pinot Blanc, Auxerrois. Roots nudge towards water in the greensand soil.

There is no one in Hardham church. There is no one, thankfully, anchored in a lean-to cell. The census finds no anchorite (though being dead-in-life he would not, in any case, have given his name). A few more weeks and visitors will find the 'OPEN' sign at the door again and step into the cool, thick-sided larder of frescoes, where the shelves on all sides are stocked with stories. For now, the painted people go on by themselves in the dark (PLATE). Adam and Eve are still having their urgent talk about the serpent. Slender angels welcome the Holy Spirit. Their bodies are contours of earthy pigments, red clay and ochre, but their haloes shine out with the sharp copper green that looks not of this earth at all. Two donkeys browse over the lozenge of a swaddled baby on the upper shelf of the north wall, born in a stable at the time of a census, or so St Luke thought, a decree that all the world should be registered.

Joseph of Nazareth, carpenter, married.
(There was no need to count Mary, his wife.)

Mary, nine months pregnant, travelled through the Judean desert to have the baby that is shown here on Hardham wall and was soon forced to leave again, for Egypt. There she is on the donkey, a woman in flight, riding over the wild brooks to Pulborough.

At Elizabeth's old house, where Caroline grew up, there's a woman talking on the phone while keeping an eye on the finest view in England. The trees in the back garden have made way for football, but there's still the sound of a wood pigeon, and a cat is lying on the drive. At the top of Church Hill, the Chequers Hotel is closed; for the first time in their lives, the owners have had the house to themselves this year. Released from the reception window and the breakfast plates, sheets folded and stored for the duration, Lissette goes down to the river to swim.

Everyone is counted on Lower Street. The willows are blowing and dunking themselves in the current beyond the garden of Templemead, where Dr Martin used to live and see his patients and investigate the ages of the earth. There's no one next door, at Waterside, where loosestrife and ragwort are taking over the land around the old lime kiln on the wharf. The red vans are lined up behind the post depot until tomorrow morning.

At Barnhouse Lane I turn down to the brooks and onto the riverbank. The winter reeds are tawny, the new growth just coming through. The downs seem close, every tree distinct on the scalloped sides of Rackham

Banks. The path is worn wide by so many people walking. There's someone coming towards me now, and then two more behind. We'll nod hello as we pass each other. Every inhabitant is fourfold. A hundredfold. Uncountable.

ABBREVIATIONS USED IN NOTES

BL British Library

ESRO East Sussex Record Office

LBS Legacies of British Slavery Database created by the Centre for the Study of the Legacies of British Slavery, University College London

ODNB *Oxford Dictionary of National Biography*

Pevsner Elizabeth Williamson, Tim Hudson, Jeremy Musson and Ian Nairn, Sussex: West, Pevsner Architectural Guides (rev. edn, New Haven: Yale UP, 2019)

SAC *Sussex Archaeological Collections* (the journal of the Sussex Archaeological Society)

SLWA State Library of Western Australia

SRS Sussex Record Society (followed by volume number for the Society's annual publications)

TGA Tate Archive

TNA The National Archives

VCH *Victoria County History*

WSRO West Sussex Record Office

Dates relating to the period before 1752, when the new year began on 25 March, have been silently modernised. Old Style January 1673, or January 1673–4, is given as January 1674.

NOTES

Squint

1 Judith Glover, *The Place Names of Sussex* (London: Batsford, 1975), 71. The re-used Roman bricks and tiles are described in F. G. Aldsworth and James Hadfield, 'Investigations at Hardham Church 1978 and 1981', *SAC* 120 (1982), 222–8.

2 Will of Richard de Wych, transcribed W. H. Blaauw, *SAC* 1 (1848), 164–92 (174), translation revised David Jones, *Saint Richard of Chichester: The Sources for His Life*, SRS 79 (1995), 68.

3 The well-documented anchoress Miliana is thought by some to have been immured at Hardham, though L. F. Salzman ('A Litigious Anchorite', *Sussex Notes & Queries* 2:5 (1929) 135–7) discusses her suing Richard 'inclusuum' of Hardham in 1272; Miliana seems to have been at Steyning. Salzman identifies this Richard as prior of Hardham Priory; Robert was his successor.

4 Terms used in the thirteenth-century guide for anchorites *Ancrene Wisse*, e.g. part 2, lines 259–62. Quoted from the edition by Robert Hasenfratz (Kalamazoo: Medieval Institute Publications, 2000).

5 Still there, though close to its end, in 1839 when it was illustrated in *The Mirror of Literature, Amusement and Instruction* (London: J. Limbird, 1839), 233, and the hollow trunk was deemed capable of holding twenty-seven people.

6 The revised Pevsner guide, 414–15, offers generous detail on the scheme of paintings; and see Christopher Aggs & John Wyatt, *The Wall Paintings at Hardham*, Otter Memorial Paper 2 (Chichester: Bishop Otter College, 1987).

7 The paintings were covered by 1637, rediscovered 1862 and the plaster fully removed 1900 as reported by Philip Mainwaring Johnston, 'Hardham Church, and Its Early Paintings', *SAC* 44 (1901), 73–115.

8 Clive Bell, 'Introduction', *Twelfth-Century Paintings at Hardham and Clayton* (Lewes: Miller's Press, 1947), 10–20.

9 *Ancrene Wisse*, ed. Hasenfratz, part 6, lines 378–80, and *Ancrene Wisse: A Guide for Anchorites*, trans. Bella Millett (Exeter: University of Exeter Press, 2009), 143.

10 *Ancrene Wisse*, ed. Hasenfratz, part 2, lines 161–3, and trans. Millett, *Guide*, 25. The question is quoted from Ecclesiasticus 31: 13.

1. The Visitor

1 One of the first texts to attract me with its local knowledge was David Bone's

booklet *The Stones of Boxgrove Priory: A Guide to the Building Stones* (Chichester: Limanda Publishing, 2010). I then turned to Historic England's *Strategic Stone Study: A Building Stone Atlas of West Sussex*, 2015.

2 W. H. Hudson, *A Shepherd's Life* (1910; London: J. M. Dent, 1923), 40.

3 As an academic discipline in England, local history emerged from the growing fields of economic and social history between the wars, offering profound challenges to accepted national narratives by examining the records of communities in particular areas. From 1948 the Centre for English Local History at the University of Leicester, headed by W. G. Hoskins, shaped the development of techniques and emphases. On the prominence of women scholars, and their methods, see e.g. Joan Thirsk, 'Women Local and Family Historians', in David Hey, ed., *The Oxford Companion to Family and Local History* (1996; Oxford: OUP, 2010), 100–10. Vibrant traditions of regional study in France and Italy lay behind the rise of 'microhistory' in the 1970s; this form of close-up focus and 'thick' description is still evolving and attracting new advocates around the world. On its current potential see especially Thomas V. Cohen, 'The Macrohistory of Microhistory', *Journal of Medieval and Early Modern Studies* 47:1 (2017), 53–73.

4 William Blake, 'Auguries of Innocence', line 1, in the Pickering Manuscript, c.1803, *Complete Writings*, ed. Geoffrey Keynes (Oxford: OUP, 1972), 431.

5 K. Jane Evans, article *SAC* 112 (1974), 97–151.

6 D. W. Crossley, 'Ralph Hogge's Ironworks Accounts, 1576–81', *SAC* 112 (1974), 48–79. Philip Henslowe retained many business and family connections with his native Sussex after he moved to London. S. R. Ceresano, 'The Geography of Henslowe's Diary', *Shakespeare Quarterly* 56:3 (2005), 328–53.

7 *The Blickling Homilies* (10th century), ed. Richard J. Kelly (London: Continuum, 2003), 48, 88.

8 Bartholomaeus Anglicus, *De Proprietatibus Rerum*, trans. John Trevisa (1398; Oxford: Clarendon, 1975), 717. Downs here include small foothills beneath higher hills; they are generally a middle ground between lowlands and highlands, and much favoured for living and farming.

9 Barnabe Googe, 'Egloga Tertia', lines 147–8, in *Eclogues, Epitaphs and Sonnets* (1563), ed. Judith M. Kennedy (Toronto: UTP, 2009).

10 LIDAR technology has recently made visible (by laser imaging) the archaeology of wooded areas. *Secrets of the High Woods*, ed. John Manley (Midhurst: SDNPA, 2016), presents research from a group of related studies in the area.

11 Matthew Dimmock, Andrew Hadfield and Paul Quinn assess the sixteenth- and seventeenth-century history of the county in Dimmock et al., eds, *Art, Literature and Religion in Early Modern Sussex* (2014; Abingdon: Routledge, 2016), 1–13. 'Sussex was an anomaly: a southern county with a religious dynamic more in

keeping with those of the north, connected to the Continent as much as to the rest of the country.'

12 A phenomenon widely discussed but see especially Keith Grieves, *Sussex in the First World War*, SRS 84 (2004), xxiv, and John Godfrey, 'Landscapes of War and Peace: Sussex, the South Downs, and the Western Front', *SAC* 152 (2014), 189–209, 204. See also chapter 26.

13 Fiona Stafford, *Local Attachments: The Province of Poetry* (Oxford: OUP, 2010), 20ff, 30.

14 Ibid., 25.

15 John Aubrey to Anthony à Wood, Bodleian MS Wood F 39, fol. 221r, quoted Ruth Scurr, *John Aubrey: My Own Life* (London: Chatto & Windus, 2015), 226, 229.

16 Several dedicated scholars were at work in the period but their research was not widely known: William Clarke, for example, librarian at Chichester cathedral. For the emergence and development of county histories in England, see C. R. J. Currie and C. P. Lewis, eds, *English County Histories: A Guide* (Stroud: Alan Sutton, 1994): the Sussex historiography (explored in a chapter by T. P. Hudson) can be seen here in the national context. The essential book on antiquarian study of Sussex, also an anthology of sources, is John Farrant, *Sussex Depicted: Views and Descriptions 1600–1800*, SRS 85 (2001).

17 Burrell's project is discussed in Farrant, *Sussex Depicted*, 25–50. The role of county historian passed to James Dallaway, who published the first substantial account of Sussex: *History of the Western Division of the County of Sussex* (London: T. Bensley, 1815), 2 vols.

18 Daniel Defoe, *A Tour through the Whole Island of Great Britain* (1724–7; London: Penguin, 1986), letter 2, 149, 148, 147.

19 Gilbert White to Daines Barrington, 9 December 1773, *The Natural History of Selborne* (1789), ed. Richard Mabey (1977; London: Penguin, 1987), 152.

20 William Gilpin, *Observations on the Coasts of Hampshire, Sussex, and Kent Etc* (London: Cadell & Davies, 1804), 39, 41.

21 Ibid., 45.

22 W. H. Hudson, *Nature in Downland* (1900; London: J. M. Dent, 1923), 7.

23 Rudyard Kipling, *Puck of Pook's Hill* (1906; London, Penguin, 1994), 14. Peter Brandon, in *The Discovery of Sussex* (Andover: Phillimore, 2010), 195, describes the 'exceptional place in England's imaginative geography' that Sussex occupied in the twentieth century.

24 *Sussex Modernism: Retreat and Rebellion*, the 2017 exhibition curated by Hope Wolf at 2 Temple Place, established the phrase and the concept. A group of cultural, commercial and tourist organisations now promote the brand 'Sussex Modern', arguing that Sussex art and thought 'helped shape our modern world' (sussexmodern.org.uk).

25 Plant lists at sussexflora.org.uk. The Sussex Botanical Recording Society has published a new county flora: *The Flora of Sussex* (Newbury, Pisces Publications, 2018).

26 Margaret Spufford, *Contrasting Communities: English Villages in the Sixteenth and Seventeenth Centuries* (1974; Stroud: Sutton, 2000), 33, considers 'neighbourhoods' or 'social areas' as the basis for historical study. On 'regions' and their distinct economic, social and religious histories see Joan Thirsk, *Agricultural Regions and Agrarian Study in England, 1500–1750* (Basingstoke: Macmillan, 1987). On counties as meaningful units of study, giving identity and sense of community, see e.g. Anthony Fletcher, *A County Community in Peace and War: Sussex 1600–1660* (London: Longman, 1975).

27 Cohen, 'Macrohistory', 66: 'Microhistory can do cultural history good service'. Writers deploying versions of the quadrat method include the ecologist David George Haskell, in *The Forest Unseen* (London: Viking, 2012), moving away from emphasis on scientific measurement towards contemplative watching, and James Attlee, in *Isolarion: A Different Oxford Journey* (Chicago: University of Chicago Press, 2007), focusing on one street.

2. High Stream of Arundel

1 Anon [William Barttelot?], *The High Stream of Arundel*, c. 1636, ed. Joseph Fowler (Littlehampton: Simson & Co., 1929), 57. Quotations follow the maunscript source text: Arundel Castle Archive, MD 170 and 178. Page numbers in the Fowler edition are given for ease of reference.

2 Ibid., 24, 'the Wild Brooks of Amberly' and 'Wiggenholt Brooks'.

3 Ibid., 21–4.

4 Ibid., 45.

5 Ibid., 40.

6 Ibid., 44.

7 The two parts are convincingly by one author, characterised by the same vigorous turn of phrase and mix of antiquarianism with practical knowledge.

8 *West Sussex Protestation Returns*, ed. R. Garraway Rice, SRS 5 (1998), 169.

9 Joseph Fowler, 'Who Wrote 'The High Stream of Arundel'?', *Sussex County Magazine*, May 1930. Fowler thinks WB was baptised 'William Bartelotte' at Pulborough, 6 July 1589. My thanks to Alice Millard for her help in analysing the sources for WB's life.

10 Arundel Castle Archive, MD 170 and 178 in Steer catalogue, vol. 2. The notebook is inscribed: 'A description of ye High Streame of Arundell as it came from Thomas Duke of Norfolk to Laurence Eliot Esq, his now Water Bayliff.'

11 *High Stream*, 20; William Camden, *Britannia*, trans. and expanded Philemon Holland (London: Bishop & Norton, 1610). The bailiff also quotes from Camden's *Annales rerum Anglicarum et Hibernicarum Regnante Elizabetha*.

12 *High Stream*, 12.

13 Cf. Karen Coke, 'Lambert Barnard, Bishop Shirburn's "Paynter"', in Matthew Dimmock, Andrew Hadfield and Paul Quinn, eds, *Art, Literature and Religion in Early Modern Sussex* (2014; Abingdon: Routledge, 2016), 61–94. The plants are part of a heraldic scheme yet reach towards naturalism. Coke, 70, suggests they may be based on illustrations in early herbals. Since the dissolution of the monastery, this decorated 'choir' has been the nave of the parish church.

14 Camden trans. Holland, *Britannia*, 310.

15 John M. Adrian, *Local Negotiations of English Nationhood, 1570–1680* (Basingstoke: Palgrave, 2011), 1–2.

16 This was the period of 'The Discovery of England' as described by Paul Slack in *The Invention of Improvement: Information and Material Progress in Seventeenth-Century England* (Oxford: OUP, 2014). Stan A. E. Mendyk shows that though much regional antiquarian and chorographic work was underway, little was published and available in the early 1600s: *Speculum Britanniae: Regional Study, Antiquarianism, and Science in Britain to 1700* (Toronto: UTP, 1989), 82ff.

17 *High Stream*, 14–15.

18 William Vallens, *A Tale of Two Swannes* (London: John Sheldrake, 1590).

19 Samuel Daniel, 'Sonnet XLVIII', *Delia* (London: Simon Waterson, 1592), n.p.

20 Peter Marchant in 'The West-Country Worlds of Samuel Daniel, 1562?–1619', *Frome Society Year Book* 15 (2012), 5–16 comments on his 'renouncing all that belongs to the social mainstream in favour of what sits on the provincial margins'.

21 *High Stream*, 42.

22 Michael Drayton, *Poly-Olbion* (1612, 1622), song 17, poly-olbion.exeter.ac.uk/the-text/full-text/song-17/.

23 *High Stream*, 41.

24 Jerome Bertram describes the Stopham memorials as 'the most outstanding example anywhere of a single family's concern for its ancestry and interest in its monuments'. 'Embellishment and Restoration: the Barttelots and their Brasses at Stopham, Sussex', *Transactions of the Monumental Brass Society*, 19:4 (2012), 334–62.

25 Walter's career was focused on local life. He was briefly a Member of Parliament but does not seem to have been a keen or active politician (Alan Davidson, 'Walter Barttelot', *History of Parliament Online*). He devoted his time to administrative local roles: as a Justice of the Peace and as Commissioner for Sewers in Sussex, which meant responsibility for the maintenance of all the coast and harbours as well as the rivers and levels inland. Water was in the blood and in the daily work of these brothers.

26 Recent commissions included a stone memorial to Drayton when the poet of *Poly-Olbion* died in 1631; the client was Lady Anne Clifford.

27 Nancy Briggs, 'Samuel Harsnett', Monumental Brass Society, Portfolio of Brasses, mbs-brasses.co.uk/index-of-brasses/samuel-harsnett.

28 R. Grosvenor Bartlet, *Our Family Surname* (privately published, 1944), 20.

29 Bertram, 'Embellishment and Restoration', examines this work in detail.

30 Stopham Parish Register, WSRO, *Sussex Parish Registers*, Par 187/1/1/1, and Wisborough Green Parish Register, WSRO, Par 210/1/1/1, via Ancestry.com. With thanks to Alice Millard.

31 Henry Cleere and David Crossley, *The Iron Industry of the Weald* (1985; rev. edn Chesterfield: Merton Priory Press, 1995); the website of the Wealden Iron Research Group offers a wealth of resources.

32 On river trade and shipping see P. A. L. Vine, *The Arun Navigation* (2000; Stroud: Tempus, 2007).

33 Evidence of other water bailiffs in the period survives, e.g. the accounts of the bailiff at Sandwich (TNA, E 101/526) and the will of Maximilian Dancey, the water bailiff for Dover (TNA, PROB 11/187/518). Bailiffs seem to have been appointed by the Crown or a Crown representative. The role of Tudor and Stuart bailiffs on the Thames was discussed in Parliament in 1884: 'Report from the Select Committee on Thames River Preservation', *UK Parliamentary Papers*, House of Commons, vol. 16 (London: HM Stationery Office, 1884), 316–22.

34 *High Stream*, 59.

35 Arthur MacGregor gives a map and illustrates a range of pictorial swan-rolls in 'Swan Rolls and Beak Markings: Husbandry, Exploitation and Regulation of *Cygnus olor* in England, c. 1100–1900', *Anthropozoologica* 22 (1996), 39–68.

36 The 1584 'Order for Swannes' was revised by the 1632 *Orders Lawes and Ancient Customes of Swanns* issued by the Royal Swan Master. See Norman Ticehurst, *The Mute Swan in England* (London: Cleaver-Hume, 1957), and MacGregor, 'Swan Rolls'.

37 *High Stream*, 57.

38 Stopham in *Protestation Returns*, 169.

39 Thomas Howard, 'Remembrances in England, for my good friend Mr John Evelinge', 1646, in Thomas Arundel, *Arundel's Remembrances of Things Worth Seeing in Italy*, ed. John Martin Robinson (London: Roxburghe Club, 1987).

40 Anthony Fletcher, *A County Community in Peace and War: Sussex 1600–1660* (London: Longman, 1975), 267: 'this was still a neutralist, even an incipiently royalist, countryside'.

41 Ibid., 268; Rosemary Hagedorn, *Arundel at War, 1642–44* (privately published, 2018), 90–118. *A Full Relation of the late Proceedings . . . at the taking of the Town and Castle of Arundel, In Sussex* (London: John Field, 1644). The young Parliamentary colonel William Springett died of an illness that was probably typhus.

42 Treasurer: see '4. Quarter Sessions'.

43 MacGregor, 'Swan Rolls', 46 n27, citing Calendar of State Papers (Domestic), 13 May 1651.

44 MacGregor, 'Swan Rolls', 46.

45 Deeds cited by George Arthur Clarkson, 'Notes on Amberley', *SAC* 17 (1865), 185–239, 218.

46 Will of William Barttelot, 30 January 1667, WSRO, STC1/23/346. Some land was to pass from the friends to WB's son Robert. His house 'the mansion house in Stopham' is named as Harme. Thanks to Alice Millard.

47 Inventory of William Barttelot, WSRO, EP I/29/187/019, and transcribed by Brian and Daphne Norton, WSRO, MP8087.

48 Arundel Castle Archive, MD 178 in Steer catalogue, vol. 2.

3. A Teacher's Books

1 Virginia Woolf, 'The Art of Biography' (1939) in *The Essays of Virginia Woolf*, vol. 6, ed. Stuart N. Clarke (London: Hogarth Press, 2011), 181–9, 186.

4. Quarter Sessions

1 *Quarter Sessions Order Book, 1642–1649*, ed. B. C. Redwood, SRS 54 (1954).

2 Redwood, introduction to *Quarter Sessions*, xxiv–xxx.

3 E.g. Arundel, Epiphany 1650, *Quarter Sessions*, 195.

4 Petworth, Michaelmas 1647 and Michaelmas 1648, *Quarter Sessions*, 135, 158.

5 Chichester 3–4 October 1642 and Arundel 14–15 April 1645, *Quarter Sessions*, 21, 71.

6 Edward Apsley, quoted Charles Thomas-Stanford, *Sussex in the Great Civil War and the Interregnum, 1642–60* (London: Chiswick Press, 1910), 74. His source is W. H. Blaauw, who transcribed the narrative from manuscript in 'Passages of the Civil War in Sussex', *SAC* 5 (1852), 29–103.

7 Cf. the judgement re Moultbridge on the Adur, taken down to prevent Royalists moving east. Petworth, Michaelmas 1647, *Quarter Sessions*, 133.

8 Petworth 6–7 April 1646, *Quarter Sessions*, 95.

9 Arundel 2–3 October 1643, *Quarter Sessions*, 40.

10 It is possible that Henry and Mary were the Henry Ouden and Mary Rose who married at Amberley (near South Stoke) in 1623. Mary is not listed in the South Stoke parish register of burials. The 'deceased kinsman' she was living with may possibly have been Isaac Hosyer, 'an old man' buried 23 November 1642, or Edward Raxhall, buried 10 October 1642. WSRO, *Sussex Parish Registers*, Par 185/1/1/1, via Ancestry.com.

11 Lewes 5–6 October 1643, *Quarter Sessions*, 41.

12 Akihito Suzuki observes that this commitment from a kinsman rather than immediate relative was rare according to the evidence of Quarter Sessions papers: 'Lunacy in Seventeenth- and Eighteenth-Century England: Analysis of Quarter Sessions records', *History of Psychiatry*, 2 (1991), 437–56.

13 South Stoke in *West Sussex Protestation Returns*, ed. R. Garraway Rice, SRS 5 (1998), 168.

14 Barttelot appointed at Chichester 2–3 April 1649, *Quarter Sessions*, 170. Richard Mill of Hardham was Treasurer for Maimed Soldiers.

15 Chichester 2–3 April 1649, *Quarter Sessions*, 171.

16 Lewes 15–16 July 1645, *Quarter Sessions*, 77. Most pensions for common soldiers were set at 40 shillings (£2) and raised to £3 from 1648. Larger payments went to those who had lost substantial property in the wars or had been prominent in the Republican army.

17 Details are available on the Civil War Petitions database: civilwarpetitions.ac.uk.

18 Petworth 6–7 April 1646, *Quarter Sessions*, 94.

19 Petition of Anne Bettesworth, April 1646, WSRO, Q/R/W 56, transcribed and discussed Helen Worthen, 'The Experience of War Widows', PhD thesis, University of Leicester, 2017, 170.

20 Arundel 6–7 October 1645 and Horsham 8–9 January 1646, *Quarter Sessions*, 83, 89.

21 Petworth 1–2 October 1649, *Quarter Sessions*, 184.

5. Sic Vita

1 T. S. Eliot, 'Dry Salvages' (1941), *Four Quartets*, in *The Complete Poems and Plays* (London: Faber & Faber, 1969), 190.

2 South Stoke in *West Sussex Protestation Returns*, ed. R. Garraway Rice, SRS 5 (1998), 168.

3 Richard Gough, *The History of Myddle*, ed. David Hey (London: Penguin, 1981). Hey's introduction is a fascinating study of Gough's life and writing. Gough's portrait of the inhabitants of Myddle included scandalous stories and many unflattering descriptions. It wasn't published in his lifetime.

4 Arundel Deanery Easter Bills 1664: South Stoke, in *Churchwardens' Presentments Part 1: Archdeaconry of Chichester*, ed. Hilda Johnstone, SRS 49 (1948), 128.

5 *VCH*: A. P. Baggs and H. M. Warne, 'South Stoke', in *A History of the County of Sussex: Volume 5 Part 1, Arundel Rape: South-Western Part*, ed. T. P. Hudson (London: VCH, 1997), 204–14, british-history.ac.uk/vch/sussex/vol5/pt1/pp204-214.

6 South Stoke Parish Register, WSRO, *Sussex Parish Registers*, Par 185/1/1/1, via Ancestry.com. *Church and People in Interregnum Britain*, ed. Fiona McCall (London: UCL Press, 2021) offers recent approaches to the complex history of the clergy at this time.

6. A Churchman's Books

1 '"Thomas Carr v William Sandham" 15 November 1638' in Chichester Diocese Deposition Book, WSRO, Ep/I/11/16, folio 146. His baptism is registered as April 1610, Bignor Parish Register, WSRO, MF 311.

2 Ellinor was Thomas' second wife, and John Sefton's stepmother.

3 Will of Thomas Sephton, made 23 February 1631, WSRO, STC/I/18/185, quoted in Annabelle Hughes, *Sussex Clergy Inventories 1600–1750*, SRS 91 (2007), 26, and A. N. Wilson, *A History of Collyer's School* (London: Edward Arnold, 1965), 60.

4 Inventory of Thomas Sephton, 3 March 1632, WSRO, Ep I/29/2027, in Hughes, *Sussex Clergy Inventories*, 23–5.

5 Licensed to teach from 14 January 1602: WSRO, STC III/EC12v.

6 Mercers' Acts, June/July 1644, quoted Wilson, *Collyer's*, 62–3.

7 John Walker, *An Attempt to Recover the Numbers and Sufferings of the Loyal Clergy* (London: Robert Knaplock, 1714), 372. Helen M. Whittle has found that 131 out of 325 Sussex parishes studied had a forced change of incumbent between 1642 and 1651. 'The Clergy of Sussex' in Fiona McCall, *Church and People in Interregnum Britain* (London: UCL, 2021), 111–34.

8 Joshua Thornton to John Walker, 18 October 1712, John Walker papers, Bodleian, and reprinted Frederick Ernest Sawyer, 'Proceedings of the Committee for Murdered Ministers Related to Sussex', *SAC* 31 (1881), 165–200 (180).

9 Hilaire Belloc, 'Lift up your hearts . . .' (1923), *Complete Verse* (London: Duckworth, 1970), 13.

10 King to Edward Bysshe, 22 January 1657, quoted 'Bishop Henry King's Library at Chichester Cathedral' in Matthew Dimmock, Andrew Hadfield and Paul Quinn, eds, *Art, Literature and Religion in Early Modern Sussex* (2014; Abingdon: Routledge, 2016), 124.

11 Mary Hobbs, 'The Cathedral Library' in Hobbs, ed., *Chichester Cathedral: An Historical Survey* (Chichester: Phillimore, 1994), 174.

12 Mary Hobbs, 'Henry King', *ODNB*.

13 Walker, *Sufferings*, 372.

14 Ibid.

15 Ibid.

16 The 'silencing' of ministers and the struggle for uniformity after 1662 are discussed in see N. H. Keeble, ed., *'Settling the Peace of the Church': 1662 Revisited* (Oxford: OUP, 2014).

17 By the time of his death in 1684 he had 'bookes 400 in number greate and small', which he left to his son. Hughes, *Sussex Clergy Inventories*, 111.

18 Edmund Calamy, *Account of the Ministers . . . Ejected or Silenc'd* (2nd edn, London: J. Lawrence, 1713), vol. 2, 694.

19 On the intellectual networks in and around Chichester cathedral, which Sefton
    clearly appreciated and contributed to, see Andrew Foster, 'Intellectual Networks
    Associated with Chichester Cathedral, c. 1558–1700', in *Early Modern Sussex*,
    95–113.

20 Will of John Sefton, 15 July 1678, TNA, PROB 11/361/335.

21 Will of Joseph Sefton, 23 January 1681, ESRO, SAS-RF/10/38 (held with papers
    relating to the prebend of Heathfield – an office Joseph had inherited from his
    brother). Yew tree: parish record cited in account of Sutton yew trees in the
    possession of Samantha Haydon.

22 With great thanks to John Barnard for his help in reading and interpreting the book
    list. This example illuminates a pattern of bequests that was common among clergy
    of Sefton's generation, many of whom gave books to help form libraries.

23 South Stoke parish register. Several of the Royalist annotations are initialled T.C.,
    perhaps Thomas Carter, rector in the 1760s. WSRO, *Sussex Parish Registers*, Par
    185/1/1/1, via Ancestry.com.

24 Thanks to Matthew Leigh for the Latin. The image of students as infants suckled by
    their college or university was conventional in the period, prompting jokes as well
    as strong association with nurture.

25 Thomas Reeve, quoted Fiona McCall, *Baal's Priests: The Loyalist Clergy and the
    English Revolution* (Farnham: Ashgate, 2013), 262. McCall considers very fully
    and vividly the experiences and writings of clergy expelled like Sefton, and the
    emphasis on memorialisation.

26 Calamy, *Account of the Ministers*, 694. Will proved Canterbury 11 August 1687,
    where he is 'of Dublin'. His connections to the Arun were still strong: he willed
    land at Warningcamp to his daughter in Arundel. Helen M. Whittle, *Sussex Clergy
    Wills*, SRS, 103 (2023), 310.

27 Hobbs, *Chichester Cathedral*, 178–9.

28 Francis Steer, *Chichester Cathedral Library*, Chichester Papers 44 (Chichester City
    Council, 1964), 10.

7. Cider in Storrington

1   The inventory taken after Richard's death in 1685 recorded four stools and thirteen
    chairs in the parlour; TNA, C 9/83/93, and see Charles R. Haines, *A Complete
    Memoir of Richard Haines* (London: Harrison & Sons, 1899), 88. Interior details
    from Melanie Backe-Hansen, 'A Poet, an Archbishop, and a Prime Minister's Wife',
    Country Life, 3 August 2011.

2   Joan Ham, *Sullington: Domesday to D-Day* (privately published, 1992), 265.
    Though the farm was just as close to Storrington, it was counted within Sullington
    for taxes and parochial duties.

3   By the terms of his marriage he no longer owned the property, but Richard, Mary

and their heirs had use of it. Ham, *Sullington*, 268. Mary, *née* Green, was also from Sullington.

4 Sullington Parish Register, WSRO, Par . Par 190/1/1/1 and Wisborough Green Parish Register, WSRO, MF 362.

5 Richard Haines, *The Prevention of Poverty* (London: Nathaniel Brooke, 1674), 8–10. On the period's culture of 'improvement', involving a multitude of published tracts and schemes, see Paul Slack, *The Invention of Improvement: Information and Material Progress in Seventeenth-Century England* (Oxford: OUP, 2014). Slack identifies Haines as one of the 'two most prolific writers of improvement tracts' (161).

6 Richard Haines, *New Lords, New Laws, or A Discovery of a Grand Usurpation* (printed for the author, 1674), 1–2. For the agricultural context in Sussex see Brian Short in Joan Thirsk, ed., *The Agrarian History of England and Wales, Vol. 5:1 Regional Farming Systems 1640–1750* (Cambridge: CUP, 1984), 273–4. Short, 298, points out that the techniques may not have been entirely unknown: John Aubrey mentioned the farmers of Worplesden as having 'an art here, not commonly known, of cleansing the seed of sanfoine and clover'.

7 Sullington Parish Register, WSRO, *Sussex Parish Registers*, Par 190/1/1/1, via Ancestry.com.

8 Jim Spivey, 'Matthew Caffyn', *ODNB*.

9 Haines, *New Lords*; Charles Haines, *Memoir*, 40–50.

10 Haines, *New Lords*: idol, 32; Machiavelli, 21; gangrene, n.p. ['The Author to the Reader'].

11 Haines, *New Lords*, 50–2.

12 Haines, *New Lords*, n.p. ['A Word to the Ingenious and Learned Perusers'].

13 Haines, *Prevention of Poverty*; Haines, *Proposals for building, in every county, a working-almshouse or hospital as the best expedient to perfect the trade and manufactory of linnen-cloth* (London: R. Harford, 1677).

14 Slack, in his *ODNB* article, says that Haines' proposals for working almshouses influenced later projects for reform of the Poor Laws.

15 Haines, *Proposals for building*, 16, 9.

16 Ibid., 3.

17 Haines' new scheme may have struck close to the bone in the enemy territory of the Caffyn household. With Matthew so often fined and imprisoned, with no secure form of income, with nine children to provide for, Elizabeth Caffyn worked at spinning to make what money she could (Spivey, 'Caffyn', *ODNB*).

18 His business partner was Richard Dereham, who had a high profile as City Remembrancer in London.

19 Patent registered 1678: *Subject-Matter Index of Patents of Invention*, ed. Bennet Woodcroft (London: Eyre and Spottiswoode, 1854), Part 2, 715. Eric Kerridge, *Textile Manufactures in Early Modern England* (Manchester: MUP, 1985), 169.

Haines, *England's Weal and Prosperity Proposed* (London: Langley Curtis, 1681), advises that all pauper children be employed from the age of six.

20 Charles Haines, *Memoir*, 71.

21 Haines, *Aphorisms Upon the New Way of Improving Cyder* . . . (printed for the author, 1684), 13.

22 Haines, *Aphorisms*, 12, 13, 5. Haines was right to see an opening for new spirits. John Chartres traces the rapid growth of the spirit market after 1685 in 'No English Calvados?: English Distillers and the Cider Industry in the Seventeenth and Eighteenth Centuries', in *English Rural Society 1500–1800: Essays in Honour of Joan Thirsk*, ed. John Chartres and David Hey (Cambridge: CUP, 1990), 313–42. Most of the spirits being consumed by the 1720s were of domestic production; even 'English brandy like French' was produced for a time, though 'Geneva' was the more popular option. Yet distilled cider never became a drink of choice for reasons (including variable harvest, distance of orchards from urban centres, and undesirable taste) that Chartres examines in detail.

23 Haines, *Aphorisms*, 9. The agreement with Goring is WSRO, Wiston 5951.

24 By the 1870s the five main cider counties would have eighty-thousand acres of apples. Chartres, *English Rural Society*, 341.

25 Haines, *Aphorisms*, 7.

26 Ibid., 12.

27 Ibid., 15.

28 Sarah Hand Meacham, *Every Home a Distillery* (Baltimore: Johns Hopkins UP, 2009), 31: 'men had assumed control of cidering in England'.

29 John Phillips, *Cyder* (London: J. Tonson, 1708), 2.

30 Ibid. On the uses of Georgic as a literary genre in this period see Paddy Bullard, ed., *A History of English Georgic Writing* (Cambridge: CUP, 2022).

31 Phillips, *Cyder*, 79–80.

32 Advertisement in *London Gazette*, 18 December 1684, 2.

33 The inventory is filed with papers for the case Weston v Haines. TNA, C 9/83/93. It was found by C. E. Gildersome-Dickinson and repr. Charles Haines, *Memoir*, 88–91.

34 The glass-seller was Charles Weston, who brought his lawsuit in 1686. Haines was 'indebted by the sum of seventy pounds for bottles and corks sold and delivered to him some short time before his death'. TNA, C 9/83/93.

35 National Planning Policy Framework, Appendix 2, 'Setting of a heritage asset'. The definition is consistent in the 2012 and revised 2018 versions of the NPPF.

36 Alan Woolnough on behalf of the Department for Communities and Local Government, Appeal Decision: APP/Z3825/A/13/2202943, Wates Development v Horsham District Council.

37 Ibid., paragraphs 32–3.

38 Ibid., paragraphs 57–65. Further significant considerations were the sustainability of the development and the effect on air quality.

39 Ibid., paragraph 34 citing Section 66 (1) of the Planning (Listed Buildings and Conservation Areas) Act 1990 as amended (the Listed Buildings Act); and paragraph 41, citing National Planning Policy Framework (2012 version), paragraphs 133–4.

40 Ibid., paragraph 51.

41 Ibid., paragraphs 47, 51, 53.

42 Ibid. paragraphs 48–50.

43 Ibid., paragraph 49.

44 Ibid., paragraphs 68, 96.

8. The London Model

1 He is first referred to as Lisbon in a will of 1721. Few details are known about his career as a merchant, though wine played at least some part in it. I am much indebted in this chapter to the research of Sibylla Jane Flower and David Coke published in *Pallant House: Its Architecture, History and Owners* (Chichester: Pallant House Gallery Trust, 1993).

2 'Sir Henry Peckham (1614–1673)', *History of Parliament Online*; entries in Redwood, ed., *Quarter Sessions*; Fletcher, *County Community*, 220.

3 Peckham v Peckham, TNA, C 11/2334/11, and discussed *Pallant House*, 30.

4 South Mundham House, described by Ian Nairn as 'an almost perfect marriage of simplicity and ornament'. Pevsner, 521 and illustrated pl. 52.

5 Flower in *Pallant House*, 26, quoting the Chichester solicitor for whom Peckham was working, Peckham v. Tawke, TNA, C 11/293/5.

6 Alan J. H. Green, *The Building of Georgian Chichester, 1690–1830* (Chichester: Phillimore, 2007), 79ff; Roy Morgan surveys the surviving evidence for buildings and their occupiers street by street in *Chichester: A Documentary History* (Chichester: Phillimore, 1992).

7 Green, 93; Morgan, 147, cites the Hearth Tax evidence for there being some prosperous houses in North Pallant as well as industry.

8 Ibid., 6, and *Pallant House*, 8.

9 The relationship between vernacular and classical building is set in a national context and among other transformations of town life in Peter Borsay, *The English Urban Renaissance* (New York: OUP, 1989), 50–9. The new houses of professionals, including Peckham, are discussed 206–10.

10 Deposition of Henry Smart, Peckham v Peckham, TNA, C 11/2334/11.

11 Deposition of John Pryor, Peckham v Peckham, ibid.

12 Deposition of John Channell, Peckham v Peckham, ibid.

13 Deposition of John Channell, ibid.

14 Deposition of John Channell, ibid.

15 Deposition of Henry Smart, ibid.

16 Green, *Georgian Chichester*, 93; *Pallant House*, 60, citing Chichester City Minute Book for 2 March 1714.

17 James Spershott, 'Spershott's Memoirs of Chichester' (1783), *SAC* 29 (1879), 219–31.

18 Flower in *Pallant House*, 30.

19 Deposition of Richard Clayton, Peckham v Peckham, TNA, C 11/2334/11.

20 Flower in *Pallant House*, 36.

21 Deposition of Henry Smart, Peckham v Peckham, TNA, C 11/2334/11.

22 Will of Elizabeth Peckham, wife of Chichester, TNA, PROB 11/774/463; Flower in *Pallant House*, 37.

23 Flower in *Pallant House*, 47. The Customer was responsible for collection of dues on goods shipped or landed within the 'lesser area' of Chichester harbour, which was nevertheless extensive, stretching from Emsworth to Felpham. *VCH*: 'The City of Chichester: The Port', in *A History of the County of Sussex: Volume 3*, ed. L. F. Salzman (London: VCH, 1935), 100–2, british-history.ac.uk/vch/sussex/vol3/pp100–2.

24 Flower in *Pallant House*, 45–7 on his work as a Tory election campaign manager.

25 Róbert Péter, ed., *British Freemasonry 1717–1813* (Abingdon: Routledge, 2016), 5 vols, vol. 5, clxxvii.

26 T. P. Connor, 'Architecture and Planting at Goodwood, 1723–50', *SAC* 117 (1979), 185–93, 186.

27 Colen Campbell, *Vitruvius Britannicus* (printed for the author, 1725), 6; Carole Fry's PhD thesis, 'The Dissemination of Neo-palladian Architecture in England, 1701–58', University of Bristol, 2006, includes an appendix listing all subscribers. Coke in *Pallant House* contrasts the Tory associations of English baroque with Whiggish Palladianism.

28 Some of Smart's time was spent in satisfying the more frivolous whims of the nobility; see Emily Lorraine De Montluzin, 'Quicksilver Ladies, Odes to Turds, and Three-Seater Privies: The Scatological Underside of the *Gentleman's Magazine*', *ANQ* 21:1 (2008), 24–34.

29 *Sussex Apprentices and Masters*, ed. R. Garraway Rice, SRS 28 (1924), 115, indenture dated 13 October 1741.

30 Timothy McCann, '"Much Troubled with Very Rude Company": The 2nd Duke of Richmond's Menagerie at Goodwood', *SAC* 132 (1994), 143–50, 145.

9. Easter Chalk

1 Andy Goldsworthy, *Chalk Stones*, 2002, commissioned by South Downs Strange Partners partnership.

2 On chalk deposition: David Robinson, *The Geology and Scenery of the South Downs National Park* (Lewes: Sussex Archaeological Society, 2013), 23–9.

3 Andy Goldsworthy quoted Andrew Graham-Dixon, 'Chalk Stones Trail by Andy Goldsworthy', *Sunday Telegraph*, 18 August 2002.

10. Native Strains

1 Richard Shenton to Thomas Warton, 16 January 1783, in *The Correspondence of Thomas Warton*, ed. David Fairer (Athens: University of Georgia Press, 1995), 474. He told the story as an indication of Collins' attachment to the Bible. Shenton was rector of nearby Racton from 1755 and one of the Vicars Choral.

2 Genesis 27: 27–8, KJV.

3 Collins, 'Ode to Simplicity', and 'Verses on a Paper', in *Odes on Several Descriptive and Allegoric Subjects* (London: A. Miller, 1747), in *Gray and Collins: Poetical Works*, ed. Roger Lonsdale (Oxford: OUP, 1977), 142, 134.

4 Collins, 'Ode to Evening', in *Gray and Collins*, 156–7. By contrast, the evening of Gray's *Elegy in a Country Churchyard* (1751) falls on the turf mounds located precisely beneath 'those rugged elms, that yew-tree's shade'; we watch in stillness as it falls in this one place that stands for many places.

5 Roy Morgan, *Chichester: A Documentary History* (Chichester: Phillimore, 2007), 91; John Wyatt in 'William Collins of Chichester' in Paul Foster, ed., *William Collins, Poet* (Chichester: University of Chichester, 2009), 14–30, 24, where he also helpfully considers the evidence for identifying Collins' school and last home.

6 Will of Roger Collins printed in P. L. Carver, *The Life of a Poet* (London: Sidgwick & Jackson, 1967), 191. Roger Collins was rector of St Olave's, and lived for a period in the Vicars' Close.

7 John Ragsdale to William Hymers, 1783, repr. Foster, ed., *Collins*, 177–80. Ragsdale was a close friend of Collins'. Mary Margaret Stewart, 'Further Notes on William Collins', *Studies in English Literature*, 10:3 (1970), 569–78, argues that Ragsdale (a London goldsmith) would have had good information about Collins' family.

8 Both parents had lived in the area all their lives. Alderman Collins was the son of a Chichester clergyman; Elizabeth had grown up on a farm near the coast at West Wittering.

9 Carver in *Life of a Poet*, 11, thinks it most likely he was taught by a local curate.

10 Lonsdale, chronology, in *Gray and Collins*, 111–13; will of William Collins, alderman, 19 September 1733, printed Carver, *Life of a Poet*, 195.

11 Stewart, 'Further Notes on William Collins', cites entries and receipts in Caryll family account books.

12 WSRO, Harris Mss 681, 683–4.

13 Collins, *Persian Eclogues* in *Gray and Collins*. Collins was reading Thomas Salmon's account of Persia in his *Modern History, or The Present State of all Nations* (1739).

14 Collins, 'Preface' to *Persian Eclogues*, in Lonsdale, ed., *Gray and Collins*, 116.

15 Oliver Goldsmith, *Beauties of English Poesy* (London: William Griffin, 1767), 2 vols, vol. 1, 239.

16 Richard Eversole looks at the 'Oriental fables' Collins may have known. 'Collins and the End of Shepherd Pastoral', in F. F. Hardin, ed., *Survivals of Pastoral* (Lawrence: University Press of Kansas, 1979), 19–32.

17 *A Literary Review* 1:1 (autumn 1744), 226, carried an advertisement for 'A Review of the Advancement of Learning, from 1300 to 1521. by Wm Collins. 4to.'.

18 Gilbert White, 'Memoirs of the Life of Mr William Collins the Poet' (*Gentlemen's Magazine*, 1781), repr. Foster, ed., *Collins*, 172–3.

19 White, ibid., and John Ragsdale to William Hymers, 1783, repr. Foster, ed., *Collins*, 177–80. Johnson found him knowledgeable and cheerful.

20 John Mulso to Gilbert White, 7 September 1745, in Rashleigh Holt-White, ed., *The Life and Letters of Gilbert White* (London: John Murray, 1901), 2 vols, vol. 1, 41. Carver, *Life of a Poet*, 35–40, details embryonic plans for his becoming a Sussex curate, and meetings with his uncle about an army post.

21 Reported in Alexander Hay, *History of Chichester* (Chichester: Joseph Seagrave, 1804), 527.

22 H. O. White, 'The Letters of William Collins', *Review of English Studies* 3:9 (1927), 12–21.

23 Samuel Johnson, 'Collins' (1763), repr. in *The Major Works*, ed. Donald Greene (Oxford: OUP, 1984, 2000), 759–61.

24 Collins, 'Ode to Evening', *Gray and Collins*, 156.

25 Marilyn Butler in *Mapping Mythologies* (finished 1984; published posthumously Cambridge: CUP, 2015) sets out the connections between 'Country party' oppositional politics and the interest in British native culture that she sees as very strong in Thomson, Collins and Gray. To emphasise British locales, antiquities, native poetic inheritance literary and oral was to counter the centralised metropolitan culture of the London Whig elite. Intriguingly, though, she does not enquire into Collins' relations with his *own* native region, or draw attention to these Arun allusions.

26 Collins, 'Ode to Pity', *Gray and Collins*, 138. Otway's plays of the 1680s (especially *The Orphan* and *Venice Preserv'd*) were popular in the 1740s.

27 Humphrey Otway was displaced as parish priest under Cromwell and took the family up to Yorkshire. He was younger than John Sefton of South Stoke, but the exiles of these clergymen ran in parallel.

28 1 May 1747, WSRO, Add. MS. 5999.

29 Collins to John Cooper, November 1747, in White, 'Letters', 12–21.

30 In Collins' 'Ode Occasioned by the Death of Mr Thomson' (Lonsdale, ed., *Gray and Collins*, 164–6) the Scottish Thomson is presented as a Druidic bard, born out of and returning to British nature, his 'airy harp' laid to rest in the whispering reeds of the Thames.

31 Edward Gay Ainsworth, *Poor Collins: His Life, His Art, His Influence* (Ithaca: Cornell UP, 1937), 20; Carver, *Life of a Poet*, 151.

32 Collins, ['An Ode on the Popular Superstitions of the Highlands of Scotland, Considered as the Subject of Poetry'], *Gray and Collins*, 168. Collins showed the manuscript to the Wartons in Chichester c.1754. It wasn't finished until long after Home's departure, and Home may never have seen it.

33 Butler, *Mapping Mythologies*, 68, calls it Collins' nearest approach to a manifesto for 'writing that is local, natural, native, popular'.

34 Collins, 'Superstitions', 170–1. Collins read *A Description of the Western Isles* by the Hebridean author Màrtainn MacGilleMhàrtainn (anglicised as Martin Martin).

35 Ibid.

36 Collins, ['No longer ask me Gentle Friends'], in *Gray and Collins*, 188–90.

37 The rise of regional and often remote places as adequate subjects for poetry is Fiona Stafford's subject in *Local Attachments*.

38 Collins to William Hayes, 8 November 1750. The music was revived in 2003 by Anthony Rooley. Collins' love of music was well attested. His uncle Charles Collins left him a large collection of scores and asked him to 'keep it for the love the Family have born to the Faculty [of music]'. Will of Charles Collins, proved 5 March 1746, printed in Carver, *Life of a Poet*, 192–4.

39 Thomas Warton to William Hymers, December 1782, *Correspondence*, 469; White in Foster, ed., *Collins*, 173, 174. White said he was 'struggling, and conveyed by force' to a madhouse.

40 Thomas Warton to William Hymers, December 1782, *Correspondence*, 469.

41 Collins, ['No longer ask me Gentle Friends'], in *Gray and Collins*, 190.

42 Thomas Warton told Thomas Percy about Collins' 'valuable collection of most curious books': 4 September 1762, *Correspondence*, 125. Warton made a series of notes about rare literary texts, apparently arising from discussion with Collins in Chichester; these are printed in William Collins, *Drafts and Fragments of Verse*, ed. J. S. Cunningham (Oxford: Clarendon, 1956), 46–8.

43 Thomas Warton to William Hymers, January 1783, *Correspondence*, 476; Fairer suggests that it was Joseph Warton to whom Collins showed the work.

44 Samuel Johnson to Joseph Warton, 24 December 1754, *Letters of Samuel Johnson*, ed. Bruce Redford (Princeton: PUP, 1992), 4 vols, vol. 1, 91.

45 Samuel Johnson to Joseph Warton, 15 April 1756, *Letters*, vol. 1, 134. 'It is dreadful', continued Johnson, thinking of Collins, 'to consider that the powers of the mind are equally liable to change, that understanding may make its appearance and depart, that it may blaze and expire.'

46 Alan J. H. Green, *The Building of Georgian Chichester*, 1690–1830 (Chichester: Phillimore, 2007), 126; Grimm drawing of Vicars' Close or 'College', 1782.

47 Thomas Park, note in his copy of Collins' poems, quoted John Mitford in his

'Additional Notes' to *The Poems of William Collins* (London: Pickering, 1827), 40.

48 *The Poetical Works of Mr William Collins*, ed. John Langhorne (London: T. Becket & P. A. de Hondt, 1765).

49 Johnson, 'Collins', *Lives*, repr. in *Major Works*, 759–61.

50 John Scott of Amwell, 'Stanzas written at Medhurst [sic], in Sussex, on the Author's return from Chichester, where he had attempted in vain to find the Burial-place of Collins', in *Poetical Works* (London: J. Buckland, 1782), 323. His Persian sequence is 'Zerad, or the Absent Lover', ibid., 127–36.

51 A setting by Benjamin Cooke was deemed too complicated for the city cellists and chorus, and Marsh's new version was played instead. Marsh, *Journals*, 463–5.

52 S. T. Coleridge to John Thelwall, 17 December 1796, in *The Major Works*, ed. H. J. Jackson (Oxford: OUP, 1985, 2000), 491.

53 William Hazlitt, 'On Swift, Young, Gray, Collins', in *Lectures on the English Poets* (London: Taylor & Hessey, 1818), 230.

11. Light Footsteps

1 Anne Francis, 'Lines, occasioned by reading Collins' Poems', in *Miscellaneous Poems* (printed for the author, 1790), 21–9. She used both Ann and Anne in her publications.

2 Ibid.

3 Ann was baptised 7 April 1738: South Stoke Parish Register, WSRO, *Sussex Parish Registers*, Par 185/1/1/1, via Ancestry.com. Gittins had been rector since 1733 and remained until his death in 1761.

4 Remembered by Ann in 'A Vision, occasioned by my visiting Cambridge, November 1787', *Miscellaneous Poems*, 30–7.

5 Subscriber list, repr. in John Farrant, *Sussex Depicted: Views and Descriptions 1600–1800*, SRS 85 (2001), 82–7.

6 Published subsequently as Daniel Gittens, *A Sermon Preached on April 11, 1744* (London: J. Bettenham, 1744).

7 Preached 18 December 1745 and published as *A Short view of some of the Principles and Practices of the Church of Rome, being the substance of a Sermon preached on occasion of the late General Fast* (London: M. Cooper, 1746). Gittens was also vicar of Lyminster, in the plain south of Arundel. On the High Church context in Sussex, Jeffrey Scott Chamberlain, *Accommodating High Churchmen: The Clergy of Sussex 1700–1745* (Champaign: University of Illinois Press, 1997).

8 E.g. WSRO, Add. MS. 14726–59.

9 Ann Francis, *A poetical translation of the Song of Solomon, from the original Hebrew, with a preliminary discourse, and notes, historical, critical, and explanatory* (London: J. Dodsley, 1781), xviii.

10 Ibid., 32–3.

11 Ibid., 33.

12 After her death, the *Gentleman's Magazine* obituarist (vol. 70 (1800), 1290) described her style of conversation ('she evinced great energies of mind and pointed wit') as well as her virtues as 'an excellent woman and a sincere Christian'.

13 In the 1790s she chose to publish in newspapers, seeking for her most expressly political poems an audience that went beyond intellectual networks and literary subscribers.

14 The poem veers off extraordinarily at the end: the last section is about Hayley's glories as a poet and about his relationship with his mother, who 'stopp'd her fair career, where Hayley's fame began'. Ann Francis was evidently thinking about the rival claims of poetry and motherhood.

15 'Ode to Melancholy', *Miscellaneous Poems*, 76–81.

16 See e.g. 'A Plain Address to My Neighbours', *Norwich Mercury*, 15 August 1798.

17 Seamus Heaney, 'Belfast', in *Preoccupations: Selected Prose 1968–1978* (London: Faber, 1980), 37, discussed Fiona Stafford, *Local Attachments* (Oxford: OUP, 2010), 15 and passim.

18 'An Ode: Written January 1790', *Miscellaneous Poems*, 271–5.

19 Ibid.

12. Midsummer Flint

1 Paul Nash, 'The Nest of the Wild Stones', in Myfanwy Evans, ed., *The Painter's Object* (London: Gerald Howe, 1937), 38–42, 38.

2 David Smith runs Flintman Company. See flintman.co.uk for architectural work and fine art.

3 Henry Vaughan, *Silex Scintillans* (London: H. Blunden, 1650); John Donne, 'Holy Sonnet 10', in *Major Works*, ed. John Carey (Oxford: OUP, 1990), 177.

13. A Teacher's Places

1 James Leeming, personal correspondence.

14. Italian Light on North Street

1 Very little has been written on the Smiths. An excellent catalogue accompanied the 1986 show at Pallant House: Sibylla Flower et al., *The Smith Brothers of Chichester* (Chichester: Pallant House, 1986). Elizabeth Wheeler Manwaring gives them substantial attention in *Italian Landscape in Eighteenth-Century England* (1925; London: Frank Cass, 1965). The main biographical source is the anonymous 'account of the author's life' prefacing the 1811 edition of George Smith's *Pastorals*. This was probably by the Chichester doctor Thomas Sanden.

2 Flower in *Smiths of Chichester*, 15; W. H. Challen, 'Baldy's Garden, the Painters

Lambert and Other Sussex Families', *SAC* 90 (1952), 102–52 (143–4), gives details of three uncles in the coopering trade but no source for George training with them.

3   George Smith (the painter's grandfather) was Elder at the Eastgate chapel in the 1670s. See chichesterbaptist.org/tn3 and James Ivimey, *A History of the English Baptists* (printed for the author, 1811–30), 4 vols, vol. 2, 563.

4   Anon [Thomas Sanden?], in George Smith, *Pastorals; to which is added Pastorella* (London: Whittingham & Rowland, 1811), 1–16. William Smith senior's will was made in 1718 and proved 29 October 1724. Challen, 'Baldy's Garden' traces the maternal family, connecting the Smiths to the Lamberts of Lewes.

5   Sanden in *Pastorals*, 14.

6   Possibly John Vanderbank whose 'Academy for the Improvement of Painters and Sculptors by drawing from the Naked' opened in 1720.

7   John Guise Bt of Elmore and Rendcomb (1701–69).

8   Sanden in *Pastorals*, 4. He gave his town as Chichester when subscribing to Benjamin Martin's *Bibliotecha Technologica: or Philosophical Library of Literary Arts and Sciences* (London: John Noon, 1737). This book by the Chichester mathematics teacher and instrument-maker covered everything from the existence of God to the habits of pastoral poetry. Henry Peckham ordered a copy too, as did James Spershott the carpenter and Henry Smart the mason.

9   George's later introduction to *Six Pastorals* (London: J. Dodsley, 1770) indicates his reading over many years.

10   Thomas Smith used 'of Derby' at about the same time, probably to distinguish himself from the Smiths of Chichester.

11   Sanden, *Pastorals*, 8, mentions the camera obscura.

12   The picture is at Pallant House. See also *Cocking Mill Pond*.

13   Sold Christie's 16 October 1987 as *A Capriccio View of Chichester*, signed and dated 1750.

14   Horace Walpole, *Anecdotes of Painting in England* (1762), ed. James Dallaway (London: 1828), 5 vols, 279. He was at Stansted. The 'Account of the Author', in Smith, *Pastorals*, 9, refers to Walpole's notion that views over Chichester resemble Claude paintings. On Walpole's idea and other comparisons of the area to Italy see Peter Brandon, *The Discovery of Sussex* (Andover: Phillimore, 2010), 24–5.

15   David Solkin, in *Richard Wilson: The Landscape of Reaction* (London: Tate, 1982), 22–3, points to British collectors' growing interest in the 'common' landscape art of seventeenth-century Holland, and examines how the gentry's 'awareness of labour' influenced tastes in landscape.

16   *Cavern Scene with Firelight and Dancers*, large version 1750, Stourhead; small version 1753, Hunterian.

17   Several were listed for most of the years he exhibited. In 1773, just before he became ill and slowed down, he was still gripped by the idea of a winter inferno and showed 'a snow-piece, with a house on fire'.

18 A full list of Premium prizes and categories is in Robert Dossie, *Memoirs of Agriculture and other Oeconomical Arts* (London: J. Nourse, 1768–82), 3 vols, vol. 3, 433–4.

19 Brian Allen, 'The Society of Arts and the First Exhibition of Contemporary Art in 1760', *Royal Society of Arts Journal* 139 (1991), 265–9.

20 Dossie, *Memoirs*, 433–4.

21 On Thomas Smith as an early English landscape artist see Trevor Brighton, 'Thomas Smith of Derby, 1723–67, Painter of the Peak District', in *Bakewell and District Historical Society Journal* 38 (2011), 15–28.

22 The Smiths' house is long gone, though it's visible in early-twentieth-century photographs, which show the four sash windows of the main rooms on the first floor. M. J. Cutten noted (WSRO, MP402) that it had a date stone 1681.

23 As well as Sanden, the Smiths knew Dr John Bayly who had several Smith landscapes hanging in his house at 5 East Pallant. In 1781 a visiting friend admired there 'several original landskips painted by the fratelli Smith of this place' – Sylas Neville in *Restricted Grandeur: Impressions of Chichester 1586–1948*, ed. Timothy McCann (Chichester: West Sussex County Council, 1974), 26.

24 The oil painting is lost, known from Pether's mezzotint. William Shayer made an oil copy in 1811, now at WSRO.

25 The graves have been moved and their inscriptions eroded but they were recorded by Mark Antony Lower in *The Worthies of Sussex* (Lewes: George Bacon, 1865), 37.

26 Will of William Smith, TNA, PROB 11/903/163.

27 Deanery of Chichester marriage licence 12 September 1766. George is a 'limner of 52', Ruth a spinster of 34. George is listed as having lived in Chichester sixteen years, which places his return in 1750.

28 *A Collection of Fifty-three Prints Consisting of Etchings and Engravings by Those Ingenious Masters Messrs. George and John Smith of Chichester after Their Own Paintings and Other Masters* (London: John Boydell, 1770). Thirty-two plates were from their own compositions, nine after Rembrandt, twelve after other Dutch painters.

29 George Smith, 'Winter: Colin and Phebe', *Pastorals* (1770), 45.

30 George Smith, 'The Country Lovers', ibid., 8.

31 Manwaring, *Italian Landscape*, 73. Few people said anything explicitly about Smith's localism, but those with geographical attachments of their own thought about what he was doing. John Scott of Amwell wished that he had the ability of a painter to catch the spirit of his own place like 'HIM, / Whom now on LAVANT's banks, in groves that breathe / Enthusiasm sublime, the Sister Nymphs / Inspire'. John Scott, *Amwell: A Descriptive Poem* (1776). This was probably published too late for Smith to read the tribute.

32 He sent four pictures to the RA in 1774, perhaps looking for a change in his sixties.

33 Addresses given in catalogue for the Society for the Encouragement of Arts exhibition 1763 and Society of Arts exhibitions 1772–4.

34 Joshua Reynolds, 'Discourse III', in *Discourses*, ed. Pat Rogers (Harmondsworth: Penguin, 1992), 102–15.

35 Reynolds, *Discourses*, 105–6.

36 Reynolds, it seems, owned at least one Smith engraving, probably more. The French collector Huber bought 'The Cott' (aquaforte) in 1775 with a Reynolds provenance.

37 Will of George Smith, TNA, PROB 11/1024/107.

38 Austen: WSRO, Add. MS. 11402 and 11406. Chaldecot was a trustee of the Baffins Lane chapel in 1763: WSRO, NC/GB1/7/4. Austen, Chaldecot and Wooldridge were all part of the Baptist group – including George Smith – who leased property together in the 1760s (Dell Hole Field deeds, WSRO, NC/GB1/7/42).

39 Sanden, in *Pastorals*, 11.

40 1784 Poll Book, WSRO, Acc 1311/MP496, referenced in notes of M. J. Cutten, WSRO, MP40; subscriptions include the local poet Daniel Foote's *Poems on Various Occasions* (1777).

41 The sign refers to three Smith sisters all dying of smallpox in 1759. This is at odds with records of the grave inscriptions. Elizabeth died in 1757; Sarah was living when William wrote his will in 1763, and died in 1769.

15. Moose

1 Gilbert White to Thomas Pennant, March 1770, in *The Natural History of Selborne* (1789), ed. Richard Mabey (1977; London: Penguin, 1987), 74. He noted the weather but not the moose in his 'Naturalist's Journal': *The Journals of Gilbert White*, vol. 1, ed. Francesca Greenoak (London: Century Hutchinson, 1986), 259.

2 White, *Selborne*, 74.

3 Estate record quoted by Timothy McCann, 'Much Troubled with Very Rude Company': The 2nd Duke of Richmond's Menagerie at Goodwood', *SAC* 132 (1994), 143–50, 145; Caroline Grigson, *Menagerie: The History of Exotic Animals in England, 1100–1837* (Oxford: OUP, 2016), 66.

4 McCann pieced together evidence from the voluminous Goodwood archives: see 'Richmond's Menagerie', 145.

5 Grigson, *Menagerie*, 67.

6 Henry Foster to 2nd Duke of Richmond, 14 October 1730, McCann, 'Richmond's Menagerie', 146.

7 2nd Duke of Richmond to Peter Collinson, BL, Add. MS. 28726 quoted by T. P. Connor, 'Architecture and Planting at Goodwood, 1723–50', *SAC* 117 (1979), 185–93, 193n, and on planting see also Rosemary Baird, *Goodwood: Art and Architecture, Sport and Family* (London: Frances Lincoln, 2007), 68–9.

8 2nd Duke of Richmond to Peter Collinson, 1742, when the contents of the late Lord Petre's nursery were being sold, quoted by Connor, 'Architecture and Planting', 189.

9 Richard Pococke in 1754, cited by Connor, 'Architecture and Planting', 189.

10 Richmond to Collinson, 1747, quoted Baird, *Goodwood*, 218n.

11 'Very bleak', quoted Connor, 'Architecture and Planting', 190.

12 Baird, *Goodwood*, 57, 65. There was also a shell grotto in the Dell with water trickling into a pool, 'a kind of antique shower house'.

13 *Nature Revisited*, Goodwood House exhibition booklet, 2014, n.p. ; McCann, 'Richmond's Menagerie'.

14 The process of appointment is described by Paul David Nelson, *General Sir Guy Carleton, Lord Dorchester* (Vancouver: Fairleigh Dickinson UP, 2000), 31.

15 Ibid., 49.

16 Given the scraps of written evidence and the limited season for sailings from the St Lawrence, it's likely that they all arrived in summer 1766. Gilbert White was told that the 'poor creature' he inspected dead in the greenhouse had at first had 'a female companion of the same species, which died the spring before'. So that female must have survived ten months in England and died in spring 1767.

17 3rd Duke to Rockingham, 14 October 1770, remembering his female moose of '3 years ago', quoted Douglas Fordham, 'George Stubbs's *Zoon Politikon*', *Oxford Art Journal* 33:1 (2010), 1–23, 13.

18 William Hunter, notes for 'The Orignal from Quebec' (1770–3), printed in W. D. Rolfe, 'William Hunter on Irish "Elk" and Stubbs's *Moose*', *Archives of Natural History* 11:2 (1983), 263–90, 265.

19 Lost eye: 3rd Duke to Rockingham, quoted Fordham, 'Stubbs'.

20 Hunter, 'Orignal', 265–6.

21 Carleton had brought a pair over as an example and Stubbs was able to copy them.

22 Rolfe suggests that Carleton gave Stubbs hints for the scenery; Lisa Vargo observes that what he painted is very unlike the Canadian moose habitat and argues that 'the romanticized landscape prospect offers a metaphor for the story of the moose in eighteenth-century Britain'. 'The Romantic Prospects of the Duke of Richmond's Moose', *European Romantic Review* 24 (2013), 297–305.

23 3rd Duke to Rockingham, quoted Fordham, 'Stubbs'.

24 Hunter, 'Quebec Orignal', 276: 'we must conclude that they were the Horns of a *much* larger Animal'.

25 The story is summarised by Kevin Jackson in *Moose* (London: Reaktion, 2008), 99–105, 113–17. Hunter's draft paper on the subject was published with notes by Rolfe in 1983; Rolfe (276) suggests that Hunter held off publication in 1773 in order to see how the bull-moose antlers developed with maturity and to see if

rumours of another moose species were correct. (They weren't.) The Irish elk was later understood to be not an elk but a deer.

26 *Journals of Gilbert White*, vol. 1, 476–7.

16. Desolate Paradise

1 Thanks to Tracey Carr for showing me the garden and sharing her knowledge of it. Details of the garden in Hayley's time are given by Stebbing Shaw in 'Description of Eartham, in Sussex', *The Topographer* 4:25 (1791), 228–32, and see Tracey Carr, 'Hayley at Eartham', in *William Hayley: Poet, Biographer and Libertarian: A Reassessment*, ed. Paul Foster and Diana Barsham (Chichester: University of Chichester, 2013), 57–79. I draw here on my article 'Cowper Away: A Summer in Sussex', *Cowper and Newton Journal* 8 (2018).

2 Morchard Bishop, *Blake's Hayley* (London: Gollancz, 1951).

3 'Elegy, 1774', in *Memoirs of the Life and Writings of William Hayley*, ed. John Johnson (London: Henry Colburn, 1823), 2 vols, vol. 1, 129.

4 William Cowper, *The Task* (1785), book 3, line 41.

5 Hayley, *Memoirs*, vol. 1, 425–8.

6 Cowper to John Newton, 27 July 1783, *The Letters and Prose Writings of William Cowper*, ed. James King and Charles Ryskamp (Oxford: Clarendon Press, 1979–86), 5 vols, vol. 2, 150.

7 Cowper to William Bull, 25 July 1792, *Letters*, vol. 4, 157.

8 Cowper to Samuel Greatheed, 6 August 1792, *Letters*, vol. 4, 165.

9 Cowper to Samuel Teedon, 5 August 1792, *Letters*, vol. 4, 163.

10 Hayley, 'Elegy, 1774', in *Memoirs*, vol. 1, 129.

11 See e.g. Hayley, *Memoirs*, vol. 1, 160.

12 Cowper to Samuel Teedon, 19 August 1792, *Letters*, vol. 4, 176.

13 See letter to Hesketh, 26 August 1792, *Letters*, vol. 4, 181.

14 John Milton, *Paradise Lost* (1667), book 4, line 75. On Cowper's varying identification with both Adam in the garden and with Satan as a damned visitor there: Dustin Griffin, 'Cowper, Milton and the Recovery of Paradise', *Essays in Criticism* 31 (1981), 15–26.

15 Cowper to Lady Hesketh, 9 September 1792, *Letters*, vol. 4, 189.

16 Cowper to Newton, 18 October 1792, *Letters*, vol. 4, 216.

17 Details from George to John Romney, 10 October 1792, in John Romney, *Memoirs of the Life and Works of George Romney* (London: Baldwin and Cradock, 1830), 226.

18 Ibid.

19 Charlotte Smith, *The Old Manor House* (London: Bell, 1793), discussed in detail as a political novel by Loraine Fletcher, *Charlotte Smith: A Critical Biography* (1998; London: Routledge, 2001), 164–89.

20 Tom Clucas, 'Editing Milton during the French Revolution: Cowper and Hayley as "Brother Editor[s]"', *Review of English Studies* 65 (2014), 866–87.

21 Cowper to Mrs Cowper, 30 September 1792, *Letters*, vol. 4, 204.

22 John Johnson to Kate, n.d., late autumn 1792, *Letters of Lady Hesketh to the Rev. John Johnson* (London: Jarrold & Sons, 1901), 22.

23 Cowper, 'Verses, supposed to be written by Alexander Selkirk, during his solitary abode in the island of Juan Fernandez' (1782), in *Poems of William Cowper*, ed. John D. Baird and Charles Ryskamp (Oxford: Clarendon, 1980–95), 3 vols, vol. 1, 403–4.

24 S. H. Grimm's two 1780 drawings of Bignor Park show the house Smith knew.

25 'To the River Arun', *Elegiac Sonnets*, in *The Poems of Charlotte Smith*, ed. Stuart Curran (Oxford: OUP, 1993), 30. Smith's allusion to Warton's poem 'The Triumph of Isis' was proposed by Bethan Roberts in *Charlotte Smith and the Sonnet* (Liverpool: LUP, 2019), 91. I am indebted to Roberts throughout my discussion of *Elegiac Sonnets* and the Arun.

26 Smith, 'To the River Arun', *Poems*, 33. On river transport and engineering schemes: P. A. L. Vine, *London's Lost Route to the Sea* (Dawlish: David & Charles, 1965), and P. A. L. Vine, *The Arun Navigation* (Stroud: Tempus, 2007). The Pallingham to Newbridge canal opened 1787. Littlehampton to London would be navigable by 1816.

27 'To the River Arun', Ibid.

28 Ibid.

29 Anne Francis, 'Lines, occasioned by reading Collins' Poems', in *Miscellaneous Poems* (printed for the author, 1790), 21–9, and see chapter 11.

30 William Wordsworth, note to 'Stanzas suggested in a Steamboat off St. Bees' Head' (1833), in *Poetical Works*, ed. E. de Selincourt and Helen Darbishire (Oxford: Clarendon, 1947), 403.

31 Smith to Joel Barlow, 3 November 1792, *Letters*, 49.

32 Smith to Joseph Cooper Walker, 20 February 1793, *Letters*, 62.

33 Ibid. and for seizure of books, *Letters*, 61n.

34 Fletcher, *Smith*, 196.

35 Charlotte Smith, *The Emigrants* (1793), Book 2, in *Poems*, 150.

36 Ibid., 160.

37 Ibid., 151.

38 Ibid., 162.

39 Ibid., 156.

40 Ibid., 132–4.

17. A Marble Head

1 S. H. Grimm, employed by William Burrell, drew the head at Bosham on his 1782 Whitsun tour: BL Add. MS. 5675, f.46 [83].

2 The identification as Trajan for the head now at the Novium, Chichester, is discussed in Miles Russell and Harry Manley, 'Trajan Places: Establishing Identity and Context for the Bosham and Hawkshaw Heads', *Britannia* 46 (2015), 151–69.

18. An Open Gate

1 Blake, *Milton*, book 1: part 15, lines 45–6, in *Complete Writings*, ed. Geoffrey Keynes (Oxford: OUP, 1972), 497.
2 Ibid., lines 47–9, *Complete*, 497.
3 Blake, *Milton*, book 2: part 39, lines 4–5, *Complete*, 530.
4 Blake's visual art in this period is discussed in context and much of it reproduced in Andrew Loukes, ed., *William Blake in Sussex: Visions of Albion*, exh. cat. (London: Paul Holberton, 2018). On Hayley's patronage see also Morchard Bishop, *Blake's Hayley* (London: Victor Gollancz, 1951).
5 Included in Catherine Blake to Anna Flaxman, 14 September 1800, *Complete*, 800.
6 Jacob's dream in Genesis 28: 12: 'He dreamed, and behold, a ladder was set up on the earth, and the top reached to heaven; and behold the angels of God ascending and descending on it.'
7 Blake to Thomas Butts, 23 September 1800, and Blake to John Flaxman, 21 September 1800, *Complete*, 803, 802.
8 Mark Crosby, '"The Sweetest Spot on Earth": Reconstructing Blake's Cottage at Felpham', *British Art Journal* 7:3 (2006), 46–53.
9 Blake to Thomas Butts, 23 September 1800, *Complete*, 803.
10 Blake to Thomas Butts, 2 October 1800, *Complete*, 804.
11 Ibid.
12 *VCH*: 'Felpham', in *A History of the County of Sussex: Volume 5 Part 1, Arundel Rape: South-Western Part, Including Arundel*, ed. T. P. Hudson (London: VCH, 1997), 160–82. british-history.ac.uk/vch/sussex/vol5/pt1/pp160-182.1997; WSRO, Add. MSs 12657; fields named on Felpham Enclosure Award Map, 1826.
13 Blake to Thomas Butts, 23 September 1800, *Complete*, 803.
14 *VCH*: 'Felpham'.
15 Owners and occupiers of property in 1785 are listed in Alan Readman et al., eds, *West Sussex Land Tax 1785*, SRS 82 (2000).
16 Felpham Parish Register, WSRO, *Sussex Parish Registers*, Par 81/1/1/4, via Ancestry.com.
17 Blake, *Milton*, book 1: part 19, line 5, *Complete*, 500.
18 Charlotte Smith, 'Written in the church-yard at Middleton in Sussex', *Elegiac Sonnets*, in *The Poems of Charlotte Smith*, ed. Stuart Curran (Oxford: OUP, 1993), 42. Blake's drawing of the village is 'Landscape near Felpham', c.1800, graphite and watercolour, Tate.

19 Blake, 'Auguries of Innocence', *Complete*, 431.

20 Blake, *Milton*, book 1: plate 25, line 11, *Complete*, 510.

21 Blake to Thomas Butts, 10 May 1801, *Complete*, 808.

22 Female space: Blake, *Milton*, book 1: plate 10, line 54, *Complete*, 490; egg: *Milton*, book 1: plate 19, line 15, *Complete*, 500.

23 1801 census figures, *Abstract . . . of the Answers and Returns made to the Population Acts of 41 Geo III*, 356. There were more than twice as many women as men in Felpham (211 women:84 men). Only the printed abstract survives and does not give names or information on individuals or houses. A fuller picture survives for an earlier moment in time: see Readman et al., eds, *Land Tax*, 107.

24 Blake, *Milton*, book 1: plate 29, lines 21–2, *Complete*, 516.

25 *The John Marsh Journals: The Life and Times of a Gentleman Composer*, ed. Brian Robins (Stuyvesant: Pendragon Press, 1998), 734. Marsh's mentions of Blake are discussed and contextualised by Robert N. Essick in 'William Blake and John Marsh', *Blake: An Illustrated Quarterly* (1991), 70–4. Marsh had bought 7 North Pallant from William Hayley, who had grown up there and inherited it.

26 Timothy McCann builds a portrait of Seagrave and his printing career in 'Poems, Posters and Poll Books: Eighteenth Century Printing in Chichester', *SAC* 130 (1992), 189–99.

27 Hayley's testimonial for Seagrave (British Library Add. MS. 29, 300x) is cited by McCann in 'Printing in Chichester', 194; Daisy Hay, *Dinner with Joseph Johnson* (London: Chatto & Windus, 2022), 385, explains why Johnson's long experience with country printers made him sceptical.

28 Morton D. Payley makes the connection between Chichester and Blake's imagery of the four gates to the world and of Los walking the walls: 'William Blake and Chichester', in *Blake in Our Time: Essays in Honour of G. E. Bentley Jr*, ed. Karen Mulhallen (Toronto: University of Toronto Press, 2010), 215–32.

29 The large paintings by Lambert Barnard have been the subject of fascinating recent scholarship; see Coke, 'Lambert Barnard', in Matthew Dimmock, Andrew Hadfield and Paul Quinn, eds, *Art, Literature and Religion in Early Modern Sussex* (2014; Abingdon: Routledge, 2016), 61–94.

30 Blake, *Jerusalem*, chapter 2, plate 40, lines 48–51, *Complete*, 667.

31 Blake, *Jerusalem*, plate 13, line 20, *Complete*, 633; *Milton*, book 1: plate 17, line 30, *Complete*, 498.

32 Blake, *Milton*, book 2: plate 31, line 32, *Complete*, 520.

33 Blake to Thomas Butts, 2 October 1800, *Complete*, 805.

34 Blake to James Blake, 30 January 1803, *Complete*, 821.

35 Felpham Parish Register, WSRO, *Sussex Parish Registers*, Par 81/1/1/4, via Ancestry.com.

36 Blake to Thomas Butts, 22 November 1802, *Complete*, 816.

37 Blake to Thomas Butts, 10 January 1802, and Blake to James Blake, 30 January 1803, *Complete*, 811, 819.

38 Blake, *Milton*, book 2: plate 36, *Complete*, 527.

39 Blake to Thomas Butts, 25 April 1803, *Complete*, 822.

40 Blake, *Milton*, book 2: plate 35, line 42, *Complete*, 526.

41 Blake to Thomas Butts, 25 April 1803, *Complete*, 823.

42 Defence return for Felpham, in Roger Pearce, *Facing Invasion: Proceedings under the Defence Acts 1801–5*, SRS 99 (2017), 82–3.

43 On the legal process and its political contexts see Jon Mee and Mark Crosby, 'The Soldierlike Danger: The Trial of William Blake for Sedition', in *Resisting Napoleon*, ed. Mark Philp (Aldershot: Ashgate, 2006), 111–24.

44 Blake to Butts, 16 August 1803, *Complete*, 828. Blake set out in this letter his version of the whole incident, his first court hearing and bail. He also wrote a Memorandum in Refutation of the Information and Complaint of John Scholfield, *Complete*, 437–9.

45 *Sussex Weekly Advertiser*, 16 January 1804.

46 Blake to Butts, 25 April 1803, *Complete*, 823, and *Jerusalem*, 'To the Public', *Complete*, 620.

47 Blake, *Milton*, book 2: plate 42, lines 20–3, *Complete*, 534.

48 Blake, *Milton*, book 2: plate 31, lines 51–63, *Complete*, 520.

49 It was painted for Elizabeth Ilive soon after she left Petworth House, where she had lived first as Lord Egremont's mistress and then as his wife. Loukes, *Blake in Sussex*, 95.

50 Blake's draft description of the picture to Ozias Humphry, 18 January 1808, *Blake in Sussex*, 96.

51 Blake, *Milton*, book 2: plate 39, line 49, *Complete*, 531.

52 Bognor Rocks are shown on Budgen's 1724 map and as a major landform on Yeakell and Gardner's large-scale map of 1783. Grimm's drawing is BL Add. MS. 5675 f.93.

19. Further Fields

1 Quarter Sessions Roll, Chichester, Michaelmas 1828, WSRO, QR/W749.

2 Alison McCann has compiled a full list of transportees in the period, WSRO, Lib 9044.

3 Michael Royall, *The Petworth House of Correction* (privately published, 1999).

4 Home Office, Convict Transportation Registers, TNA via Ancestry.com: register for *Waterloo*.

5 freesettlerorfelon.com record for *Waterloo* 1829 voyage.

6 He survived the years of penal labour. A record from 1837 shows him being assigned to the Australian Agricultural Company to begin a new phase of his labouring life. freesettlerorfelon.com item 133630.

7 'Rev. Richard Smith', LBS, ucl.ac.uk/lbs/. His father, Richard Smith the Elder, became owner of the estate when he married Mary Mapp in 1764, and bequeathed either the estate or the mortgage over it in his will.

8 'Mapp's Estate [Barbados | St Philip]', LBS; Slave Registers of Former British Colonial Dependencies via Ancestry.com, Barbados, St Philip, TNA, T71/536 (1826), T71/544 (1829).

9 A complex doubleness that finds varying expression in her work; see e.g. *The Letters of a Solitary Wanderer: The Story of Henrietta* (1800), presenting a critique of West Indian slavery.

10 The sand box tree fell in the 1831 hurricane. Anon [Samuel Hyde?], *An Account of the Fatal Hurricane* (Bridgetown: Samuel Hyde, 1831), 139.

11 *Report from a Select Committee of the House of Assembly, appointed to inquire into the origin, causes, and progress of the late insurrection* (Barbados: W. Walker for the Legislature, 1817), 50–2.

12 Ibid., 35. Modern historians are reaching for ways to make such archival silences speak out; see especially Marisa Fuentes' work on records of enslaved people in Barbados and her challenge to the 'reproduction of invisibility and commodification': *Dispossessed Lives: Enslaved Women, Violence and the Archive* (Philadelphia: University of Pennsylvania Press, 2016), 147ff.

13 'John Duer of Chichester', LBS; *Hampshire Chronicle*, 21 February 1825.

14 Alice Millard, 'Stories from the Parish Registers: Black Residents of West Sussex', 2021, westsussexrecordofficeblog.com. 'James Sholto Douglas', LBS.

15 Edward Long, *The History of Jamaica* (London: T. Lowndes, 1774); on Long's use of landscape aesthetics and local commemoration of him, see Catherine Hall, 'Whose Memories? Edward Long and the Work of Re-remembering', in Katie Donnington et al., eds, *British History and Memory of Transatlantic Slavery* (Liverpool: LUP, 2016), 129–49.

16 Richard Dally, *The Bognor Guide* (Chichester: William Mason, 1828), 172.

17 Elizabeth A. Bohls, *Slavery and the Politics of Place: Representing the Colonial Caribbean* (Cambridge: CUP, 2016), discusses the Picturesque used by both Long and Hakewill, emphasising an 'eminently portable means of place-making' transposed from Europe to the West Indies (23). On the visual languages used to depict these industrial landscapes see Tim Barringer, 'Picturesque Prospects and the Labor of the Enslaved', in Barringer, Gillian Forrester and Barbaro Martinez Ruiz, *Art and Emancipation in Jamaica: Isaac Mendes Belisario and His Worlds* (New Haven: Yale UP, 2007), 41–64.

18 Tim Barringer and Alexander Lee in *Art and Emancipation*, 318–21.

19 *Hampshire Telegraph and Sussex Chronicle*, 6 February 1826, 13 February 1826.

20 Richard Huzzey studies the networks involved in this local work in 'A Microhistory of British Antislavery Petitioning', *Social Science History* 43 (2019), 599–623.

21 'Return of William Sharp of slaves the joint property of Richard Smith and Robert Allen', 27 May 1829, Slave Registers of Former British Colonial Dependencies via Ancestry.com, Barbados, St Philip, 1829, TNA, T71/544, image 179.

22 'Negro Slavery', report of a lecture in Chichester, *Hampshire Telegraph and Sussex Chronicle*, 12 December 1831.

23 Ashton Warner with Susanna Strickland, *Negro Slavery Described by a Negro* (London: Samuel Maunder, 1831), 33–4, 46.

24 Mary Prince with Susanna Strickland, *The History of Mary Prince*, ed. Thomas Pringle (London: F. Westley & A. H. Davis, 1831), 23.

25 Elizabeth Dolan, 'Lionel Smith in Barbados, 1833–1836: Imperialist and Abolitionist Rhetoric in Emancipation-era Caribbean Governance', *Slavery and Abolition*, 39:2 (2018), 333–56.

26 LBS lists 112 claimants with Sussex addresses.

27 'Rev. Richard Smith', LBS.

20. New South Downs

1 *Hampshire Chronicle*, 2 March 1829.

2 Joan Ham, *Storrington in Georgian and Victorian Times* (privately published, 1987), 230–40, on this Sullington group. Family History of Western Australia dataset for *Lotus*: data.fhwa.org.au.

3 Marnie Bassett, *The Hentys: An Australian Colonial Tapestry* (Oxford: OUP, 1954), 38–43.

4 *Sussex Advertiser*, 15 June 1829, 3, describes the embarkation on 4 June; William Henty wrote an account in an exercise book: SLWA, MN610.

5 The words were recorded by one of the cabin passengers – with an imitation of Gee's spelling, which I have standardised. See Graeme Skinner, 'A Chronological Checklist of Australian Colonial Musical Works 1826–1830', sydney.edu.au/paradisec/australharmony/checklist1826-1830.php; Bassett, *Hentys*, 43, makes the link with shepherds' ballads.

6 James to Thomas Henty, 15 November 1829, Papers of James Henty, Acc. 597A, Battye Library, SLWA, MN610.

7 James to Thomas Henty, 1 November 1829, SLWA, MN610.

8 Bassett, *Hentys*, 117. James to Thomas Henty, writing from Fremantle 15 November 1830, SLWA, MN610.

9 James to William Henty, 11 February 1830 and (for clocks) James to Thomas Henty, 19 January 1830. SLWA, MN610.

10 James to Thomas Henty, 20 March 1830, SLWA, MN610.

11 Ibid.

12 Ibid.

13 James to Thomas Henty, 12 March 1831, SLWA, MN610.

14 James to William Henty, 6 April 1831, SLWA, MN610.

15 Louisa Woods *née* Charman to John Charman, 3 May 1831, *Letters and Extracts of Letters from Settlers at the Swan River and in the United States to their friends in the Western part of Sussex* (Petworth: John Phillips, 1832).

16 Amina Marzouk Chouchene, 'Fear, Anxiety, Panic and Settler Consciousness', *Settler Colonial Studies* 10 (2020), 443–60, 444.

17 James to William Henty, 27 May 1831, SLWA, 597A/22.

18 Auction advertisement, Bassett, *Hentys*, plate 24.

19 Thomas Gallop to his sons, 15 October 1832, SLWA, 1862A/15 ; his descendant, Geoff Gallop, quoted this letter in his first parliamentary speech, 1986.

20 Edward Henty, diary, 2 and 4 December 1834, swvic.org/merino/hentyset.htm. Edward made a copy of this expedition diary for his brother Charles; this copy was later found and much of it printed in *Portland Guardian*, 13 January 1927, 4.

21 Report of lecture by Thomas Henty (junior), given at Tarring, 28 November 1882, printed *Mission Field: A Monthly Record of the Proceedings of the Society for the Propagation of the Gospel in Foreign Parts*, January 1883 (London: G. Bell, 1883).

22 Merino Downs Homestead Complex: vhd.heritagecouncil.vic.gov.au.

23 Joan Ham, *Sullington: Domesday to D-Day* (privately published, 1992), 226–7; Alan Atkinson, *The Europeans in Australia* (2004; Sydney: NewSouth Publishing, 2016), 284.

24 Nicholas Dean Brodie in 'Relics of the Tasmanian Gothic', *Limina* (2013), 1–15, shows that it was not the only font taken from England to Australia. A photograph is reproduced Bassett, *Hentys*, plate 5.

25 Pevsner, 751. The refurbishment is described *Gentleman's Magazine*, 1854, 517–18. For Thomas Henty and the rectory garden font see Edward Orger, *The Life of Henry Bailey* (London: no publisher given, 1912), 125. Bailey was the West Tarring rector. Bassett, *Hentys*, plate 5, records that it did not go to Melbourne cathedral but stood in several Henty gardens until 1953 when it was accidentally destroyed.

26 Reproduced Bassett, *Hentys*, plate 59.

21. The Fat of the Land

1 Richard Dally, *The Bognor, Arundel and Littlehampton Guide* (Chichester: William Mason, 1828), 42–3, 55, 37.

2 The Petworth Emigration Scheme assisted about 1800 people. The majority were from West Sussex parishes close to Petworth where Lord Egremont held lands, but when berths were available these were joined by emigrants from parishes in East Sussex, Surrey and the Isle of Wight. The scheme is comprehensively described and documented in Wendy Cameron and Mary McDougall Maude, *Assisting Emigration to Upper Canada: The Petworth Project, 1832–1837* (Montreal: McGill-Queen's UP, 2000).

3 Rainer Baehre, 'Pauper Emigration to Upper Canada in the 1830s', *Histoire sociale/ Social History* 14:28 (1981), 339–67: numbers (rounded to the thousand), 345.

4 On Colborne and immigration policy in Upper Canada see *Assisting Emigration*, 113ff.

5 Parliament Select Committee, *The Parish and the Union* (London: Charles Knight, 1837), 22.

6 Emigrants on Petworth ships are listed *Assisting Emigration*, 211–90.

7 Elias Elliott to Richard Elliott, 24 September 1832, *English Voices*, 54.

8 Martin Martin to Mr Sparks, 24 September 1832, *English Voices*, 55–8. Later Martin tried being a publican again: he and Fanny moved to Elora, a village north of Guelph, about 1837 and for a time ran a tavern there. See *English Voices*, 58, and *Assisting Emigration*, 253.

9 *Emigration: Letters from Sussex Emigrants* (Petworth: John Phillips, and London: Longman, 1833). There was a good deal of contemporary worry over whether published emigrant letters (in Sussex and elsewhere) could be trusted. Had they been doctored or faked to lure further travellers? Fariha Shaikh in *Nineteenth-Century Settler Emigration in British Literature and Art* (Edinburgh: Edinburgh UP, 2018), 50–7, gives a moving account of the steps taken to prove authenticity.

10 Cameron and Maude, *Assisting Emigration*, xiv.

11 *Quarter Sessions Order Book, 1642–1649*, ed. B. C. Redwood, SRS 54 (1954), 94.

12 Richard Neal to friends and relations, 20 July 1832, *English Voices*, 16–18.

13 Cameron, Haines and Maude, *English Voices*, 81.

14 Thomas Adsett to Thomas Scutt, 9 September 1832, *English Voices*, 46.

15 George to James and Sarah Carver, 18 August 1833, *English Voices*, 148.

16 George to James and Sarah Carver, 30 June 1834, *English Voices*, 165.

17 Quarter Sessions, Petworth, Easter 1821, WSRO, QR/W719.

18 Brian Short, 'The Decline of Living-In Servants in the Transition to Capitalist Farming: A Critique of the Sussex Evidence', *SAC* 122 (1984), 147–64.

19 'The farmer can now command any labour when he wants it, without burthening himself permanently, with indoor labourers', explained one respondent to the Royal Commission on Poor Law cited by Short in 'Decline of Living-In Servants', 152.

20 Mike Matthews, *Captain Swing in Kent and Sussex* (Hastings: Hastings Press, 2006), 72–3. Petworth Quarter Sessions Roll (WSRO, QR/W758) gives the Swing Riot offences brought before magistrates in 1830–1.

21 Witness depositions, 15 December 1830, Quarter Sessions, Petworth, Epiphany 1831, WSRO, QR/W758/219–20.

22 Edward Goble, witness deposition, 19 November 1830, Quarter Sessions, Petworth, Epiphany 1831, WSRO, QR/W758/201.

23 Ibid., 74. On the national context and impact of the Swing Riots, see Eric Hobsbawm and George Rudé, *Captain Swing* (1969; London: Verso, 2014).

Subsequent records of transported convicts, including seventeen from Sussex, are given by Bruce W. Brown in 'The Machine Breaker Convicts from the *Proteus* and the *Eliza*', MA thesis, University of Tasmania, 2004.

24 Baehre, 'Pauper Emigration', 340.

25 Stephen to Elizabeth Goatcher, 6 July 1832, *English Voices*, 13–16.

26 Ibid., 17 January 1833, *English Voices*, 96–7.

27 Edward and Catharine Boxall to Mrs Boxall, 9 February 1833, *English Voices*, 100–1.

28 Edward Heming to Anna Maria Heming, 25 September 1832, *English Voices*, 59.

29 Colin Pooley suggests that ties of language, culture and kinship have a stronger influence on migration decisions than 'intrinsic place features' such as climate and landscape, but also that these cannot always be separated: 'The Influence of Locality on Migration: A Comparative Study of Britain and Sweden in the Nineteenth Century', *Local Population Studies* 90 (2013), 13–27. In the case of emigration from Sussex, the continuation of established rural culture depended on a move to agricultural areas.

30 David McNab discusses early-nineteenth-century 'amalgamation' policy and its implementation in *No Place for Fairness: Indigenous Land Rights and Policy in the Bear Island Case and Beyond* (Montreal: McGill-Queen's UP, 2009), 20–38. Aboriginal people 'became entrapped in a kind of social and economic limbo, losing their original skills and at the same time finding it almost impossible, in the competition with white farmers, to adapt to an agricultural economy' (29).

31 William Cooper to Christopher Cooper, 5 February 1833, *English Voices*, 99.

32 Thomas Adsett to his father Thomas Adsett, re William Davis, 25 June 1833, *English Voices*, 122.

33 Martin Doyle, *Hints on Emigration to Upper Canada, Especially Addressed to the Middle and Lower Classes in Great Britain and Ireland*, 2nd edn (London: Simpkin & Marshall, 1832), 36, 39, 42.

34 George Carver to James and Sarah Carver, 30 June 1834, *English Voices*, 165.

35 Francis Bond Head, *The Emigrant* (London: John Murray, 1846), 90.

36 Doyle, *Hints*, 46, 49. An Irish clergyman tied to his parishes in Wexford, Doyle was no more used to procuring buffalo blankets than the people he wrote for. But he saw himself as a 'sincere advisor' to the poor.

37 David A. Gerber discusses the narrative conventions of 'first letters' (from shipboard struggles to new fortunes) in *Authors of Their Lives: The Personal Correspondence of British Immigrants to North America in the Nineteenth Century* (New York: NYU Press, 2006).

38 The correspondence of emigrants from 'the letter-writing classes' could be much fuller and more personal; Elizabeth Jane Errington discusses this and other patterns of communication in *Emigrant Worlds and Transatlantic Communities: Migration to*

Upper Canada in the First Half of the Nineteenth Century (Montreal: McGill-Queen's UP, 2007), 136–58.

39 James Rapson to Philip Rapson, 16 October 1832, *English Voices*, 70.

40 Edward and Catharine Boxall to Mrs Boxall, 28 July 1832, *English Voices*, 20.

41 Edward Heming to Anna Maria Heming, 25 September 1832, *English Voices*, 59. On lists see also Shaikh, *Emigration in British Literature*, 48, who stresses the ordinariness of the things itemised: 'the information . . . is meant to make the unfamiliar familiar.'

42 James Cooper to James Cooper, 26 May 1838, *English Voices*, 271.

43 James and Hannah Tilley to Thomas Lucas, 29 July 1833, *English Voices*, 143.

44 John and Ruth Waldon to James Cooper, 9 January 1836, *English Voices*, 197.

45 Interesting comparisons can be made with the way more literary emigrants tried to understand similar landscapes in Canada. See e.g. Susanna Moodie's self-conscious trialling of landscape aesthetics in *Roughing It in the Bush* (1852). For discussion: Shaikh, *Emigration in British Literature*, 106–11, and Susan Glickman, *The Picturesque and the Sublime: A Poetics of the Canadian Landscape* (Montreal: McGill-Queen's University Press, 1998), 38–49.

46 Charlotte and William Willard to Maria Wolgar, 26 August 1832, *English Voices*, 39.

47 Edward and Catharine Boxall to Mrs Boxall, 9 February 1833, *English Voices*, 100.

48 Martin Martin to Mr Sparks, 25 September 1832, *English Voices*, 56.

49 James Rapson to Philip Rapson, 16 October 1832, *English Voices*, 71.

50 William Phillips to Mrs Newell, 5 August 1832, *English Voices*, 29.

51 William Cobbett, 2 August 1823, in *Rural Rides* (1830), ed. Ian Dyck (London: Penguin, 2001), 87–8.

52 Ibid., 87. By 1829 Cobbett was advocating emigration for farmers as well as labourers. 'The state of the country is now such, that no man, except by mere accident, can avoid ruin, unless he can get a share of the taxes.' *The Emigrant's Guide: In Ten Letters* (printed for the author, 1829), 7.

53 William Phillips to Thomas Phillips, 14 July 1839, *English Voices*, 293–4.

54 *The Champion and Weekly Herald*, 10 June 1837.

55 Elizabeth Hooker to Richard Pullen, 22 April 1838, *English Voices*, 405–6. It would be a 'blank', too, for Charles' sons, who tried to follow him as gamekeepers, found no work, and eventually emigrated to America.

56 Ibid.

57 Elizabeth Hooker to Richard Pullen, 4 April 1839, *English Voices*, 289. Conditions remained desperate in Sussex through the 1840s. Jane Cobden recorded testimonies of Sussex workers in *The Hungry Forties: Life under the Bread Tax* (London: T. Fisher Unwin, 1904). Emigration was still being encouraged in the 1870s.

58 William Phillips to Thomas Phillips, 14 July 1839, *English Voices*, 293–4.

22. A Historian's Books

1 Fiona MacCarthy, *Eric Gill* (London: Faber & Faber, 1990), 58, quoting Gill's diaries (Clark Library); Linda Grace and Margaret Nicolle, 'Introduction' to *A Woman in the Shadow of the Second World War: Helena Hall's Journal from the Home Front* (Pen & Sword, 2015). Drafts and papers from Hall's later life are at ESRO.

2 She is mentioned as a student in Justin Howes, 'Edward Johnston's First Class at the Central School on 21 September 1899', in *Object Lessons: Central Saint Martin's Art and Design Archive*, ed. Sylvia Backemeyer (London: Lethaby Press, 1996).

3 *Journal of the Ex Libris Society* 11 (1902), 46. The 1907 issue includes (90) a list of heraldic silks and cloths shown by Hall at the Ex Libris exhibition.

4 Helena Hall, 1911 Census of England and Wales.

5 Stuart N. Clarke gives the census data for this and other addresses connected with Woolf and her family in 'The 1911 Census', *Virginia Woolf Bulletin* 31 (2009), 34–7. 22 HPG was co-owned by Virginia Stephen, her brother Adrian, sister Vanessa and half-sister Laura.

6 Virginia Woolf to Violet Dickinson, 29? January 1911, *The Letters of Virginia Woolf*, ed. Nigel Nicolson and Joanne Trautmann, vol. 1 (London: Hogarth Press, 1983), 451.

7 Virginia Stephen to Jacques Raverat, [late March 1911], *Letters*, vol. 1, 455 (for train on Saturday); VS to Jacques Raverat, 9 April 1911, *Letters*, vol. 1, 459; VS to Vanessa Bell, 8 April 1911, *Letters*, vol. 1, 458.

8 William Hamilton Hall, *Calendar of Wills and Administrations in the Archdeaconry Court of Lewes* etc (London: British Record Society, 1901).

9 Cf. Pauline Phillips, 'The Participation of Women in the Journal *Sussex Archaeological Collections*, 1900–1950', *SAC* 136 (1998), 133–47.

10 See e.g. Helena Hall, 'Ornamental Sussex Ironwork', *Sussex County Magazine* 1:12 (1927), 509–10. Over 350 of her drawings of ironwork were left to Brighton Museum.

11 Hall, *Journal from the Home Front*, 64, 197.

12 Helena Hall, *William Allen, 1770–1843: Member of the Society of Friends* (Haywards Heath: Charles Clarke, 1953).

13 William Allen, *Colonies at Home, or the means for rendering the industrious poor independent of parish relief* (1826; printed for the author, 1832). For modern discussion: Barbara Arneil, 'The Failure of Planned Happiness', in Georgios Varouxakis and Mark Philp, eds, *Happiness and Utility* (London: UCL Press, 2019), 269–88.

14 W. D. Parish, revised and expanded by Helena Hall, *A Dictionary of the Sussex Dialect* (Bexhill: Gardner's, 1957).

15 Grace and Nicolle, 'Introduction' to Hall, *Journal*, 1.

23. Mill and Castle

1 C. R. Leslie, *Memoirs of the Life of John Constable Esq. RA* (1843; London: Longmans, Brown, 1845), 258.

2 The two artists' responses to Petworth are explored by Andrew Loukes in the exhibition booklets *Turner's Sussex* (2013) and *Constable at Petworth* (2014), both produced by the National Trust to accompany exhibitions at Petworth House.

3 Constable to C. R. Leslie, 14 January 1832, *John Constable's Correspondence*, vol. 3, ed. R. B. Beckett, Suffolk Records Society 8, 1965, 59. Egremont had been critical of Constable's work in Brighton in 1824, which seems to have left Constable cautious about further meetings.

4 Their itinerary for this and future visits can be traced with reference to the many drawings Constable made along the way as detailed by Graham Reynolds in *The Later Paintings and Drawings of John Constable* (New Haven: Yale UP, 1984), 2 vols, vol. 2, 259–68, 276–9.

5 John Constable's notes beside canoe wash drawing, British Library Egerton MS 3253. With thanks to Stephen Daniels for the reference. 'Cwch' is a Celtic word for boat.

6 British Museum catalogue entry for object number 1834,0801.1.

7 Constable to Leslie, 30 August 1834, *Correspondence*, vol. 3, 113. Thomas Phillips, 'Account of the Discovery of an Ancient Canoe at North Stoke in Sussex', *Archaeologia* 26 (1836), 257–64.

8 Edward Turner, 'British Boat Found at North Stoke', *SAC* 12 (1860), 261.

9 Constable to Leslie, 16 July 1834, *Correspondence*, vol. 3, 111.

10 Sims Williams sale particulars.

11 Constable to Leslie, 16 July 1834, *Correspondence*, vol. 3, 111–12.

12 Ibid., 111.

13 In his fourth lecture at the Royal Institution in 1836 he praised Richard Wilson, who 'looked at nature entirely for himself', regretting an imitative culture in which 'the Smiths of Chichester, whose names are now nearly forgotten, accumulated wealth, while Wilson might have starved'. Reported in Leslie, *Memoirs*, 353.

14 Constable to Leslie, 16 July 1834, *Correspondence*, vol. 3, 112. The drawing shows Tortington Priory barn and is now in the British Museum.

15 Near the end of Grove Lane and now called Soanes.

16 Reported by George Constable to Leslie, in Leslie, *Memoirs*, 259.

17 George Constable to John Constable, 22 May 1835, *John Constable's Correspondence*, vol. 5, ed. R. B. Beckett, Suffolk Records Society 9, 1967, 21. On the emigration of Susan Boniface, who became Mrs Charles Shum Henty: Marnie Bassett, *The Hentys: An Australian Colonial Tapestry* (Oxford: OUP, 1954), 340–3.

18 Constable to George Constable, 2 July 1835, *Correspondence*, vol. 5, 23.

19 Sketchbook used in Sussex, 1835, V&A 316–1888; Charlotte Smith, 'Sonnet XLIV: Written at the Church Yard in Middleton in Sussex', in *The Poems of Charlotte*

Smith, ed. Stuart Curran (Oxford: OUP, 1993), 42; and see Bethan Roberts, *Charlotte Smith and the Sonnet* (Liverpool: LUP, 2019), 125.

20 Constable to George Constable, 16 December 1835, *Correspondence*, vol. 5, 29; Mark Tierney, *The History and Antiquities of the Castle and Town of Arundel* (London: G. & W. Nicol, 1834), 2 vols, vol. 2, 725.

21 Leslie explained the situation to Constable's children: Leslie to Maria and Isabel Constable, 27 August 1844, *Correspondence*, vol. 5, 38–9.

22 *The Arundel Roads: Report of the appeal tried at West Sussex Epiphany Quarter Sessions* (Brighton: printed by Curtis & Co, 1851).

23 Ibid., 16.

24 Ibid., 47, 48.

24. New Timetables

1 P. I. Martin, *A Geological Memoir on a Part of Western Sussex* (London: John Booth, 1828), viii.

2 Gideon Mantell, *Fossils of the South Downs* (London: Lupton Relph, 1822), 283; Mantell, *The Journal of Gideon Mantell*, ed. E. Cecil Curwen (Oxford: OUP, 1940), 48.

3 Martin to Mantell, 7 January 1827, microfilm of papers of Gideon Mantell at National Library of New Zealand, ESRO, XA/64/6, folder 68. Several Pulborough visits are recorded, e.g. *Journal*, 24 May 1833: 'After dinner walked with Mr Martin to several quarries near the village.'

4 Gideon Mantell, *The Geology of the South-East of England* (London: Longman, 1833), 179 for the species found by Martin in the sands near Pulborough; 268–281 for Iguanodon.

5 The geologist Thomas Bonney, who wrote entries for geologists with surnames M–Z, respectfully summed up Martin's career in the *Dictionary of National Biography*. Valuable evidence of his life is pieced together by David Morris in *The Doctors of Pulborough, 1731–1997* (privately published, 1997).

6 William Fitton, 'The Strata below the Chalk', *Transactions of the Geological Society* 4 (1836), with many Stopham identifications attributed to Martin.

7 Martin, *Memoir*, 22.

8 Ibid., 60.

9 P. A. L. Vine, *Around Pulborough* (Stroud: Tempus, 2002), 20–1.

10 Pulborough, Lower Street, 1841 Census of England. *The Arundel Roads: Report of the appeal tried at West Sussex Epiphany Quarter Sessions* (Brighton: printed by Curtis & Co, 1851), 49.

11 Ibid., 67, and Historic England Official List Entry. The kiln is still there, behind Waterside House. It was built before 1724 and in use until the 1870s when the dock beside it silted up.

12 This must have been before 1851 when the widely hated window tax was abolished. Ivy Strudwick, in *Pulborough: A Pictorial History* (Chichester: Phillimore, 1983), n.p., suggests the house ('Henley's') may have been built without the windows in the first place, leaving spaces for sashes to be let in at a later date.

13 The paper was found and published: P. J. Martin, 'On the anticlinal line of the London and Hampshire basins', *London, Edinburgh, and Dublin Philosophical Magazine and Journal of Science* 2:8 (1851), 41–51.

14 Mantell, 28 November 1848, *The Unpublished Journal of Gideon Mantell*, ed. John A. Cooper, 126, at gideonmantell.files.wordpress.com.

15 Martin to Mantell, e.g. 22 September 1850, ESRO, XA/64/6, folder 68. Martin's only son Robert (1827–91) became a doctor, practising at St Bartholomew's hospital in London, and (1854–6) co-directing the field hospital at Smyrna in the Crimean War.

16 'P. P.' [Peter Martin], *The Gardeners' Chronicle*, 15 January 1842.

17 Ibid., 17 December 1842.

18 From the paper Martin wrote in 1834 and reprinted with additional commentary as 'Notice of a British Settlement and Walled Tumulus, near Pulborough', *SAC* 9 (1857), 109–18.

19 Ibid.

20 P. J. Martin, 'Some Recollections of a Part of the "Stane Street Causeway"', *SAC* 11 (1859), 127–46, 137.

21 *Bradshaw's Monthly Railway Guide*, 1861.

22 W. Boyd Dawkins, 'On a Romano-British Cemetery and a Roman Camp at Hardham, in West Sussex', *SAC* 16 (1864), 52–64.

23 The Arun Valley Line was complete with the opening of Littlehampton station in August and a dinner and fête in Arundel for the railway builders and stationmasters. On the stages of planning and building, including the Stoke cuts, see Adrian Gray, *The Railways of Mid-Sussex* (Blandford Forum: Oakwood Press, 1975), 36–48.

25. A Teacher's History

1 David Morris, ed., with Pulborough History Group, *Pulborough Before the Great War: A Brief Guide to Lower Street* (privately published, 1986).

26. Just Country

1 At Selsey, Ford's German name (Hueffer) and espousal of close ties with Germany, made him a figure of suspicion to the extent that Edward Heron-Allen, from whom the cottage was rented, tried to get him forcibly removed; Ford satirised Heron-Allen's spy-hunting in his story 'The Scaremonger'.

2 On an uninvited visit to D. H. Lawrence's house at Greatham in 1915.

3 Stella Bowen, *Drawn from Life* (1940; Maidstone: George Mann, 1974), 65. Bowen's life and work in these years are discussed by Drusilla Modjeska in *Stravinsky's Lunch* (Sydney: Pan Macmillan Australia, 1999), 56–67.

4 Ford generally called it Red Ford, though before and since it has been Redford.

5 Ford to Stella Bowen, 3–4 April 1919, *The Correspondence of Ford Madox Ford and Stella Bowen* (Bloomington: Indiana University Press, 1993), 60.

6 Max Saunders explores in detail the different versions of this first night in *Ford Madox Ford: A Dual Life* (Oxford: OUP, 1996), 2 vols, vol. 2, 61–4.

7 Ford Madox Ford, *It Was the Nightingale* (London: William Heinemann, 1933), 101. Thanks to Jordan Dobbins who taught me a good deal about Ford.

8 Ford, *Nightingale*, 101.

9 Ford to his mother from Rouen, 15 December 1916, cited Saunders, *Ford*, 23.

10 Ford to Iris Barry, 4 July 1918, *Letters of Ford Madox Ford*, ed. Richard M. Ludwig (Princeton: PUP, 1965), 87; the novel was 'Mr Croyd'.

11 Bowen, *Drawn from Life*, 61: 'He was the only intellectual I had met to whom army discipline provided a conscious release from the torments and indecisions of a super-sensitive brain. To obey orders was, for him, a positive holiday.'

12 Ford to Bowen, 18 May 1919, *Correspondence*, 131.

13 Ford, *Nightingale*, 49.

14 Ford to Bowen, 7 April 1919, *Correspondence*, 71.

15 Ford to Bowen, 19 May 1919, *Correspondence*, 133; Bowen, *Drawn from Life*, 78.

16 Ford to Bowen, 4 April 1919, *Correspondence*, 64.

17 Ford to Bowen, 21 May 1919, *Correspondence*, 137.

18 Ford to Bowen, 9 April 1919, *Correspondence*, 77.

19 George Heyler, Redford, Cootham, Pulborough, 1911 Census of England and Wales.

20 William Figg, 'Roman Coins at Storrington', *SAC* 8 (1856), 277–8; Peter J. Martin, 'Some Recollections of a Part of "Stane Street Causeway"', *SAC* 11 (1858), 127–46, 140.

21 Ford to Bowen, 2 June 1919, *Correspondence*, 163.

22 Ford Madox Ford, *The Heart of the Country* (London: Alston Rivers, 1906), 94.

23 Ford to Bowen, 7 April and 21 May 1919, *Correspondence*, 71, 137.

24 Ford Madox Ford, 'The Work of W. H. Hudson', *English Review* 2 (1909), 157–64, 157.

25 Ford Madox Ford, *Parade's End: Last Post* (1928; London: Penguin, 2015), 812. Ford would have known William Dyce's painting of Herbert in his garden, painted with a Pre-Raphaelite reverence for detail and stillness; the turf is fresh and spotted with primroses, a fishing basket lies beside the river.

26 Ford Madox Ford, *No Enemy: A Tale of Reconstruction*, ed. Paul Skinner (written 1919; published 1929; Manchester: Carcanet, 2002), 13.

27 Ford Madox Ford, 'The Iron Music', in *Selected Poems*, ed. Max Saunders (Manchester: Carcanet, 1997), 87.

28 Ford, *Nightingale*, 48.

29 Edward Thomas to Helen Thomas, 24 March 1917, in *Letters to Helen*, ed. R. George Thomas (Manchester: Carcanet, 2000), 88–90; John Godfrey, 'Landscapes of War and Peace: Sussex, the South Downs, and the Western Front', *SAC* 152 (2014), 189–209, 202–4, cites other soldiers' comparisons between Sussex chalk and the Western Front.

30 Ford, *No Enemy*, 31.

31 Ibid., 19.

32 Ibid., 37.

33 Ibid., 43.

34 Ibid., 24.

35 Ibid., 7. The name invoked a whole company of French writers, summoned by Ford into Sussex. Victor Hugo's troubadour narrator in *Notre-Dame de Paris* is loosely based on the sixteenth-century poet Gringoire; Alphonse Daudet in *Lettres de mon moulin*, an important book for Ford's sense of place, addressed the story of 'Monsieur Seguin's Goat' to a fictive Pierre Gringoire.

36 Ford, *Last Post*, 799.

37 Ford, *Nightingale*, 94.

38 Ibid., 48.

39 Ford Madox Hueffer, 'A House', *The Chapbook* 21, March 1921, in *Poems*, 133–6.

40 On Bowen's illustrations and book jackets: Joseph Wiesenfarth, *Ford Madox Ford and the Regiment of Women* (Madison: University of Wisconsin Press, 2005), 97.

41 Bowen describes the house and her feelings about it in *Drawn from Life*, 69–73.

42 Bowen, *Drawn from Life*, 69.

43 At the centre of Fittleworth's artistic life was the painter Rex Vicat Cole who owned Brinkwells on Bedham lane. On his pre-war landscape 'rhapsodies' and their post-war ending, see Tim Barringer, '1908: Deep in the Maze of Summer Woods', *The Royal Academy Summer Exhibition: A Chronicle*, Chronicle250.com. For images of art at the Swan: fittleworth.wordpress.com/art/.

44 Ruth Tittensor has written a historical and ecological portrait of the place: 'A History of The Mens: A Sussex Woodland Common', *SAC* 116 (1978), 347–74.

45 Rhoda Leigh, *Past and Passing* (London: Heath Cranton, 1932), 110: 'to hold a rheumatic limb under this gushing flow is considered an infallible cure'.

46 On Elgar's explorations of the woods, interest in learning forestry techniques, and the influence of the area on his music, see Jerrold Northrop Moore, *Elgar: A Creative Life* (Oxford: OUP, 1999), 720–6.

47 Royal College of Music collection, and see W. H. Reed, *Elgar as I Knew Him* (London: Gollancz, 1936), 62–3.

48 Ford has it in *Nightingale*, 143, that the encounter with Elgar was the occasion for certain phrases appearing in his mind and that these were the beginning of his war novel. 'There came into my mind suddenly the words: "The band will play: *Land of Hope and Glory . . .*" The adjutant will say: "There will be no more parades" . . .'

49 Ford, *Nightingale*, 143.

50 Bowen, *Drawn from Life*, 78.

51 Ibid.

52 Ford, *The Heart of the Country*, 227.

53 Ford to Herbert Read, 24 July 1920, *Letters of Ford Madox Ford*, ed. Richard Ludwig (Princeton: PUP, 1965), 115.

54 Ford, *Nightingale*, 111.

55 Ibid. On Ford's husbandry, and his literary ways of describing it, see Harriet Walters, 'Rural Ritual, Gardened Faith: Ford Madox Ford's Memorial Plots', *Modernist Cultures* 16:2 (2021), 242–64. My thanks to Hattie for rich conversations on this subject.

56 Ford tells the story in *Nightingale*, 141, though he omits from the book any word of Stella.

57 Ford, '*Ulysses* and the Handling of Indecencies', *English Review* 35 (1922), 538–48.

58 Thanks to Ed Shingles. Bowen (*Drawn from Life*, 76–7) remembers the cauldron, and how she hung up hams to smoke in the open chimney.

59 In her native Adelaide, she remembered (and she would make it the opening observation of *Drawn from Life*) 'the air is so dry that the distance has the same quality as the foreground'. She discovered with 'surprised delight' 'the separate veils of blue which define each stage of the English distance'.

60 Ford, *No Enemy*, 35.

61 Ford, *Last Post*, 713.

62 Ford, *No Enemy*, 33.

63 Ford to Anthony Bertram, 24 October 1922, *Letters*, 145.

64 Bowen to Ford, 3 January 1928, *Correspondence*, 372.

27. Tank Tracks

1 James Roffey, *A Schoolboy's War in Sussex* (Stroud: History Press, 2010), 26. Photographs of Burchell Stores are at gravelroots.net, ref. 243 and 253. The building is still there, with an extension housing the Station Fryer.

2 Ibid., 27; on the psychological effect on children, see Maud Ellmann, 'Vaccies Go Home: Evacuation, Psychoanalysis and Fiction in World War II Britain', *Oxford Literary Review* 38:2 (2016), 240–61.

3 Roffey, *Schoolboy's War*, 40.

4 Ibid., 49.

5 Hilary Greenwood, 'The Defence of Littlehampton during the Second World War', project.littlehamptonfort.co.uk.

6 John Piper, 'Pre-history from the Air', *Axis* 8 (1937), 4–8; W. H. Auden, 'Consider this and in our time' (1930), *The English Auden*, ed. Edward Mendelson (London: Faber and Faber, 1977, 1986), 46.

7 Historic England research record for monument number 1465086 (accessed at heritagegateway.org.uk). Gumber's military history has been pieced together from many sources by the author of slindonatwarmyblog.wordpress.com, including photographs of soldiers manning the decoy. Chris Butler in *West Sussex under Attack* (Stroud: Tempus, 2008) suggests the runway took its line from the Roman road. The planes were designed by a decoy unit based at Shepperton Studios and made by a garden-furniture manufacturer.

8 Laurie Lee, diary, 18 August 1940, quoted Valerie Grove, *Laurie Lee: The Well-Loved Stranger* (1999; London: Penguin, 2000), 127; on Lorna's love of Binsted Woods see Emma Tristram, binsted.org/wishartists.

9 Roffey, *Schoolboy's War*, 56.

10 Ibid., 51, 63.

11 Grove, *Laurie Lee*, 131.

12 Vera Pragnell, *The Story of The Sanctuary* (Steyning: Vine Press, 1928). Pragnell herself is vividly evoked by Franz Wilfrid Walter in the Storrington and District Museum magazine *Times Past* 41 (spring 2012). On experimental communities between the wars see Anna Neima, *The Utopians* (London: Picador, 2021).

13 Ronald Hutton, *The Triumph of the Moon: A History of Modern Pagan Witchcraft* (Oxford: OUP, 1999, rev. 2019), 175.

14 Quoted Grove, *Laurie Lee*, 132.

15 *West Sussex Gazette*, 17 October 1940. By all accounts he had been much loved in the parish for seven years, always taking an active part, for instance in opening the old Stopham schoolroom for evacuee children. *Gazette* 10 October 1940 records his long interest in the murals at Hardham and their preservation. His brother was the poet John Masefield.

16 *West Sussex Gazette*, 28 November 1940.

17 Joan Ham, *Storrington in Living Memory* (London: Phillimore, 1982), 81.

18 Ibid.

19 Ann Salmon et al., *Voices of the Village: A History of West Chiltington during the 20th Century* (privately published, 1999), 154.

20 Beryl Callon with Ron Callon, *But for the Sake of a Tiny Wasp* (Kibworth Beauchamp: Matador, 2019), 120.

21 Ibid., 72. The published memoir was written by Ron's wife, Beryl, who used the notes she had made over decades as Ron 'told and retold' stories from his time as an evacuee in Sussex. Ron described it as a record 'compiled from [his] spoken memories'.

22 Ibid., 75–6. Wordsworth, 'Lines Written a Few Miles above Tintern Abbey' (1798), in *Major Works* (Oxford: OUP, 1984, rev. 2000), 131–5.

23 C. P. Stacey, *Six Years of War: The Canadian Army in Canada, Britain, and the Pacific* (Ottawa: Edmond Cloutier, 1957), 92ff. C. P. Stacey and Barbara M. Wilson, *The Half-Million: The Canadians in Britain, 1939–46* (Toronto: University of Toronto Press, 1987).

24 Regimental Diary, qormuseum.org/history/timeline-1925-1949/the-second-world-war/war-diaries-1942. Thanks to John M. Stephens at the Regimental Museum in Toronto.

25 Salmon, *Voices of the Village*, 368.

26 Gerald Smedley Andrews to Jean Andrews, 30 November 1941; also May 1942, July 1942. canadianletters.ca/collections/all/collection/20892.

27 The nursery was run by Arthur Linfield, and its history is described by Malcolm Linfield in 'A Brief History of Mushroom Growing at Thakeham', 2019, thakehamparish.co.uk/wp-content/uploads/2019/05/A-brief-history-of-mushroom-growing-at-Thakeham-1.pdf.

28 Discussed in Anne Marie Peatrik, 'Jomo Kenyatta's *Facing Mount Kenya* and Its Rival Ethnographies', *Bérose*, 2021.

29 Malcolm Linfield gives a detailed account of Kenyatta's wartime life: 'Jomo Kenyatta and His Connections with West Sussex', 2019, lindfield.org. See also W. O. Maloba, *Kenyatta and Britain* (Cham: Palgrave, 2017), 81–106, and Jeremy Murray-Brown, *Kenyatta* (London: Allen & Unwin, 1972), 210–17. Armstrong would be a prominent figure in fostering Sussex history after the war: he was one of the founders of the pioneering Weald and Downland Museum. His commitment to understanding local communities went hand in hand with his involvement in international socialist politics.

30 Salmon, *Voices of the Village*, 382.

31 Kenyatta to Edna Grace Clarke, quoted Murray-Brown, *Kenyatta*, 216.

32 White Hart: Linfield, 'Kenyatta'. The question of representing 'the Kikuyu', and different Kikuyu communities, is examined by Bruce J. Berman and John M. Lonsdale in 'The Labours of Muigwithania: Jomo Kenyatta as Author, 1928–45', *Research in African Literatures* 29:1 (1998), 16–42.

33 Maloba, *Kenyatta and Britain*, 82.

34 Grove, *Laurie Lee*, 141. 'We heard all about the black man's burden,' Lee wrote, 'and joined in reviling the Commonwealth.'

35 The novel 'White Man's Magic' was never finished. *My People of Kikuyu* was published: United Society for Christian Literature, 1942.

36 Murray-Brown, *Kenyatta*, 210.

37 Ibid., *Kenyatta*, 211–12.

38 They divorced in 1946, soon after Kenyatta's return to Kenya, though they corresponded. Their son Peter was brought up by his mother in England. Edna stayed on at the Armstrong house for a time, and after the war taught at Pinewood

School in Hertfordshire.

39 Linfield, 'Kenyatta'.

40 Kenyatta, *Facing Mount Kenya* (1938; London: Mercury, 1961), 236.

41 Linfield, 'Mushroom Growing'; Salmon, *Voices of the Village*, 382 quotes Gwen Smith: 'it was a mystery who bought them'.

42 *West Sussex Gazette*, adverts running across various issues, 1942.

43 *West Sussex Gazette*, 12 March 1942.

44 Helena Hall, *Journal*, 14 and 16 July 1942.

45 Roffey, *Schoolboy's War*, 46.

46 Salmon, *Voices of the Village*, 369, 370; Ham, *Storrington*, 86.

47 Roffey, *Schoolboy's War*, 97.

48 For English memories of these soldiers, including the 'huge, generous men' of the Canadian Black Watch, and the French Canadians camped at Angmering, see project.littlehamptonfort.co.uk.

49 Stewart Hastings Bull, audio memoir 2002, transcribed canadianletters.ca/document-6001.

50 Callon, *But for the Sake*, 130, 149.

51 Ham, *Storrington*, 92–3.

52 WSRO, 1/4/10/3/3. Discussed Emma Barnard, 'Parham in the War', westsussexrecordofficeblog.com.

53 Peter Khoroche, *Ivon Hitchens* (London: Lund Humphries, 1990), 48, writes that they found the land for sale and bought the caravan while staying at Barnett's Farm, East Lavington, in 1939.

54 Correspondence with John Hitchens, 2023.

55 *Petworth Society Magazine* 169 (2017).

56 Ibid.; Terry Lucas, audio recording, *Wartime West Sussex* resources, West Sussex County Council, www2.westsussex.gov.uk

57 John C. Hatt, former sergeant with Canadian 104th Anti-tank Battery, speech reproduced *Petworth Society Magazine* 81 (1995).

58 Roffey, *Schoolboy's War*, 37.

59 Ibid., 105.

60 Barbara Bertram, *Memoirs* (Oxford: Oxuniprint, 2001); Anthony and Barbara Bertram, *The Secret of Bignor Manor* (privately published, 2014); Edward Wake-Walker, *A House for Spies: SIS Operations into Occupied France from a Sussex Farmhouse* (London: Robert Hale, 2011); A. W. M. Smith, 'Eclipse in the Dark Years: Pick-Up Flights, Routes of Resistance and the Free French', *European Review of History* 25:2 (2018), 392–414.

61 Bertram, *Memoirs*, 30, 39.

62 Bertram, *Secret*, 128; memoresist.org/resistant/pierre-delaye/.

63 Smith, 'Eclipse in the Dark Years', discusses these 'tokens and symbolic echoes',

and compares the 'allusions to local and regional history found throughout the resistance press in France'.

64 Bertram, *Memoirs*, 45.

65 Marie-Madeleine Fourcade, *L'Arche de Noé*, 1968, trans. Kenneth Morgan, *Noah's Ark* (London: Penguin, 1974), 253.

66 Fourcade, *Noah's Ark*, 254.

67 Ibid., 263.

68 Ibid., 264.

69 Barbara was not told when her visitors were later captured, though she took note of those who did not return. British SIS eventually allowed Fourcade to return to France in July 1944; she evaded capture.

70 Roffey, *Schoolboy's War*, 90.

71 Captain Bryan Hilton-Jones, 'No. 3 Troop, No. 10 Commando', TNA, DEFE 2/977, printed in Michael S. Goodman, 'In Search of a Lost Commando', *Journal of Intelligence History* 15 (2016), 53. 'The training at this period', he explained, 'was exemplified by load-carrying when parachuting, dory and dinghy landings, the use of silenced weapons, shooting at night, lying up and concealed bivouacking, abseiling (roping down) on cliffs, practice parachute jumps, the use of homing pigeons, the use of the S-phone.'

72 Ibid., 55.

73 Manfred Gans reports the trialling of ropes in the Black Rabbit quarry, *Life Gave Me a Chance* (privately published, 2009), 118, 123.

74 'Swimming tanks' and other vehicles were waterproofed: Ian Greig, et al., *D-Day West Sussex* (Chichester: West Sussex County Council, 1994), 13–14.

75 Ibid.

76 Richard Harris, quoted Peter Craddick-Adams, *Sand and Steel: The D-Day Invasions and the Liberation of France* (Oxford: OUP, 2019), 254.

77 On Fabius: Craddick-Adams, *Sand and Steel*, 251–9.

78 All recorded by the Army Film Unit: '3rd Division Rehearses Fabius IV, Parts 1–3', Imperial War Museum A70 14–18.

79 Craddick-Adams, *Sand and Steel*, 254.

80 Roffey, *Schoolboy's War*, 127.

81 Greig et al., *D-Day West Sussex*, 62.

82 *Tatler*, 25 September 1940.

83 Picnics: e.g. photograph 17 June 1944, WSRO, PH/4/96.

84 Flora MacDonald Brown, memories printed in Greig et al., *D-Day West Sussex*, 80–1, and WSRO, MP 3730/47.

85 Mission Keokuck and Mission Elmira involved large numbers of gliders though both were later in the day than the gliders Flora Brown remembered seeing.

86 See film footage of QA nurses unpacking supplies outside Bayeux, IWM A70, 53–2.

28. The Pine Tree

1 Joan Ham, *Storrington in Living Memory* (London: Phillimore, 1982), 93.

2 'The Ignacy Paderewski Grammar School in West Chiltington', polishresettlementcampsintheuk.co.uk, and see Zosia and Jurek Biegus, *Polish Resettlement Camps in England and Wales 1946–69* (privately published, 2013), 274–7. The name honoured the former prime minister and passionate champion of Poland's independence from its neighbours after World War I, the man who had signed the Treaty of Versailles for Poland and who had died in exile in 1941 while another war laid waste to his native land.

3 Polish Forces Official Committee papers, TNA, ED128/141, cited and discussed by Agata Blaszczyk in 'War and Resettlement: Polish Resettlement Camps in the UK after the Second World War', Refugee Law Initiative Working Paper 45.

4 Teofila Rumun, *née* Jaroszyńska, interviewed in London, November 2006, and transcribed (in Polish) for the online archive of the Warsaw Rising Museum, 1944.pl/archiwum-historii-mowionej/teofila-rumun,956.html. See also (in English) 'Tosia Jaroszyńska's Journey from Poland to Stowell Park', polishresettlementcampsintheuk.co.uk.

5 Ibid.: interview for Warsaw Rising Museum.

6 Ibid.

7 Ibid.

8 Warsaw Rising Museum: 1944.pl/powstancze-biogramy/zofia-burzycka,5181.html.

9 Rumun, interview for Warsaw Rising Museum.

10 Bogna Domańska, contribution to *Out of the Inferno: Poles Remember the Holocaust*, ed. Richard C. Lukas (Lexington: University Press of Kentucky, 1989), 56–8.

11 *London Gazette*, deceased estate notice, 4 July 1988.

12 *London Gazette*, notice of naturalisation, 24 July 1959.

13 Ibid.

14 Ibid.

15 Major Corburn to Arthur Duncan Jones, Dean of Chichester, reported *West Sussex Gazette*, 9 January 1947.

16 J.A.S., 'A Village of Women and Children', *Worthing Herald*, 21 February 1947, 9.

17 Norman Davies, *Trail of Hope: The Anders Army, an Odyssey across Three Continents* (Oxford: Osprey, 2015), 17.

18 Ibid., 254.

19 Documents released in 2012 indicate he was killed in the Katyn massacre.

20 Franciszek Herzog, *Herzog Family Chronicle*, trans. Franciszek Herzog and Ivona Verbeke, 2003, polishexilesofww2.org. Franciszek died in 2017.

21 For discussion of the Indian context see Anuradha Bhattacharjee, *The Second Homeland: Polish Refugees in India* (New Delhi: Sage, 2012).

22 *Herzog Family Chronicle*.

23 The maharaja's orphanage has become legendary in both Poland and India. See
for example the documentary film *A Little Poland in India*, dir. Amu Radah and
Sumit Osmand Shaw, 2018, in which some of those who were children there revisit
Balachadi and remember.

24 *Herzog Family Chronicle*.

25 *Empire Brent* passenger list: polishresettlementcampsintheuk.co.uk/passengerlist/
empbrent1947nov.htm.

26 Tadek to Franciszek Herzog, letters 20 October 1945 and spring 1945. Such signs
were much less common by 1947.

27 *Herzog Family Chronicle*.

28 Stasha Martin *née* Starzec, 'Stasha Starzec's Story', *Petworth Society Magazine*, issue
175, 31–6, and petworthpolishcamp.com.

29 Ziggi Janiec with Miles Costello, 'Petworth Polish Camp – 1', *Petworth Society
Magazine* 174, 22–6 and petworthpolishcamp.com.

30 Martin, 'Stasha Starzec's Story'.

31 'Lydia Gardner née Stefanska's Story', petworthpolishcamp.com.

32 *The Evacuation of Haifa*, British Pathé (unissued film, 1948), britishpathe.com/
video. Maria Bassara docked at Liverpool in March 1948, with West Chiltington
marked as her destination. polishresettlementcampsintheuk.co.uk/passengerlist/
franconia1948mar.htm.

33 Tadeusz Dudzicki, interview with Theo Cronin, 'Hidden History of West
Chiltington Revealed by Polish Soldier That Escaped Stalin's Gulags', *West Sussex
Gazette*, 21 April 2013.

34 Dudzicki wrote a substantial memoir, which was lodged with the Polish Institute.
Adam Czesław Dobroński introduces it and reproduces extracts in 'Sniła mu się
po nocach Lida', *Polski Magazyn w UK* 6:149 (2018).

35 Ibid.

36 Dudzicki, *West Sussex Gazette*.

37 Dudzicki, *Polski Magazyn*.

38 No. 5 Polish Field Hospital had been relocated from Italy in November 1946, and
from summer 1948 was a PRC 'General Hospital'.

39 Dudzicki, *West Sussex Gazette*.

29. An Open Window

1 Mark Cocker and Richard Mabey, *Birds Britannica* (London: Chatto & Windus,
2005), 77. Thanks to Tim Dee.

2 Ann Salmon et al., *Voices of the Village: A History of West Chiltington during the 20th
Century* (privately published, 1999), 142.

3 Ibid., 143–4.

4 Monkmead House, 1911, designed by Percy Morley Horder, prolific architect of

pubs, country houses and university buildings.

5 Ibid., 105. On the long-established geography of atchin tans, especially in the Sussex area, see Damian Le Bas, *The Stopping Places* (London: Chatto & Windus, 2018).

6 The mill was dismantled c.1830 and carried up into the village, where it worked until 1921 before being converted to a home. Richard and Richard McDermott, *The Standing Windmills of West Sussex* (Worthing: Betford, 1978), 45–8.

7 Ordnance Survey First Series, sheet 9, from visionofbritain.co.uk. It may have been one of many mills built to answer domestic wheat demand during the Napoleonic wars, or it may have been there earlier.

8 Midhurst Quarter Sessions Roll, WSRO, QR/W629/113; McDermott, *Windmills*, 46.

9 *The Book of John Rowe*, ed. Walter H. Godfrey, SRS 34 (1928), 102. Sylvia Saunders-Jacobs, *West Chiltington in the County of Sussex* (privately published, 1965), 11–12. Enclosure was widespread in Sussex in this period. 'Substantial areas of common were taken in during the sixteenth century, and further extensive acreages both of common and of common field were inclosed in the seventeenth century.' W. E. Tate, 'Sussex Enclosure Acts and Awards', *SAC* 88 (1949), 114–56, 136.

10 *Rowe*, 93.

11 Ibid., 102.

12 Women were among the freeholders and customary tenants in West Chiltington though: *Rowe* lists Elizabeth Cherriman as a freeholder, and Margareta Swan a tenant at Swan's Yard.

13 There are dole stone survivals in the meadows at Coates.

14 *Rowe*, 102.

30. Shadow and Blaze

1 On Hitchens and Cézanne see David Gervais, 'Ivon Hitchens and the Harmony of Colour', *Cambridge Quarterly* 38:1 (March 2009), 87–94.

2 Bishop to Kit Barker, 1954, *One Art: Letters*, ed. Robert Giroux (Farrar, Straus & Giroux, 1994), 291.

3 Hitchens, 23 November 1957, quoted Mary Chamot, Dennis Farr and Martin Butlin, *The Modern British Paintings, Drawings and Sculpture* (London: Oldbourne Press, 1964), 2 vols, vol. 1, 288. Peter Khoroche links the 'special pull' of the Petworth and Midhurst area with the places Hitchens had known as a child: *Ivon Hitchens* (London: Lund Humphries: 1990, rev. 2007), 48.

4 Thanks to John and Ros Hitchens for details here and throughout this chapter. Alfred Hitchens gave up oil painting and turned to pastel drawing when his wife became ill and they moved to live in a hotel in Hove with very limited space.

5 Hitchens to Kit Barker, 9 June 1979, TGA, 943.

6   Hitchens to Michael Ayrton, 24 November 1945, TGA, 811.

7   Patrick Heron, *Ivon Hitchens*, Penguin Modern Painters (Harmondsworth: Penguin, 1955), 11.

8   Hitchens to Keynes, 27 November 1940, reproduced David Scrase, 'A Theoretical Letter from Ivon Hitchens to Maynard Keynes', *Burlington Magazine*, July 1983, 420–3, 422.

9   Ibid., and publicly stated later in 'Notes on Painting', *Ark* 18 (1956), 51–2.

10 Hitchens to Michael Ayrton, 8 December 1945, TGA, 811.

11 Quoted T. G. Rosenthal, *On Art and Artists* (London: Unicorn Press, 2014), n.p.

12 Ted Floate interviewed for a Goldmark Gallery film, *Ivon Hitchens: Encounter in the Woods*, 2014.

13 The story is related in Khoroche's introduction to *Encounter in the Woods*, exhib. cat., Goldmark Gallery, 2014. Interviews with Floate in the film of the same name.

14 Hitchens to Michael Ayrton, 15 December 1945, TGA, 811.

15 Ibid., 8 December 1945.

16 Hitchens to Veronica Wedgwood (C. V. Wedgwood, historian, biographer of William of Orange of William the Silent), Bodleian, MS. Eng. c. 6829.

17 Hitchens to Michael Ayrton, 8 December 1945, TGA, 811.

31. A Teacher's Return

1   Wilfred Campbell, 'The End of the Furrow', in *Poems of Wilfred Campbell* (London and Toronto: Holder & Stoughton, 1923), 202.

32. A Census

1   Marie-Madeleine Fourcade, *L'Arche de Noé*, 1968, trans. Kenneth Morgan, *Noah's Ark* (London: Penguin, 1974), 254.

2   Anon [William Barttelot?], *The High Stream of Arundel*, c. 1636, ed. Joseph Fowler (Littlehampton: Simson & Co., 1929), 63.

LIST OF ILLUSTRATIONS

191 George Stubbs, *The Moose, or The Duke of Richmond's Bull-Moose*, 1770, oil on canvas. Courtesy Hunterian Art Gallery, University of Glasgow.

194 Eric Ravilious, wood engraving from *The Writings of Gilbert White of Selborne*, ed. by H. J. Massingham (London: Nonesuch Press, 1938).

200 William Harvey, *Cowper's Favourite Seat at Eartham*, engraved by Joseph Goodyear for *The Works of William Cowper*, ed. Robert Southey, 1833–7, reproduced here from the edition published London: H. G. Bohn, 1854.

209 Unknown sculptor, the Bosham Head, thought to represent the emperor Trajan, AD 121–22, Novium Museum, Chichester. Photograph by Udimu, 2022. CC BY-SA 4.0.

210 James Rouse, *Boseham* [Bosham] *Parsonage House from Beauties and Antiquities of the County of Sussex*, 2 vols (London: privately published, 1825).

213 The new rail bridge over the Arun at Ford, *Illustrated London News*, 14 November 1846, 320, engraving by Ebenezer Landells.

216 William Blake, *Blake's Cottage at Felpham*, detail from plate 36 of Milton: A Poem, c.1804–11, hand-coloured etching. British Museum.

228 William Gardner, *An accurate plan of the city of Chichester, with the suburbs and liberty thereof*, 1769. Courtesy British Library, Maps K. Top.42.18.

235 William Blake, *Colinet's Fond Desire Strange Lands to Know*, wood engraving, from Robert Thornton, *The Pastorals of Virgil* (third edition London: F. C. & J. Rivington and others, 1821). Southampton City Art Gallery/Bridgeman Images.

244 James Hakewill, *View of Montpelier Estate Old Works*, etching and aquatint, from *A Picturesque Tour of the Island of Jamaica* (London: Hurst, Robinson & Co, 1824).

257 James Rouse, *South view of the residence of Mr Henty, Tarring, from Beauties and Antiquities of the County of Sussex*, 2 vols (London: published by the artist, 1825).

258 John Helder Wedge, *Mr Henty's House, Portland Bay*, 6 October 1835, field book sketch in pencil and pen and ink, State Library of Victoria, MS10768. Courtesy State Library of Victoria.

259 Believed to be Edward Henty's telescope and used at the early Portland settlement. Courtesy Dunkeld Museum Inc.

273 James Pattison Cockburn, *The Road between Kingston and York*, Upper Canada, c.1830, pencil, ink and watercolour. Library and Archives Canada, acc. no. 1934-402.

278. John George Howard, *King Street West, Toronto*, 1835. Photograph courtesy Digital Archive Ontario, E6-8. The Chewett Building shown here (completed 1833) housed shops, offices, and the British Coffee Shop.

285 Helena Hall, bookplate, 1900, shown here in a volume of the *Sussex Archaeological Collections*.

293 John Constable, ancient canoe at North Stoke, 12 July 1834, pen and ink and watercolour. British Library, Egerton MS 3253, folio 16. Photograph © British Library Board. All Rights Reserved/Bridgeman Images.

396 Ordnance Survey, first series, 1813, detail showing West Chiltington Common. National Library of Scotland.

406 George Garland, Ivon Hitchens painting in the woods, 1952, photograph. © West Sussex County Council. West Sussex Record Office, Garland N37771. The picture on the easel is *Trees and Bushes*.

Plate section

1 The downs from Pulborough Brooks. Photograph AH.

2 Chancel arch at St Mary the Virgin, North Stoke, probably early fourteenth century. Photograph AH.

3 St Botolph's, Hardham, south wall. Photograph AH.

4 Samuel Hieronymus Grimm, *Pulborough, Upper Mount*, 1780, ink and watercolour on paper. British Library, Add. MS. 5674, f.44 [80].

5 Samuel Hieronymus Grimm, *Hardham Priory and Chapel*, 1780, ink and watercolour on paper. British Library, Add. MS. 5674, f.42 [76]. Photograph © British Library Board. All Rights Reserved / Bridgeman Images.

6 George Garland, Rabbit catching, c.1931, photograph. © West Sussex County Council. West Sussex Record Office, Garland N5057.

7 George Garland, reed cutting at Amberley, December 1931, photograph. © West Sussex County Council. West Sussex Record Office, Garland N8429.

8 Bargemaster Henry Doick with his sons Percy and Tom on Barge No. 64, below Pulborough Bridge, c.1898. Photographer unknown. Image courtesy Tony Pratt and the Arun Valley Postcard Trail.

9 George Smith, *Landscape*, 1763, oil on canvas. By permission of the Trustees of the Goodwood Collection.

10 George Romney, *Charlotte Smith*, 1792, pastel. Abbot Hall, Lakeland Arts.

11 George Romney, *William Cowper*, 1792, pastel. National Portrait Gallery, NPG 1423.

12 William Blake, *Jacob's Dream, or Jacob's Ladder*, c.1799–1806, ink and watercolour on paper. British Museum, 1949, 1112.2. Photograph © The Trustees of the British Museum.

13 John Constable, *Arundel Mill and Castle*, 1837, oil on canvas. Photograph courtesy Toledo Museum of Art.

14 Ivon Hitchens, *September Trees and Pond by House*, 1956, oil on canvas. © Estate of Ivon Hitchens.

15 The Studio at Greenleaves. Photograph AH, used courtesy John Hitchens.

16 Ivon Hitchens, *John by Jordan*, 1942, oil on canvas. © Estate of Ivon Hitchens.

17 Edward Elgar, map showing the way from Pulborough to Bedham, drawn for W. H. Reed, 1921, coloured inks on paper. © Royal College of Music / ArenaPAL.

18 Adam and Eve, wall painting at St Botolph's, Hardham, early twelfth century. Photograph AH.

ACKNOWLEDGEMENTS

This book is the result of a Philip Leverhulme Prize, which gave me the great gift of time and autonomy. It allowed me to be exploratory in thought and ambitious with form in ways I could never have justified and costed in advance. My first thanks is therefore to the Leverhulme Trust and its reviewers for showing such faith in what writers do. I have also been extremely fortunate to hold a Professorial Fellowship at the University of Birmingham. It's an honour to keep company with the outstanding scholars and teachers who inhabit Birmingham's College of Arts and Law. I've incurred many debts and am glad of many friendships, but I record here special thanks to Jessica Fay, Andrew Hodgson, Oliver Herford, Matthew Ward, David James, and Tom Lockwood; to all who have brought their energy and interest to the Arts of Place group; and to the graduate students whose own giant projects have taken shape in these years. I've loved the concurrent effort and imagining.

I am grateful to all those who have shared their knowledge, showed me their places, answered queries and read my work. For invaluable help with particular subjects I thank Andrew Loukes, Christopher Whittick, John and Ros Hitchens, Hope Wolf, Ed Shingles, Jan Parkinson, David and Karen Coke, Simon Bonvoisin, Raymond Smith, James Brookes, Tracey Carr, Colin Stepney, Lissette Trembling, Stephen Daniels, Adam Nicolson, Fred Gray, James Leeming, Max Saunders, Lisa Gee, Peter Jerrome, Miles Costello, Zosia Biegus, Ryszard Starzec, and Krystyna Szypowska. Richard Dudzicki made time, at no notice at all, to describe his father's feelings for West Chiltington Polish camp and long, complex attachment to the Arun Valley. Special thanks to Jonathan Newdick and Fulvia Zavan for introducing me to people and places, and for drawings that save up the work of centuries in their pencil lines; to James Simpson for showing me some of what he sees and hears on Heyshott Down; to Suzanne Joinson for exhilarating conversation on country lanes; to Simon Martin and all at Pallant House for their part in making Sussex an exciting place to think about the arts.

I thank my oldest Sussex friends and family. Thanks to Susan Venning and the late Christopher Venning, remembered with love; at their book-lined home I encountered rural and literary life at one and the same time. To Catherine, Louise, and Barbara Buchanan, for all the shared history in Storrington. To the teachers and contemporaries who shaped my early ideas of place: I'm sorry my quadrat didn't quite reach Horsham but all the stories of booklists and shared knowledge are told here with intense appreciation for what I received. From early gifts to recent ones: after years as a wandering visitor, uncertainly but unshakeably attached to places where I didn't really belong, I was made welcome by Samantha Haydon in a landscape that had come to matter to me. My time there illuminates my time everywhere. To Samantha, and to David Munns: thank you.

I am grateful to the staff of the Bodleian Libraries, where I have been a fortunate reader for more than twenty years and where, this time round, I was able to put *Sussex Notes & Queries* side by side with histories of the world. I thank the staff at Arundel Castle, Storrington and District Museum, Petworth House, and Goodwood House. My debts to many writers on Sussex history are indicated in the endnotes, but I want to say what an education it has been to engage with the scholarship of local historians and archivists. I thank Wendy Walker, Jennifer Mason, and their superb team at West Sussex Record Office. I was tremendously lucky to be able to work with the archivist Alice Millard, who brought her experience and ingenuity to bear on what I'd done; thank you, Alice, for suggestions at once calming and thrilling.

The more difficult aspects of this project had to do with the altered rhythms that became necessary through periods of fragile health. I won't forget the help of friends and colleagues who saw that the two-hour days were much harder work than the twelve-hour days, or the professionals who broke through various kinds of impasse to change things: Timothy Hinks, Ian Pavord, and their transformative research team in Oxford, and, later, Sarah Ledingham and Steve Foley.

Warm thanks to my agent Caroline Dawnay for her uplifting advocacy, and to both Kat Aitken and Sophie Scard. It has been a privilege to work with Ella Griffiths and Laura Hassan as my editors at Faber; with great insight and panache they helped me towards the patterning of image and voice that I was striving for, and never doubted that local subjects have the power to travel. Thanks to Martin Smith for his work on the pictures, Djinn von Noorden for copy-editing, Victoria Hunt for proofreading, Melanie Gee for the intricate index, Pete Adlington for the depths and distances of the cover. This book has been more challenging than anything I've previously written; six years proved a short time in which to research elusive lives and left me feeling just about ready to begin. I want to thank everyone at Faber for the care they have given to the project, and the production manager Kate Ward, in particular, for collaborative efforts that were really above and beyond. I hope we'll make more books together.

Thank you to friends who have helped in many personal and professional ways, and inspired me with their own work: Tim Dee, Richard Mabey, Olivia Horsfall

Turner, Fiona Stafford, Jenny Uglow, Robert Macfarlane, Paddy Bullard, Laurence Scott, Michelle Kelly, Ben Morgan, Nicholas Roe, Lucy Powell, Ali Smith, Peter Conrad, and Kate McLoughlin. Peter Davidson came to the rescue with erudition and kindness. John Barnard was always encouraging, and when I had been staring hour on hour at illegible documents, there he was, offering to look. Ruth Scurr lifted my spirits, read my words, and sharpened my thoughts. Loving thanks to Dinah Birch, who never gave up on me for a moment. Will May and Andrew Blades, best of topographers and winter explorers, brought joy in the flinty places and everywhere else. Robert Harris has heard far too much about this book; he'll be glad it's done, but I hope he'll be glad to have it and will see that his forty-three years of support made it possible. His influence is on every page as I try to be patient and look closely.

My early readers responded to the manuscript in ways that stretched and delighted me, and made it all feel new. Lara Feigel brought to it her great clarity of insight. Felicity James heard rhythms I'd missed and guided me among the nonconformists. Daisy Hay made judicious observations that deeply informed my work. I am so grateful for their time, their friendship, and for the sense of common purpose that has kept us all writing and thinking. Hermione Lee, most appreciative and life-giving of friends and critics, was my first reader, and she is the reader for whom I'm still trying to get it right. My gratitude to Caroline Garrett for our long familial friendship is recorded in the dedication. Thank you all.

A first version of 'Squint' was written for the International Literature Showcase in 2016: that commission got me started. Tim Dee commissioned an essay for *Ground Work: Writings on People and Places* (Jonathan Cape, 2018) in which I first ventured to write about the wild brooks. My thinking about Cowper on the downs was developed for the excellent *Cowper and Newton Journal* and appeared in the penultimate issue. I first wrote about Ivon Hitchens' places for *Ivon Hitchens: Space through Colour* (Pallant House Gallery, 2019). I wrote about flint for *Archipelago*, and thank its editor, Andrew McNeillie. 'Easter Chalk' appeared, richly illustrated, in *Sussex Landscape: Chalk, Wood and Water* (Pallant House Gallery, 2022).

Quarter Sessions and Chancery records, census returns, probate documents and Colonial Office registers are Crown Copyright, waived, and quoted under the terms of the Open Government Licence. 'Consider this . . .' © W. H. Auden, renewed, from *The English Auden*, ed. Edward Mendelson (Faber and Faber, 1977), © 1977 Estate of W. H. Auden, renewed, and reprinted by permission of

Curtis Brown Ltd. Quotations from Laurie Lee are © The Estate of Laurie Lee and used by kind permission. Quotations from the essays and letters of Ivon Hitchens are © Estate of Ivon Hitchens and used by kind permission. For their efforts in helping me to trace copyright holders I thank: Zosia Biegus (site curator at polishresettlementcampsintheuk.com), Krystyna Szypowska (site curator at polishexilesofww2.org), Richard Dudzicki, Troubador Publishing, John M. Stephens (at The Queen's Own Rifles of Canada Regimental Museum), Matthew Jones (at West Sussex Record Office), Alice Millard and Norah Perkins.

INDEX